HSP Math

SCHOOL PUBLISHERS

Visit *The Learning Site!*
www.harcourtschool.com

ISBN 13: 978-0-15-341258-5
ISBN 10: 0-15-341258-5

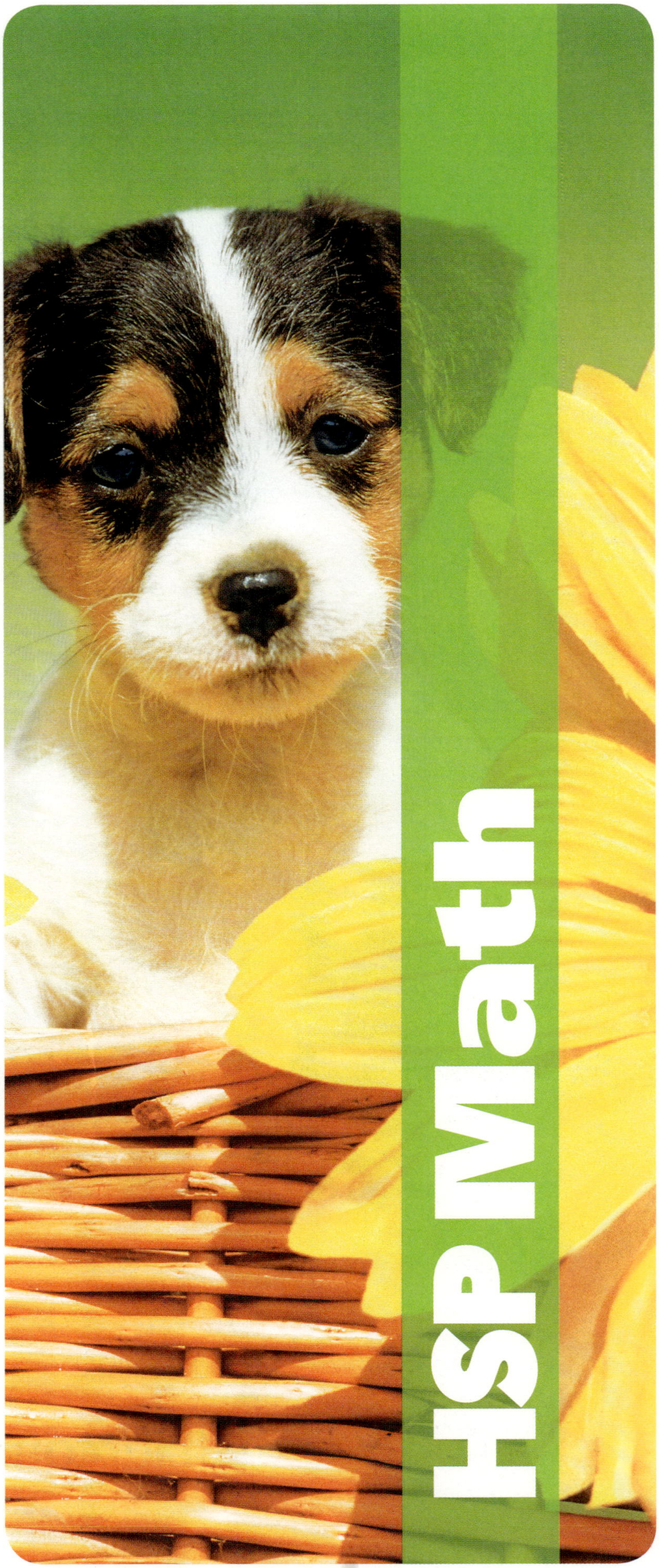

5 6 7 8 9 10 030 16 15 14 13 12 11 10

© Harcourt

Senior Authors

Evan M. Maletsky
Professor Emeritus
Montclair State University
Upper Montclair, New Jersey

Joyce McLeod
Visiting Professor, Retired
Rollins College
Winter Park, Florida

Authors

Karen S. Norwood
Associate Professor of
    Mathematics Education
North Carolina State University
Raleigh, North Carolina

Tom Roby
Associate Professor
    of Mathematics
Director, Quantitative
    Learning Center
University of Connecticut
Storrs, Connecticut

James A. Mendoza Epperson
Associate Professor
Department of Mathematics
The University of Texas
    at Arlington
Arlington, Texas

Juli K. Dixon
Associate Professor of
    Mathematics Education
University of Central Florida
Orlando, Florida

Janet K. Scheer
Executive Director
Create-A-Vision
Foster City, California

David G. Wright
Professor
Department of Mathematics
Brigham Young University
Provo, Utah

David D. Molina
Program Director, Retired
The Charles A. Dana Center
The University of Texas
    at Austin

Jennie M. Bennett
Mathematics Teacher
Houston Independent
    School District
Houston, Texas

Lynda Luckie
Director, K–12 Mathematics
Gwinnett County Public Schools
Suwanee, Georgia

Angela G. Andrews
Assistant Professor of
    Math Education
National Louis University
Lisle, Illinois

Vicki Newman
Classroom Teacher
McGaugh Elementary School
Los Alamitos Unified
    School District
Seal Beach, California

Barbara Montalto
Mathematics Consultant
Assistant Director of
    Mathematics, Retired
Texas Education Agency
Austin, Texas

Minerva Cordero-Epperson
Associate Professor of Mathematics
    and Associate Dean of the
    Honors College
The University of Texas
    at Arlington
Arlington, Texas

Program Consultants and Specialists

Russell Gersten
Director, Instructional
    Research Group
Long Beach, California
Professor Emeritus of
    Special Education
University of Oregon
Eugene, Oregon

Michael DiSpezio
Writer and On-Air Host,
    JASON Project
North Falmouth,
    Massachusetts

Concepcion Molina
Southwest Educational
    Development Lab
Austin, Texas

Rebecca Valbuena
Language Development
    Specialist
Stanton Elementary School
Glendora, California

Valerie Johse
Elementary Math Specialist
Office of Curriculum
    & Instruction
Pearland I.S.D.
Pearland, Texas

Robin C. Scarcella
Professor and Director,
    Program of Academic
    English and ESL
University of California, Irvine
Irvine, California

Lydia Song
Mathematics Program
    Specialist
Costa Mesa, California

Tyrone Howard
Assistant Professor,
    UCLA Graduate School
    of Education—
    Information Studies
University of California
    at Los Angeles
Los Angeles, California

Anne M. Goodrow
Associate Professor,
    Elementary Education
Rhode Island College
Providence, Rhode Island

iii

Back to School Fun

Literature

Back to School Fun A-H

READ Math
Workshop . . . . A-F

WRITE Math
Workshop . . . . . . G-H

THE WORLD ALMANAC FOR KIDS

Chapter 1

Theme: In the Classroom

Sort and Classify   3

v

At the Market

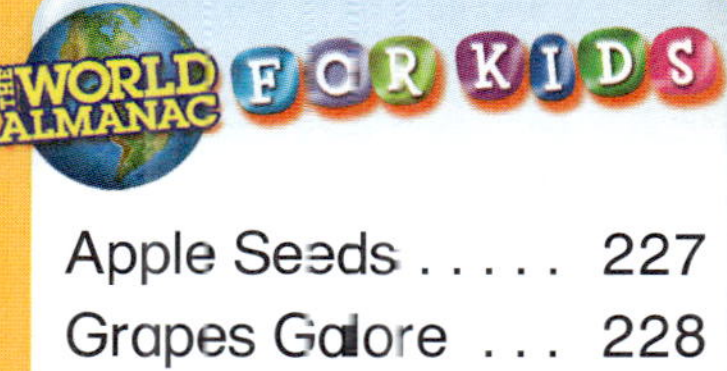

ix

Helping Hands

Chapter 9

Theme: How Does Your Garden Grow?

xi

Back to School Fun

written by Ann Dickson

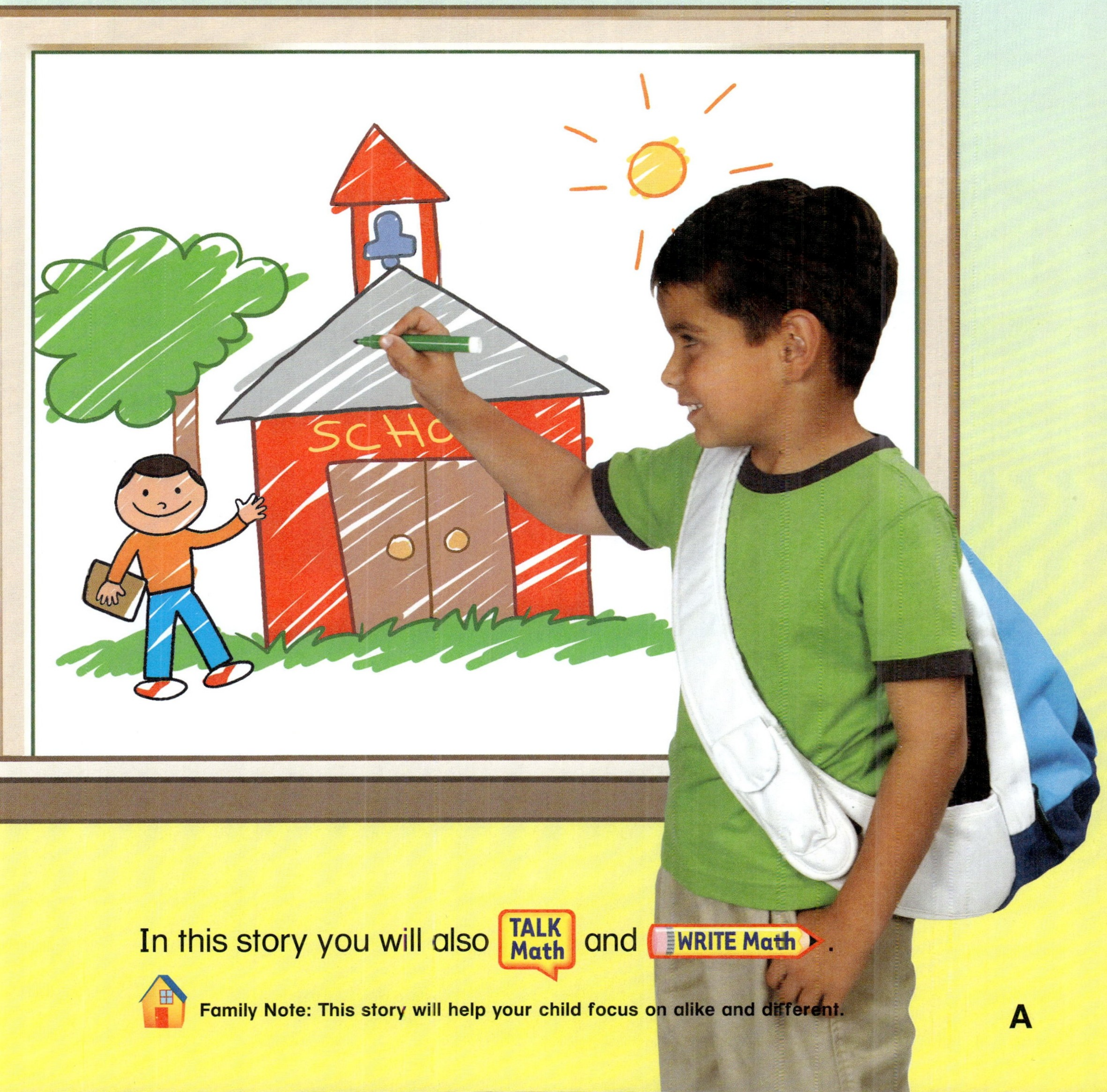

In this story you will also  and .

 **Family Note:** This story will help your child focus on alike and different.

A

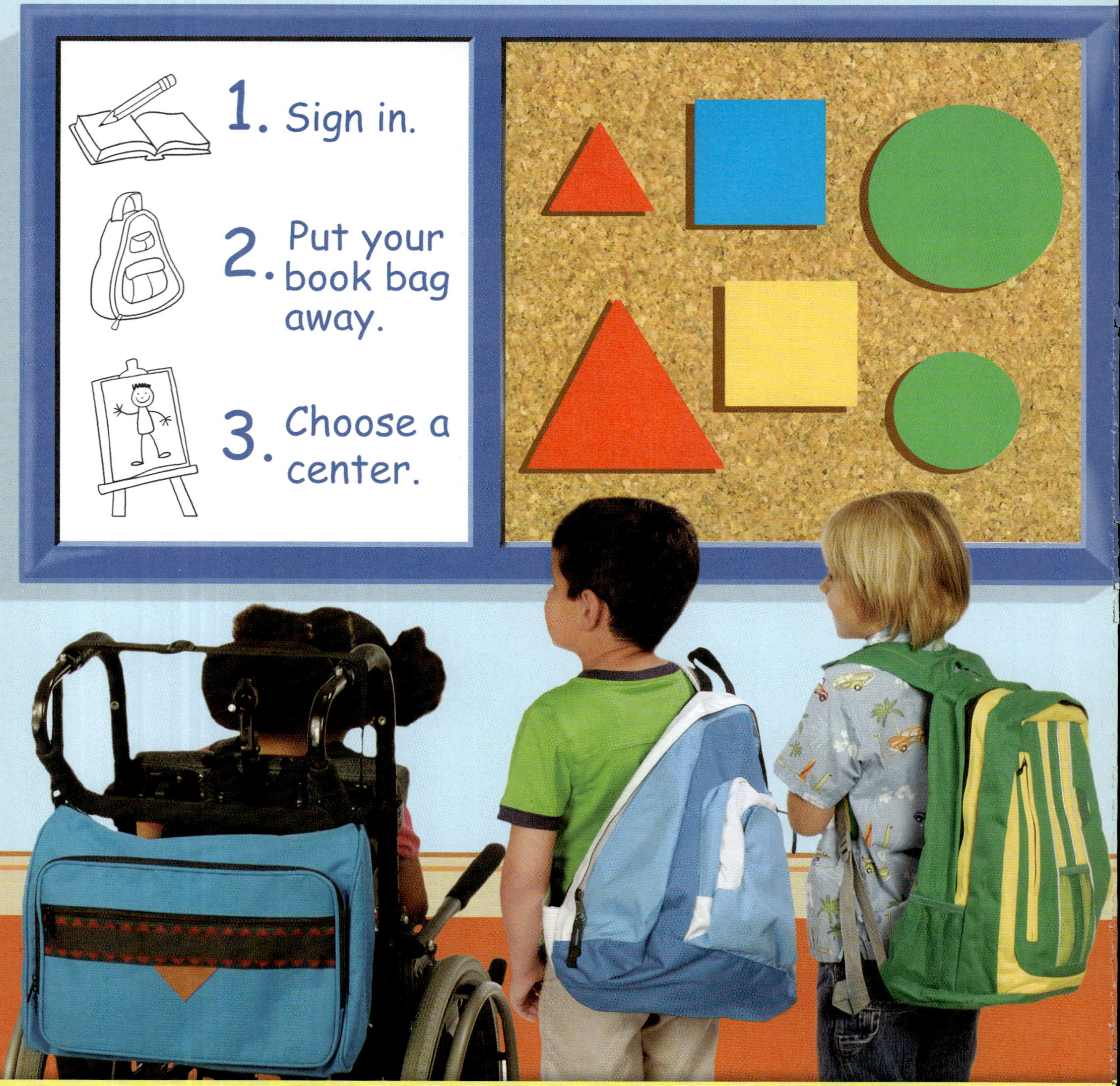

1. Sign in.

2. Put your book bag away.

3. Choose a center.

Here is my classroom, come on in.

Learning time is about to begin.

Why do we have rules?

© Harcourt

These are the book bags

we hang by our names.

Circle the ones that look the same.

Why do we learn names?

c

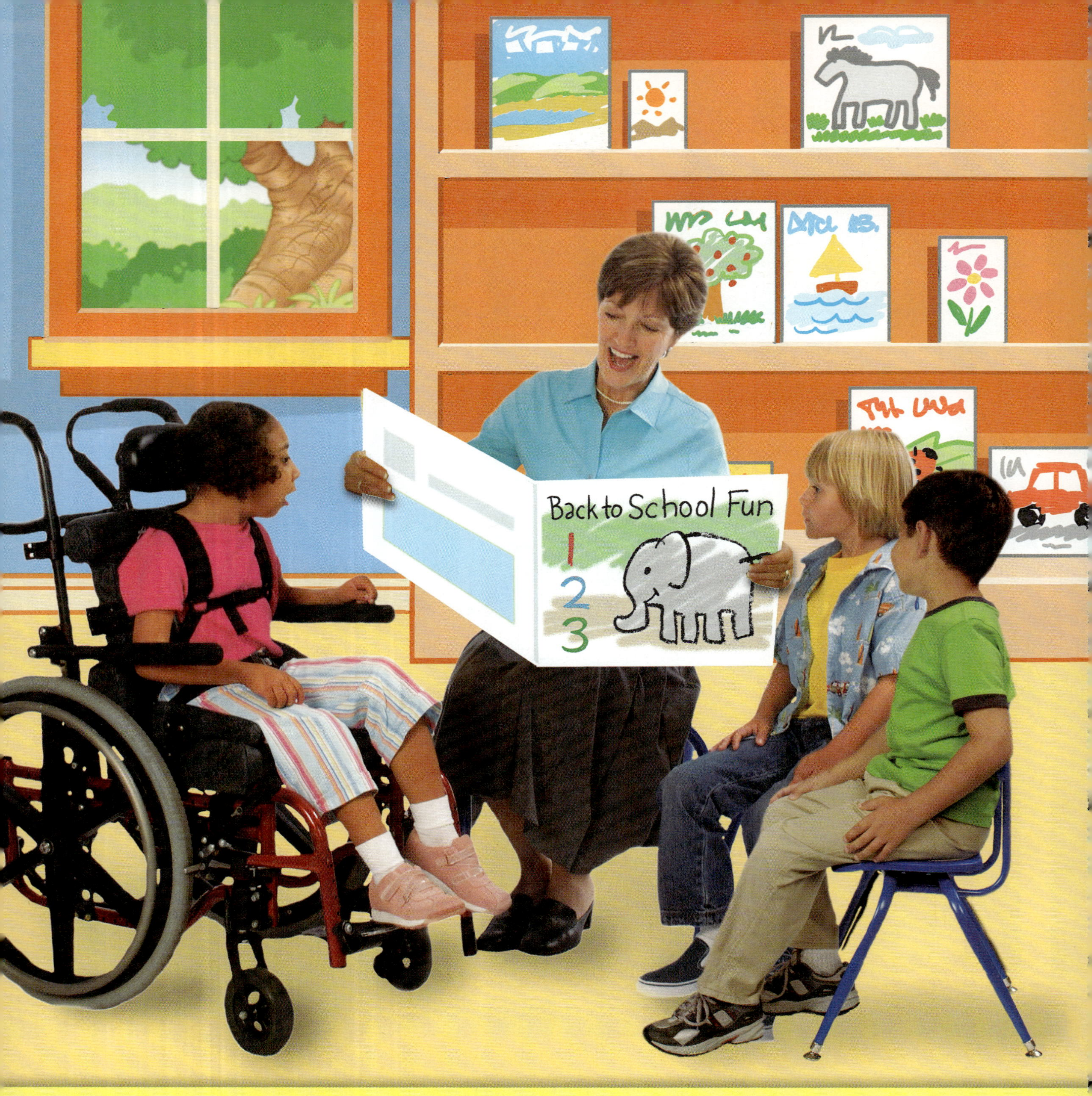

Here are the books. We read them all!

Which books are big?

Which books are small?

Why do we help others?

D

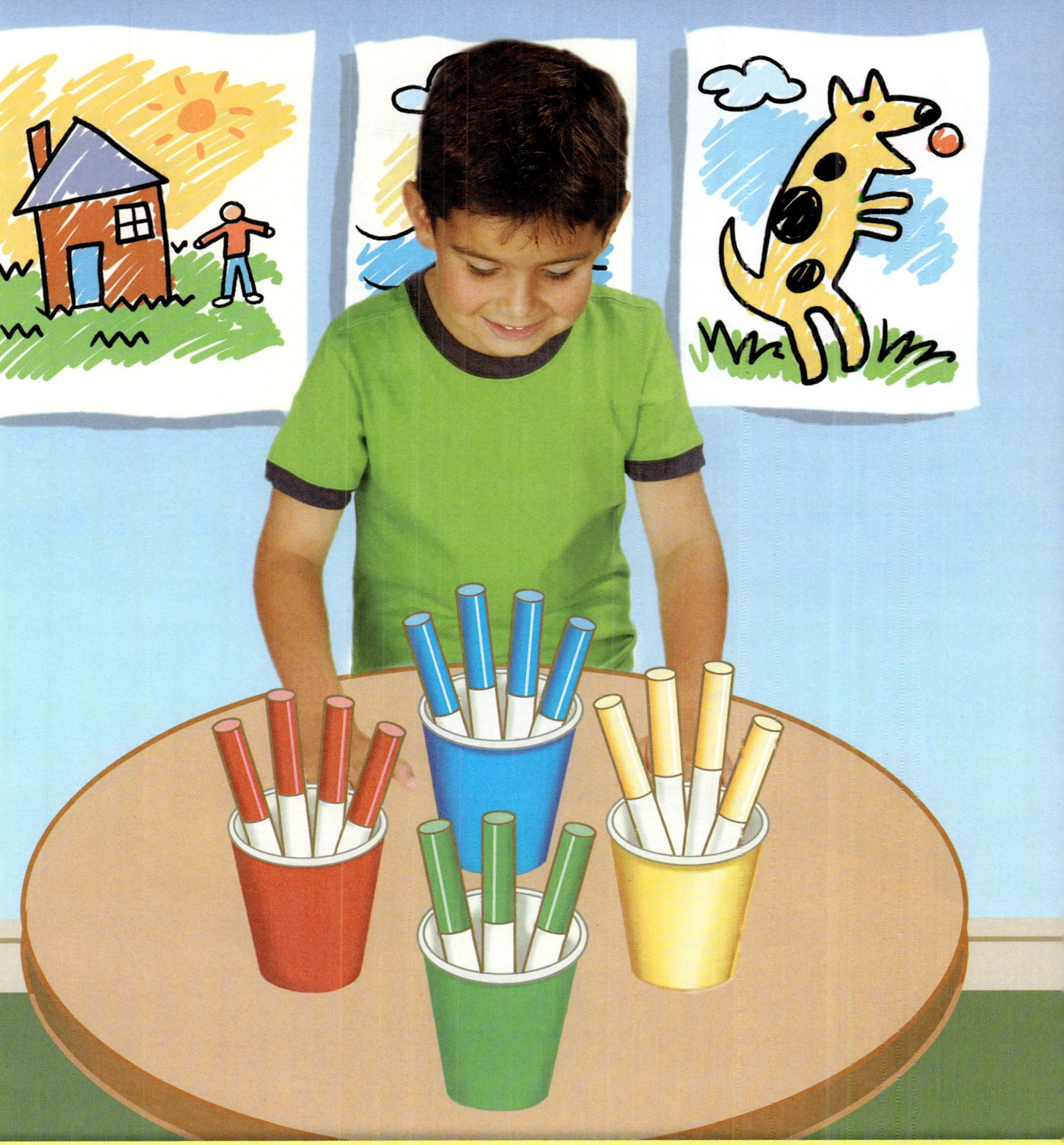

Here are markers of every kind.

Name all the colors you can find.

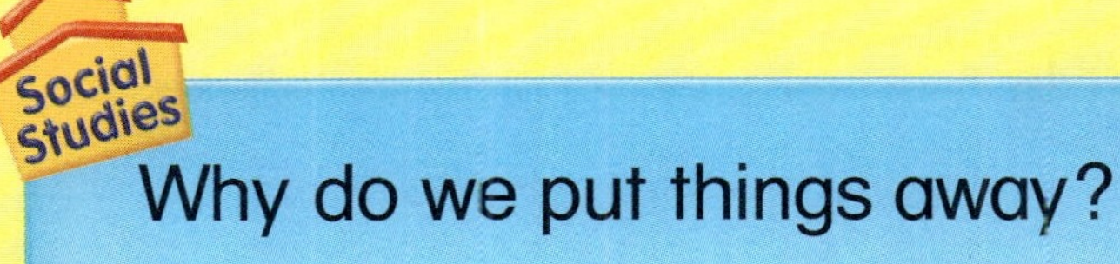

E

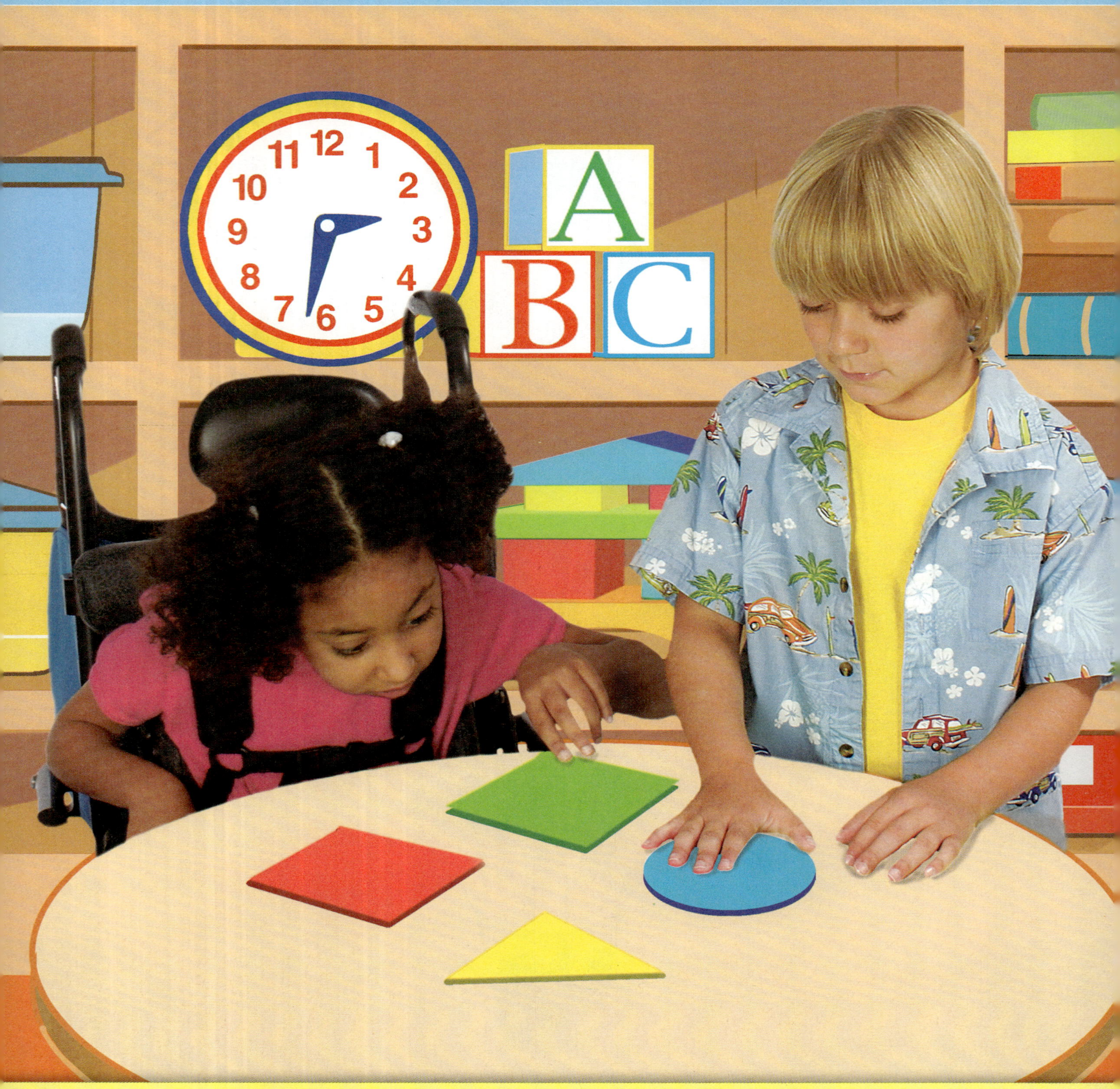

Our blocks and toys are over there.

Which figures are round?

Which figures are square?

Why do we share?

Name ____

My Math Story
Literature Activity

Vocabulary Review
alike
different

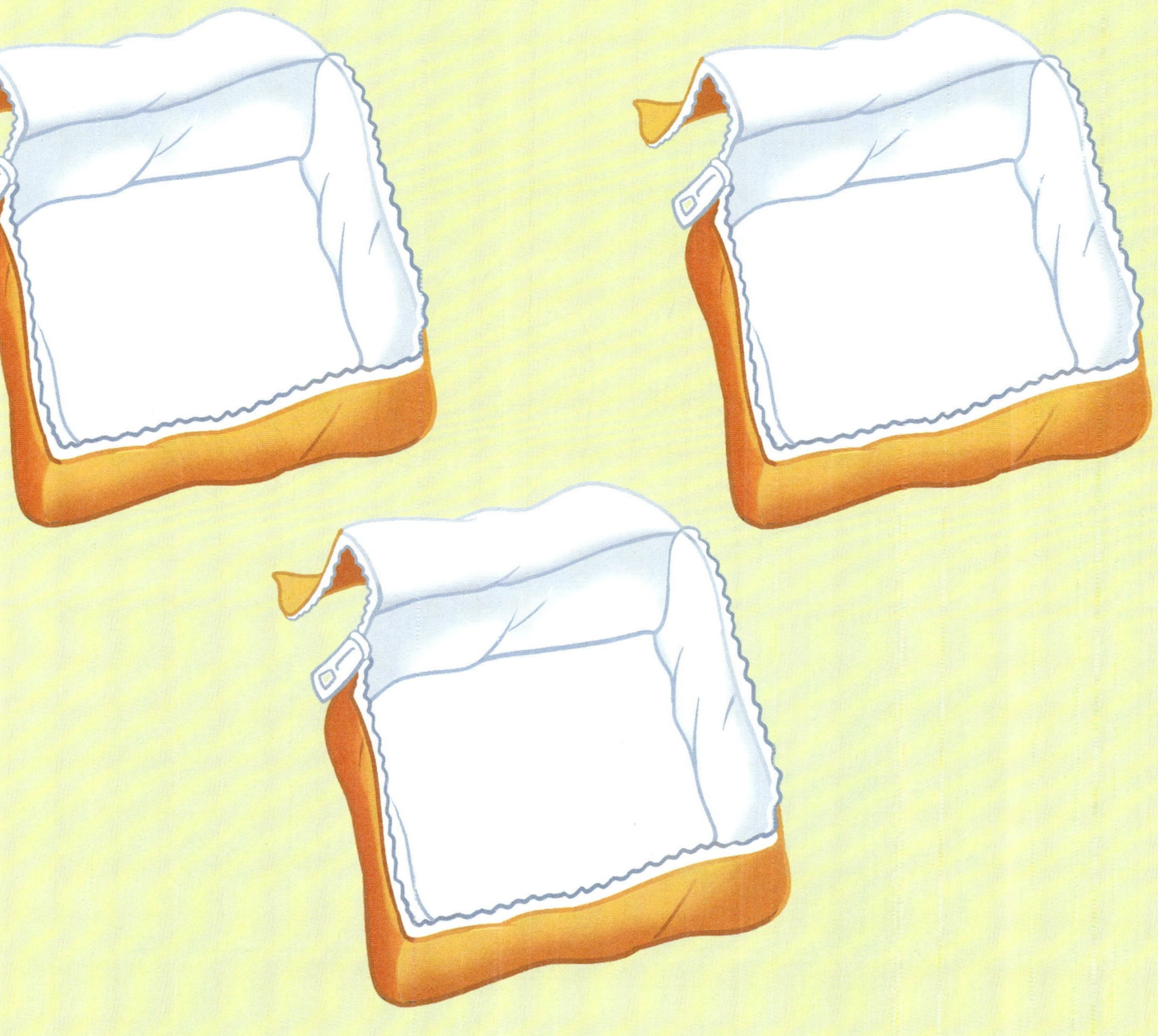

DIRECTIONS These lunch boxes are alike. Draw in one lunch box something that you like to eat. Now circle the lunch box that is different.

G

Alike and Different

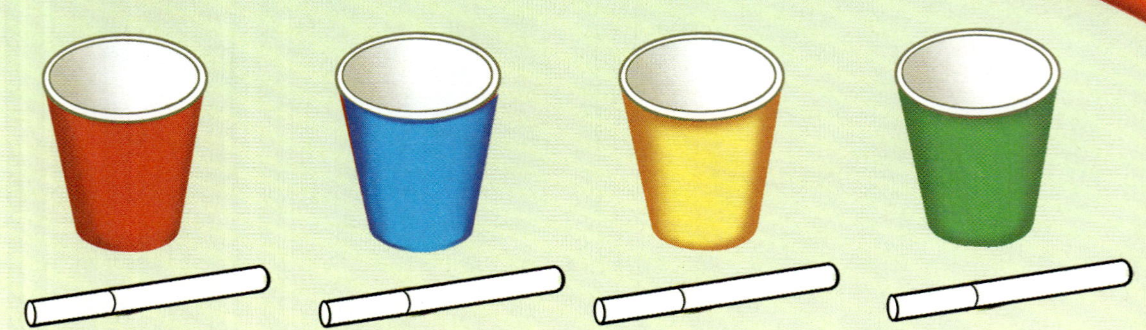

DIRECTIONS I. Color the markers so they match the color of the cup.
2. Color the book bags that are alike by shape.
3. This classroom needs some books. Draw a book that is a different size.

H

Dear Family,

My class started Unit 1 today. I will learn how to sort objects that are alike and count objects up to 5. Here are some vocabulary words and activities for us to share.

Love, _______________________________

Vocabulary Power

Key Math Vocabulary

Sort to put objects into groups by attributes

Graph a way of displaying objects in columns and rows so that the groups can be compared to show information

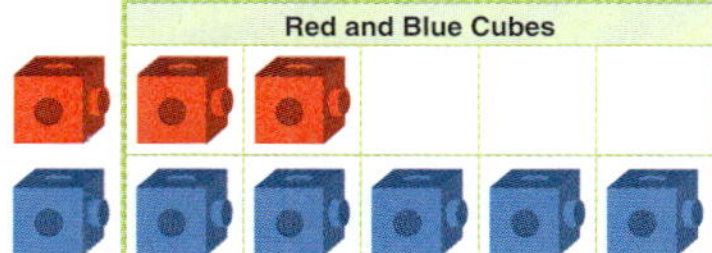

Equal sets the same number of objects in each set

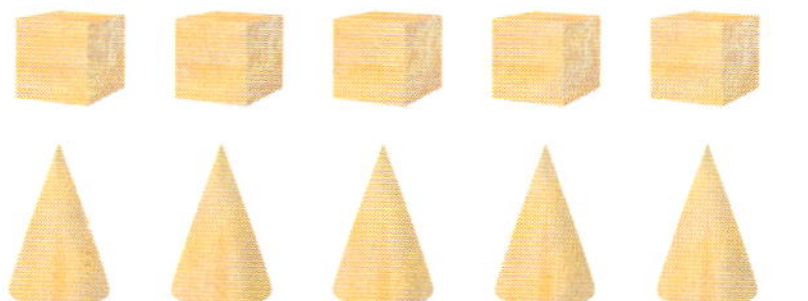

Vocabulary Activity

Math on the Move

Provide opportunities for your child to sort objects, such as the laundry. Have him or her sort the clothes by color, by kind, or by whom they belong. Then have your child show you how he or she can count a set of up to five objects.

GO ONLINE

Technology
Multimedia Math Glossary link at
www.harcourtschool.com/hspmath

School Home CONNECTION

Remember This Your child may already know how to match objects in a one-to-one correspondence, such as one napkin for every place setting at the table. Ask your child to match a set of four objects of one kind to another set of four objects.

Calendar Activity

September

Sunday	Monday	Tuesday	Wednesday	Thursday	Friday	Saturday
		1	2	3	4	5
6	7	8	9	10	11	12
13	14	15	16	17	18	19
20	21	22	23	24	25	26
27	28	29	30			

Ask your child to look at the calendar and tell you what they know about the calendar. Talk about the different colored leaves.

Practice (after pages 7 and 8)
Have your child sort the leaves on the calendar by color.

Practice (after pages 39 and 40)
Have your child count how many of each color leaf there is on the calendar.

Literature

Look for these books in a library. Ask your child to point out math vocabulary words as you read each book together.

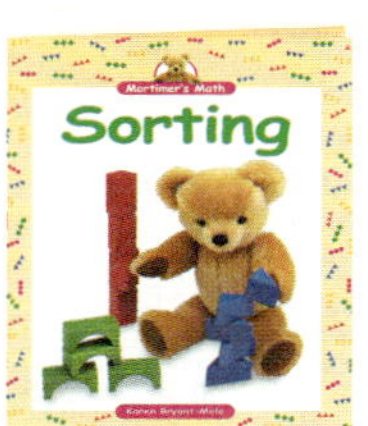

Mortimer's Math: Sorting.
Bryant-Mole, Karen.
Gareth Stevens, 2000.

Seaweed Soup.
Murphy, Stuart J.
HarperCollins, 2001.

Big and Little.
Miller, Margaret.
Greenwillow, 1998.

Sort and Classify
Theme: In the Classroom

Name ______________________________________

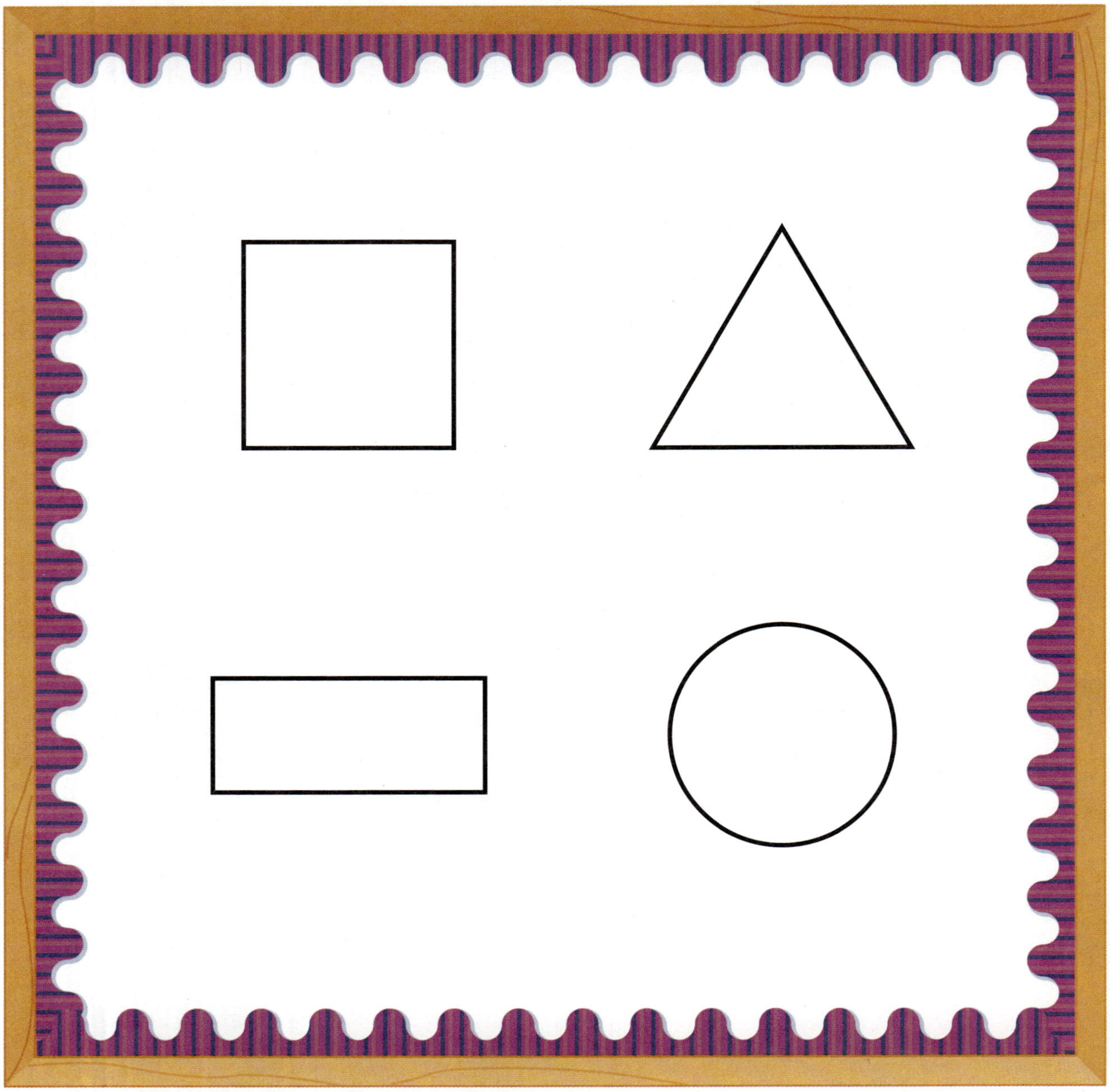

DIRECTIONS Color the figures on the board to match the figures at the top of the page.

FAMILY NOTE: This page checks your child's understanding of important concepts and skills needed for success in Chapter 1.

4 four

© Harcourt

Alike and Different

 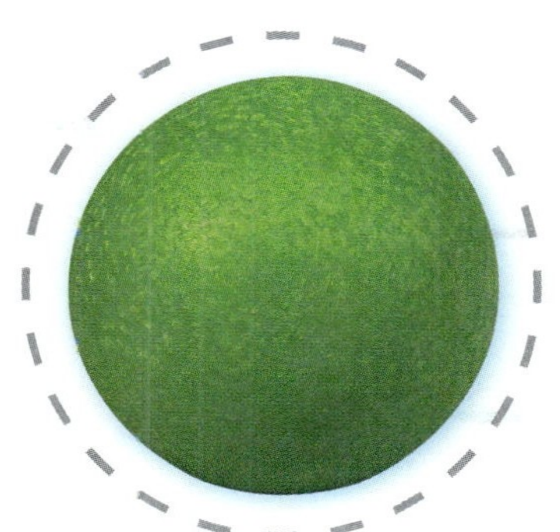 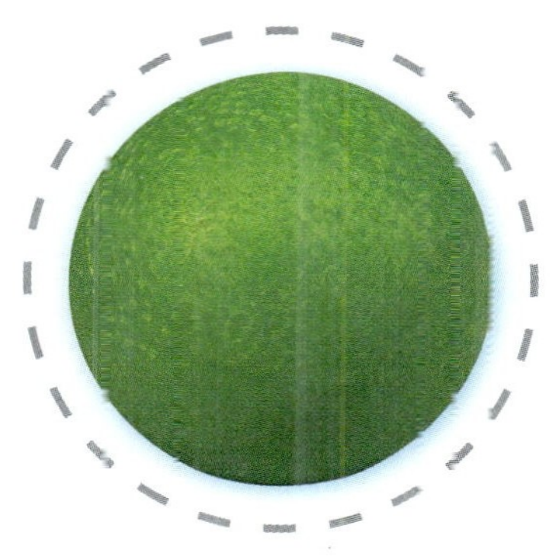

DIRECTIONS 1–4. Circle the objects that are alike.

OBJECTIVE • Use attributes to determine how objects are alike and different.

DIRECTIONS 1–4. Mark an X on the object that is different.

HOME ACTIVITY · Show your child two objects in your home that are alike and one that is different from the other two such as a can of soup, a can of vegetables, and a bar of soap. Have your child tell you how the objects are alike or different.

6 six

Sort and Classify by Color

DIRECTIONS   Sort a handful of figures. Draw and color one more figure that belongs in each group. Tell how the figures are alike.

OBJECTIVE • Sort objects according to the attribute of color.

Chapter I • Lesson 2

seven **7**

1

2

3

4

DIRECTIONS **1–4.** Look at the group of figures at the beginning of the row. Tell how the figures are alike. Circle the figure that belongs in the group.

 **HOME ACTIVITY** • Ask your child to sort household objects such as shirts, socks, or shoes into groups according to color. Have your child tell how he or she sorted the groups.

8 eight

Sort and Classify by Size

1

2

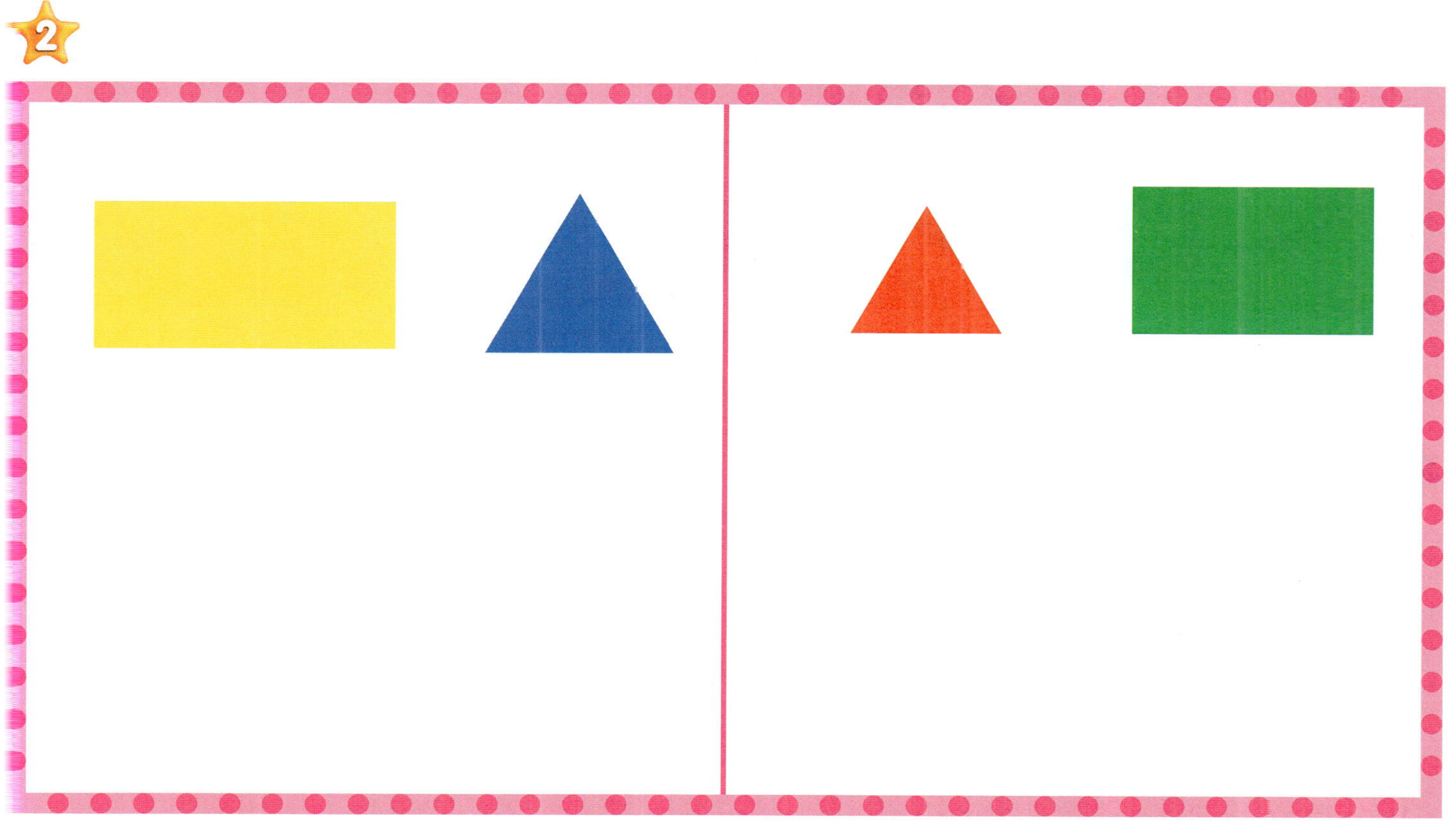

DIRECTIONS 1–2. Sort a handful of figures. Draw and color one more figure that belongs in each group. Tell how the figures are alike.

OBJECTIVE • Sort objects according to the attribute of size.

DIRECTIONS 1–4. Mark an X on the object that does not belong.

HOME ACTIVITY · Provide your child with big and small versions of the same objects, such as spoons, shoes, shirts, or stuffed animals. Ask your child to tell which objects are big and which are small.

10 ten

Sort and Classify by Shape

1

2

DIRECTIONS 1–2. Use figures to match each figure. Circle the two figures that are alike. Draw that figure in the workspace. Tell what you know about that figure.

OBJECTIVE • Sort objects according to the attribute of shape.

Chapter 1 • Lesson 4

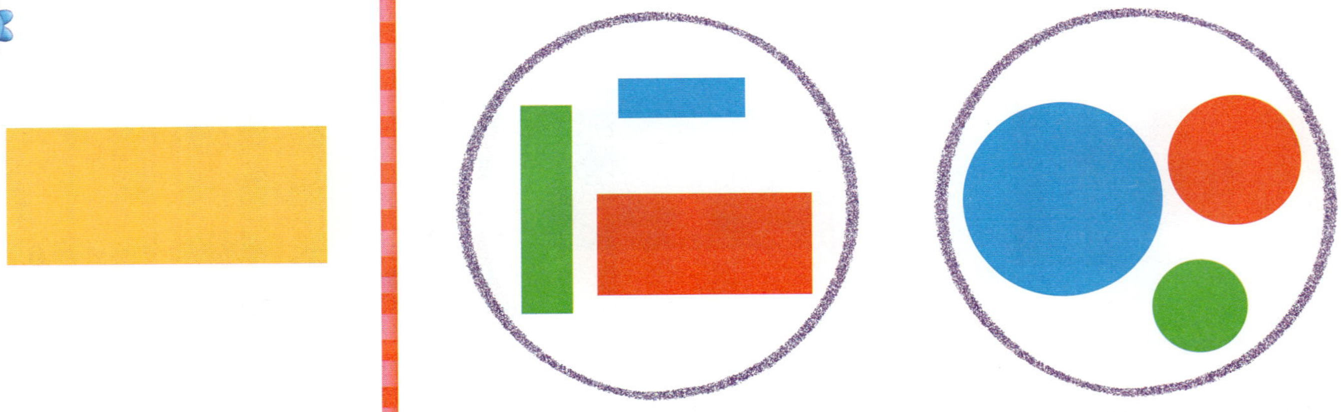

DIRECTIONS   1–4. Look at the figure at the beginning of the row. Tell what you know about the figure. Mark an X on the group in which the figure belongs.

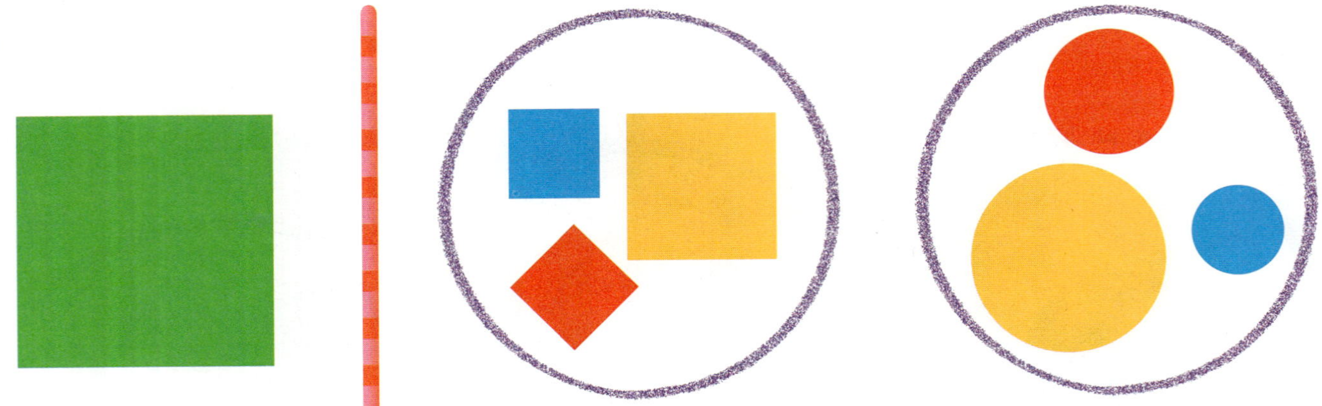

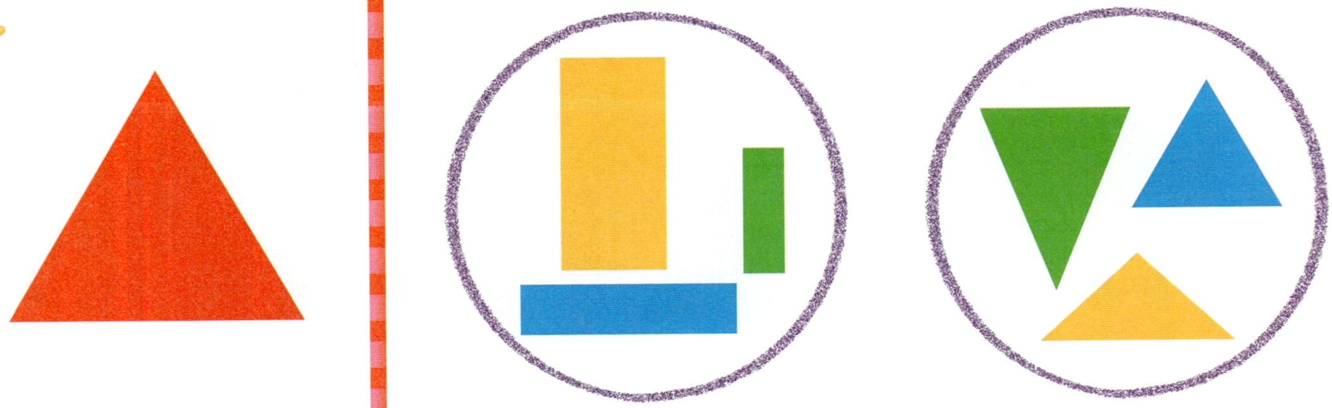

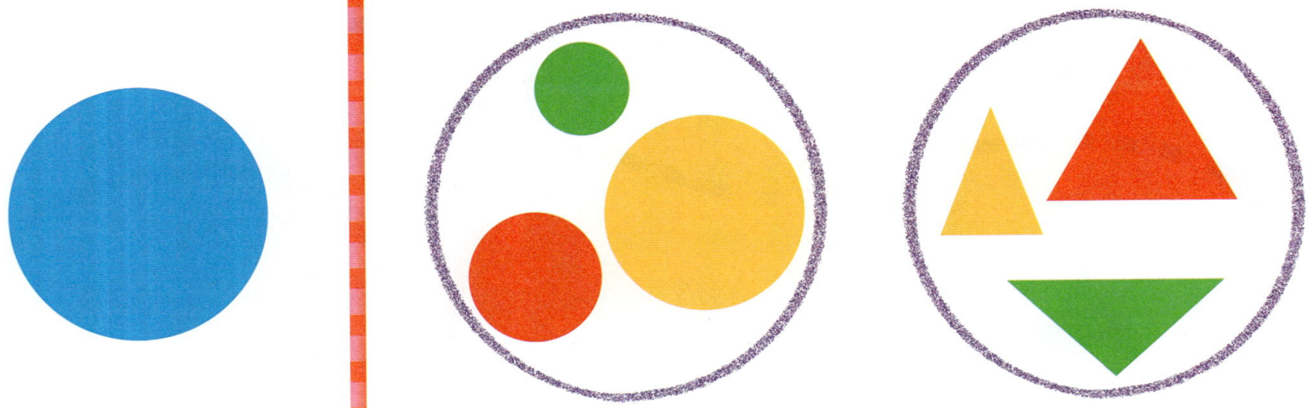

 **HOME ACTIVITY** • Help your child find a household object to match each of the following figures: a square, a triangle, a rectangle, and a circle.

✓ Mid Chapter I Review

DIRECTIONS **I.** Mark an X on the object that is different. **2.** Look at the group of figures at the beginning of the row. Circle the figure that belongs in the group. **3.** Mark an X on the object that does not belong. **4.** Look at the figure at the beginning of the row. Mark an X on the group in which the figure belongs.

Chapter I

Cumulative Review

DIRECTIONS **1.** Mark an X on the object that is different.
2–3. Sort a handful of figures. Draw and color one more figure that belongs in each group. **4.** Look at the fugure at the beginning of the row. Mark an X on the group in which the figure belongs.

Sort in Different Ways

DIRECTIONS **1.** Circle all the red figures. **2.** Circle all the triangles. **3.** Mark an X on the figure that is circled in both groups. Draw and color the figure.

OBJECTIVE • Sort and classify in more than one way.

Chapter 1 • Lesson 5

DIRECTIONS   **1.** Circle all the green figures.
2. Circle all the squares.   **3.** Mark an X on the figure that is circled in both groups. Draw and color the figure.

 **HOME ACTIVITY** · Ask your child to find two objects in your home that are alike in two of these ways: color, shape, and size. For example, different-size dishes of the same set may have the same color and shape. Have your child tell ways the objects are alike.

16 sixteen

Name _______________________________

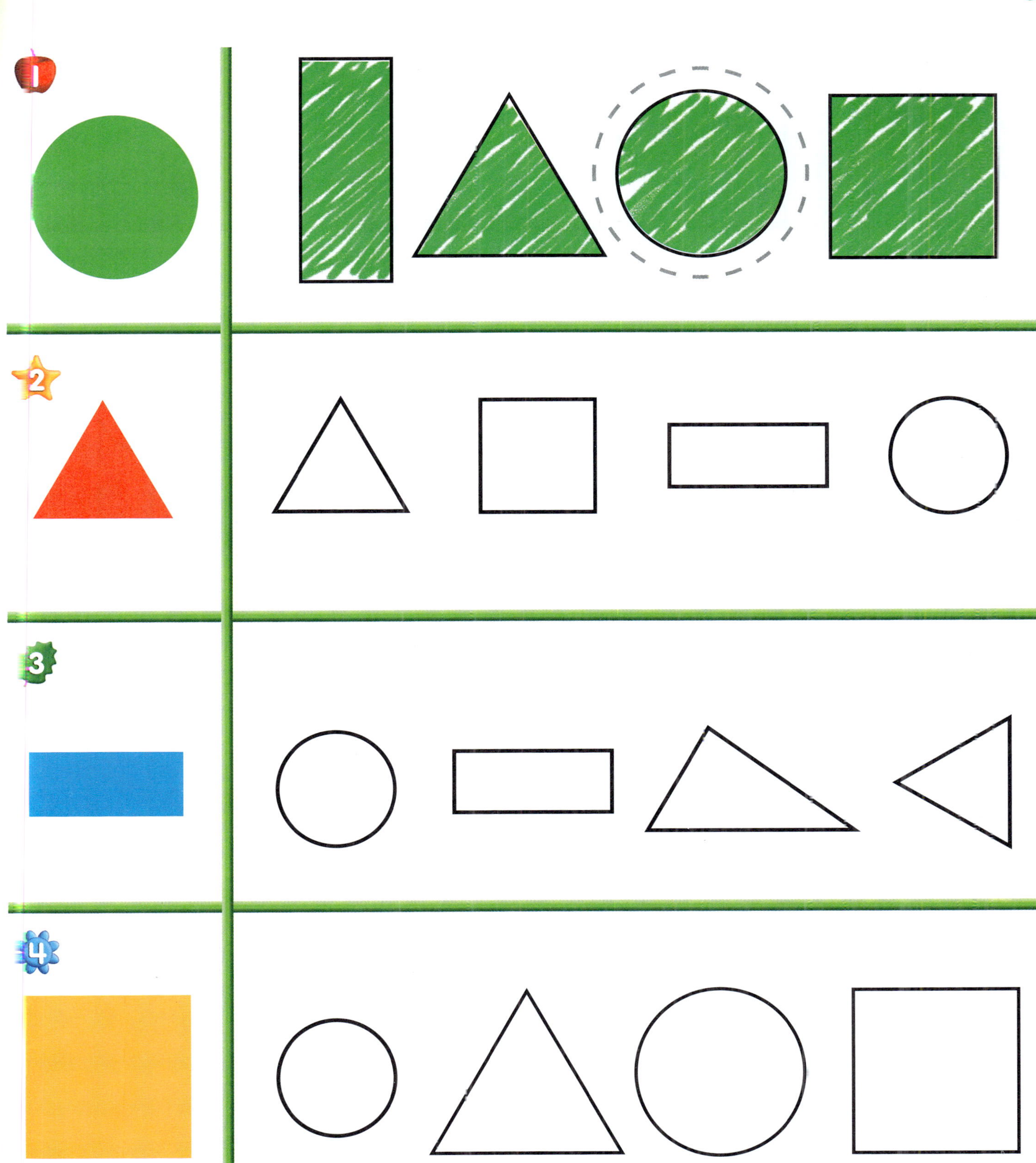

DIRECTIONS **1–4.** Color all the figures to match the color of the figure at the beginning of the row. Circle one figure that matches in more than one way. Tell how the figure matches.

OBJECTIVE • Solve problems by using the skill *use visual thinking.*

Chapter 1 • Lesson 6

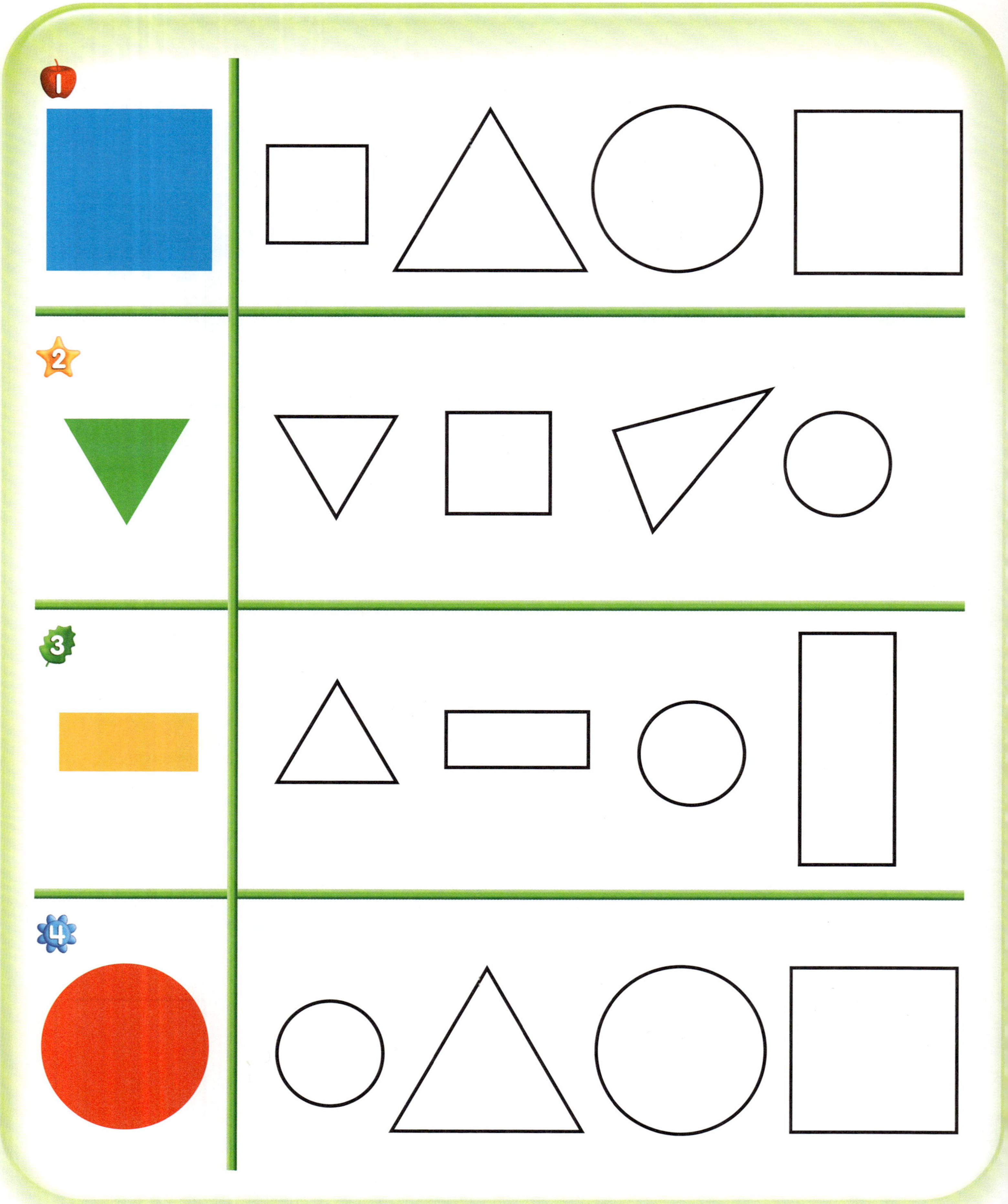

1

2

3

4

Identify Sorting Rules

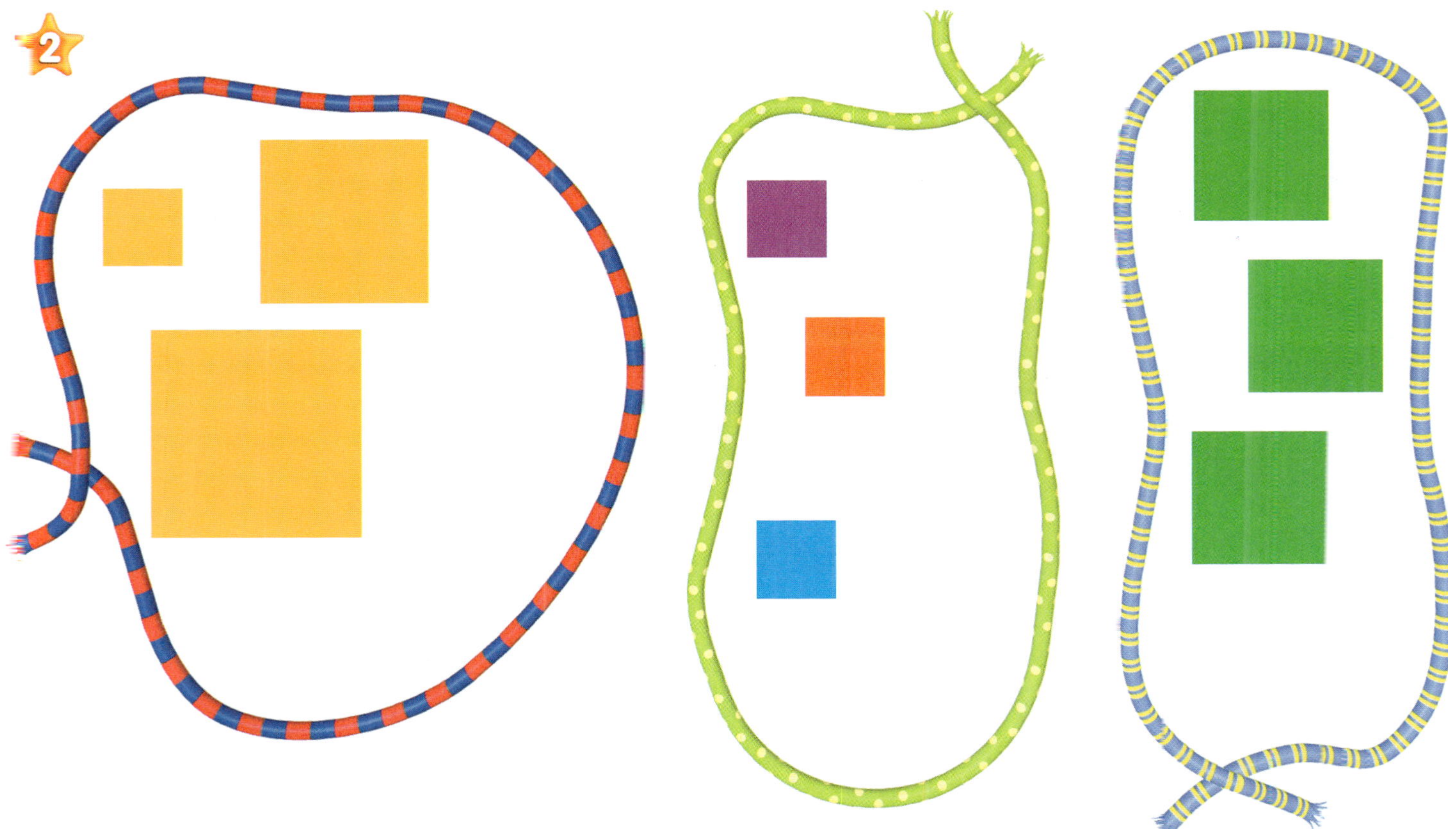

DIRECTIONS **1.** Trace the figure in the group that is sorted by shape and color.
2. Draw and color one more figure in the group that is sorted by size and color.

OBJECTIVE • Describe how groups of objects are formed.

Chapter 1 • Lesson 7

nineteen **19**

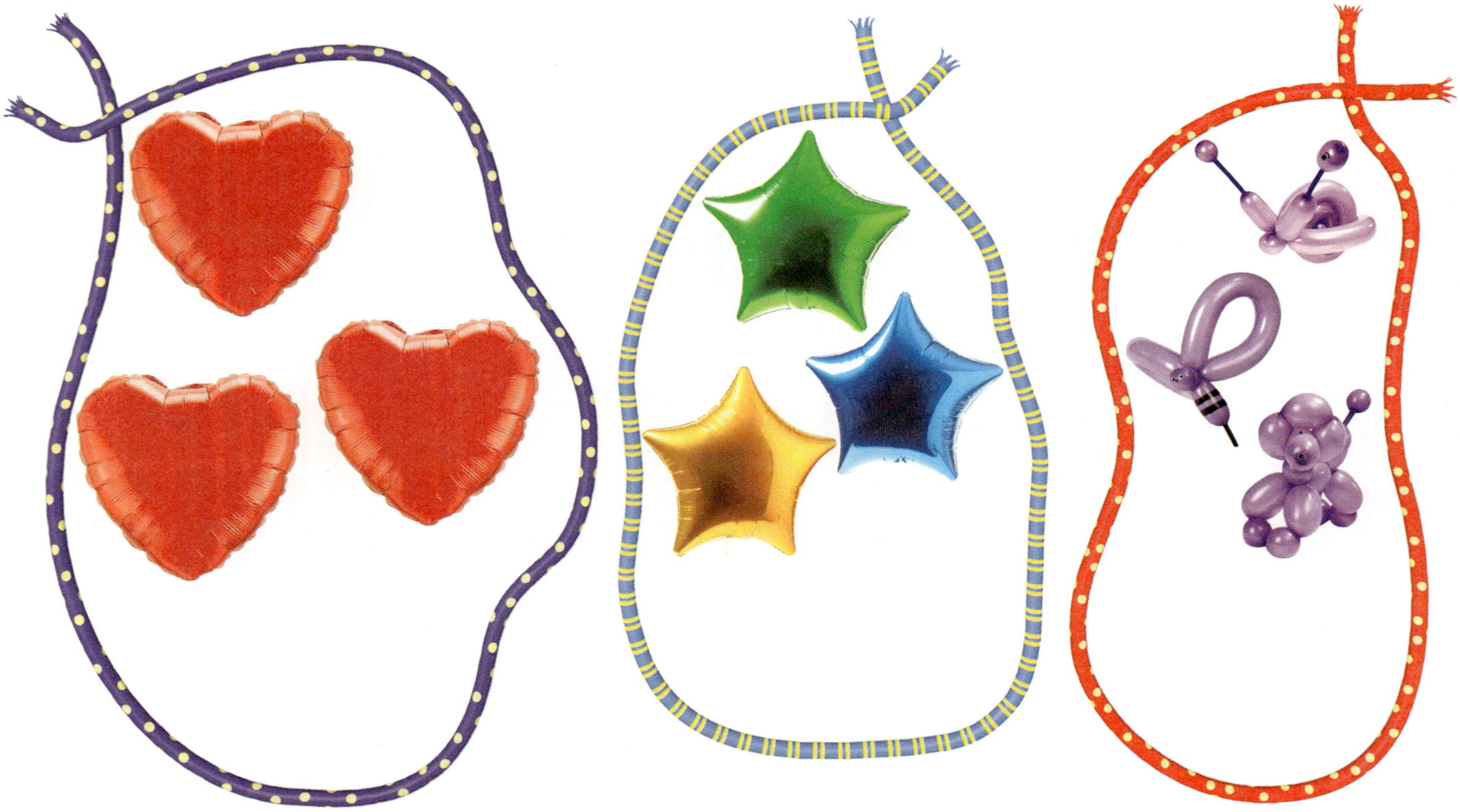

DIRECTIONS **1.** Draw and color one more ball in the group that is sorted by color and size. **2.** Draw and color one more balloon in the group that is sorted by color and shape.

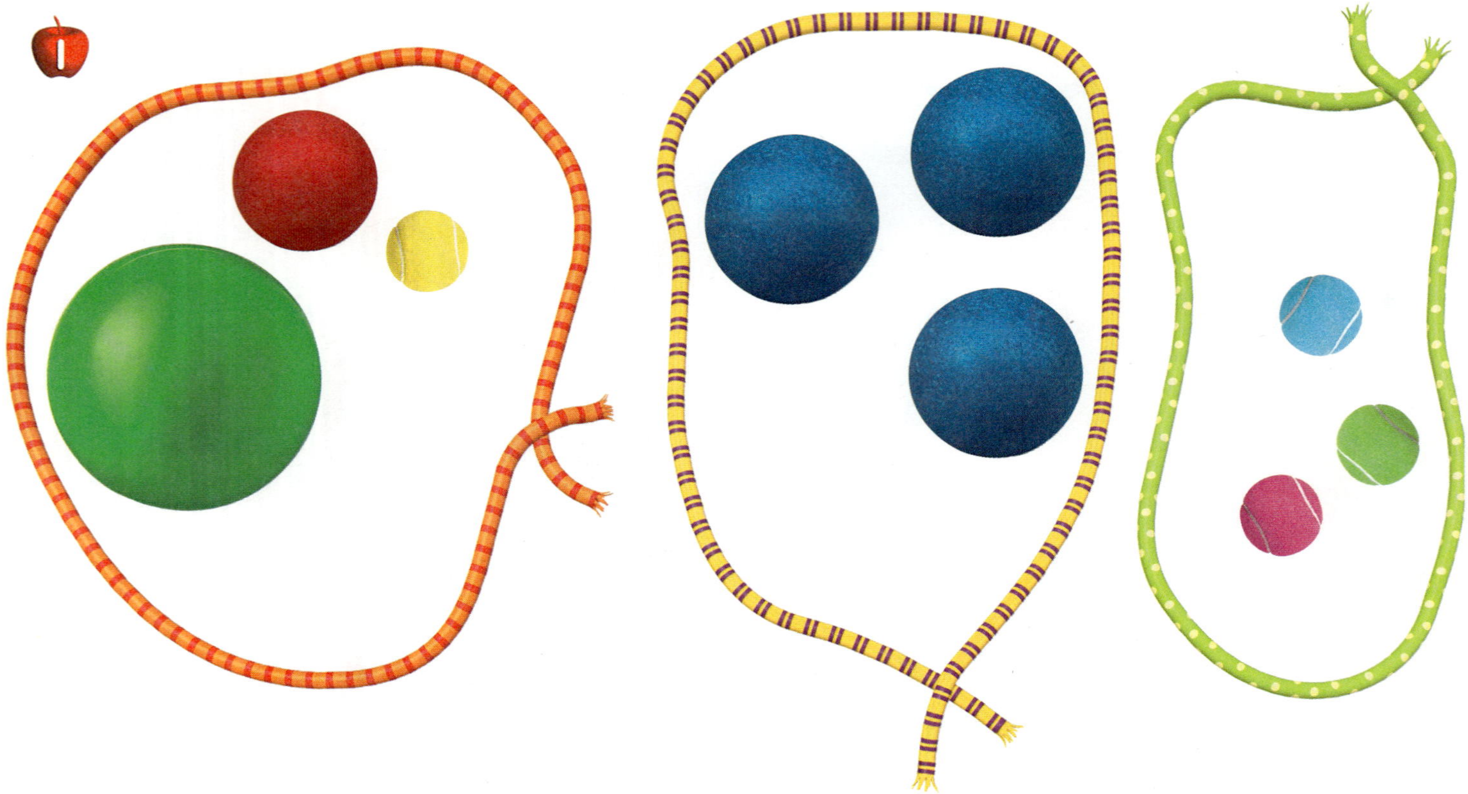

 **HOME ACTIVITY** · Ask your child to sort his or her toys into groups in which all the toys are alike in two ways and to explain how the toys in each group are alike. For example, they all are small and have wheels.

20 twenty

Problem Solving Workshop
Strategy • Use Logical Reasoning

1

2

3

4

DIRECTIONS 1. We want to sort fruit. Trace the X on the object that should not be included. **2–4.** Three of the objects are alike. Mark an X on the one that does not belong. Tell why it does not belong.

OBJECTIVE • Solve problems by using the strategy *use logical reasoning.*

Chapter 1 • Lesson 8

DIRECTIONS 1–4. Three of the objects are alike. Mark on X on the one that does not belong. Tell why.

HOME ACTIVITY · Show your child three household items that are alike in some way and a fourth that is different. Ask your child to identify the item that does not belong and to explain why it does not belong.

22 twenty-two

Sort to Make a Graph

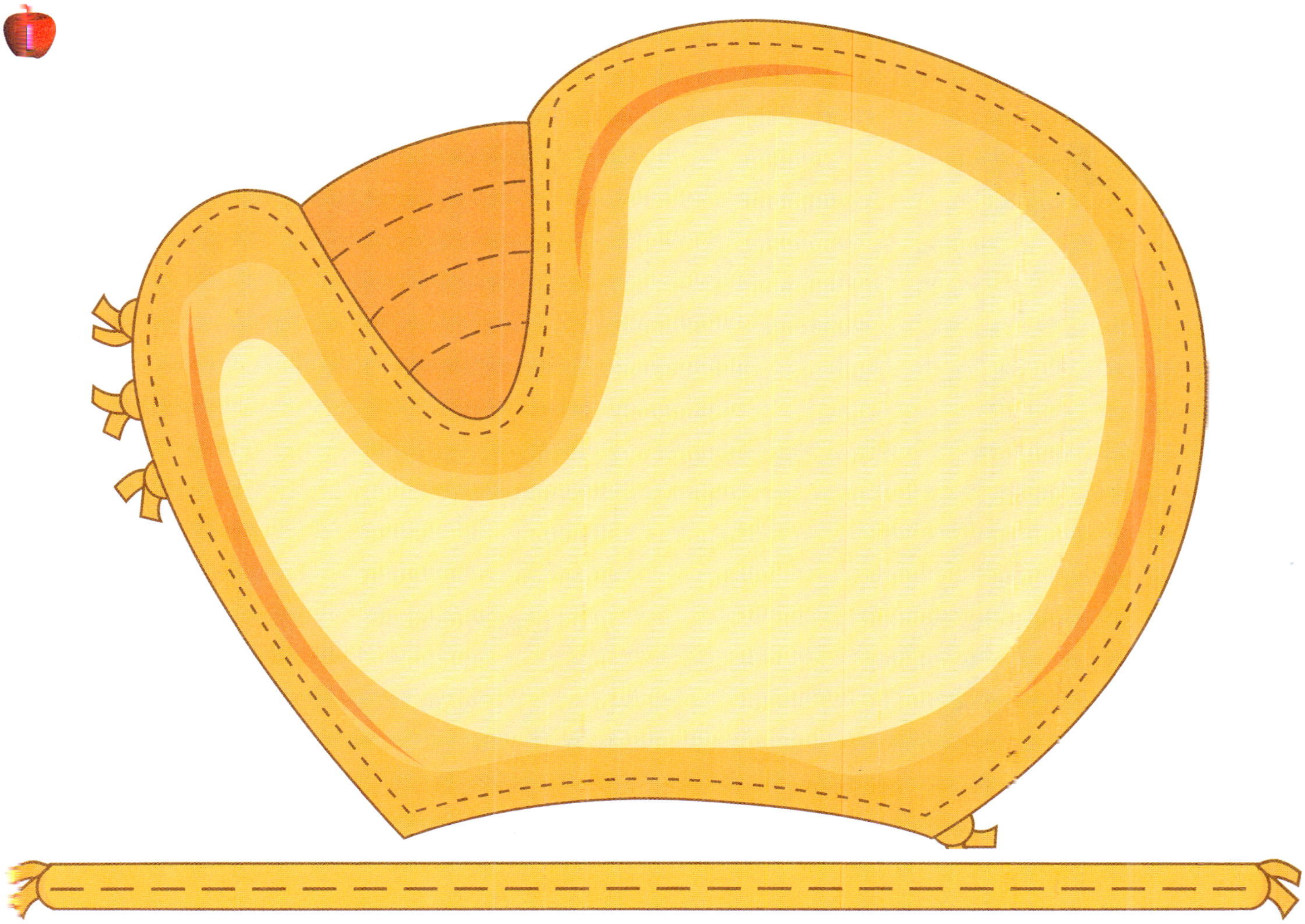

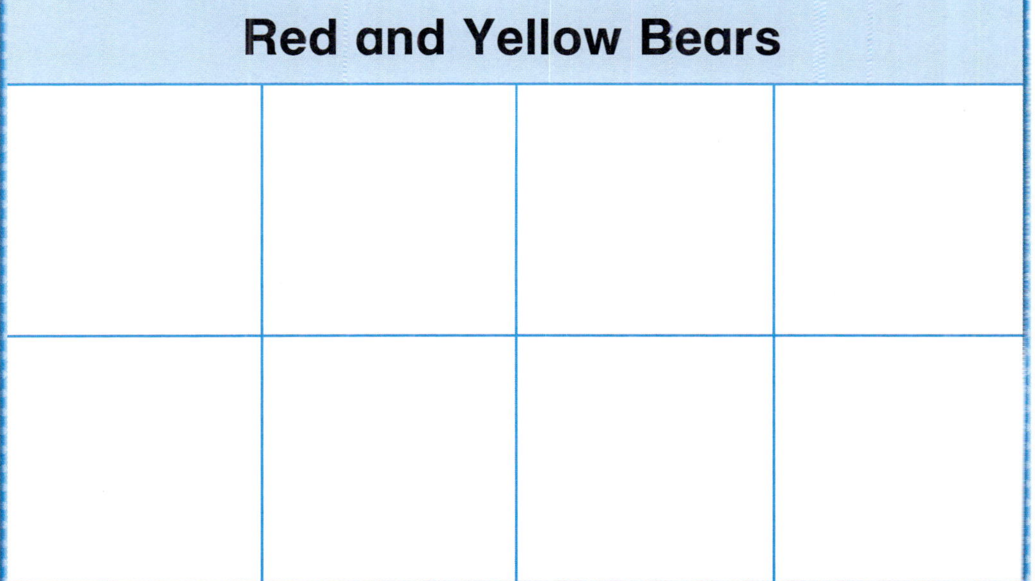

2

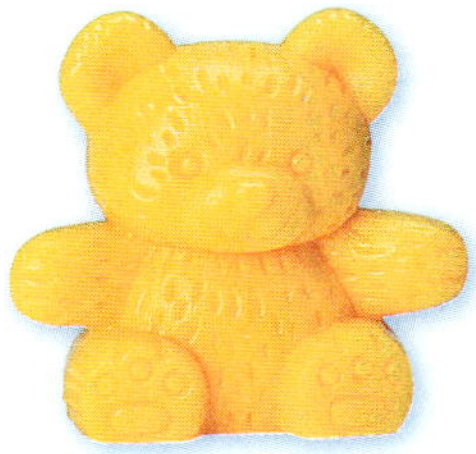 Red and Yellow Bears			

DIRECTIONS **1.** Place a handful of red and yellow bear counters on the baseball glove. Sort the counters by color. **2.** Move the red counters to the top row on the graph. Move the yellow counters to the bottom row on the graph. Draw and color the counters. Explain the graph.

OBJECTIVE • Sort objects into groups to make a graph.

DIRECTIONS   **I.** Place a handful of bear counters on the lunch box. Sort the bear counters by size.   **2.** Move the small bear counters to the top row on the graph. Move the big bear counters to the bottom row on the graph. Draw and color the counters. Explain the graph.

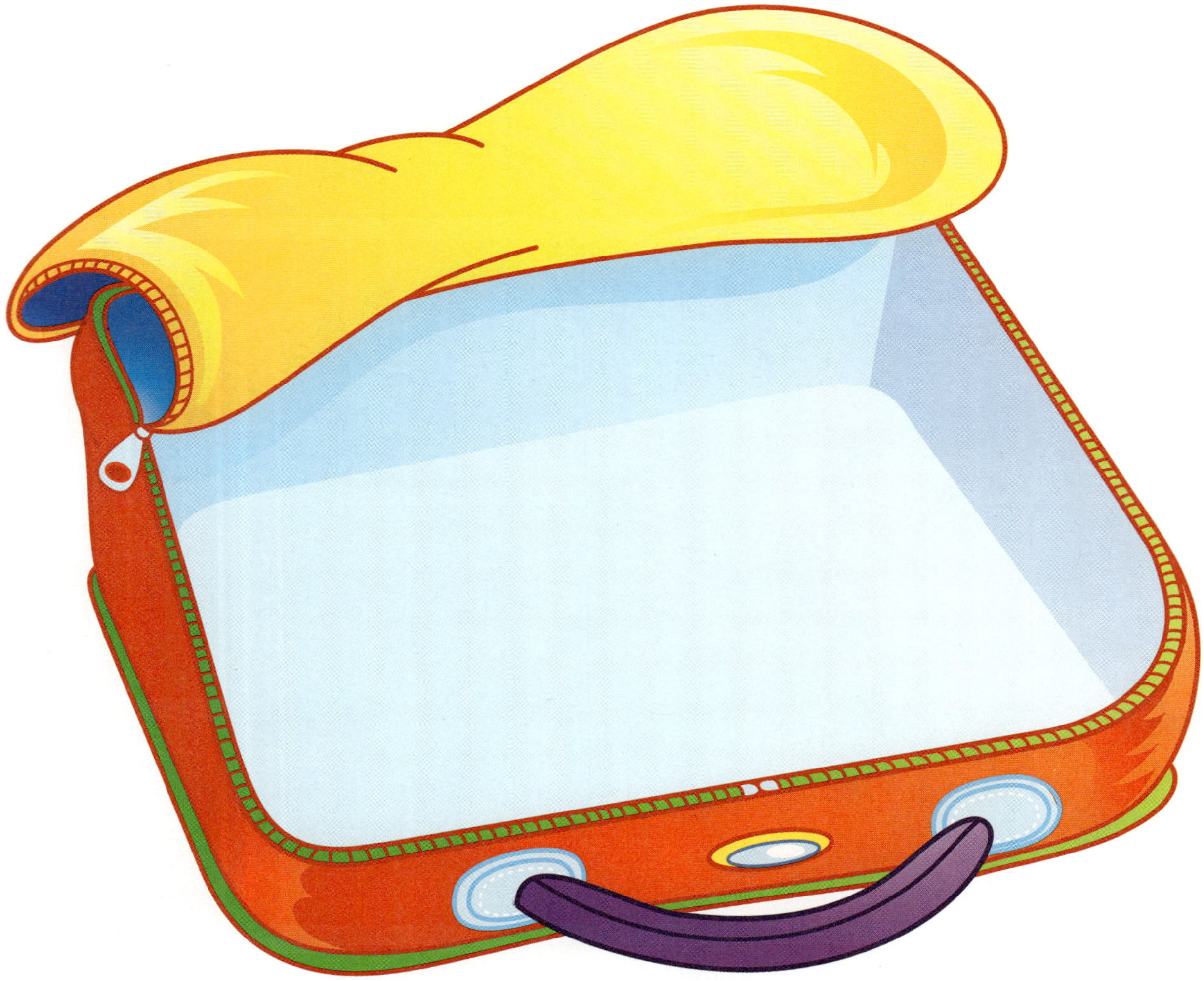

HOME ACTIVITY • Help your child make a similar graph in which to sort small objects such as paper clips or buttons by size or color.

24 twenty-four

Follow the Figures

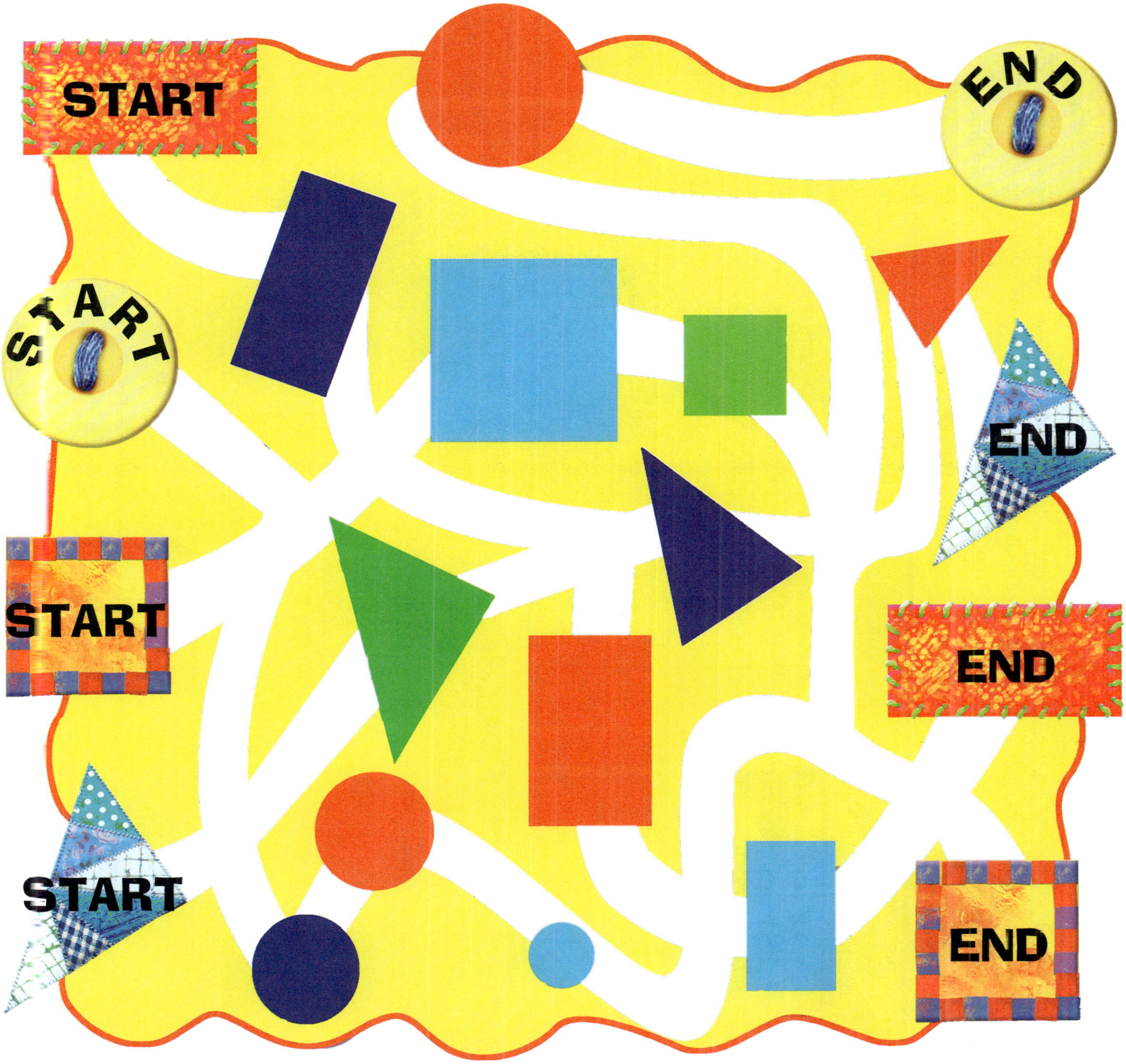

DIRECTIONS Choose a figure from Start. Follow the path that has the same figures. Draw a line to show the path.

Math Power • Figures That Do Not Belong

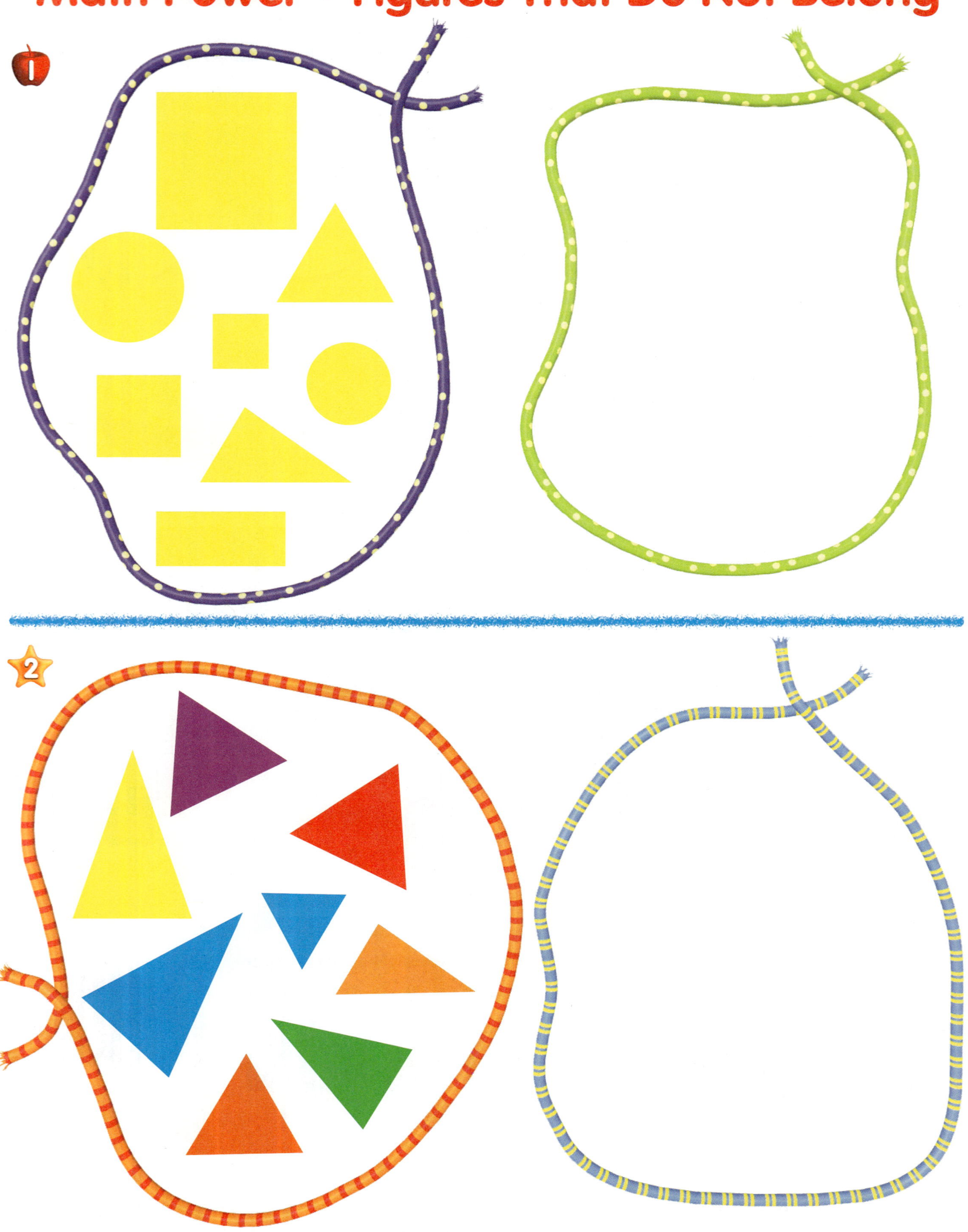

DIRECTIONS **1–2.** Tell how the figures in the group are alike. Draw and color a figure that does not belong in the group.

26 twenty-six

✓ Chapter I Review/Test

1 

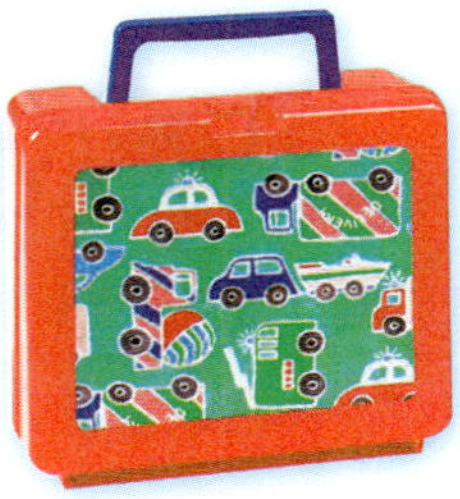

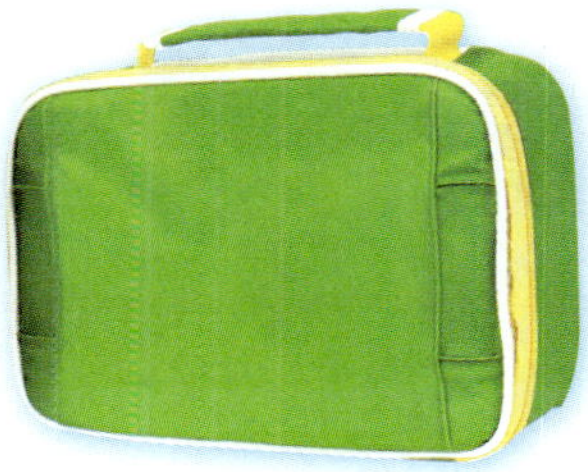

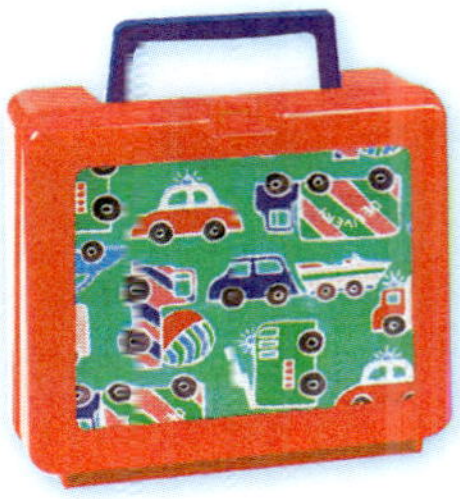

2

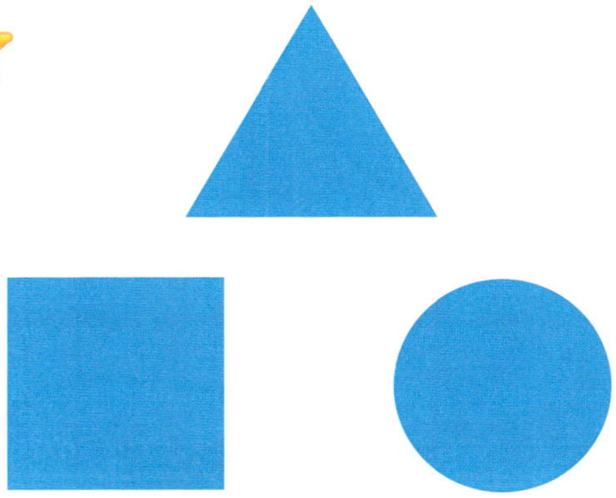

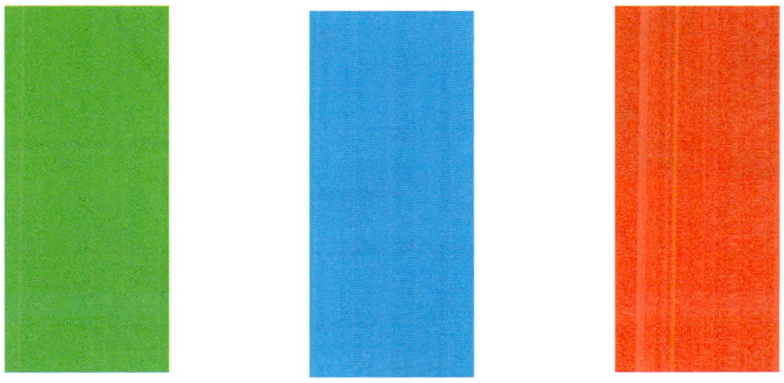

3

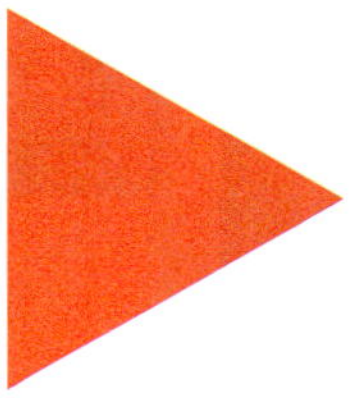

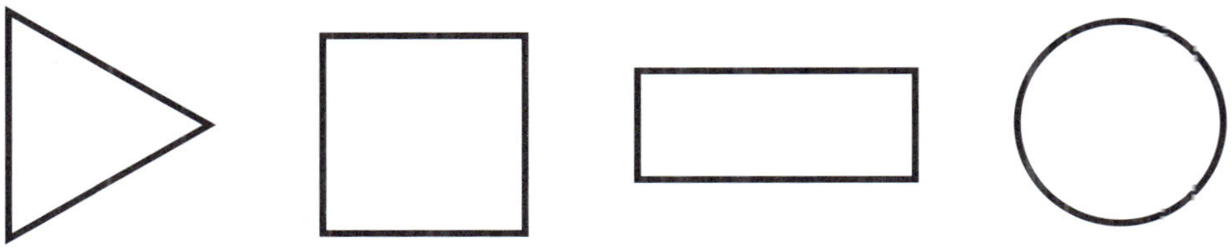

4

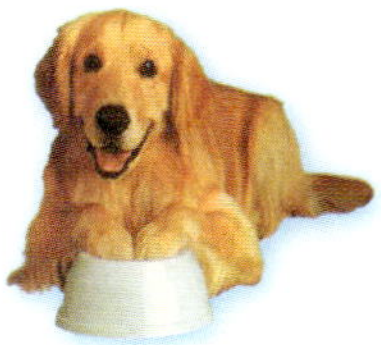

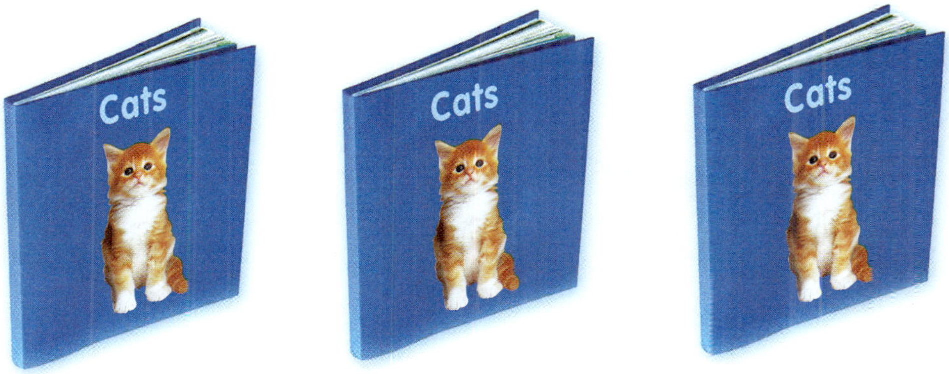

DIRECTIONS **I.** Mark an X on the object that is different.
2. Look at the group of figures at the beginning of the row. Circle the figure that belongs in the group. **3.** Color the figures to match the figure at the beginning of the row. Circle one figure that matches in more than one way. **4.** Three of the objects are alike. Mark an X on the one that does not belong.

✓ Cumulative Review

DIRECTIONS   **I.** Mark an X on the object that does not belong.
2. Color the figures to match the figure at the beginning of the row. Circle one figure that matches in more than one way.   **3.** Draw and color one more figure in the group that is sorted by color and size.   **4.** Three of the objects are alike. Mark an X on the one that does not belong.

28   twenty-eight

Numbers 0 to 5
Theme: My Friends and I

Name ___________________________________

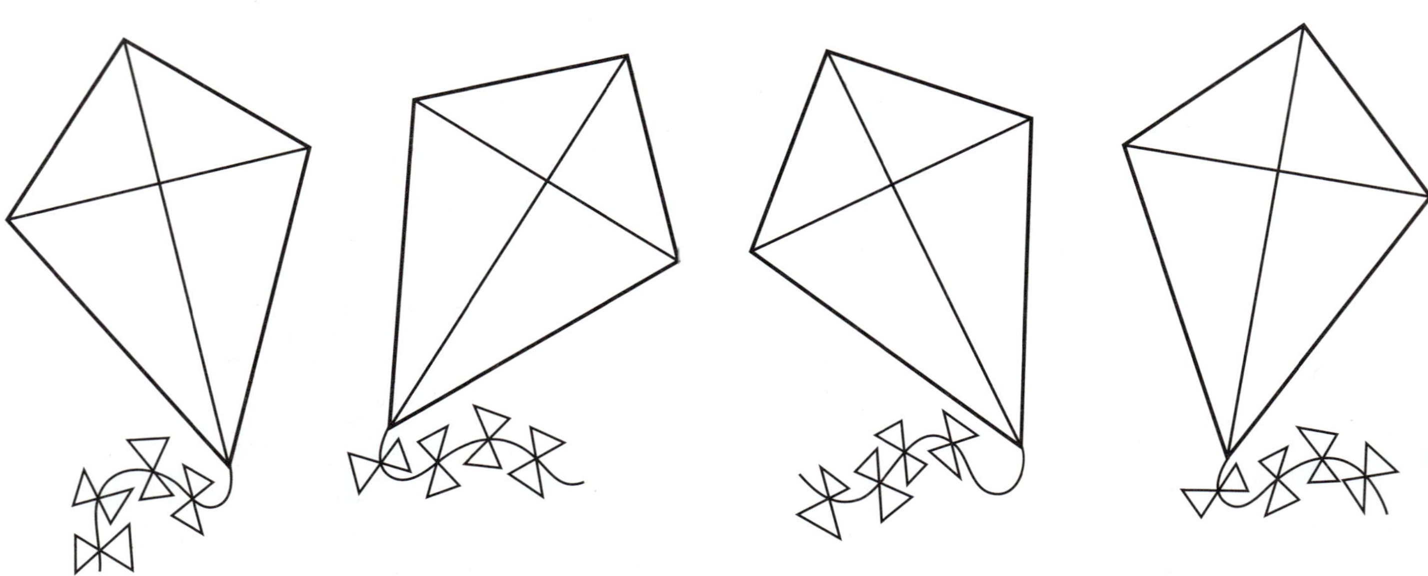

DIRECTIONS Draw a string from each child to his or her kite. Color the kites.

 **FAMILY NOTE:** This page checks your child's understanding of important concepts and skills needed for success in Chapter 2.

1

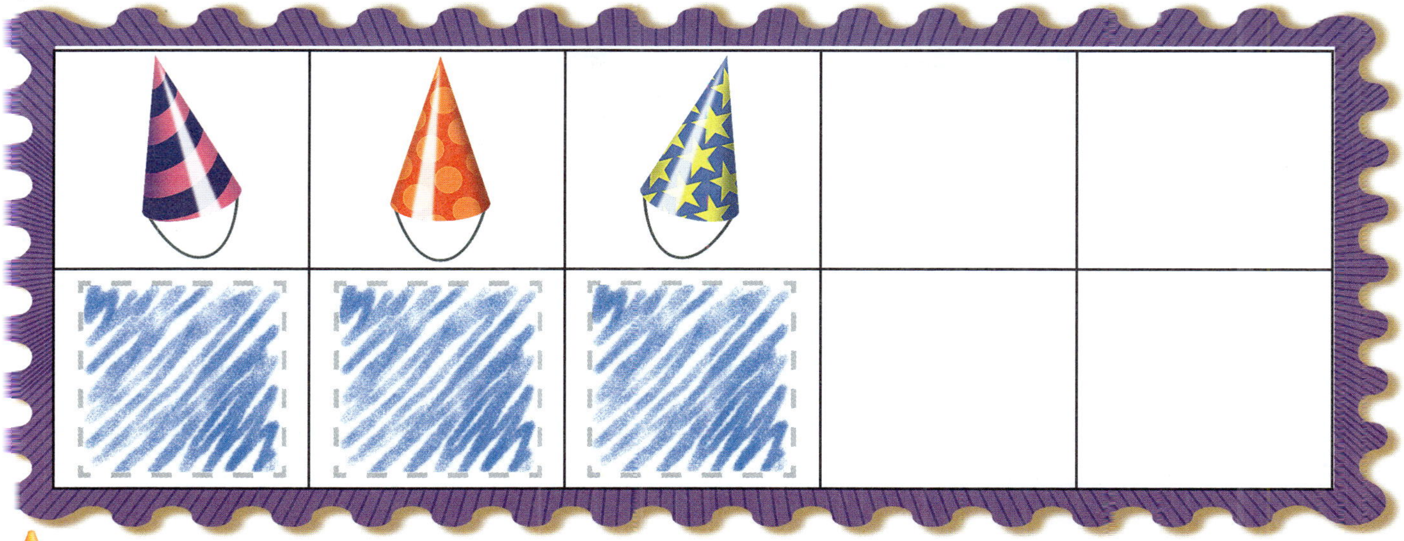

2

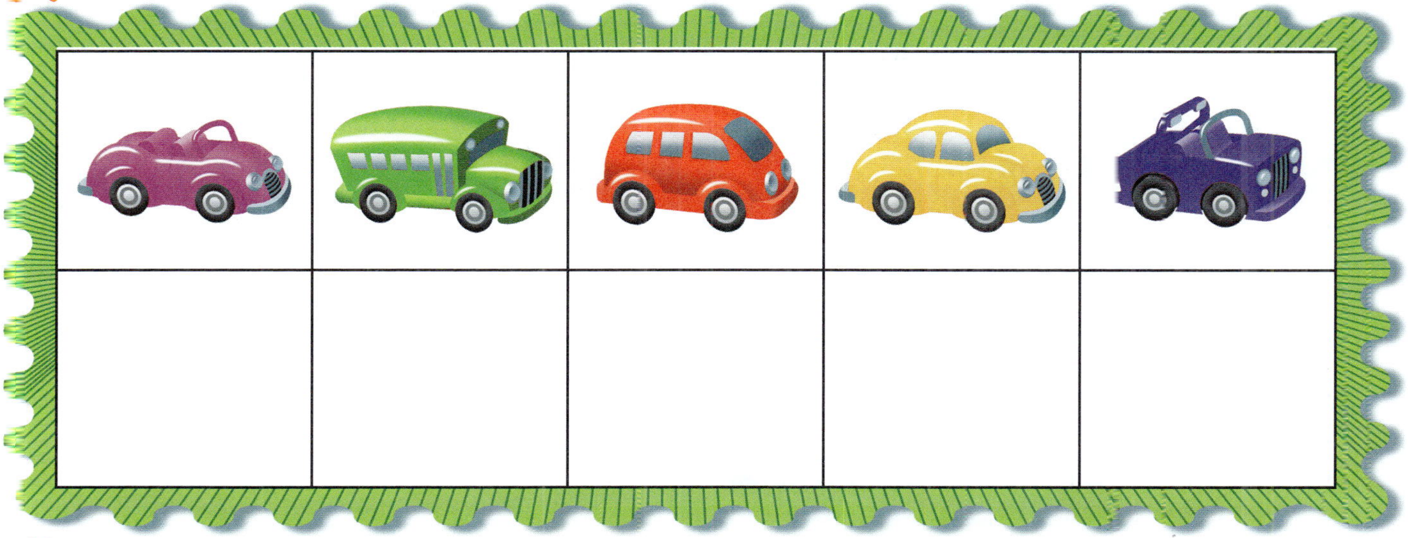

3

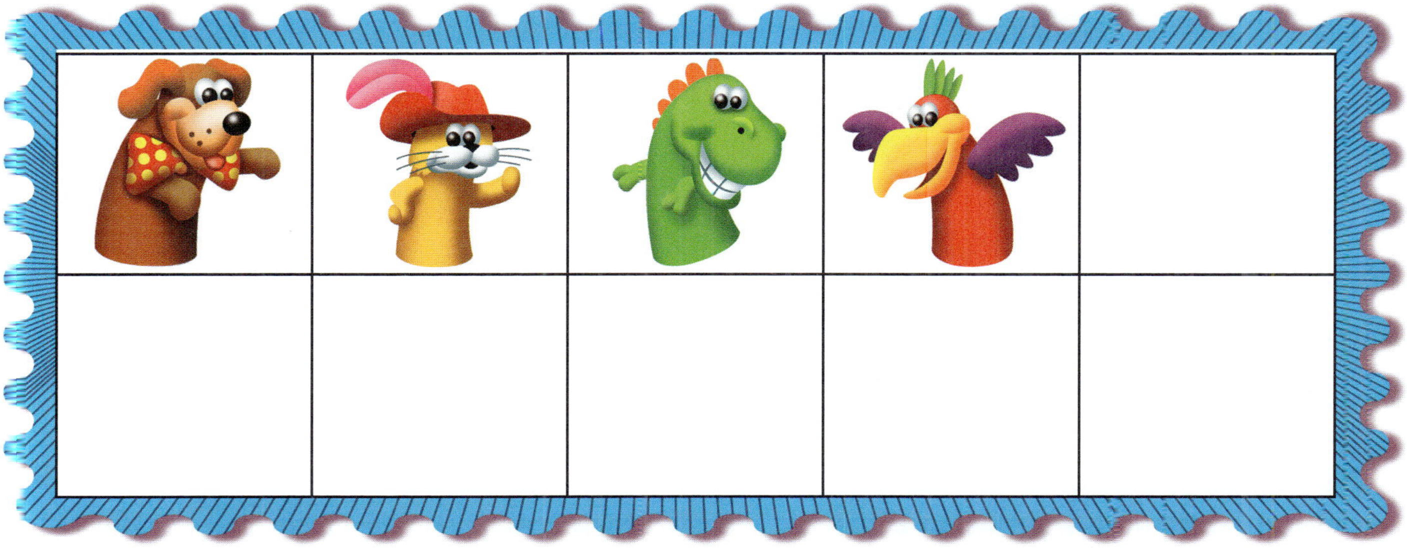

DIRECTIONS **1–3.** Place a color tile below each object to show an equal set. Draw and color each color tile.

OBJECTIVE • Use one-to-one correspondence to make equal sets.

Chapter 2 • Lesson 1

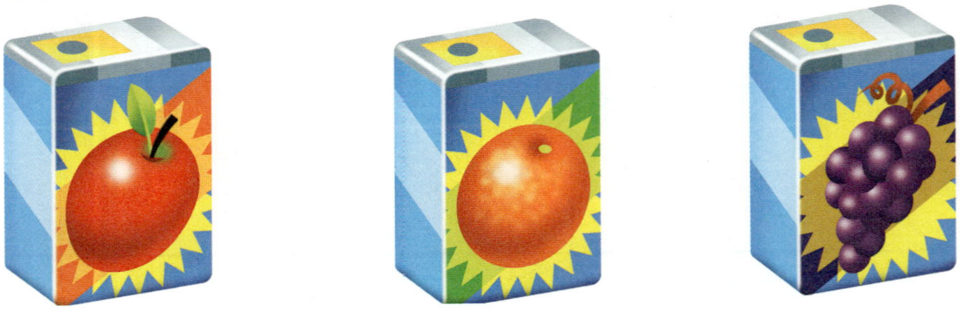

Problem Solving Workshop
Skill • Use a Model

DIRECTIONS **1–3.** Use bear counters to show a set with fewer bears than stuffed toys. Draw the counters.

HOME ACTIVITY · Draw a row of shapes (all alike), and ask your child to draw a set that has more shapes. Draw another row of shapes, and ask your child to draw a set with fewer shapes.

34 thirty-four

Model, Read, and Write 1, 2, 3, 4

DIRECTIONS Use cubes to show how many there are of each object or animal. **1.** Say the number. Trace the cube. Trace the number. **2–4.** Say the number. Draw the cubes. Trace the number.

OBJECTIVE • Use one-to-one correspondence to model and describe sets of 1 to 4.

Chapter 2 • Lesson 3

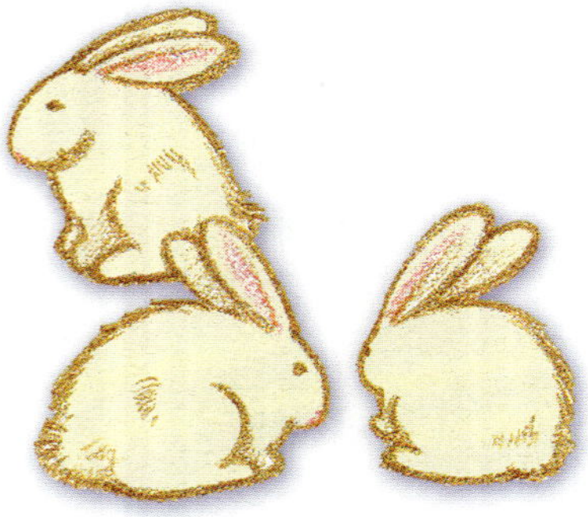

DIRECTIONS   1–4. **Place a cube on each object or animal in the set as you count. Draw the cubes. Write the number.**

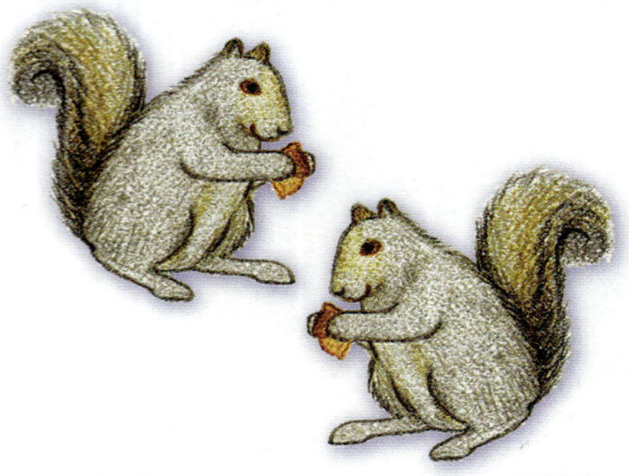

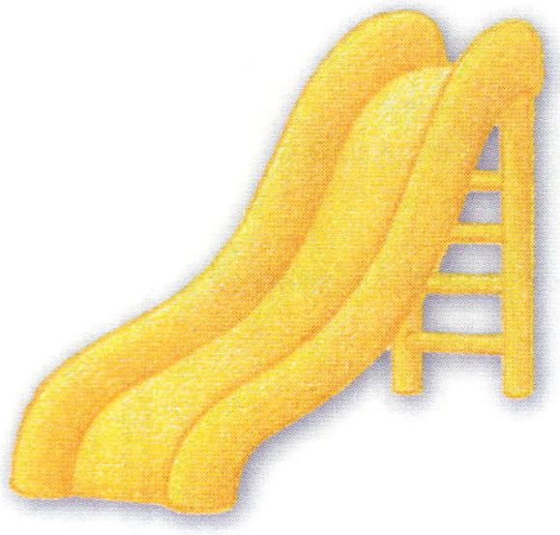

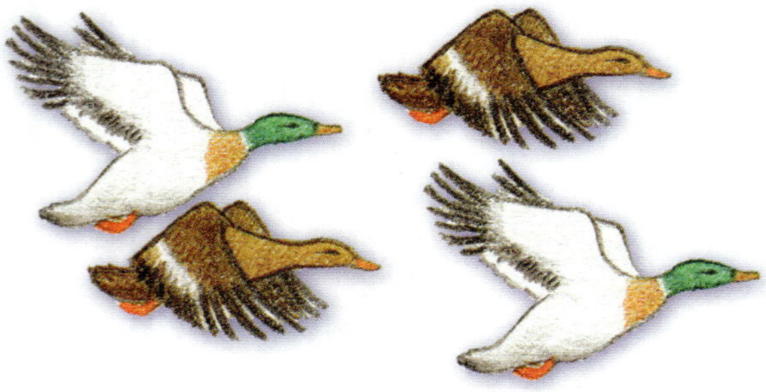

 **HOME ACTIVITY** • Ask your child to count a set of one to four household objects, such as books or buttons, and then write the number. Repeat with more sets of objects.

Model on a Five Frame

1

1 2 3 4 5

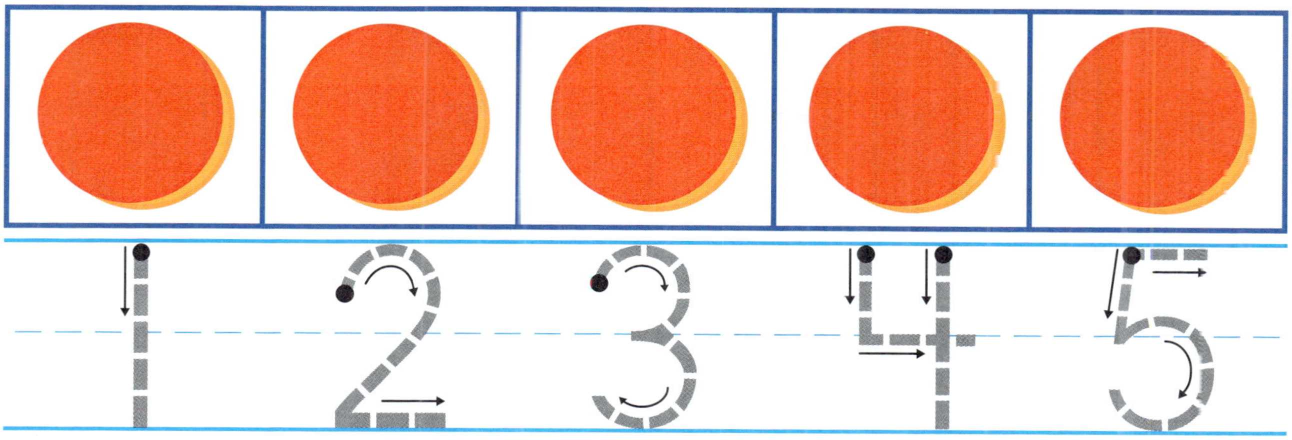

2

3

3

2

4

5

DIRECTIONS **1.** Trace each number as you count. **2–4.** Use counters on the five frame to model the number shown. Draw the counters. Trace the number.

OBJECTIVE • Use concrete objects to represent quantities.

Chapter 2 • Lesson 4

1

2

3

4

DIRECTIONS 1. Use counters to model five. Draw the counters. Write the number. 2. Use counters to model four. Draw the counters. Write the number. 3. Use counters to model five. Draw the counters. Write the number. 4. Use counters to model three. Draw the counters. Write the number.

HOME ACTIVITY • Draw a five frame as shown on this page. Write a number from 1 to 5. Ask your child to model the number by using objects on the five frame. Now have your child write the number.

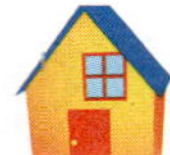

5 5 5 5 5

five

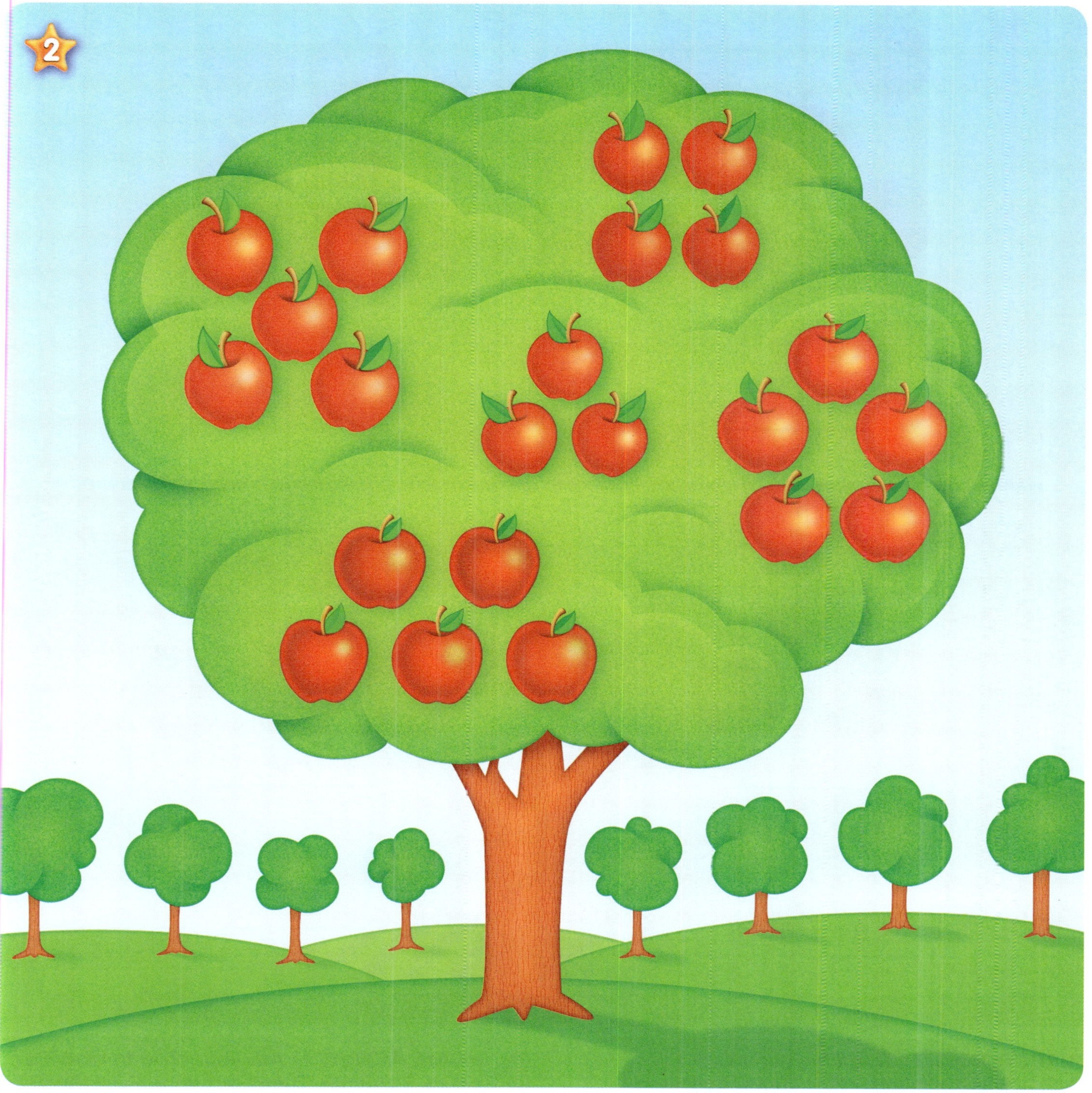

DIRECTIONS 1. Trace the number 5.
2. Circle the sets of five apples.

OBJECTIVE • Recognize and write the numeral that describes the quantity 5.

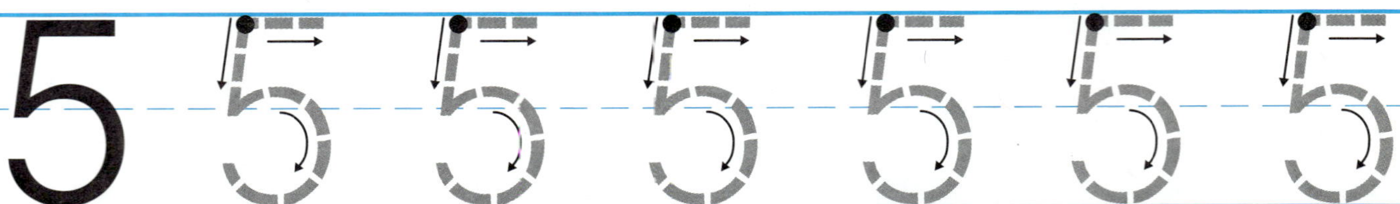

DIRECTIONS I. Trace the number 5.
2–5. Write the number that shows how many in the set.

 HOME ACTIVITY · Ask your child to model a set of 5 objects. Then have your child show you a set with one less than the first set. Ask how many are in the second set.

40 forty

 Mid Chapter 2 Review

2

3

4

DIRECTIONS 1. Draw a straw below each drink to show equal sets.
2. Use bear counters to show a set with fewer bears than stuffed toys. Draw the counters.
3. Place a cube on each animal in the set as you count. Draw the cubes. Write the number.   4. Use counters to model 4. Draw the counters. Write the number.

✓ Cumulative Review

1

2

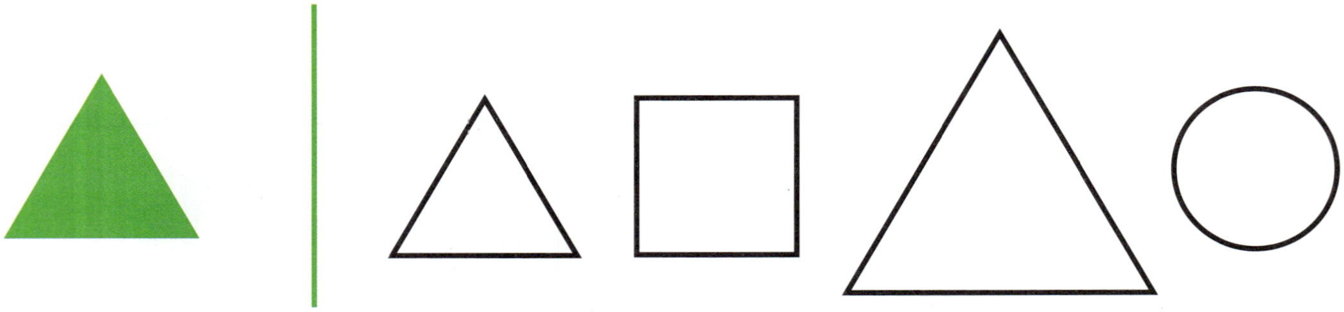

3

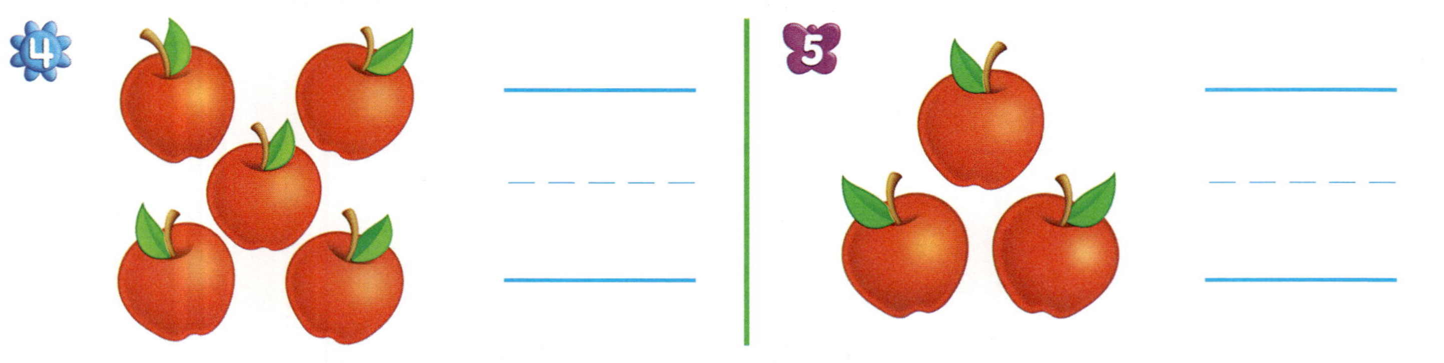

4   **5**

DIRECTIONS   1. Look at the figure at the beginning of the row. Mark an X on the group where the figure belongs.   **2.** Color all the figures to match the color of the figure at the beginning of the row. Circle one figure that matches in more than one way.   **3.** Draw a ball below each cap to show equal sets.   **4–5.** Write the number that shows how many in the set.

42 forty-two

1 

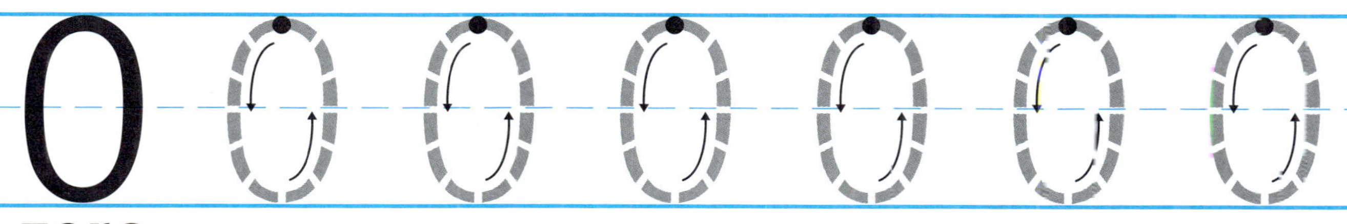

0
zero

2 

3 

4 

5

DIRECTIONS 1. Say the number. Trace the number 0. 2–5. Write the number to show how many fish are in the set.

OBJECTIVE • Recognize and write the numeral that describes the quantity 0.

four

zero

zero

one

zero

three

DIRECTIONS   1–6. Write the number that shows how many fish are in the bowl.

HOME ACTIVITY • Provide six bowls, each containing from 0 to 5 objects. Ask your child to write the number that shows how many objects are in each bowl.

44 forty-four

Write Numbers to 5

DIRECTIONS I-6. Trace the number that shows how many backpacks are on the hooks. Then write the number.

OBJECTIVE • Use numbers to describe in writing how many objects are in a set.

Chapter 2 • Lesson 7

DIRECTIONS 1–6. Trace the number that shows how many toys are on the shelf. Then write the number.

HOME ACTIVITY · Help your child write the numbers 0 to 5 on separate slips of paper. Then have your child make a set of blocks or paper clips to model each number.

Name _______________________________

 **1**

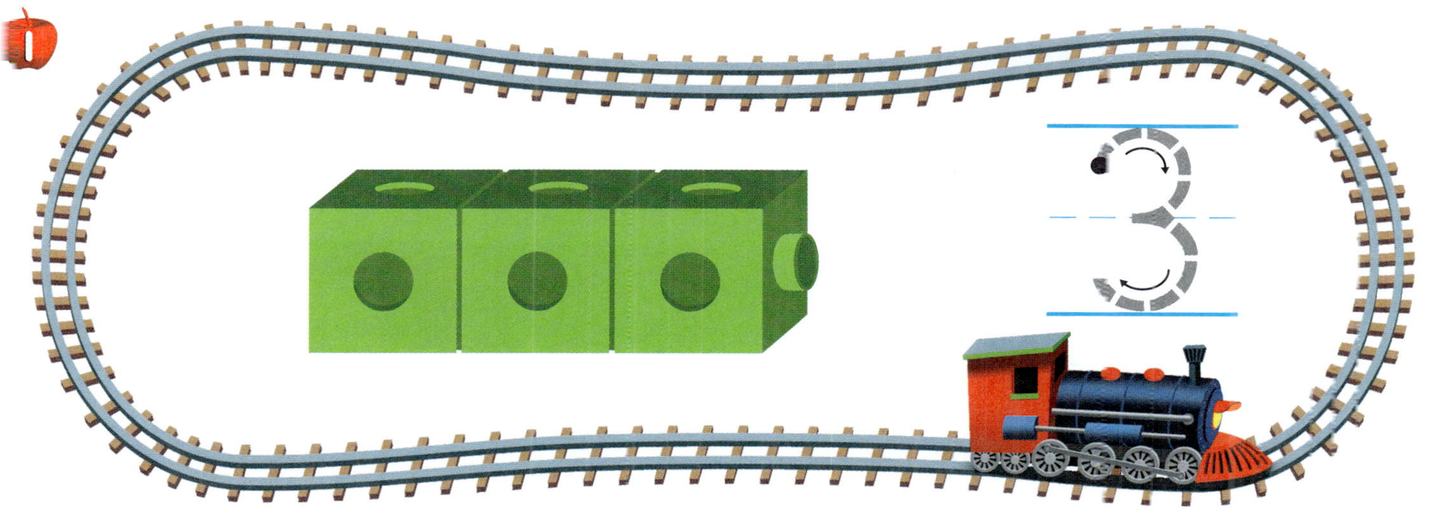

 **2**

3

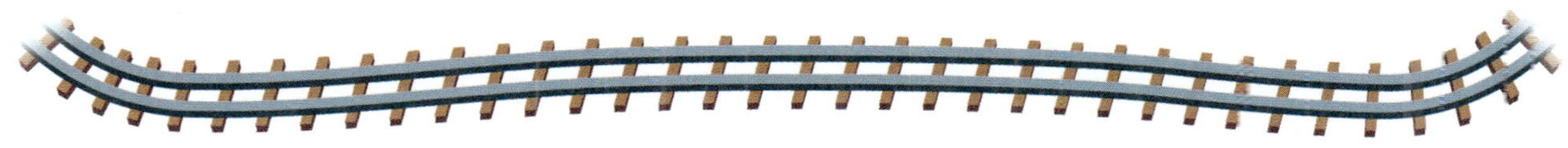

DIRECTIONS **1.** Trace the number of cubes.
2. Build a cube train that has 1 cube more
than 3. Draw the cube train. Write the number.
3. Build a cube train that has 2 cubes more
than 3. Draw the cube train. Write the number.

OBJECTIVE • Solve problems by using the
strategy *make a model.*

HOME ACTIVITY · Draw a domino block with up to 3 dots on one end. Ask your child to draw on the other end a set of dots that has more than the set you drew.

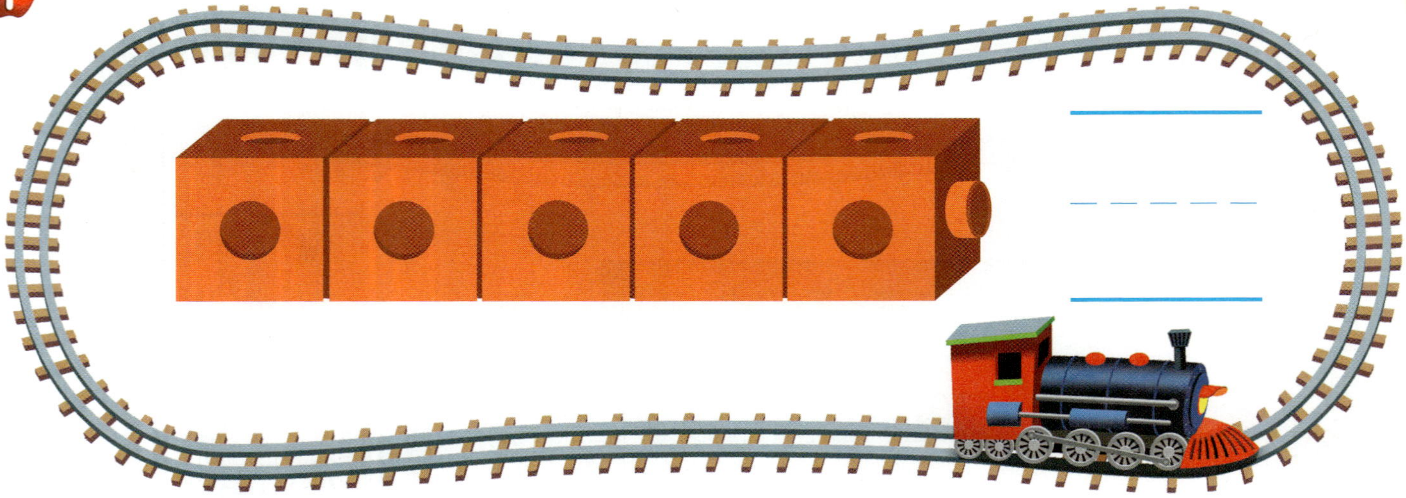

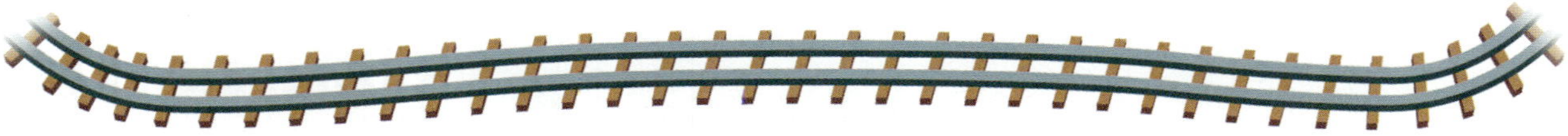

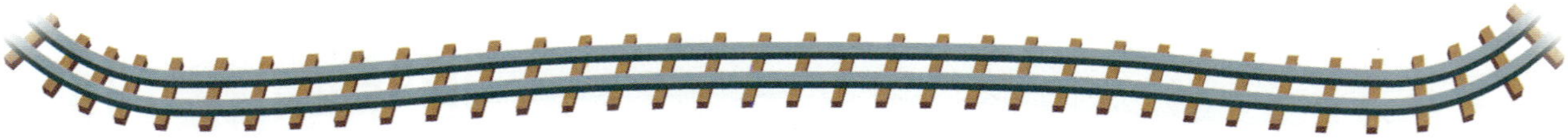

48 forty-eight

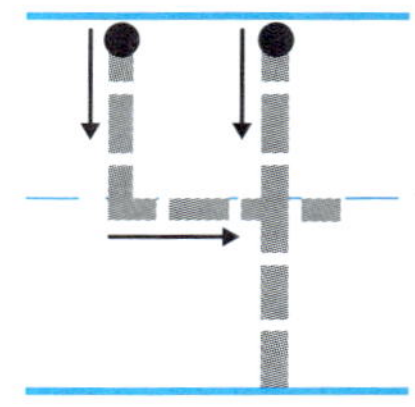
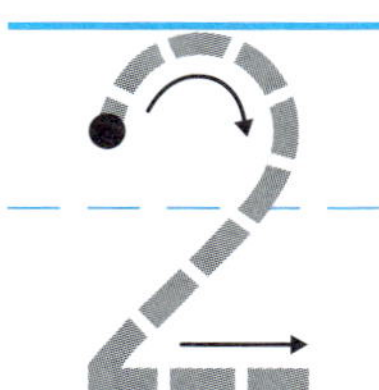
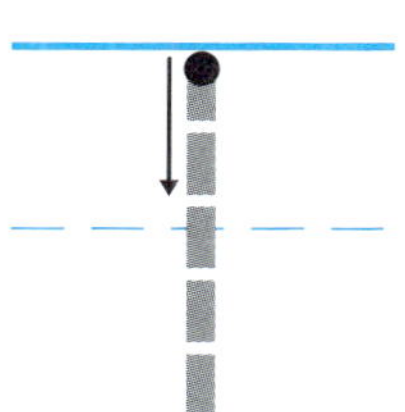
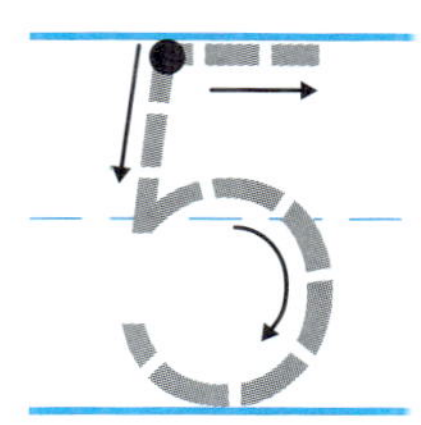

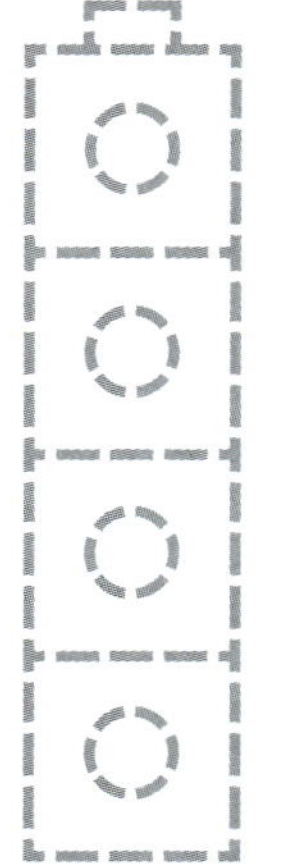

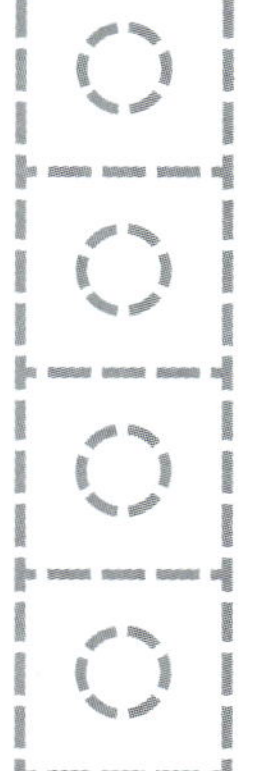
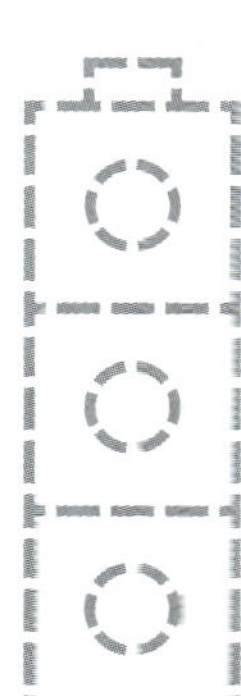

DIRECTIONS **1.** Trace the numbers.
Make a cube train to model each number.
2. Place the cube trains in order. Draw the
cube trains. Write the number for each train.

OBJECTIVE • Order objects by number.

Chapter 2 • Lesson 9

forty-nine **49**

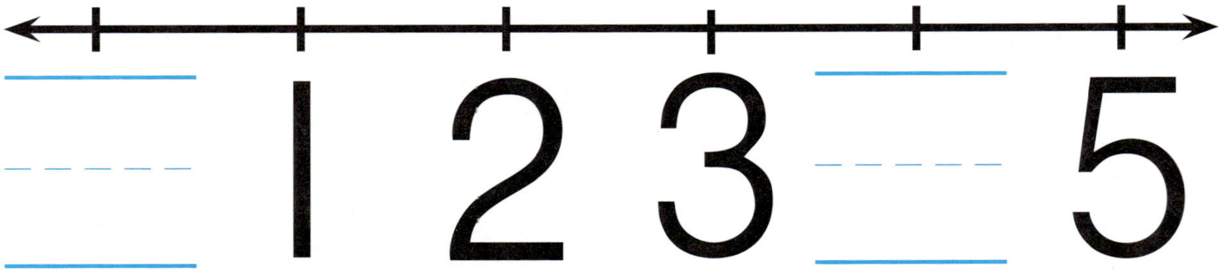

DIRECTIONS   1. Trace the number that is before 3. Trace the number that is after 4. **2.** Write the number that is before 2. Write the number that is after 2.   **3.** Write the number that is before 1. Write the number that is after 3.

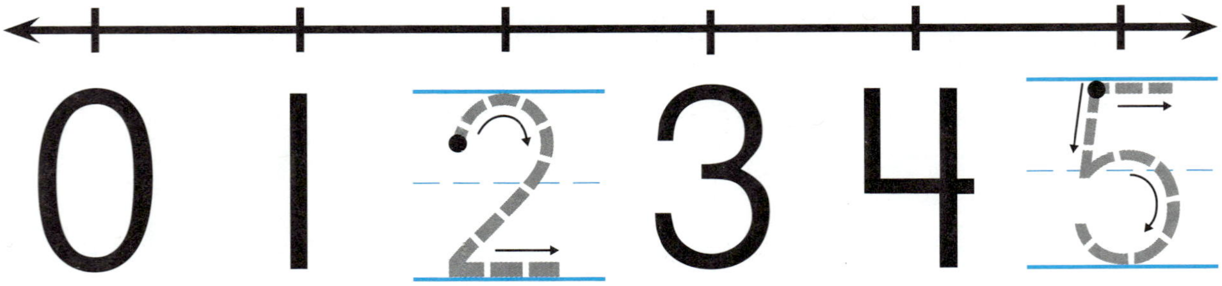

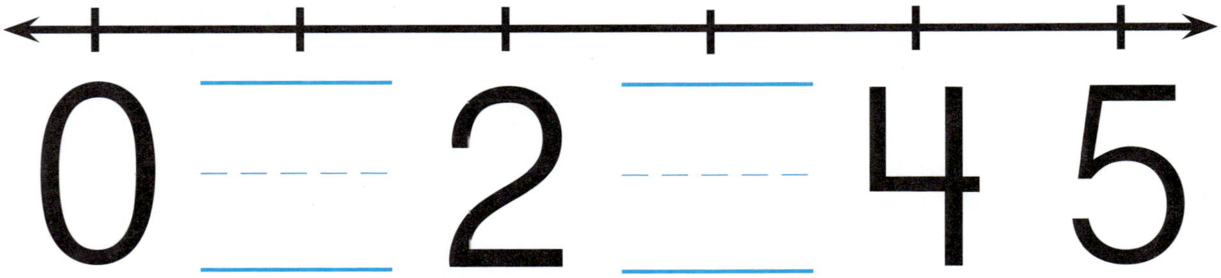

HOME ACTIVITY • Write the numbers 0-5 on separate self-stick notes or on slips of paper. Have your child place the numbers in order from 0 to 5.

50 fifty

Bus Stop

PRACTICE GAME

DIRECTIONS Each partner rolls the number cube and models his or her number with cubes. Compare the sets. The player with the greater set moves to the next bus stop. If the sets are the same, no one moves. The first player to reach the end wins the game.

MATERIALS connecting cubes; game marker for each player; number cube (0-5)

Math Power • Number Cards

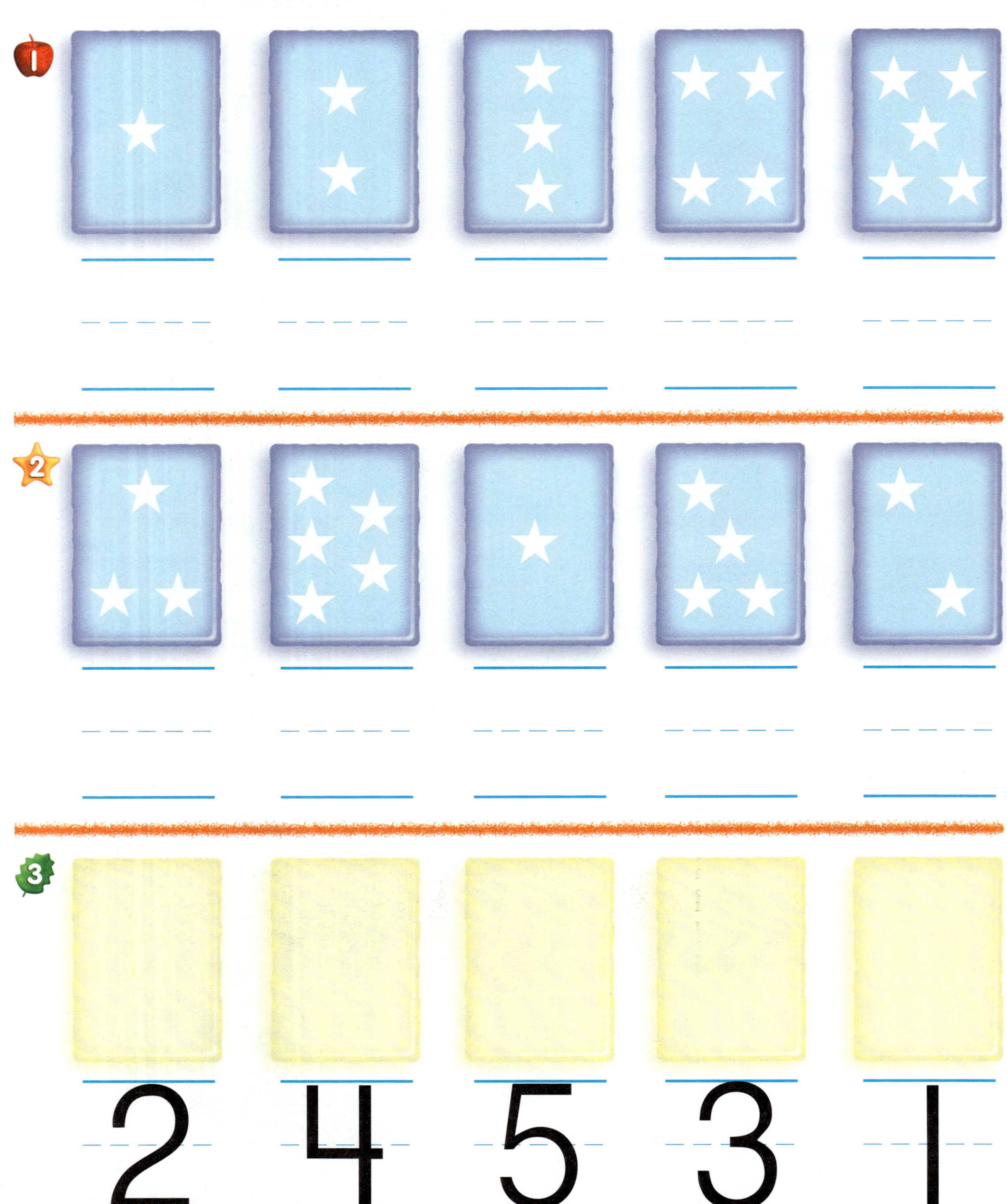

DIRECTIONS 1–2. How many stars on each card? Write the number of stars for each card. 3. Draw dots on each card to show the number.

52 fifty-two

✓ Chapter 2 Review/Test

ZERO

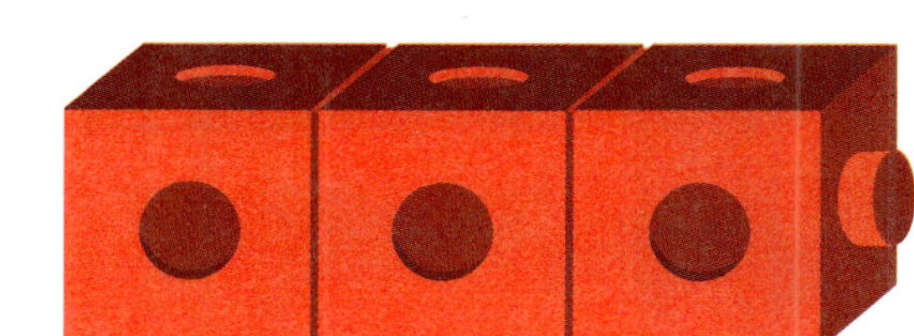

---

0   I   3   5

DIRECTIONS **1.** Place a cube on each animal in the set as you count. Draw the cubes. Write the number. **2.** Write how many fish in the bowl. **3.** Build a cube train that has two cubes more than 3. Draw the cube train. Write the number. **4.** Write the number that is before 3. Write the number that is after 3.

Chapter 2

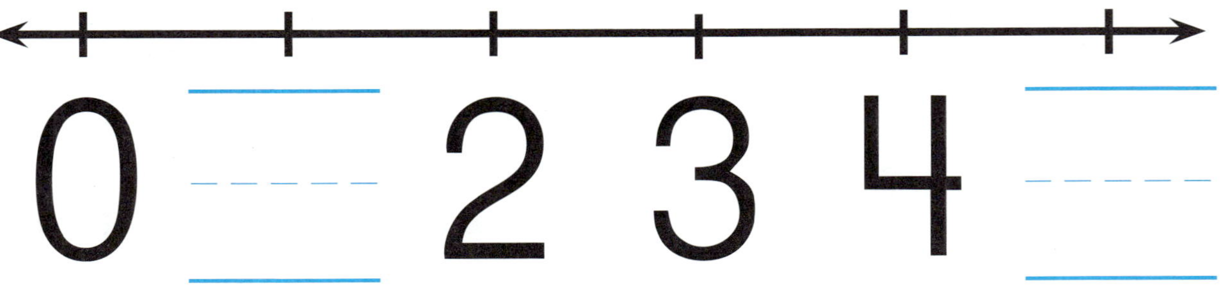

DIRECTIONS   **1.** Mark an X on the object that does not belong.
2. Three of the objects are alike. Mark an X on the one that does not belong.   **3.** Write how many fish in the set.   **4.** Write the number that is before 2. Write the number that is after 4.

THE WORLD ALMANAC FOR KIDS

Healthful Snacks

ALMANAC Fact

Eating foods from each group every day will help you stay healthy.

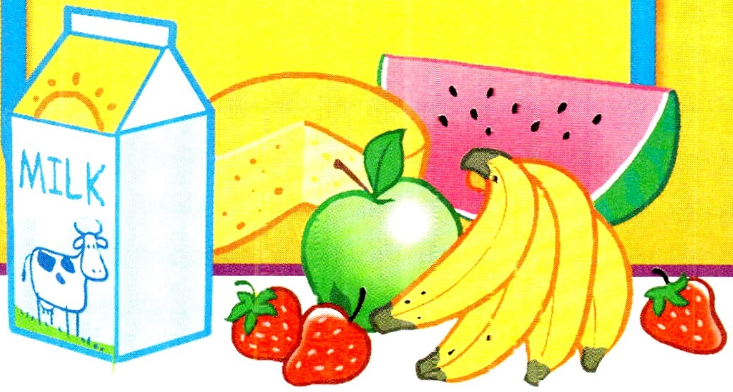

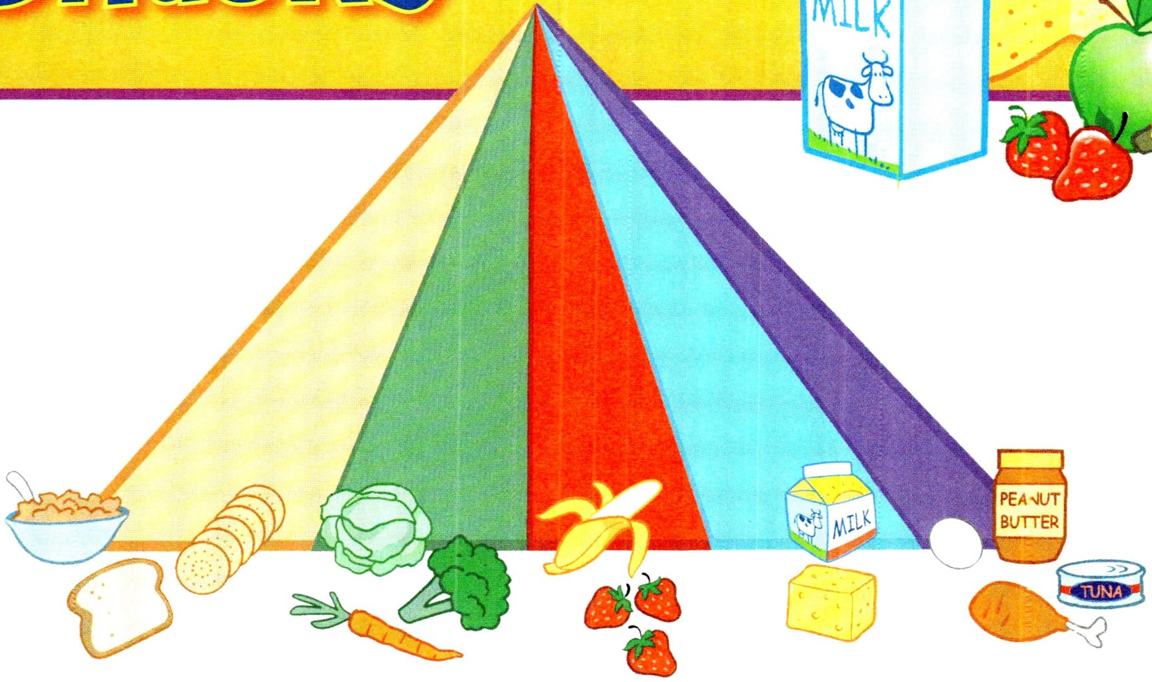

Cows & Milk

Milk, cheese, and yogurt help make your teeth and bones strong. Milk comes from cows that live on dairy farms.

1

2

3

• 4

5 •———————• 3

1 •   • 2

Milk

Yogurt

Cheese

DIRECTIONS   **1–2.** How many? Write the number.   **3.** Beginning with 1, connect the dots in order. Use yellow to color inside the outline. Circle what you drew.

TALK Math Are there more containers of milk or more containers of yogurt? Are there fewer containers of milk or fewer containers of yogurt?

© Harcourt

Fall Festival!

written by Alison Juliano

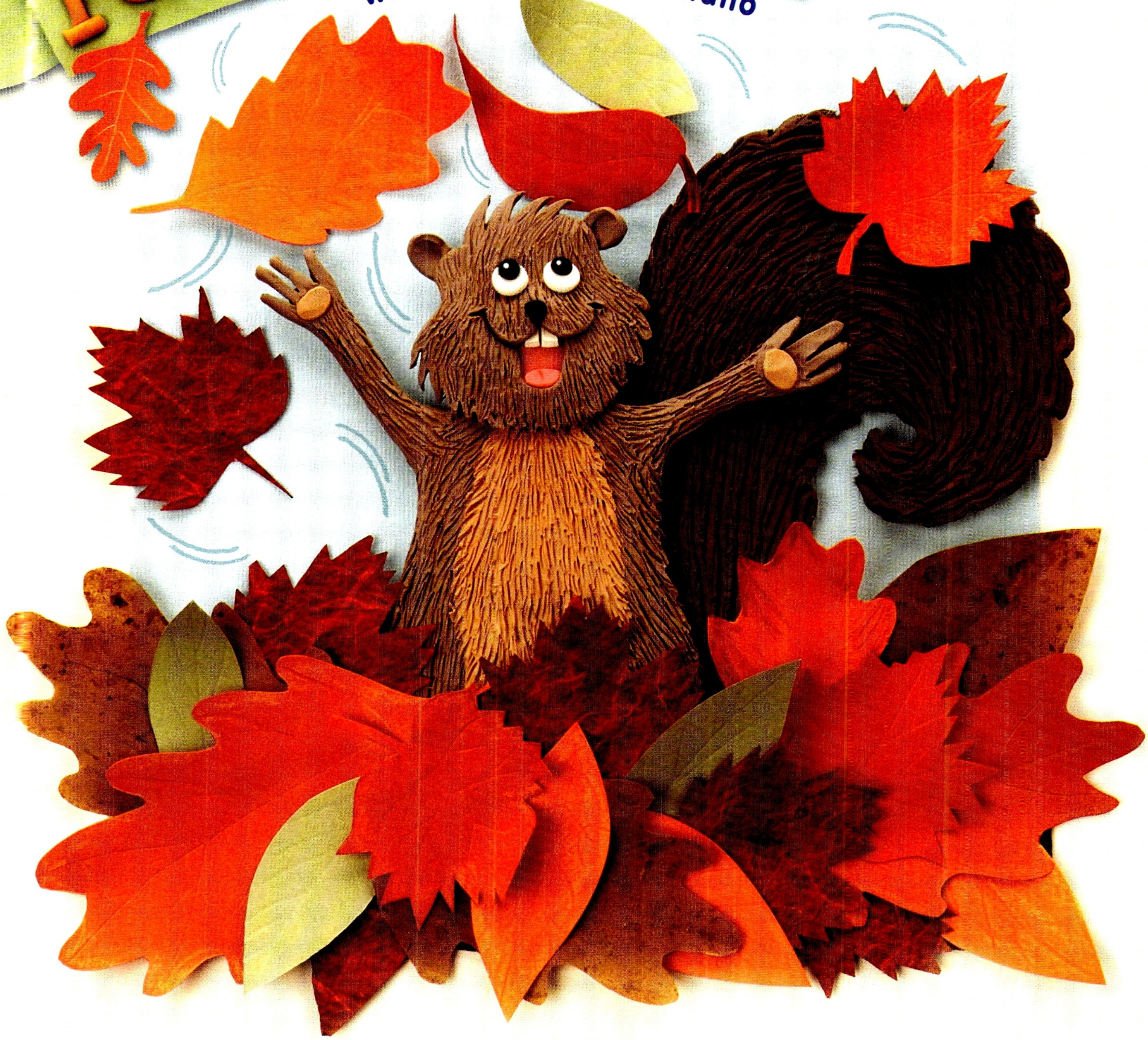

In this story you will also  and .

 Family Note: This story will help your child review numbers to 5.

A

Fall is here! What do you see?
___ big apple tree.
Science
What season is this?
B
© Harcourt

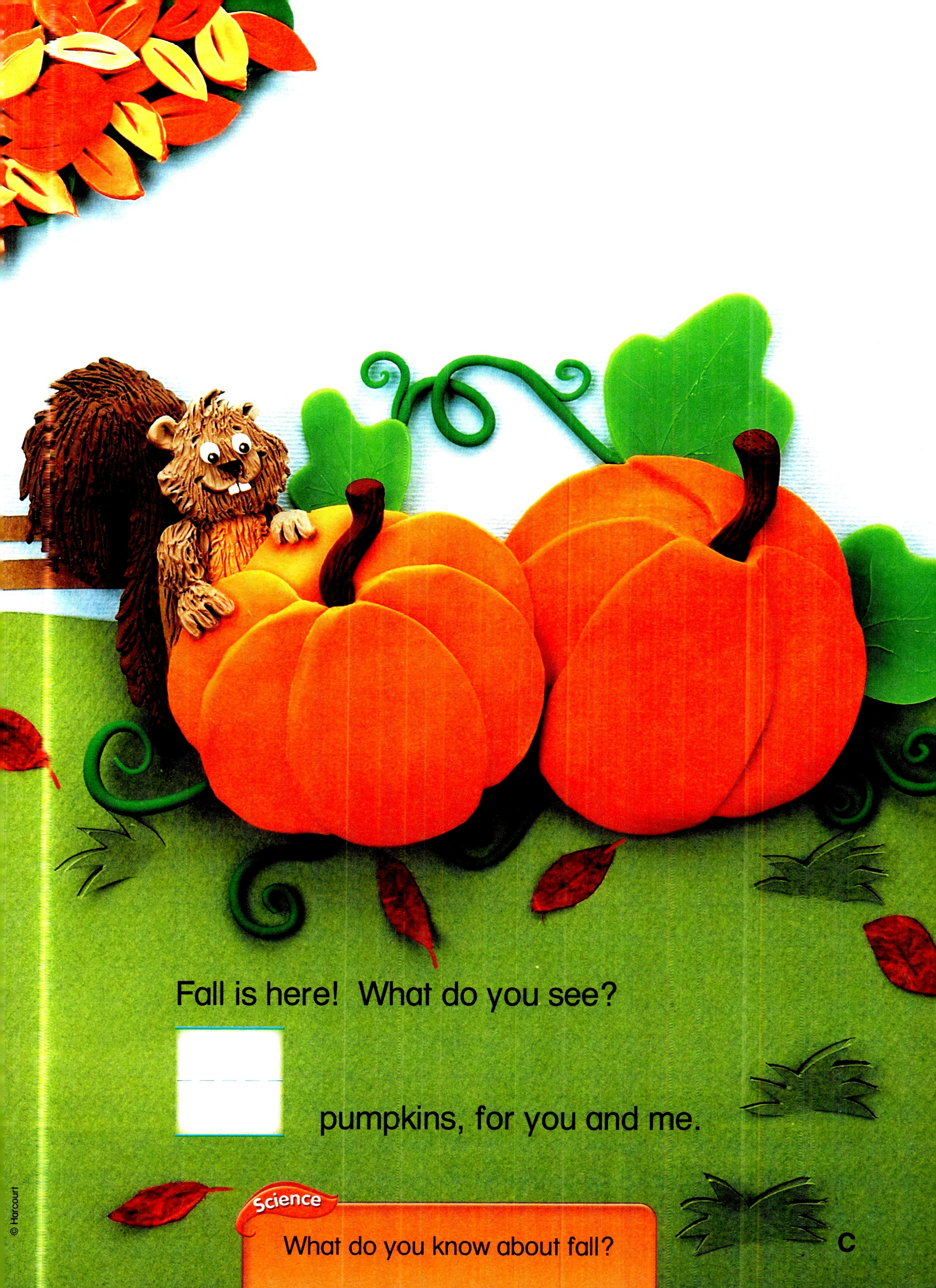

Fall is here! What do you see?

pumpkins, for you and me.

Science

What do you know about fall?

C

Fall is here! What do you see?
Bales of hay — 1, 2, ___ !
Science
What do people wear in fall?

Fall is here! What do you see?

__________ leaves falling from a tree.

Science

What changes in fall?

Fall is here! What do you see?

stalks of corn. Do you see me?

Science

What is different about fall
and other seasons?

F

My Math Story
Literature Activity

Math Words

ore	four
two	five
three	

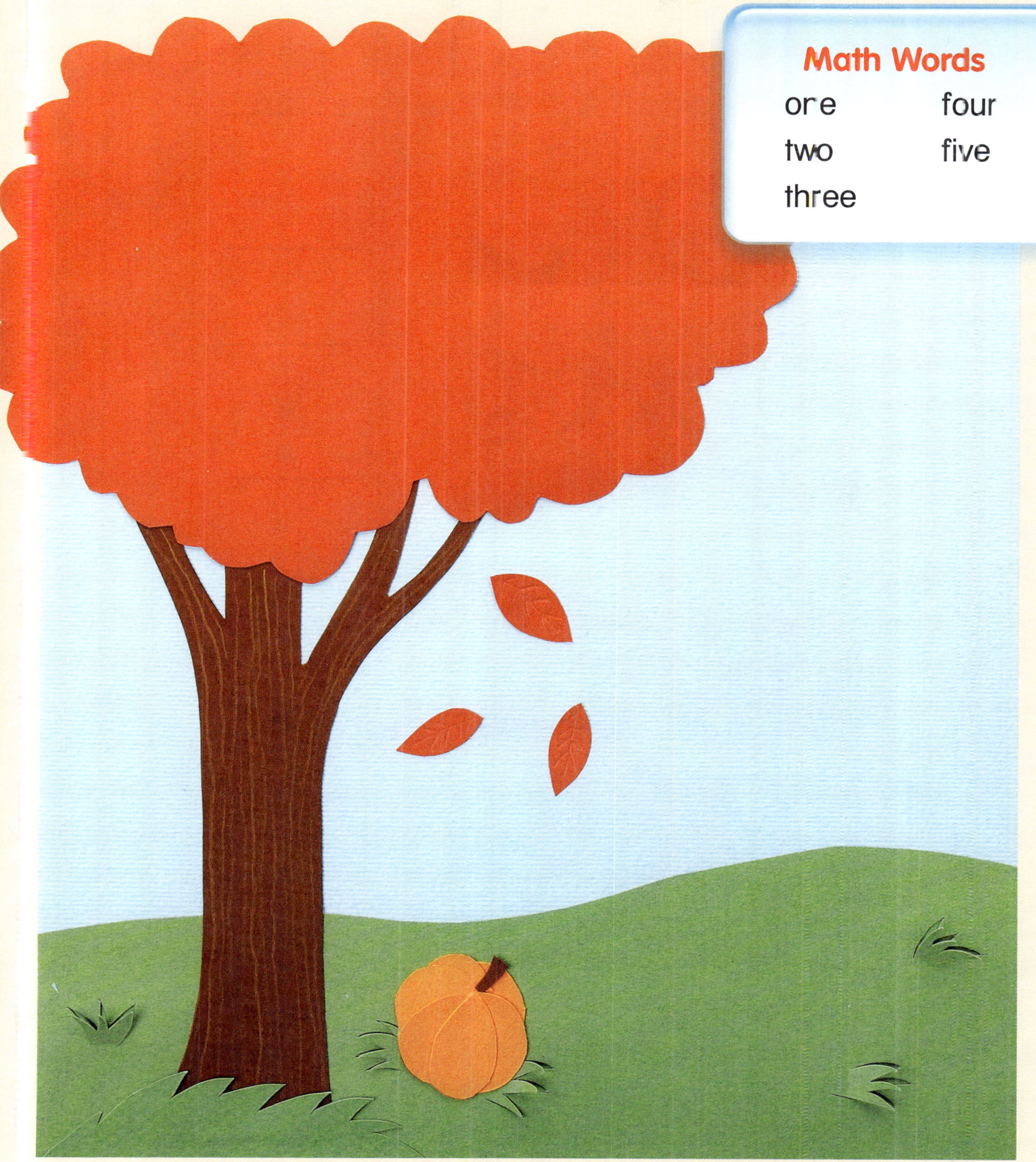

DIRECTIONS Look at the picture of the fall scene. Draw a story about fall using the numbers you have learned. Invite a classmate to count the objects in your story.

G

How Many Do You See?

1.
2.
3.
4.
5.

DIRECTIONS 1–5. Look at the picture. Write how many you see.

H

Dear Family,

My class started Unit 2 today. I will learn how to identify patterns and count objects up to 10. Here are some vocabulary words and activities for us to share.

Love, _______________________________

Vocabulary Power

Key Math Vocabulary

Pattern a repeated sequence or design

Ten one more than nine

Vocabulary Activity

Math on the Move

Provide opportunities for your child to make a pattern using grocery items. Have him or her choose two kinds of objects such as canned goods and boxed goods and create a pattern using those objects.

GO ONLINE

Technology
Multimedia Math Glossary link at
www.harcourtschool.com/hspmath

School Home CONNECTION

Remember This

Your child may already know how to count objects up to ten. Ask your child to point to each object as he or she counts.

Calendar Activity

October

Sunday	Monday	Tuesday	Wednesday	Thursday	Friday	Saturday
				1	2	3
4	5	6	7	8	9	10
11	12	13	14	15	16	17
18	19	20	21	22	23	24
25	26	27	28	29	30	31

Use 10 cards with a number from 1 – 10 on each card. Ask your child to look at the numeral card and place it on the appropriate numeral on the calendar.

Practice (after pages 91 and 92)

Have your child point to the numbers 6 and 7 on the calendar.

Practice (after pages 107 and 108)

Have your child point to the number that is one more than 8 on the calendar.

Literature

Look for these books in a library. Ask your child to point out math vocabulary words as you read each book together.

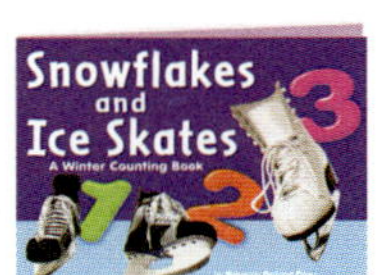

Snowflakes and Ice Skates: A Winter Counting Book.
Davis, Rebecca Fjelland.
Capstone, 2006.

Pattern Bugs.
Harris, Trudy.
Millbrook, 2001.

Mortimer's Math: Patterns.
Bryant-Mole, Karen.
Gareth Stevens, 2000.

CHAPTER
3
Positions and Patterns
Theme: Lots of Pumpkins

✓ Show What You Know

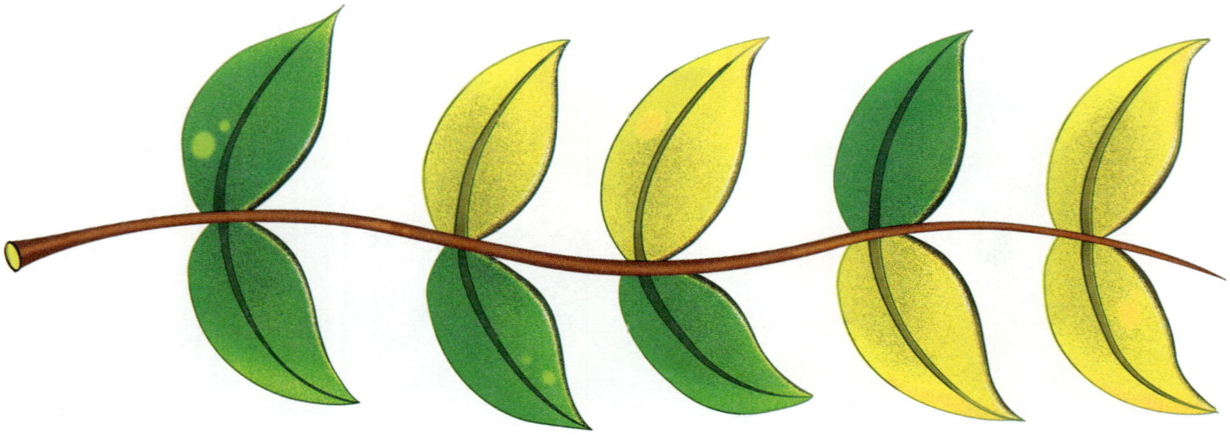

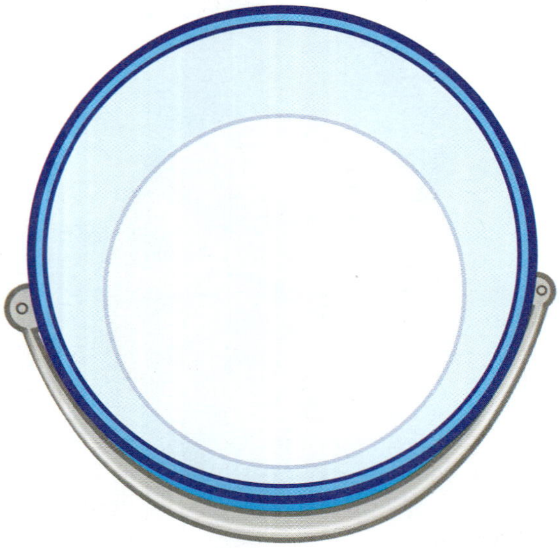

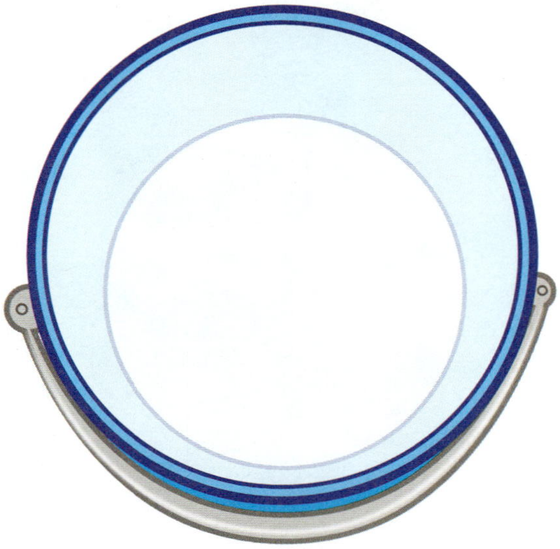

DIRECTIONS Sort the leaves by color. Draw the leaves in the sorting rings. Use yellow to color a square for each yellow leaf on the top row. Use green to color a square for each green leaf on the bottom row.

FAMILY NOTE: This page checks your child's understanding of important concepts and skills needed for success in Chapter 3.

Above, Below, Over, and Under

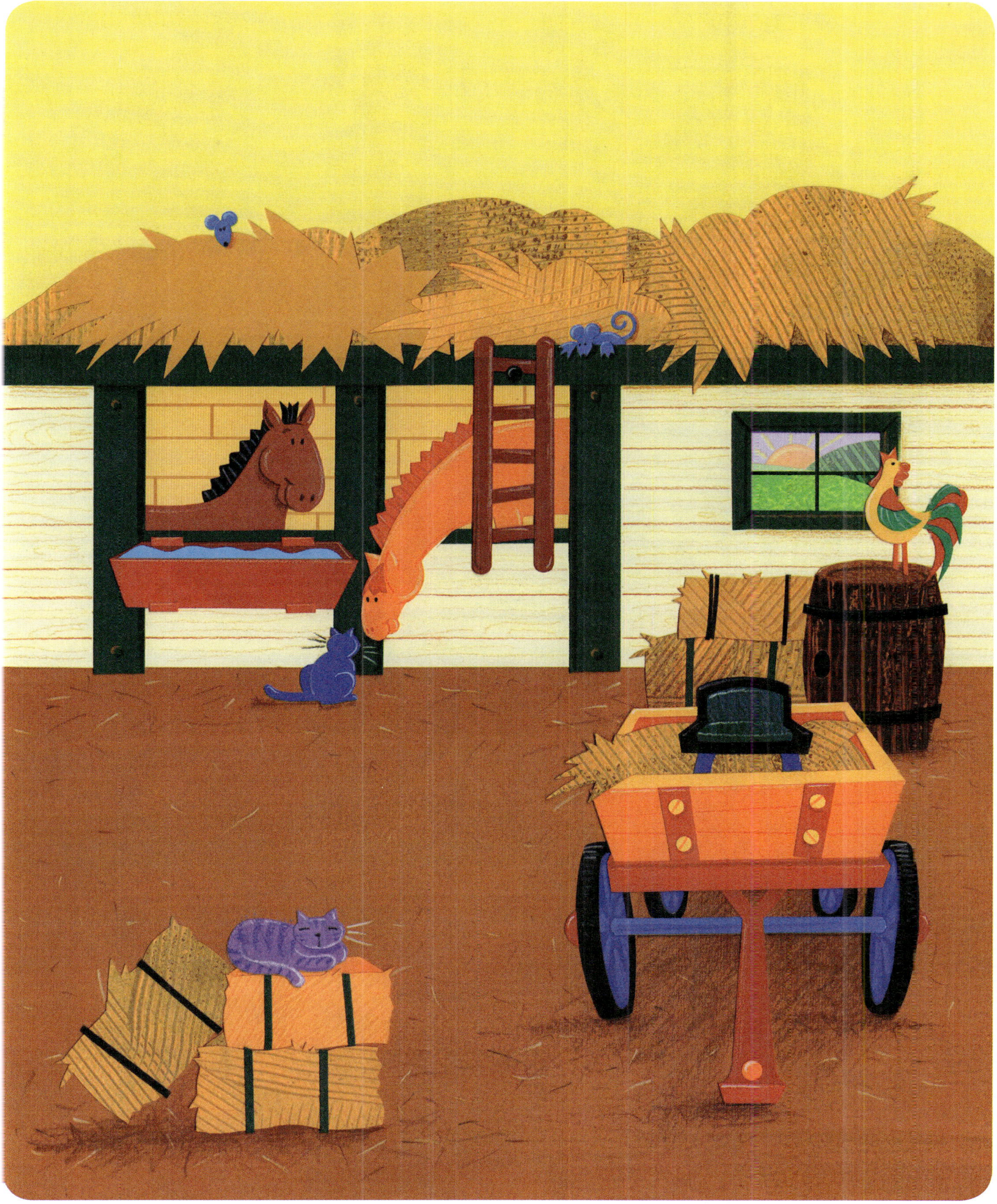

DIRECTIONS Place a red cube below the water. Place a red cube under the ladder. Use red to draw the cubes. Place a blue cube over the window. Place a blue cube above the horses. Use blue to draw the cubes.

OBJECTIVE • Place an object in a specified position, such as *above*, *below*, *over*, or *under*.

DIRECTIONS   I. Draw a bird over the pond.
Draw a pumpkin below the table.   2. Draw
an apple under the tree. Draw a sun above
the house.

HOME ACTIVITY • Tell your child you are
thinking of something in the room that is
above, below, over, or under another object.
Have your child tell you what the object is.

62 sixty-two

Beside, Next To, and Between

DIRECTIONS **I.** Circle the football that is next to the basket. Mark an X on the football that is beside the pumpkin. **2.** Mark an X on the pumpkin that is between two paint cans. **3.** Circle the ball that is beside a cap. Mark an X on the bucket that is between two balls.

OBJECTIVE • Place three objects, such as a book, a toy, and a cup, in a row. Ask your child questions that will lead him or her to use the words *beside*, *next to*, or *between* to describe the positions of the various objects.

DIRECTIONS   Circle the pumpkin that is between two other pumpkins. Mark an X on the pumpkin that is beside the tree. Draw a pumpkin next to the hay.

HOME ACTIVITY · Use language such as *beside*, *next to*, and *between* to describe the position of one object in relation to another.

In Front Of and Behind

1 

2 

3 

4 

DIRECTIONS   **1.** Circle the child in front of the fence.   **2.** Circle the chick behind the pumpkin.   **3.** Circle the dog in front of the hay bale.   **4.** Circle the child behind the wheel.

OBJECTIVE • Describe the position of objects using the terms *in front of* and *behind*.

DIRECTIONS   Circle the child behind the wagon. Draw a pumpkin in front of the hay. Mark an X on the squirrel in front of the wagon.

 **HOME ACTIVITY** · Place a stuffed animal or doll in the middle of a table. Direct your child to place a cup behind the toy and a spoon in front of the toy. Repeat the activity, using different objects.

1 

2 

3 

4 

DIRECTIONS 1. Circle the child who is outside the house. 2. Circle the bird that is inside the nest. 3. Circle the squirrel that is inside the tree. 4. Circle the dog that is outside the dog house.

OBJECTIVE • Use language such as *inside* and *outside* to describe the position of one object in relation to another.

Chapter 3 • Lesson 4

DIRECTIONS Draw a banana inside the basket. Draw an apple outside the basket.

 **HOME ACTIVITY** · Provide your child with a block and a dish that is large enough to hold the block. Ask your child to place the block inside the dish. Then ask your child to place the block outside the dish.

68 sixty-eight

Problem Solving Workshop
Skill • Use a Picture

DIRECTIONS Mark an X on the bird that is over the corn plants. Circle the corn that is below the ground. Mark an X on the fox that is above the ground.

OBJECTIVE • Solve problems by using the skill *use a picture*.

DIRECTIONS **1.** Draw a gift under the table. Draw a balloon over the table. **2.** Draw a kite above the tree. Draw a duck below the bridge.

HOME ACTIVITY · Place a block or other toy above or below another object, such as a table. Ask your child to tell whether the toy is above or below the table. Repeat the activity using the words *under* and *over*.

70 seventy

✓ Mid Chapter 3 Review

1

2

3

4

DIRECTIONS   **1.** Draw a butterfly over the pond. Draw a ball under the table.   **2.** Mark an X on the football that is next to the basket. Circle the football that is beside the pumpkin.   **3.** Circle the bird that is outside the nest.   **4.** Draw a raft below the bridge.

Cumulative Review

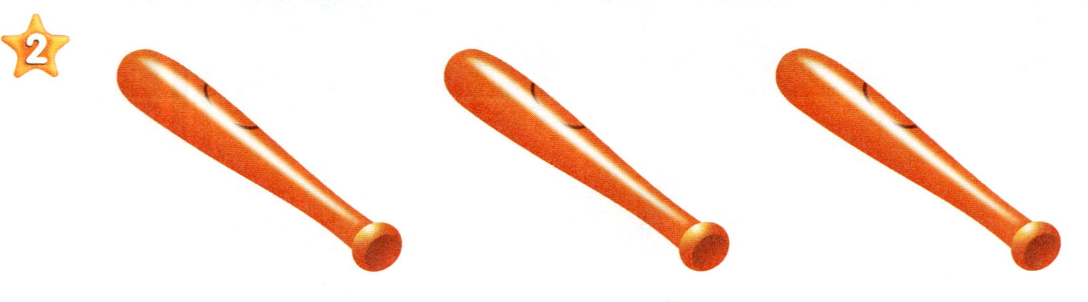

DIRECTIONS 1. Use figures to match each figure. Circle the two figures that are alike. Draw that figure in the workspace. Tell what you know about that figure. **2.** Draw a ball below each bat to show equal sets. **3.** Draw a bird above the fence.

72 seventy-two

DIRECTIONS 1–3. Read the pattern. Place bear counters to identify the pattern. Color the pattern.

OBJECTIVE • Identify and copy patterns of concrete objects.

1

2

3

DIRECTIONS 1–3. Read the pattern. Place figures to identify the pattern. Draw and color the pattern.

 **HOME ACTIVITY** • Create a pattern by using two different kinds of objects, such as flower / leaf, flower/leaf, flower/leaf. Ask your child to use flowers and leaves to copy the pattern.

1

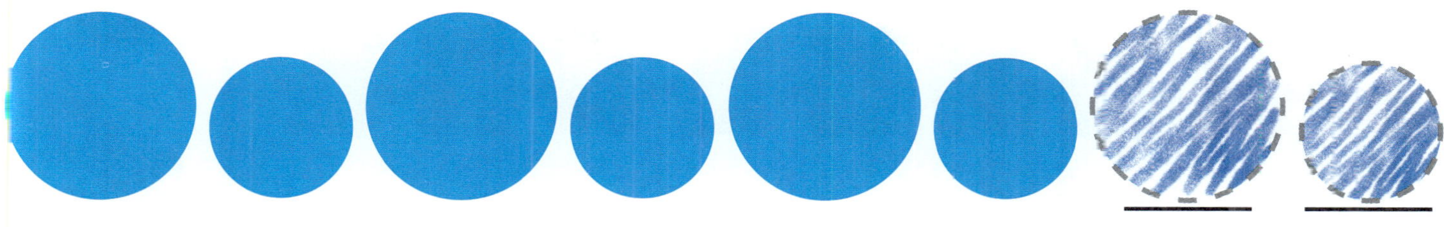

2

3

4

DIRECTIONS **1–4.** Use figures to identify the pattern. Find the two figures that most likely come next. Draw and color the figures.

OBJECTIVE • Identify and extend patterns of concrete objects.

DIRECTIONS   1–4. Circle the bear that most likely comes next in the pattern.

HOME ACTIVITY • Create a pattern, using two different kinds of objects, for example spoon/fork, spoon/fork, spoon/fork. Ask your child to extend the pattern, using more spoons and forks.

76   seventy-six

Problem Solving Workshop
Strategy • Act It Out

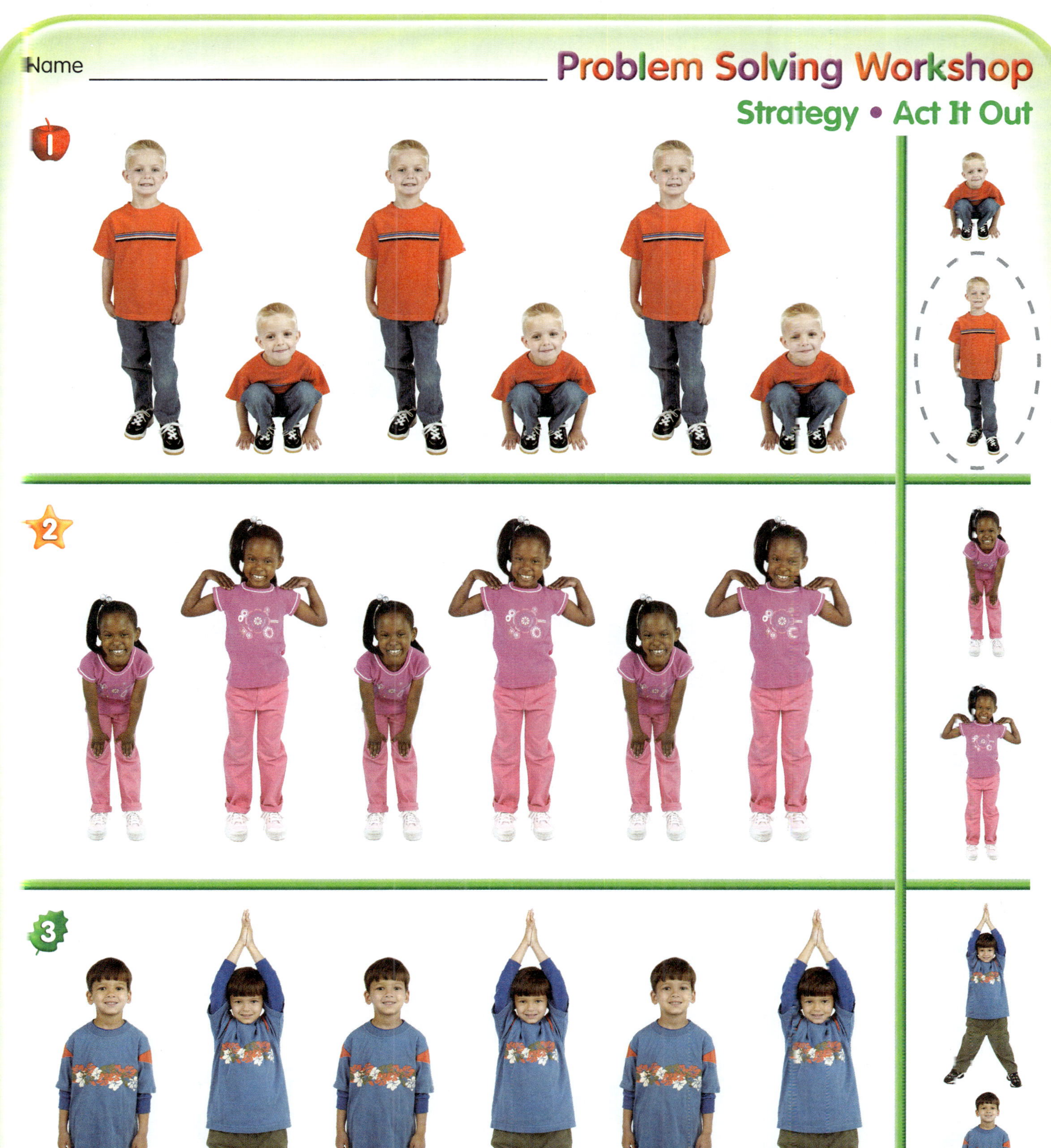

DIRECTIONS **I–3.** Act out the pattern. Say the pattern as you act out each part. Circle what you would most likely do next.

OBJECTIVE • Solve problems by using the strategy *act it out*.

DIRECTIONS   I–3. Act out the pattern. Say the pattern as you act out each part. Circle the action that you would most likely do next.

HOME ACTIVITY • Have your child follow a movement pattern that you show him or her, such as arms at sides/arms above head. Repeat the movement pattern until your child can tell you the movement that most likely comes next.

78 seventy-eight

Identify the Pattern Rule

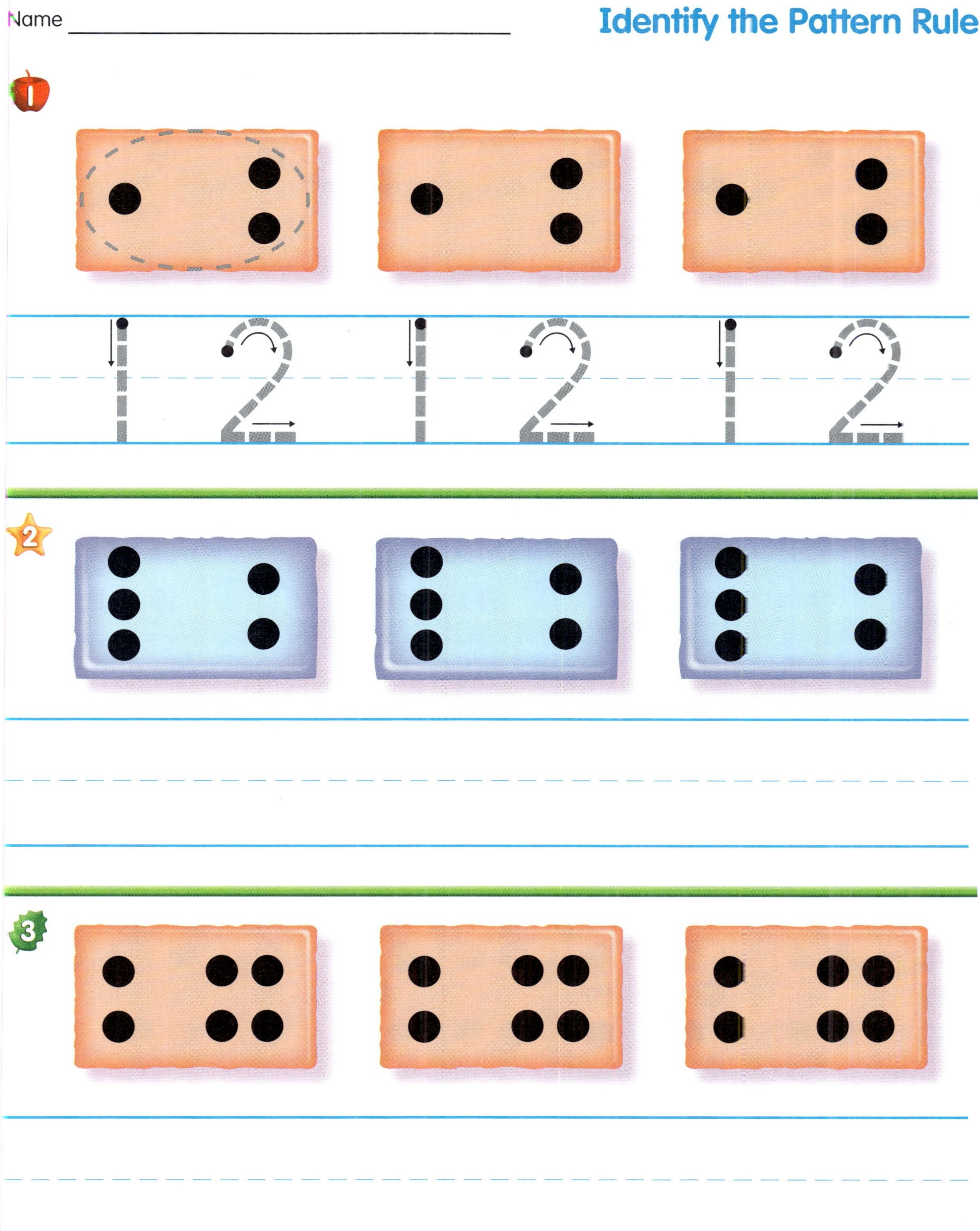

DIRECTIONS 1–3. Look at the pattern. Write the numbers below the dot cards. Circle the part that repeats again and again.

OBJECTIVE • Identify the pattern rule.

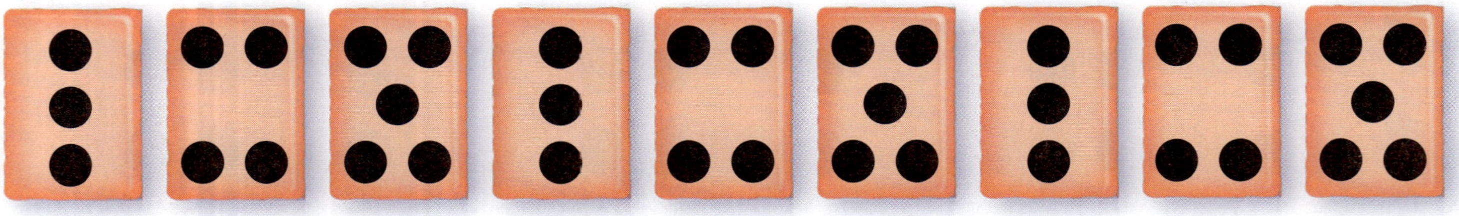

DIRECTIONS **1–3.** Look at the pattern. Write the numbers below the dot cards. Circle the part that repeats again and again.

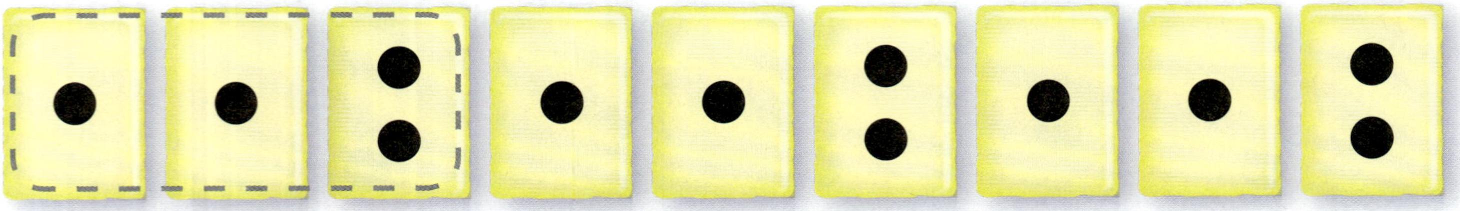

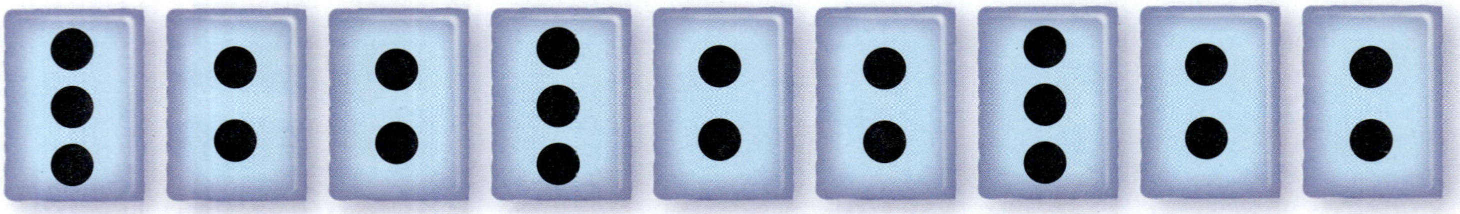

 **HOME ACTIVITY** • Cut out pieces of colored paper to make a red/blue/yellow pattern. Repeat the pattern three times. Have your child tell which part of the pattern repeats again and again.

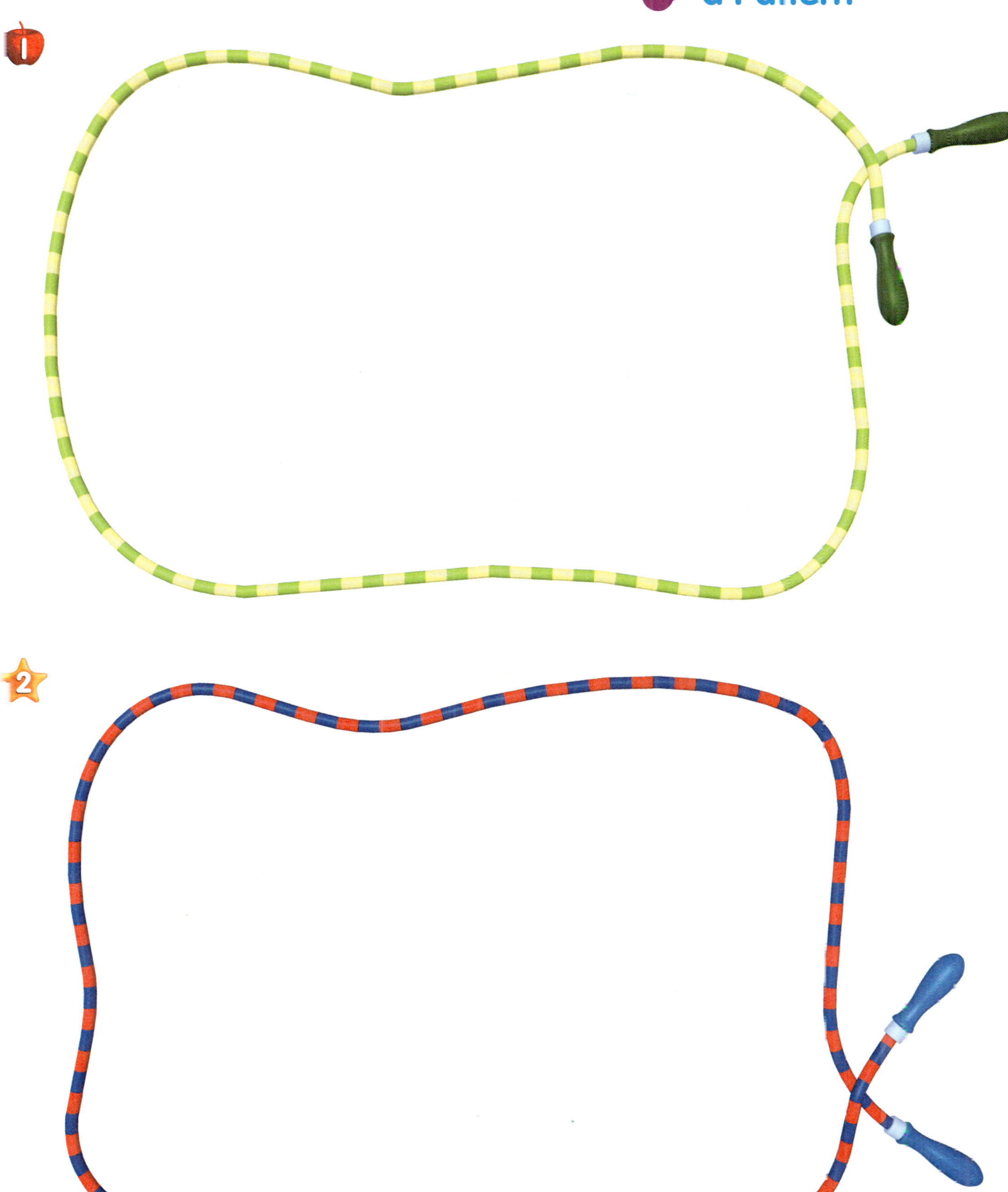

1

2

DIRECTIONS **1.** Use two colors of counters to make a pattern. Draw and color your pattern. Circle the part that repeats again and again. **2.** Use two colors of pattern blocks to make a pattern. Draw and color your pattern. Circle the part that repeats again and again.

OBJECTIVE • Identify and create patterns of concrete objects.

82 eighty-two

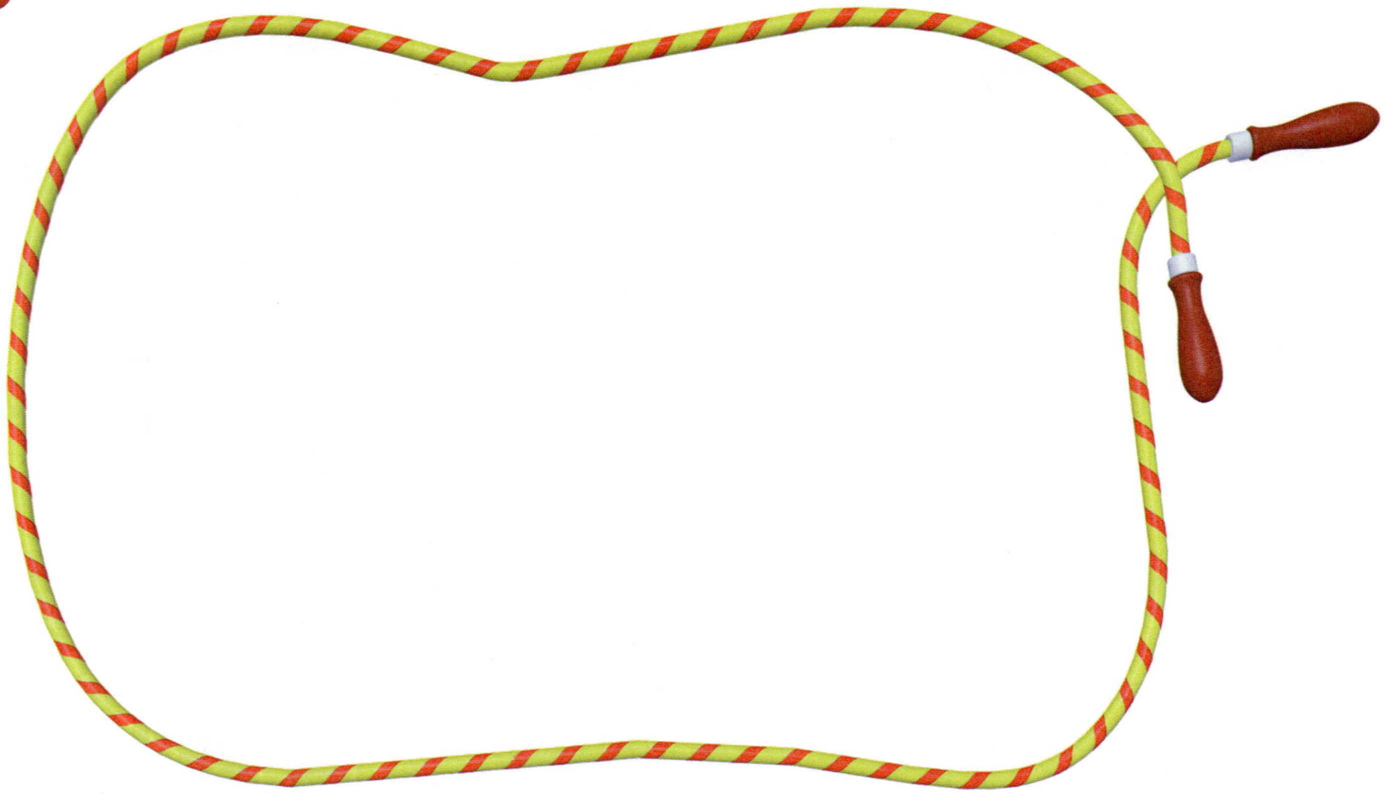

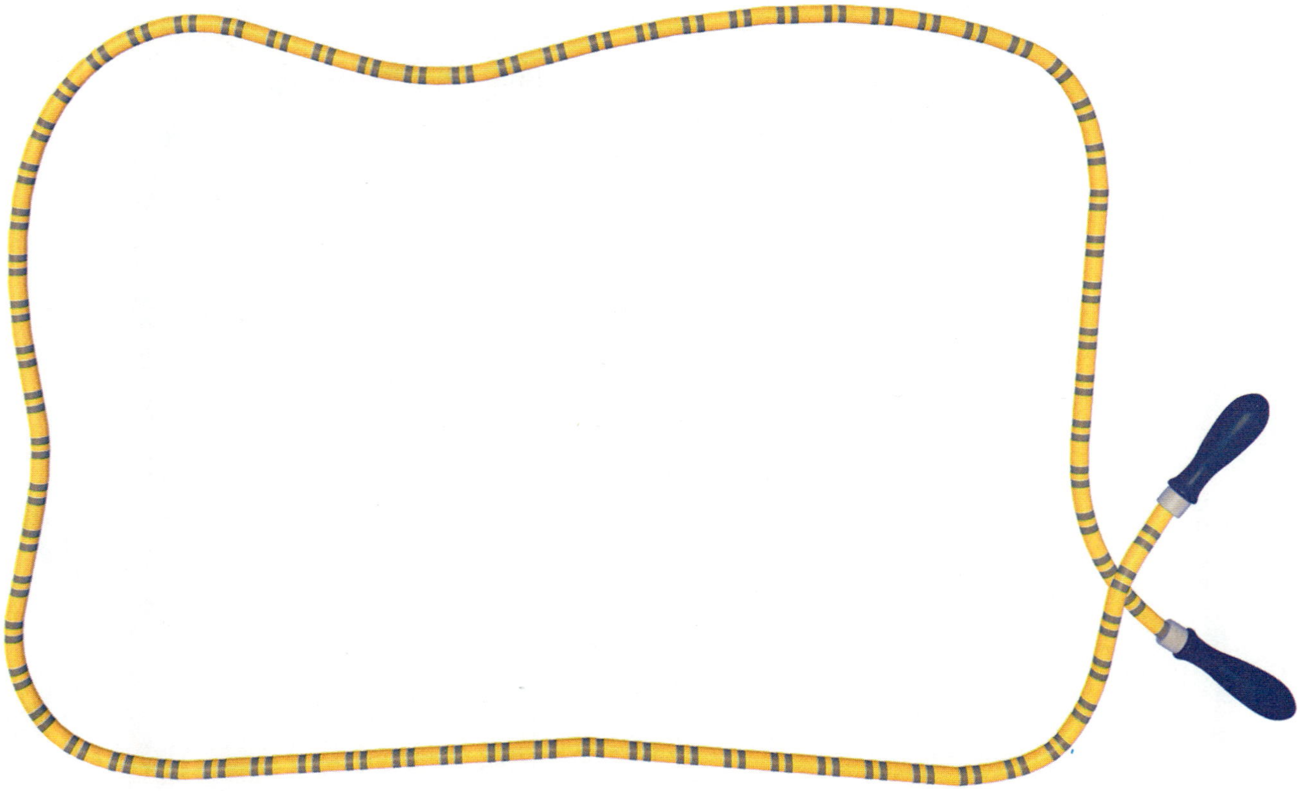

Growing Patterns

DIRECTIONS Look at the pattern. Describe the pattern. Use connecting cubes to extend the pattern. Draw and color the cubes.

OBJECTIVE • Identify and extend growing patterns.

Chapter 3 • Lesson 11

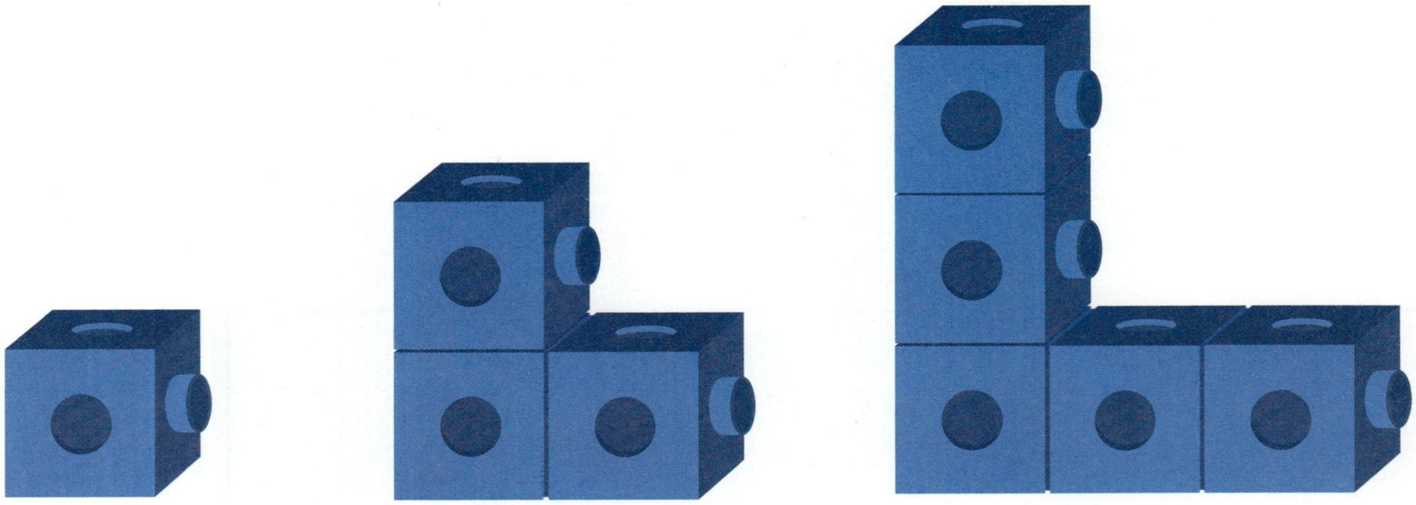

Pattern path

PRACTICE GAME

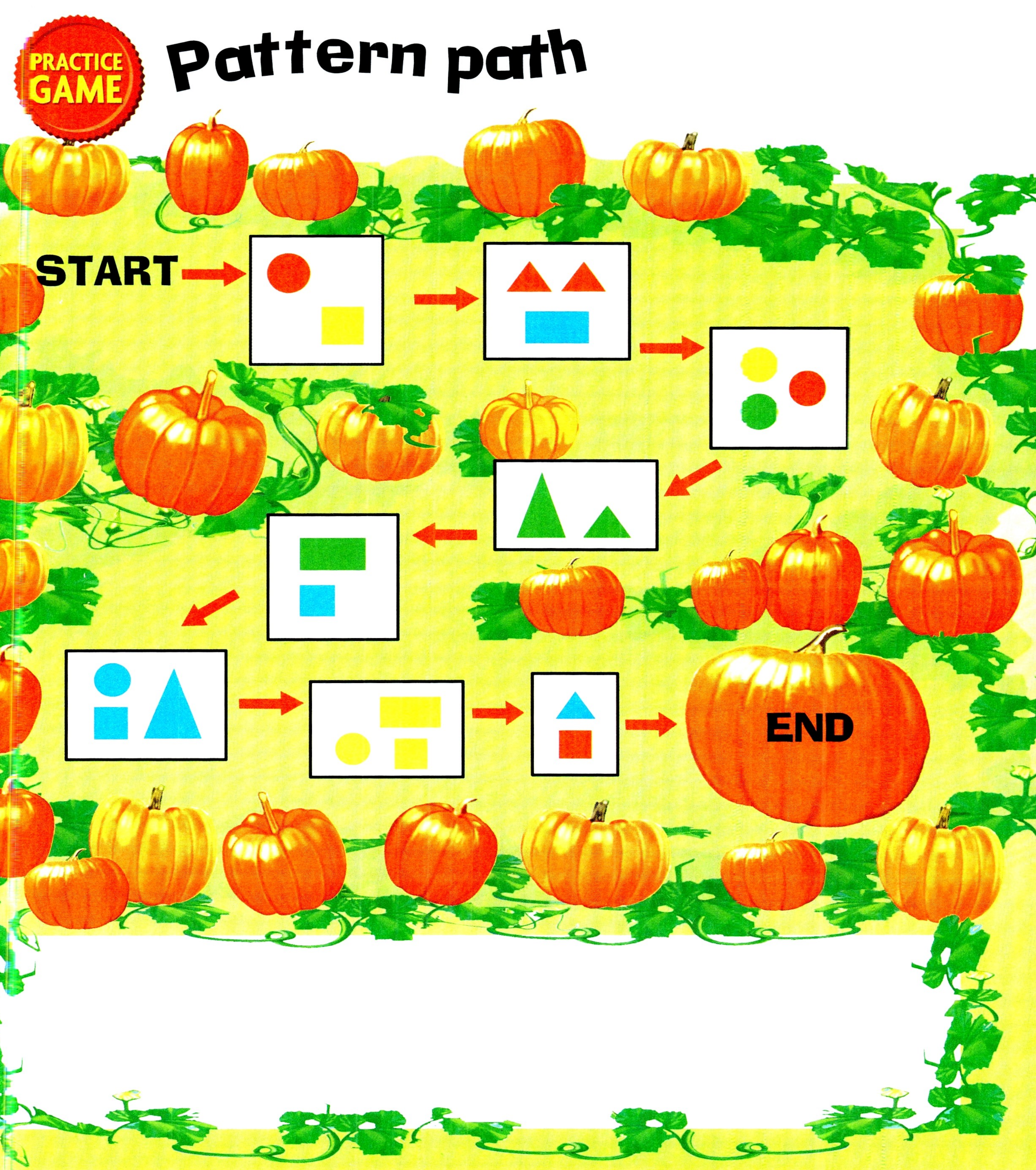

DIRECTIONS   Play with a partner. Decide who goes first. Put your marker on Start. Toss the number cube. Move that number of spaces. Take some of each figure shown on that space. Use those figures to make a pattern in the workspace. Read the pattern to your partner. Take turns until both players reach the end.

MATERIALS   markers, number cube, plane figures

Math Power • Transfer a Pattern

DIRECTIONS 1–2. Read the pattern. Use figures to show the same pattern. Draw the pattern.

86 eighty-six

✓ Chapter 3 Review/Test

DIRECTIONS **1.** Read the pattern. Place bear counters to make the pattern. Color the pattern. **2.** Use figures to identify the pattern. Find the two figures that most likely come next. Draw and color the figures. **3.** Act out the pattern. Say the pattern as you act out each part. Circle what you would most likely do next.

✓ Cumulative Review

DIRECTIONS   1. Three of the objects are alike. Mark an X on the one that does not belong.   **2. How many backpacks? Write the number of backpacks in the set.   3. Write the number that is before 3. Write the number that is after 3.   4. Look at the pattern. Write the numbers below the dot cards. Circle the part that repeats again and again.**

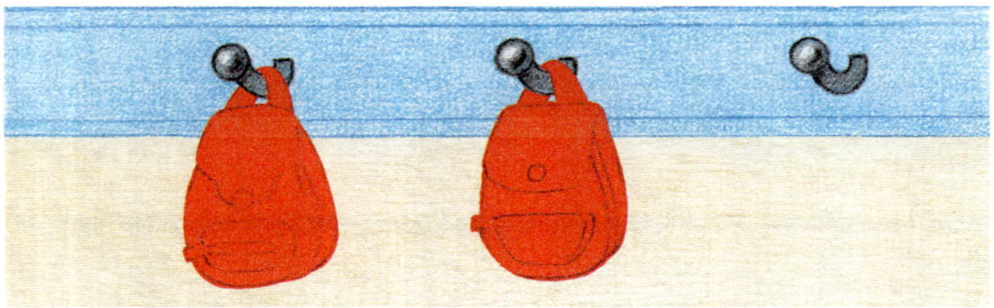

88   eighty-eight

CHAPTER 4

Numbers 6 to 10

Theme: At the Fair

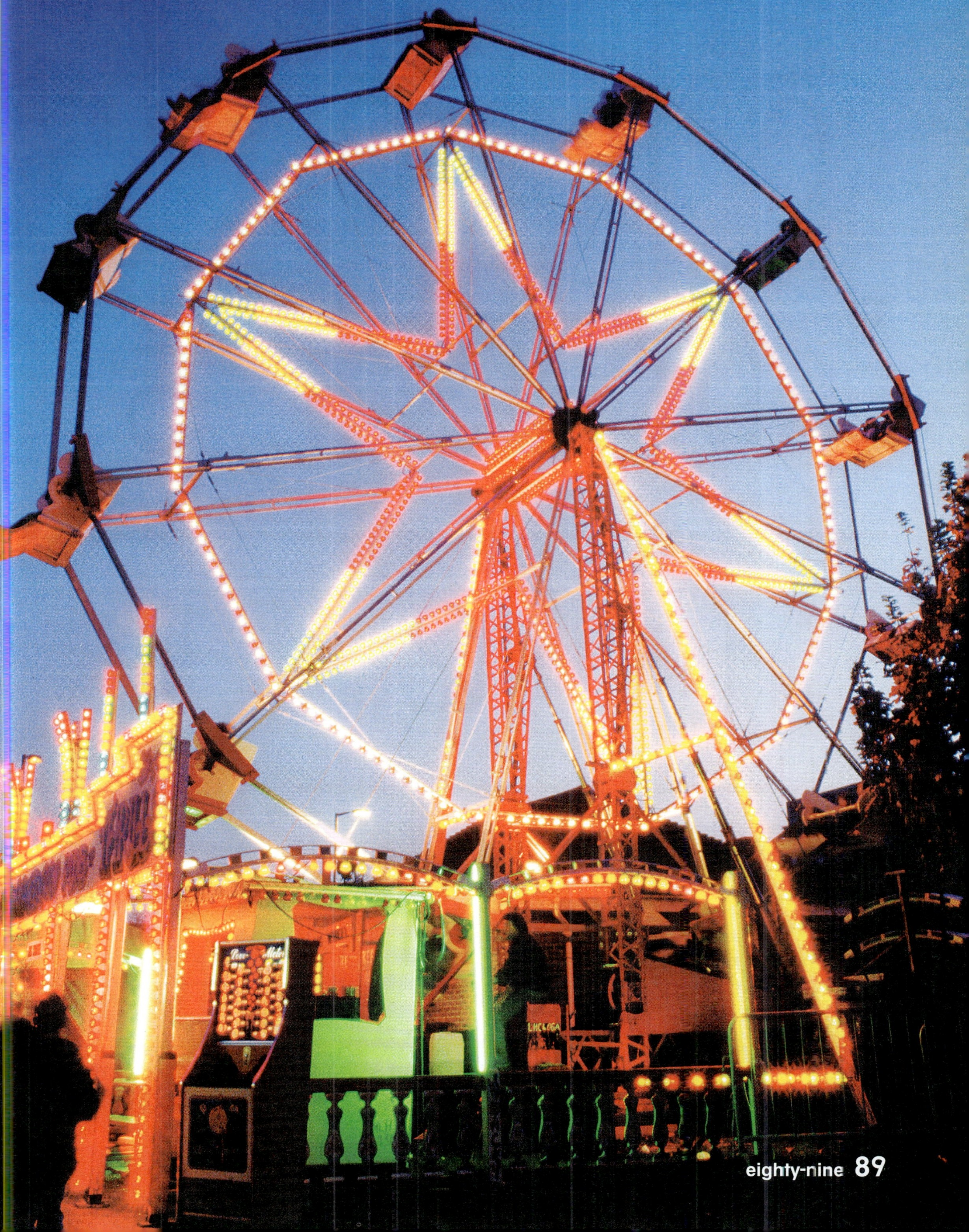

0 1 2 3 4 5

1.

0   3   5

2.

1   2   4

3.    **4.** 

FAMILY NOTE: This page checks your child's understanding of important concepts and skills needed for success in Chapter 4.

HANDS ON

Model, Read, and Write 6 and 7

 **1**

3

4

DIRECTIONS 1–2. Count the objects in the set. Trace the number. Write the number. 3–4. How many objects in the set? Write the number.

 **HOME ACTIVITY** • Have your child look around your home for a set of six objects. Write the number 6 on a piece of paper and place it beside the set. Repeat for seven.

92 ninety-two

Model, Read, and Write 8 and 9

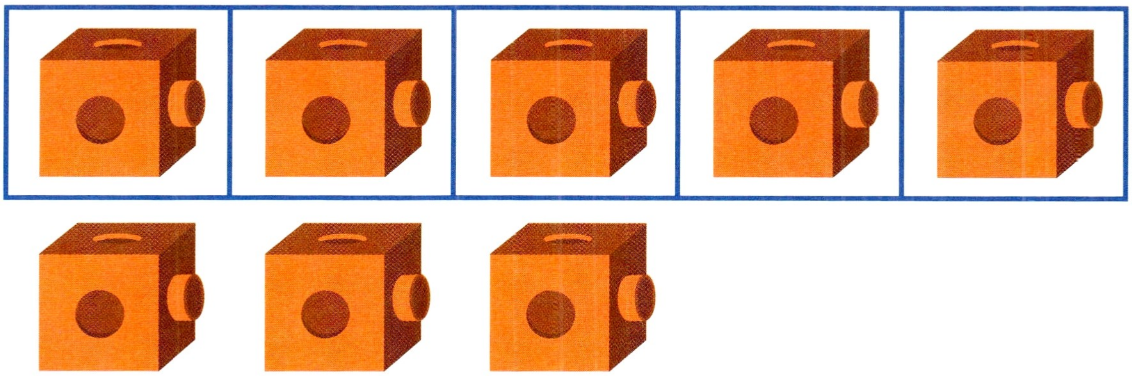

8
eight

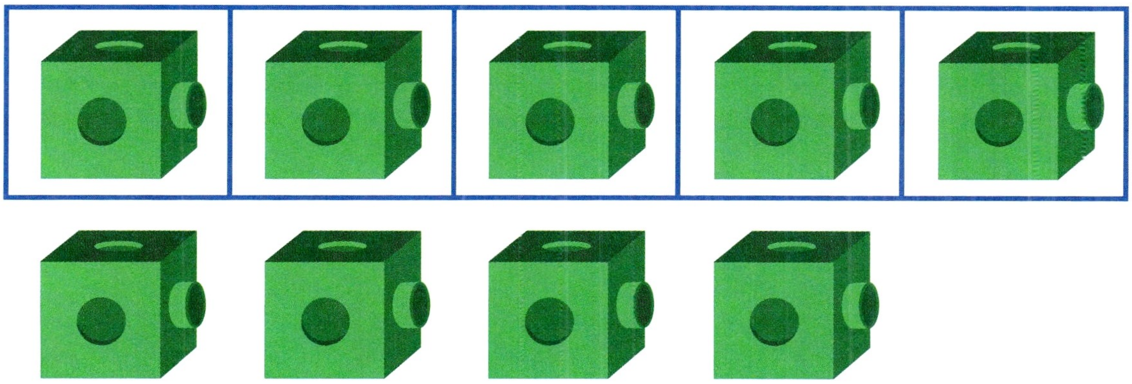

9
nine

1

8

2

9

3
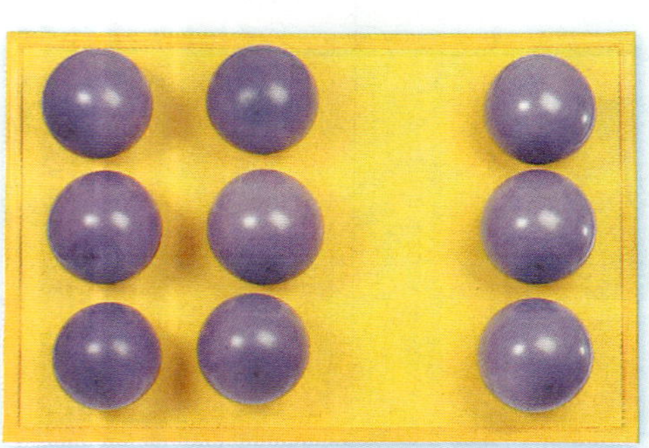

4

5

6

DIRECTIONS 1–2. Say the number. Trace and write the number. 3–6. How many objects in the set? Write the number.

HOME ACTIVITY · Ask your child to count a set of nine objects. Then have your child show you a set with one less than the set just counted. Ask how many are in the second set.

94 ninety-four

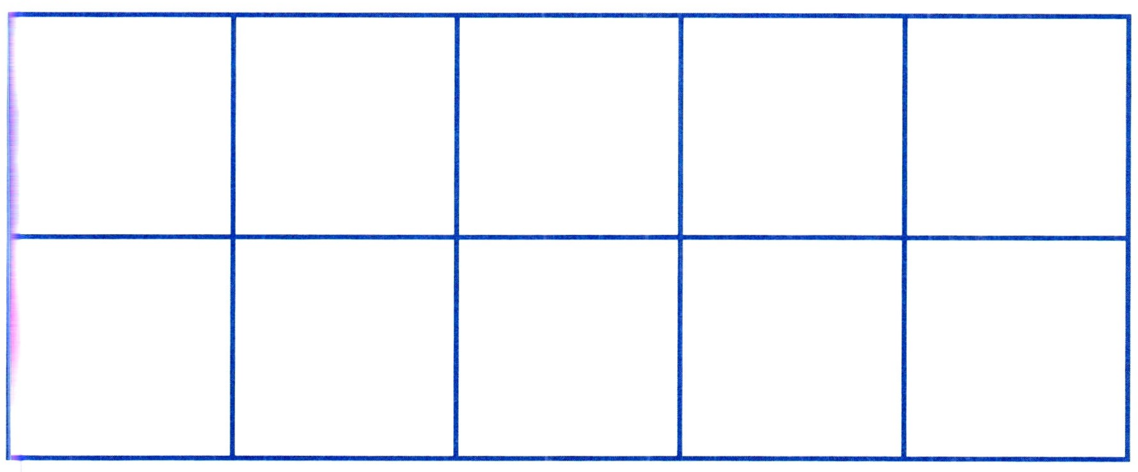

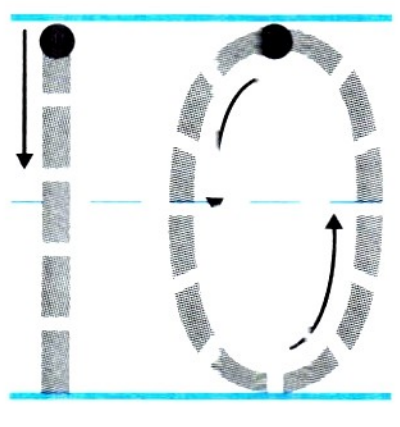

ten

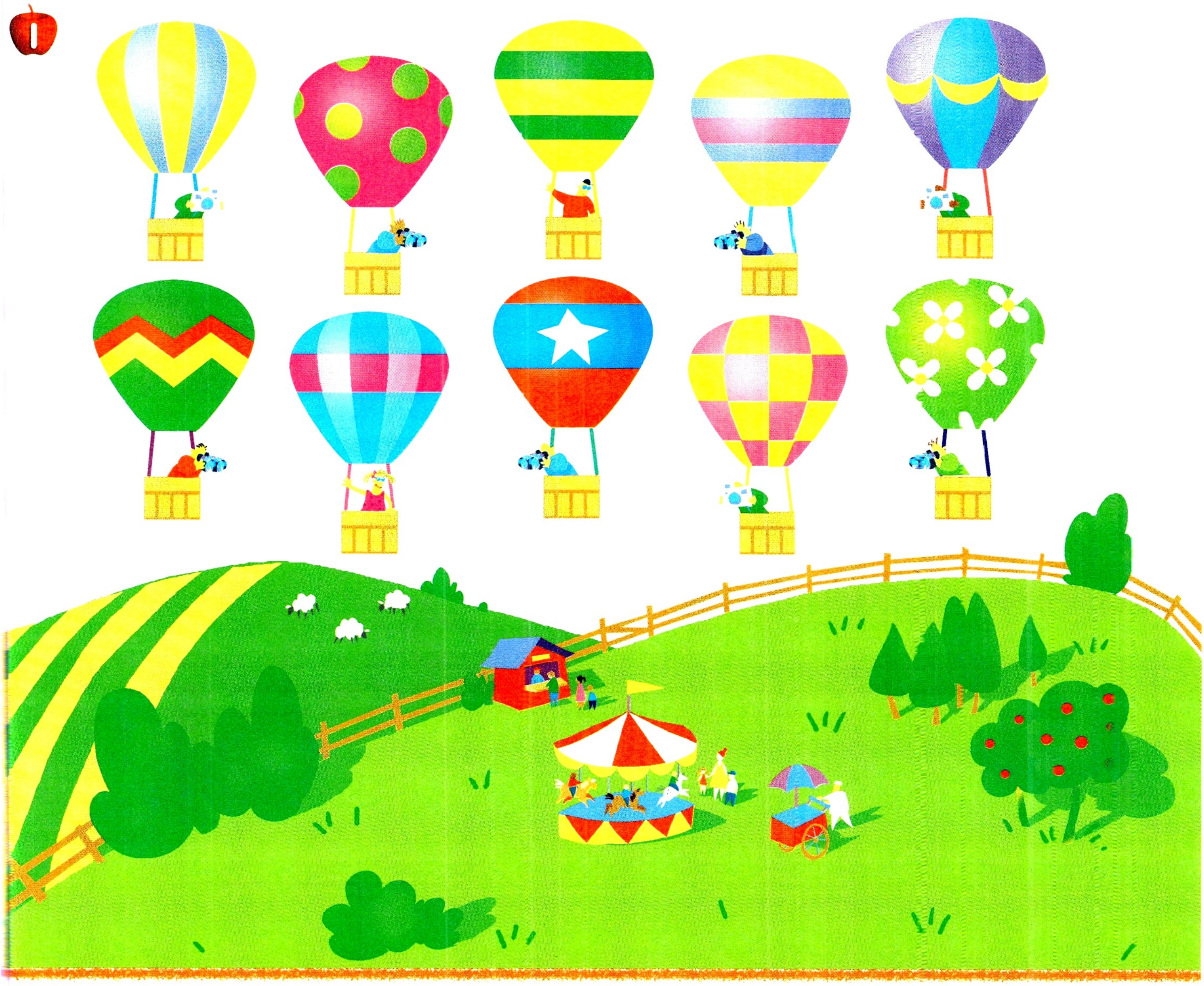

1

7

2

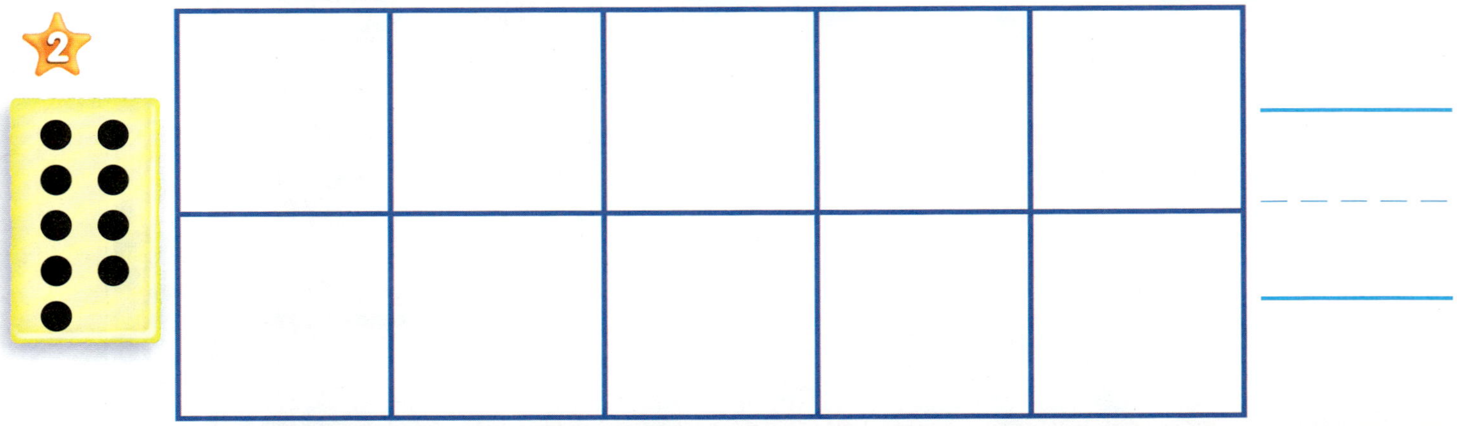

3

4

DIRECTIONS **1.** How many dots? Trace the counters in the ten frame. Trace the number. **2–4.** How many dots? Place counters in the ten frame to model that number. Draw the counters in the ten frame. Write the number.

HOME ACTIVITY • Trace around your child's hands. Have your child place a penny on each finger while counting to ten. Then have your child write the number.

© Harcourt

96 ninety-six

Read and Write 10

1

10
ten

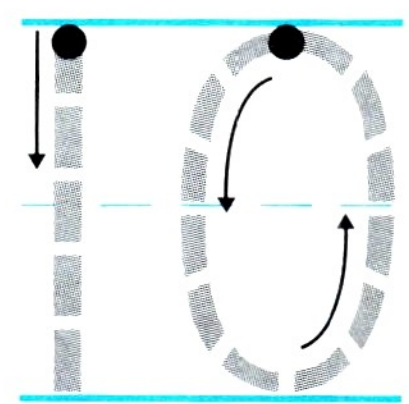

2

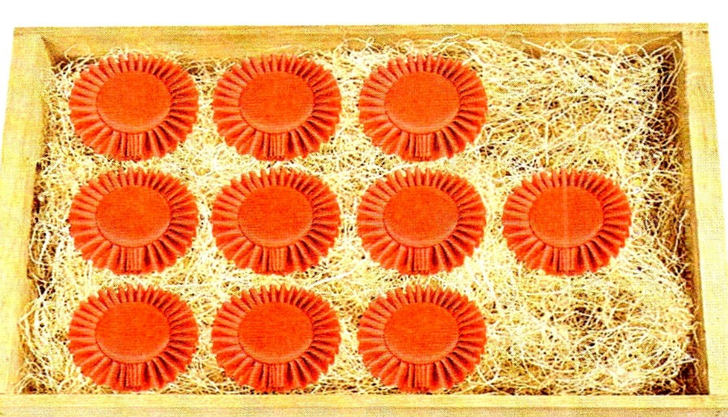

3

4

5

DIRECTIONS **1.** How many objects? Trace the number. **2–5.** How many objects? Write the number. Circle the sets that have ten objects.

OBJECTIVE • Use numbers to name the quantity 10.

Chapter 4 • Lesson 4

DIRECTIONS **1.** Trace and write the number 10. **2–7.** How many objects? Draw more to make a set of ten.

HOME ACTIVITY · Ask your child to use stickers or small slips of paper to make a set of ten and a set with one less than ten. Have your child count the stickers in both sets and point to the set with ten.

98 ninety-eight

 Mid Chapter 4 Review

____

- - - - -

____

_______   _______

- - - - -   - - - - -

_______   _______

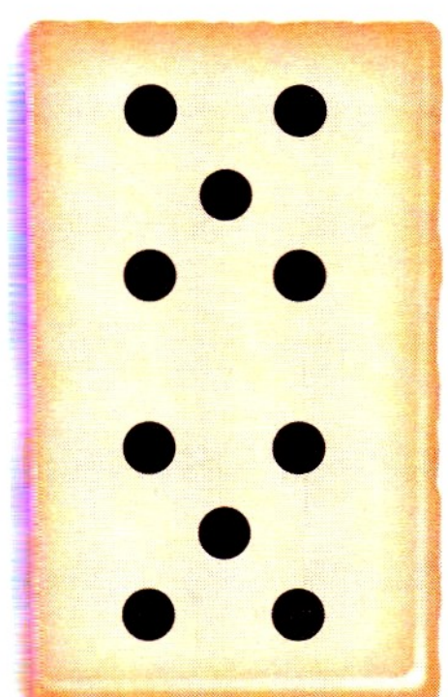

____

- - - - -

____

DIRECTIONS   **I–3. How many objects in the set? Write the number.**
4. How many dots? Draw counters in the ten frame. Write the number.

Cumulative Review

          _______ _______

DIRECTIONS   **1. Circle the objects that are alike.**
2. Draw bear counters to show a set of more bears.   3. Use figures to identify the pattern. Draw and color the two figures that most likely come next.   4–5. Write how many objects. Circle the set that has ten objects.

100 one hundred

Write Numbers to 10

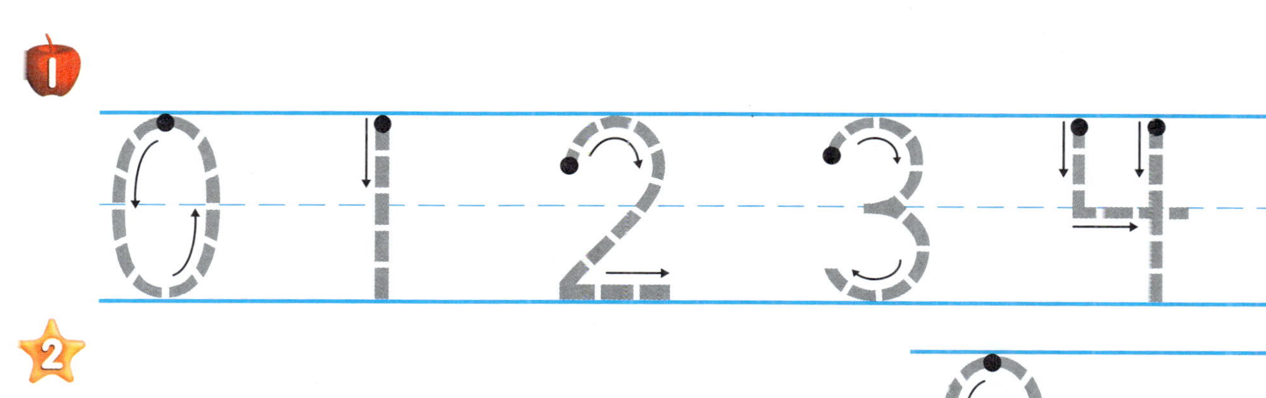

DIRECTIONS I. Say the number as you trace it.
2–7. How many animals? Write the number.

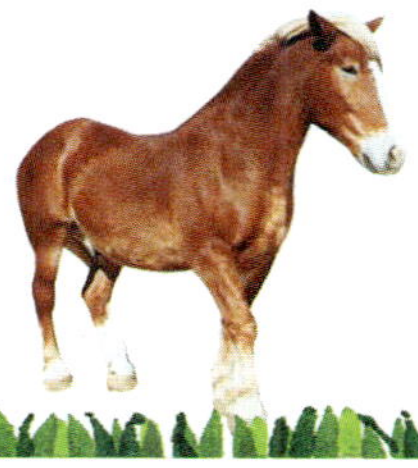

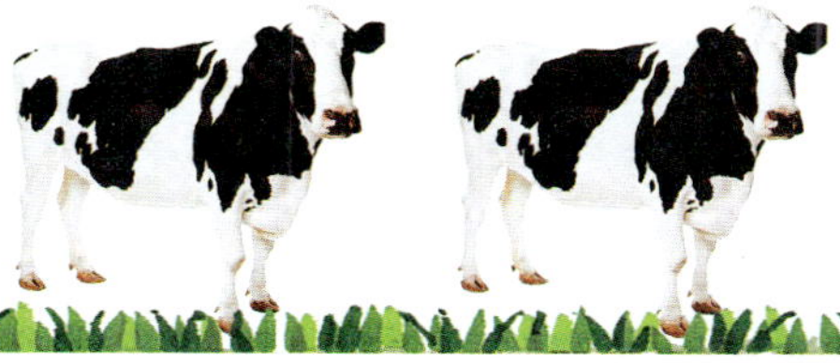

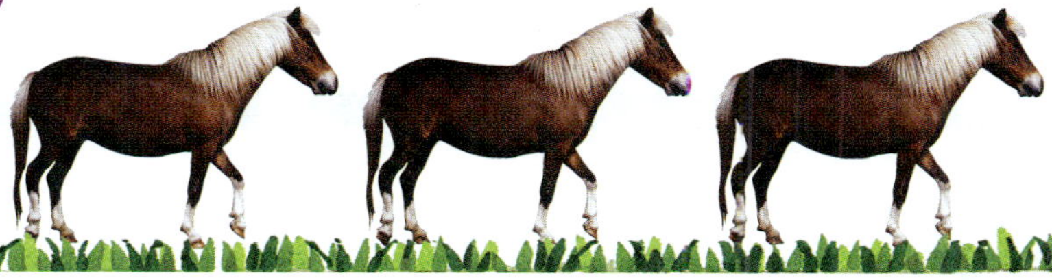

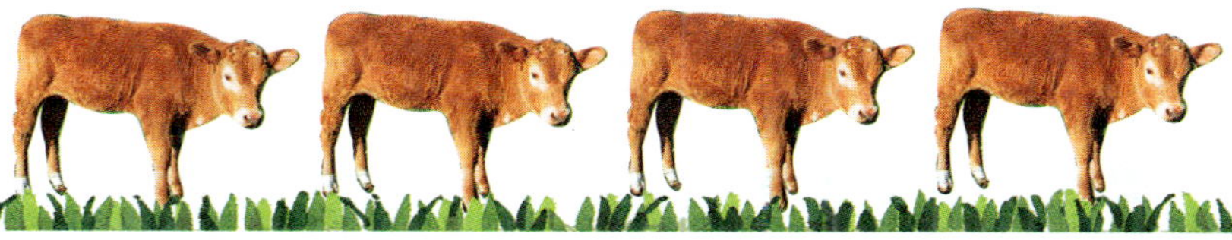

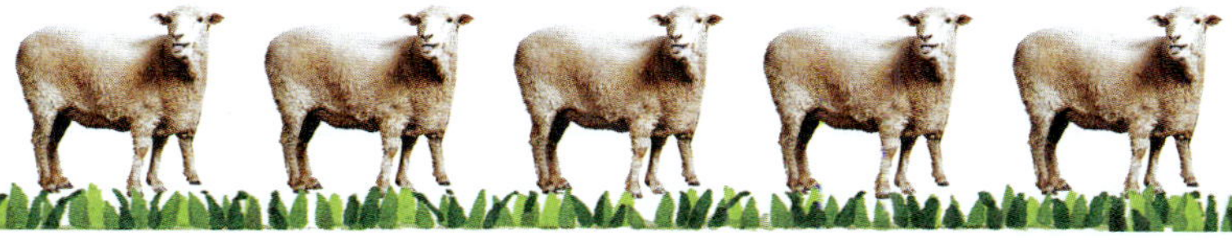

OBJECTIVE • Read and write numerals to 10.

6 7 8 9 10

DIRECTIONS 1. Say the number as you trace it. 2–6. How many animals? Write the number.

HOME ACTIVITY • Hold up from 1-10 fingers. Ask your child to say the number of fingers you are holding up and write the number.

102 one hundred two

Name ______________________________

Compare Sets to 10

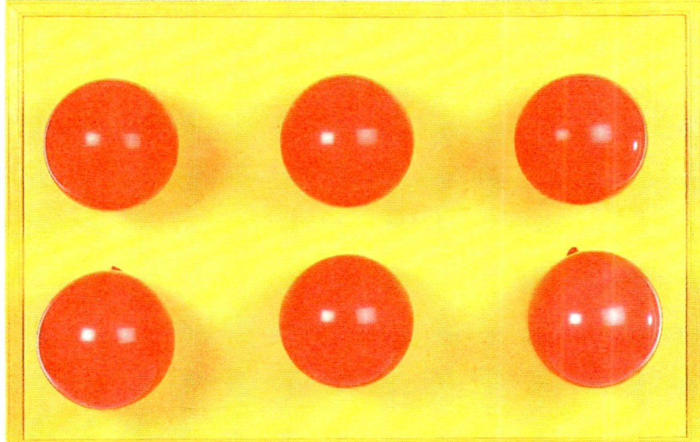

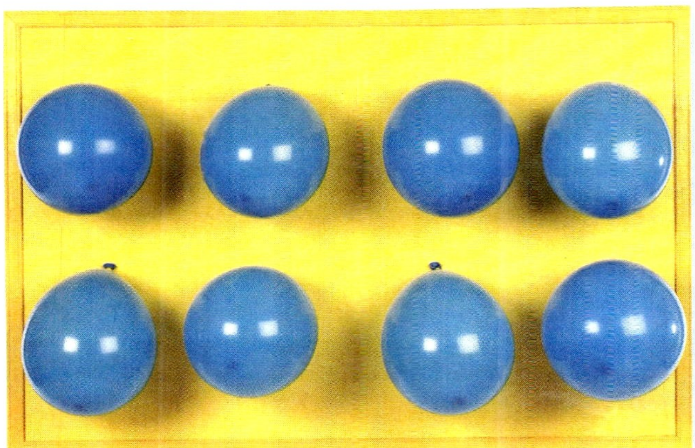

DIRECTIONS Place a red cube on each red balloon. Place a blue cube on each blue balloon. Join the cubes for each set and place each cube train in the workspace. Draw and compare the cube trains. Write how many in each cube train. Circle the set that has more.

OBJECTIVE • Use objects to compare sets up to 10.

DIRECTIONS 1–3. How many flowers in each set? Write the number. Circle the row that has more. Circle the number that is greater.

 **HOME ACTIVITY ·** Place six to ten pennies in each hand. Watch how your child determines which hand has more. Does your child count them, or line them up and compare them? Have your child write the number that is greater.

104 one hundred four

Problem Solving Workshop
Strategy • Make a Model

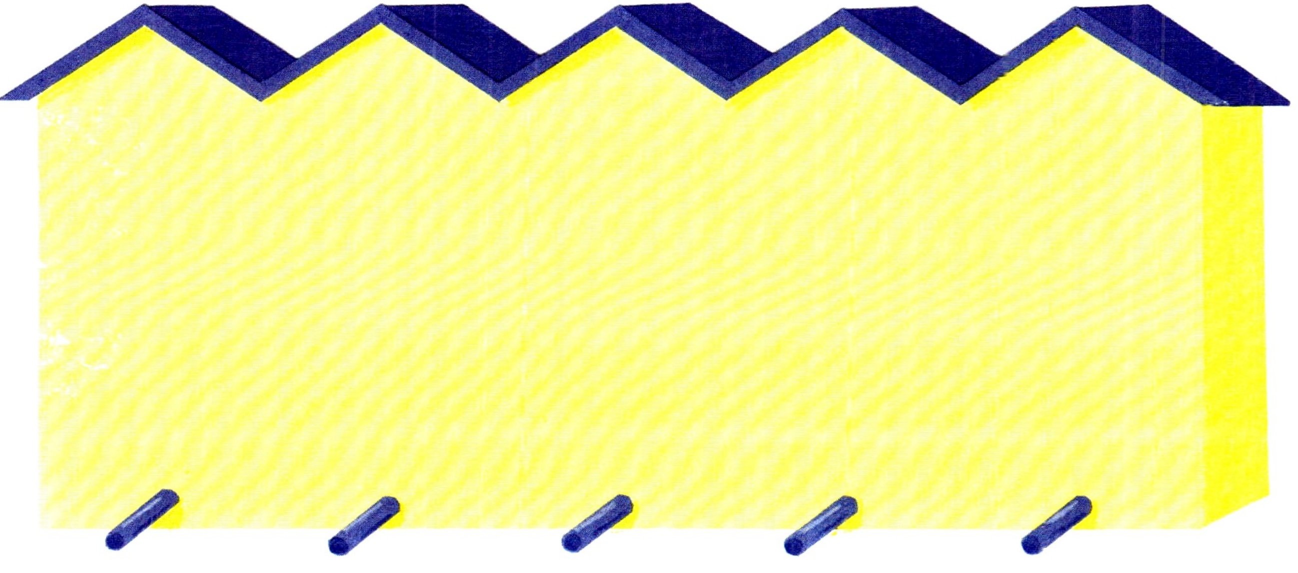

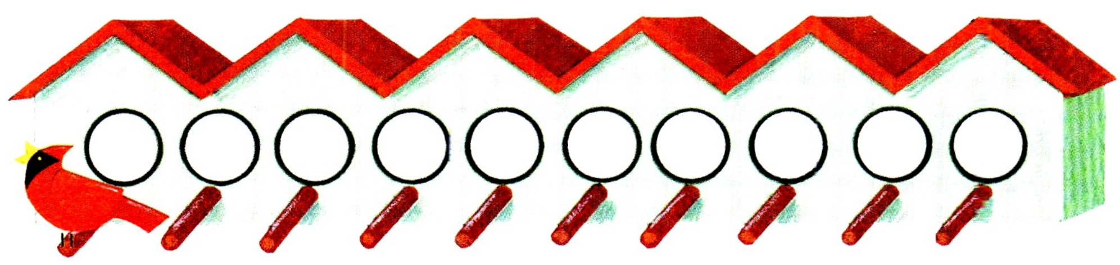

DIRECTIONS Spill ten two-color counters on the page. Sort by color. **1–2.** Beginning with the bird on the left, color the holes to match the counters of one color, then continue coloring the holes for the other color. Write how many of each color.

OBJECTIVE • Solve problems by using the strategy *make a model*.

DIRECTIONS Spill ten two-color counters on the page. Sort by color. Beginning with the head on the left, color the sections to match the counters of one color, then continue coloring the sections for the other color. Write how many of each color.

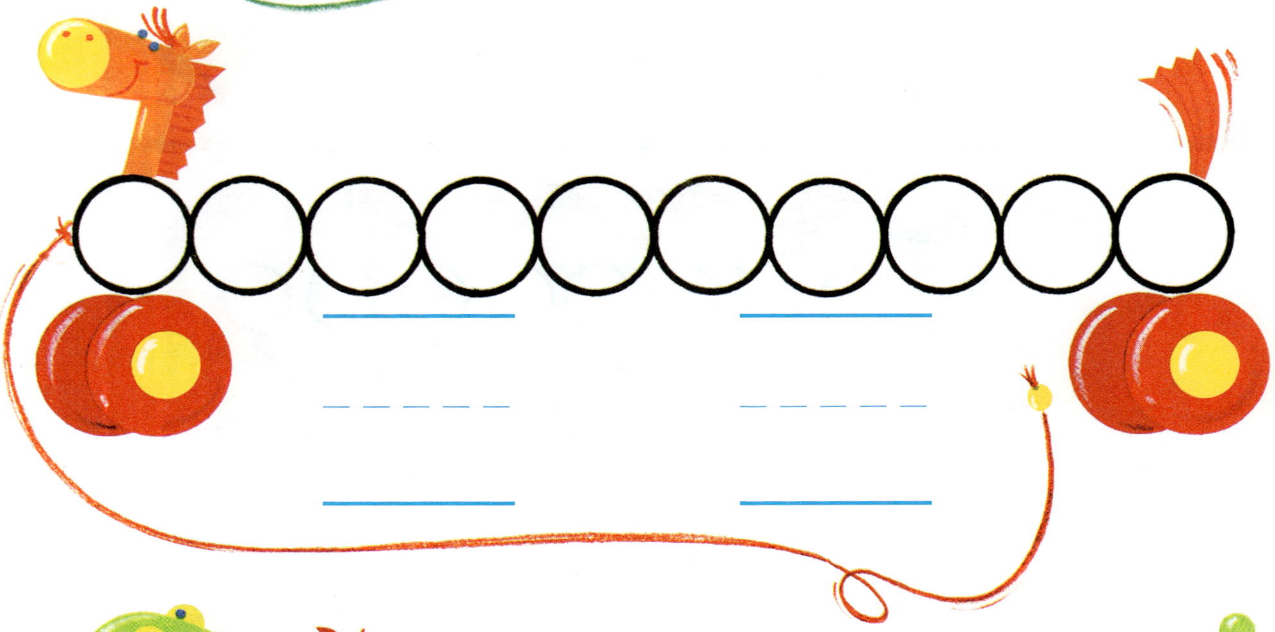

 **HOME ACTIVITY** · Place ten pennies in a cup, and have your child spill them on a table, then sort them by heads or tails. Have him or her write the number of pennies in each group, and compare the groups.

DIRECTIONS 1. How many windows on each rocket? Write the number. 2. Write those numbers in order on the number line. Use *before* and *after* to tell about the number 3.

OBJECTIVE • Use a number line to order numbers to 10.

1

2

108 one hundred eight

Ordinal Numbers to 10th

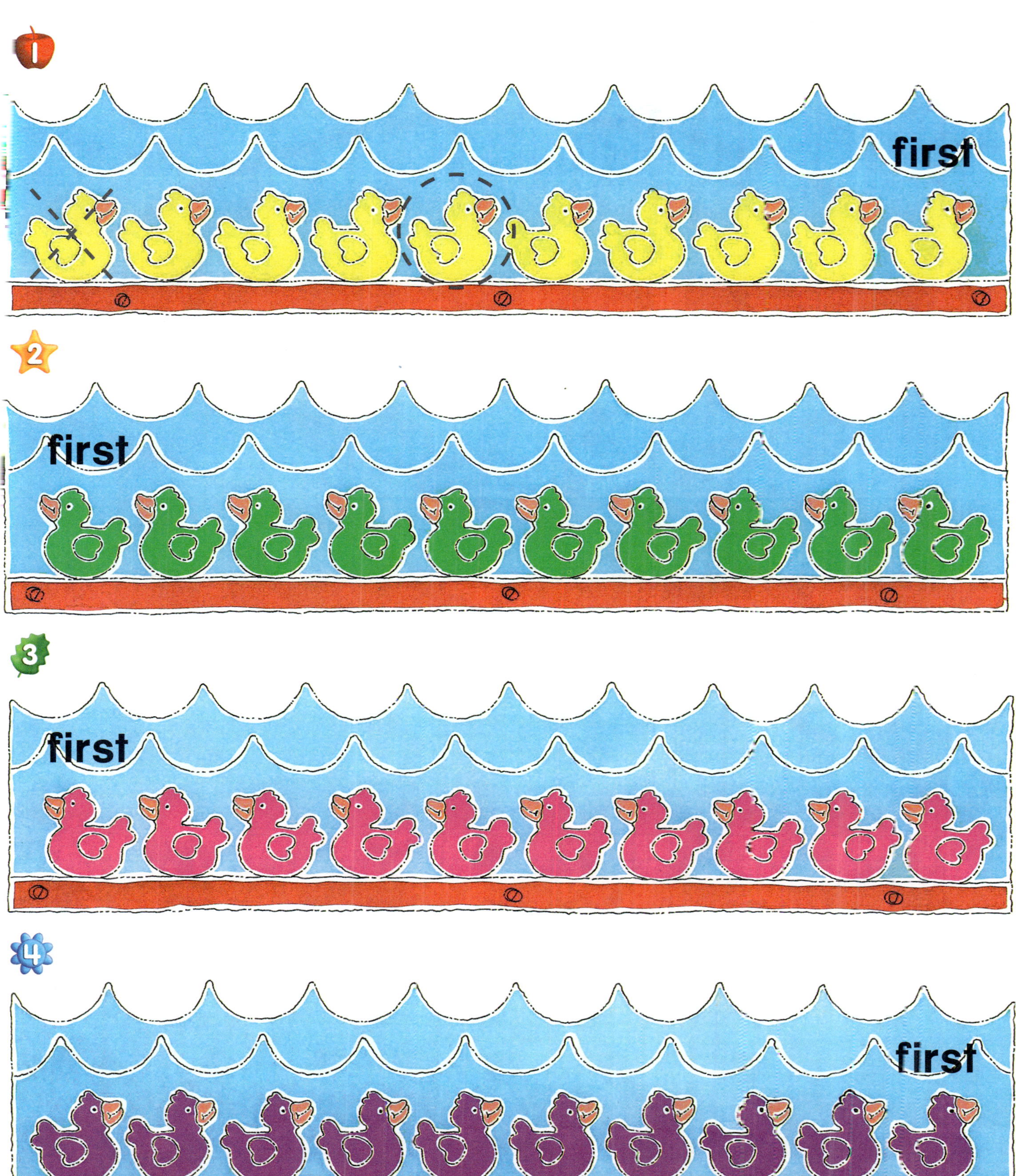

DIRECTIONS **1.** Trace the circle on the sixth duck. Trace the X on the tenth duck. **2.** Circle the eighth duck. Mark an X on the second duck. **3.** Circle the fifth duck. Mark an X on the ninth duck. **4.** Circle the seventh duck. Mark an X on the last duck.

OBJECTIVE • Describe order of objects.

Chapter 4 • Lesson 9

one hundred nine **109**

DIRECTIONS   Circle the fourth bird. Mark an X on the seventh bird. Circle the eighth car on the ride. Mark an X on the fifth car on the ride. Circle the third child standing in line. Mark an X on the tenth child standing in line. Circle the ninth duck. Mark an X on the sixth duck.

HOME ACTIVITY · Have your child line up ten objects. Point to the objects in order and have your child use the words *first, second, third, fourth, fifth, sixth, seventh, eighth, ninth,* and *tenth* to tell the position of each object. Then ask your child to point to the third object, the last object, the seventh object, and so on.

110   one hundred ten

© Harcourt

Problem Solving Workshop
Skill • Use Estimation

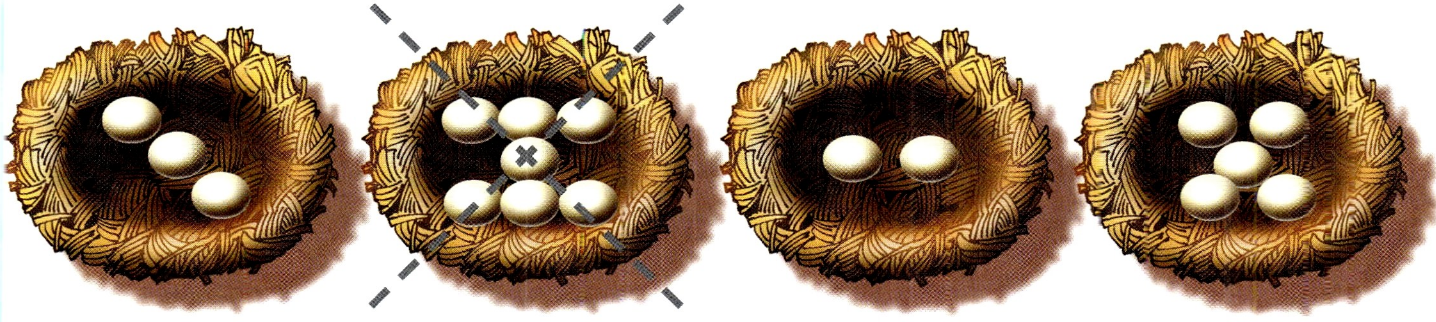

DIRECTIONS Look at the nest at the top of the page. It has 5 eggs. Without counting, mark an X on the nests that have more than 5 eggs.

OBJECTIVE • Solve problems by using the skill *use estimation*.

Chapter 4 • Lesson 10

one hundred eleven **111**

DIRECTIONS   Look at the horse at the top of the page. It has 10 spots. Without counting, mark an X on the horses that have fewer than 10 spots.

 **HOME ACTIVITY** · Take turns seeing if you can pick up 10 raisins or cereal pieces without actually counting. After you have tried, count the items to see if you were close.

Number Line Up

DIRECTIONS Play with a partner. Place the 5's on the board. Shuffle the remaining cards. Lay 9 cards face up in front of each player. Players take turns putting down one card at a time to form a number line to the right or left of each 5 without skipping any numbers. If a player cannot put down a card, he or she misses a turn. The first player to place all their cards wins the game.

MATERIALS 2 sets of numeral cards 1-10

Math Power • Most and Fewest

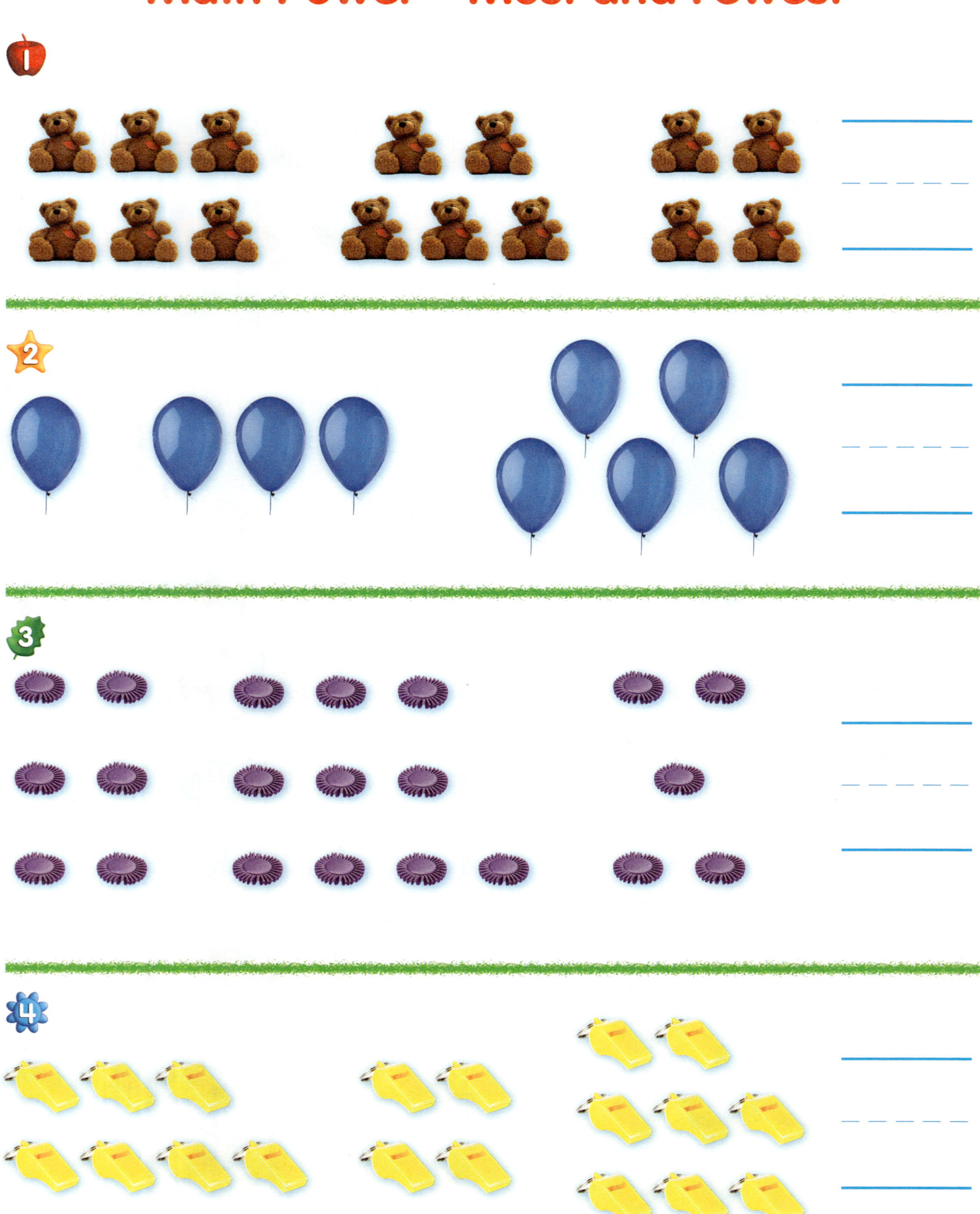

DIRECTIONS 1–2. Circle the group that has the most objects. Write that number.   3–4. Circle the group that has the fewest objects. Write that number.

114 one hundred fourteen

✓ Chapter 4 Review/Test

1

2

3

DIRECTIONS   1. How many flowers in each set? Write the number. Circle the row that has more. Circle the number that is greater.   **2.** Spill ten two-color counters on the page. Sort by color. Beginning with the head on the left, color the sections to match the counters of one color, then continue coloring the sections for the other color. Write how many of each color.   **3.** Look at the first nest. It has 5 eggs. Without counting, mark an X on the nest that has more than 5 eggs.

Chapter 4

DIRECTIONS **1.** Look at the group of figures at the beginning of the row. Tell how the figures are alike. Circle the figure that belongs in the group. **2.** Place a cube on each animal in the set as you count. Draw the cubes. Write the number. **3.** Look at the pattern. Write the numbers below the dot cards. Circle the part that repeats again and again. **4.** How many animals? Write the number.

THE WORLD ALMANAC FOR KIDS

Fall Finds

ALMANAC Fact

Problem Solving

There are 1, 2, or 3 ears of corn on a cornstalk.

DIRECTIONS   Draw a bird above the cornstalk with one ear.
Circle the animal between the pumpkins. Mark an x on the animal under the wheelbarrow.

TALK Math   Use the words above, between, and under to tell about this picture.

Popcorn

TALK Math How many pieces of popcorn did you draw? Count the pieces aloud.

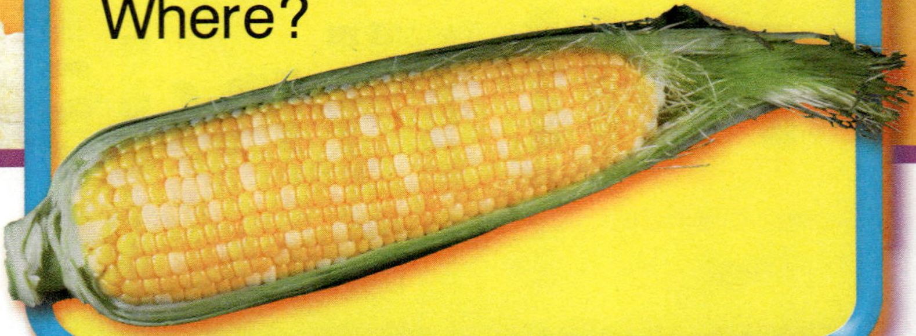

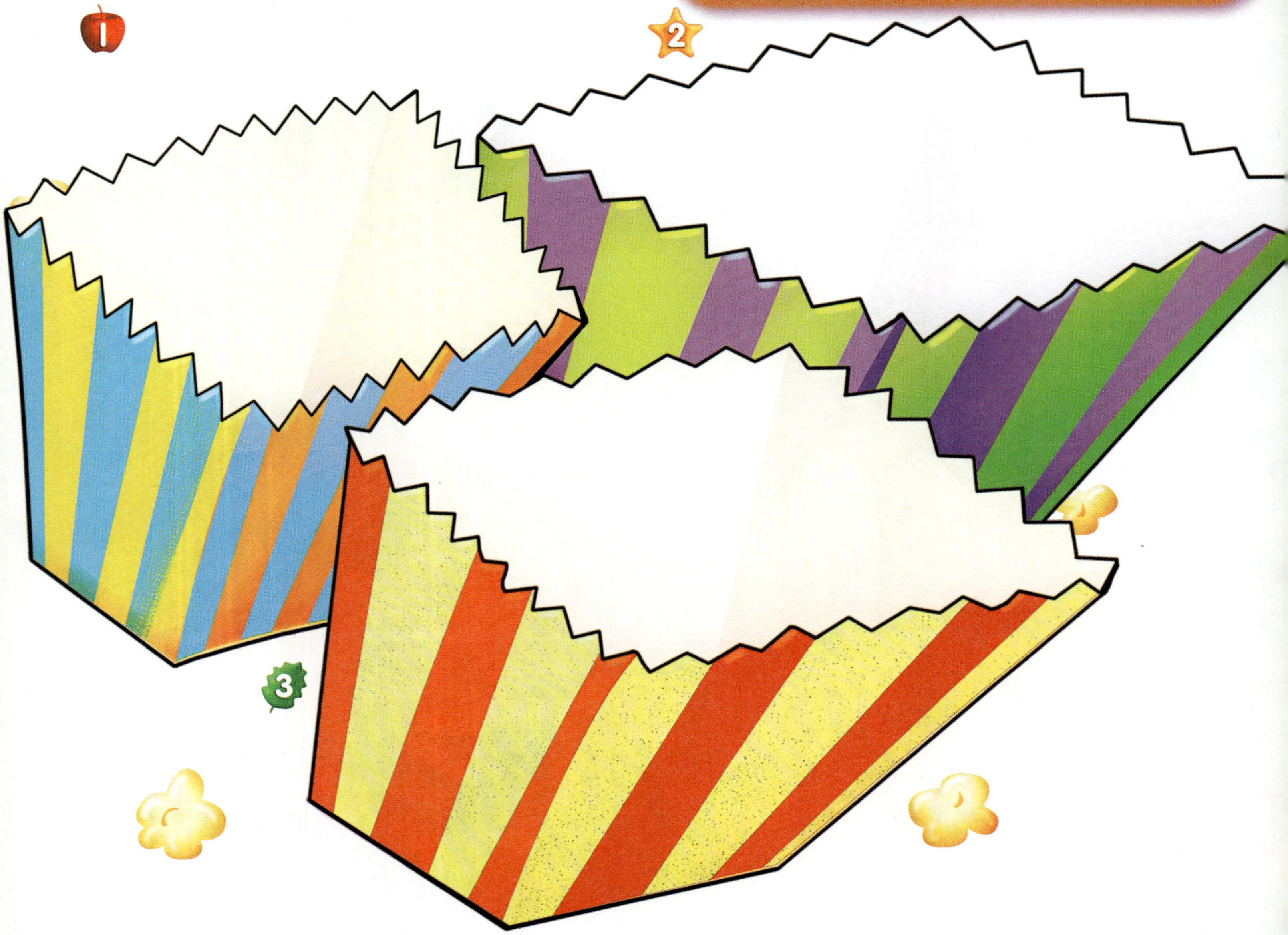

Unit 2 • The World Almanac For Kids

Unit 3
READ Math
Workshop
Animals
written by Ann Dickson
In this story you will also TALK Math and WRITE Math.
Family Note: This story will help your child review groups with more and fewer objects.
A

Look at the ducks through the viewer!

Which group has fewer?

Science

Can you find a duck's bill?

B

© Harcourt

The cubs are younger as they are newer.

Which group has fewer?

Science

Do you see the lion cubs' paws?

C

Alligators sleep and snore.

Which group has more?

Science

Where are the alligators' tails?

D

Young eagles learn to soar.

Which group has more?

Science

Find the eagles' wings.

E

Can you name these
for sure?
Which group has more?
Map
Science
Find the hedgehogs' noses.
F

My Math Story
Literature Activity

Vocabulary Review
more
fewer

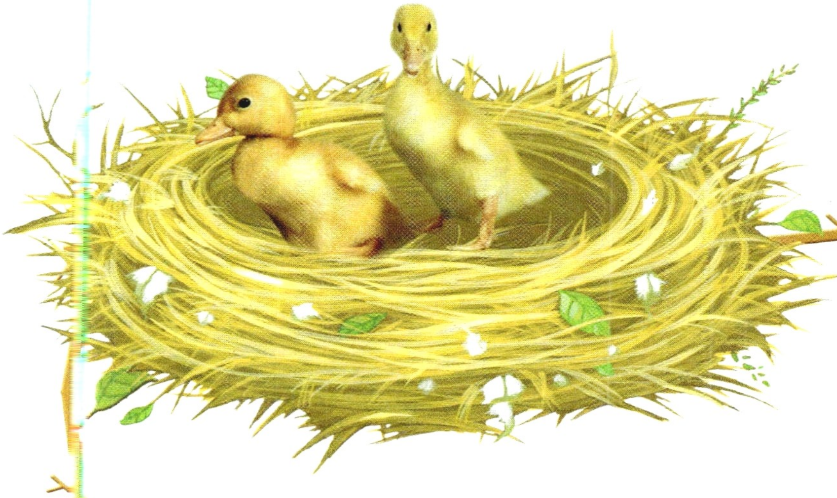

DIRECTIONS Look at the ducklings in the nest. Draw a nest with another group of ducklings. Tell a story. Use more or fewer to describe your group.

G

Which Has More?
Which Has Fewer?

DIRECTIONS **1.** Look at the pictures. Draw a circle around the family that has more lions. **2.** Look at the pictures. Draw a cirle around the family that has fewer alligators. **3.** Make up a story about two alligator mothers and their babies. Share the story with a classmate.

H

School Home CONNECTION

Dear Family,

My class started Unit 3 today. I will learn how to make a graph and identify geometric figures. Here are some vocabulary words and activities for us to share.

Love, ____

Vocabulary Power

Key Math Vocabulary

Solid Figures: **sphere, cube, cylinder, cone, rectangular prism, pyramid**

sphere   cube   cylinder   cone   rectangular prism   pyramid

Plane Figures: **circle, square, triangle, rectangle**

circle   square

triangle   rectangle

Vocabulary Activity

Math on the Move

Provide your child with straws or toothpicks and have them make plane figures such as a square, a rectangle, or a triangle.

Technology
Multimedia Math Glossary link at:
www.harcourtschool.com/hspmath

School Home CONNECTION

Remember This Your child may already know how to identify solid figures in your home such as blocks, balls, and cones.

Calendar Activity

December						
Sunday	Monday	Tuesday	Wednesday	Thursday	Friday	Saturday
		1	2	3	4	5
6	7	8	9	10	11	12
13	14	15	16	17	18	19
20	21	22	23	24	25	26
27	28	29	30	31		

Have your child place an object such as a button on all the Mondays and place another object such as a paper clip on all the Fridays. Then have your child make a graph. Have him or her explain the graph.

Practice (after pages 123 and 124)

Are there more buttons or more paper clip on your graph?

Practice (after pages 129 and 130)

Have your child chart the weather on the calendar and then draw a graph to show the data.

Literature

Look for these books in a library. Ask your child to point out math vocabulary words as you read each book together.

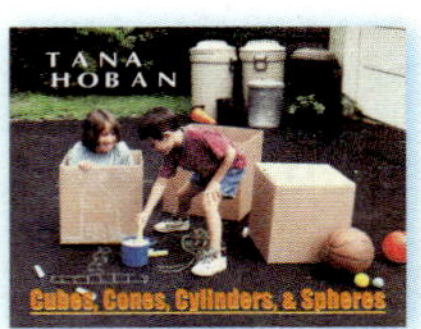

Cubes, Cones, Cylinders, & Spheres.
Hoban, Tana.
Greenwillow, 2000.

How Many Snails?
A Counting Book.
Giganti, Paul Jr.
Greenwillow, 1994.

So Many Circles,
So Many Squares.
Hoban, Tana.
Greenwillow, 1998.

School Home Connection

Graphing
Theme: Animals

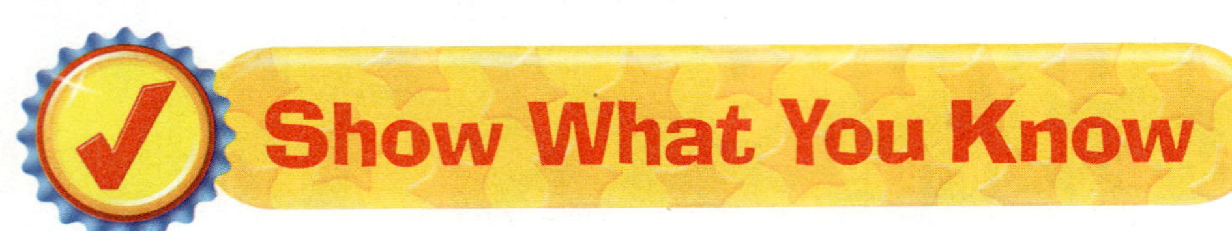

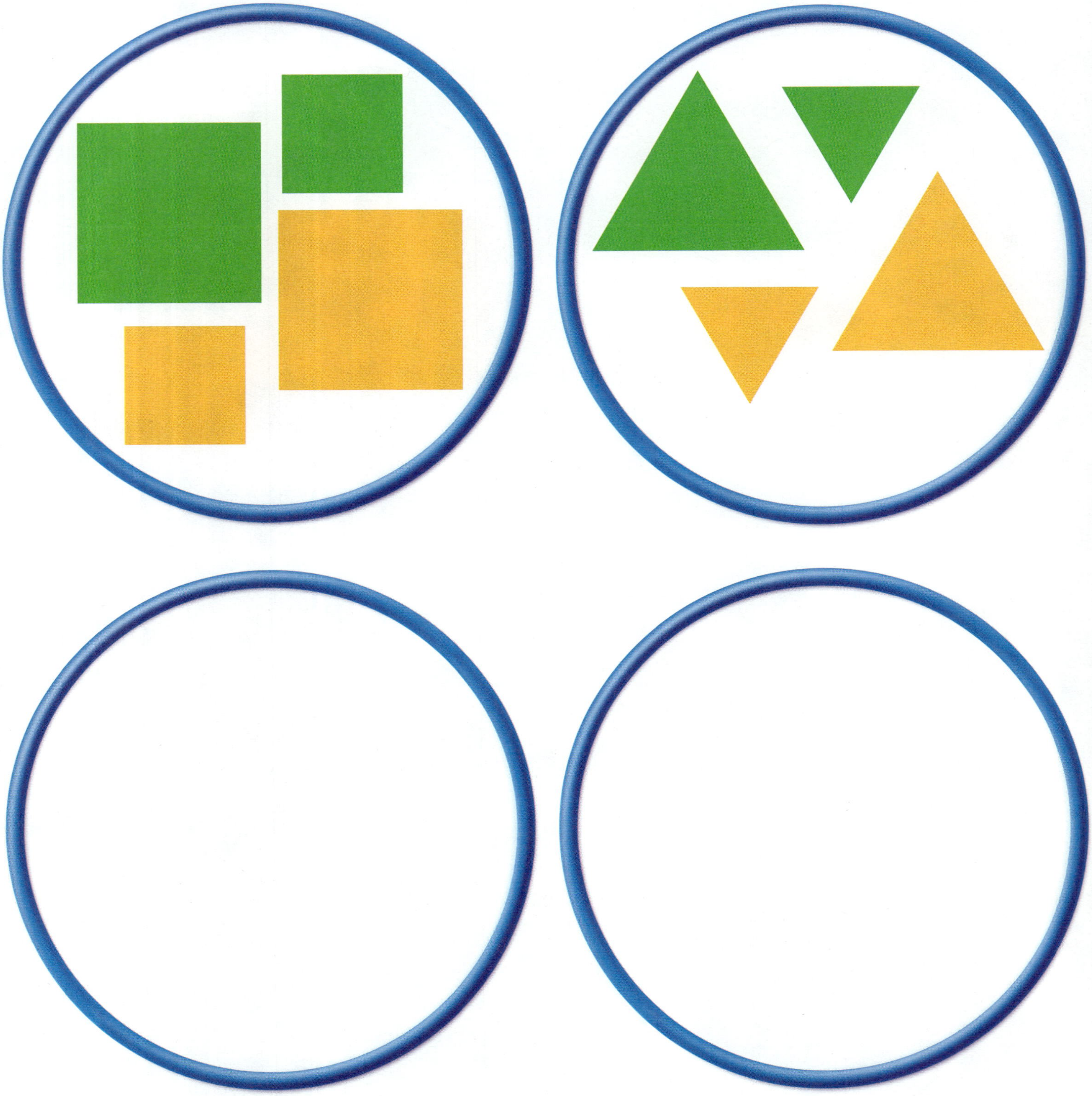

DIRECTIONS Place plane figures on the figures in the sorting rings at the top of the page. Discuss how the figures are sorted. Move the figures to the bottom sorting rings to show another way to sort these figures. Draw how the figures are sorted.

FAMILY NOTE • This page checks your child's understanding of important concepts and skills needed for success in Chapter 5.

122 one hundred twenty-two

DIRECTIONS   1. Make a graph with blue and green bears. Color the bears.   **2.** Count the bears. Write how many there are of each color. Circle the greater number.   **3.** Circle the kind of bear that there are more of on the graph.

OBJECTIVE • Construct graphs of real objects and use them to answer questions.

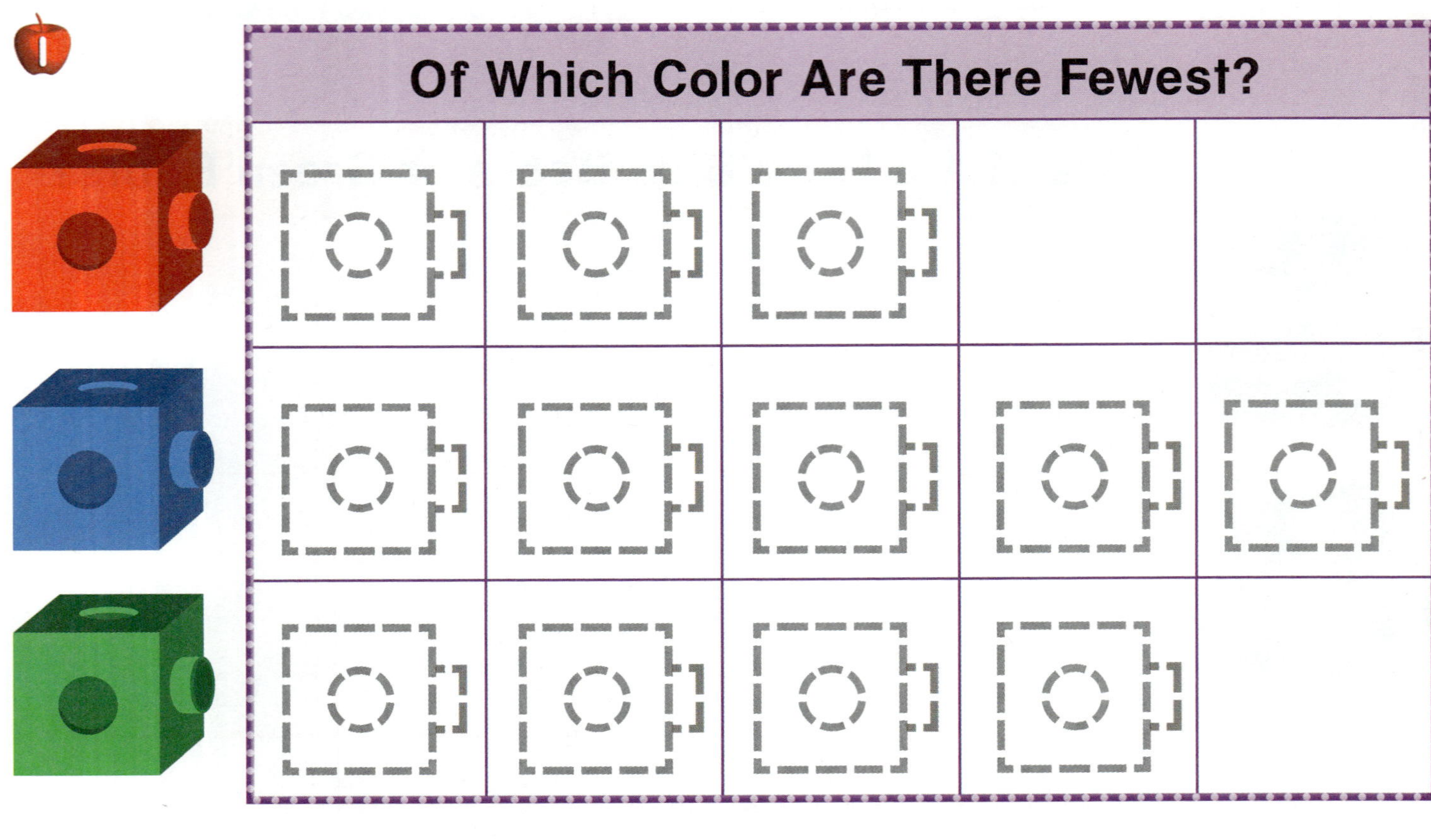

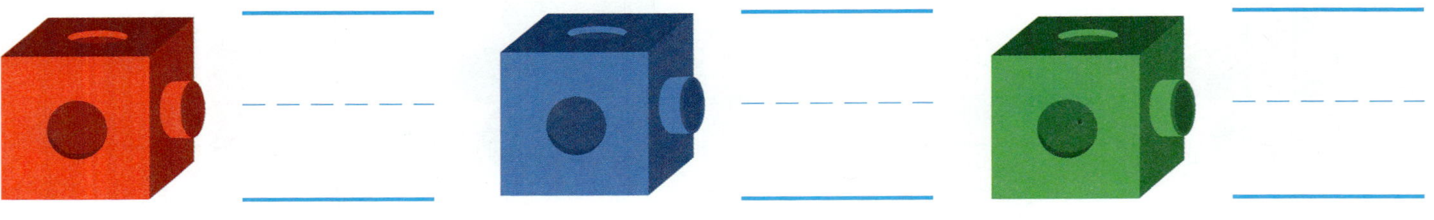

DIRECTIONS **1.** Make a graph with red, blue, and green cubes. Color the cubes. **2.** Count the cubes. Write how many there are of each color. Circle the least number. **3.** Circle the kind of cube that there are fewest of in the graph.

HOME ACTIVITY · Have your child explain how this graph would be different if there were two fewer green cubes.

124 one hundred twenty-four

Read Concrete Graphs

Name ______________________________

1 

2 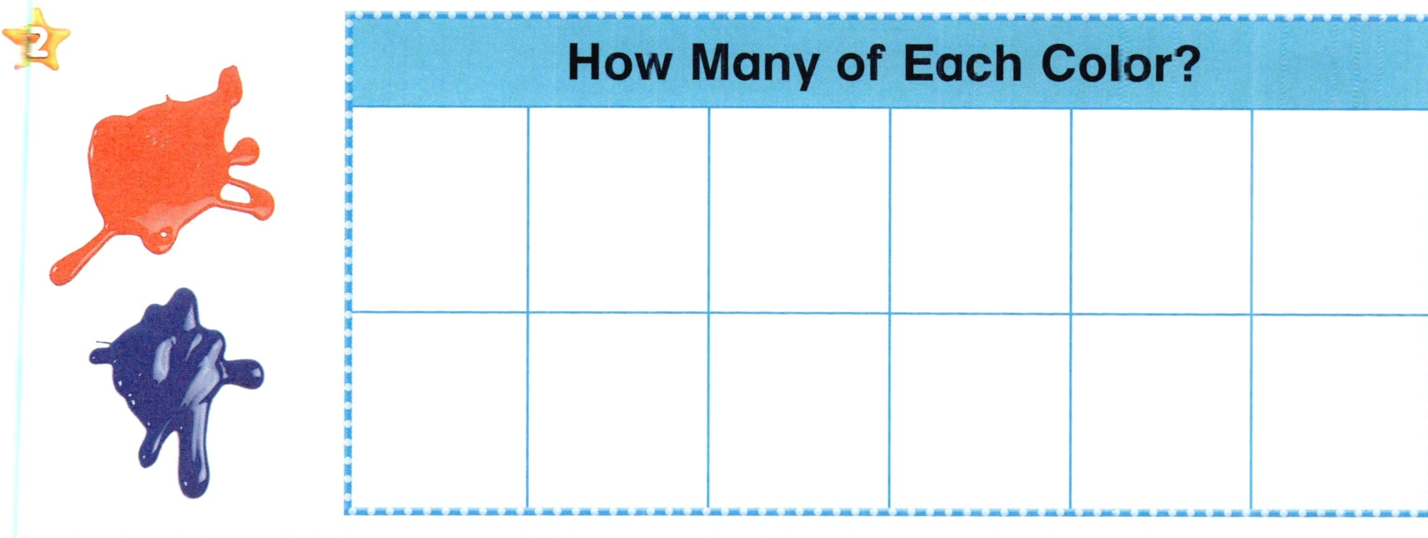

How Many of Each Color?

3 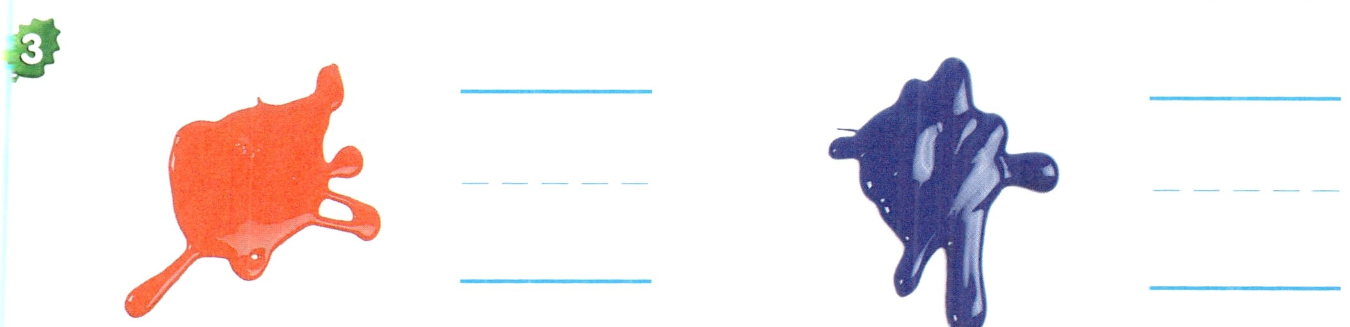

DIRECTIONS **1.** Place 6 small red and blue figures on the workspace. Sort the figures by color. **2.** Make a graph with the figures. Draw and color the figures in the graph. **3.** Read the graph. Write how many figures there are of each color.

OBJECTIVE • Construct graphs of real objects and use them to answer questions.

Chapter 5 • Lesson 2

one hundred twenty-five **125**

How Many of Each Figure?

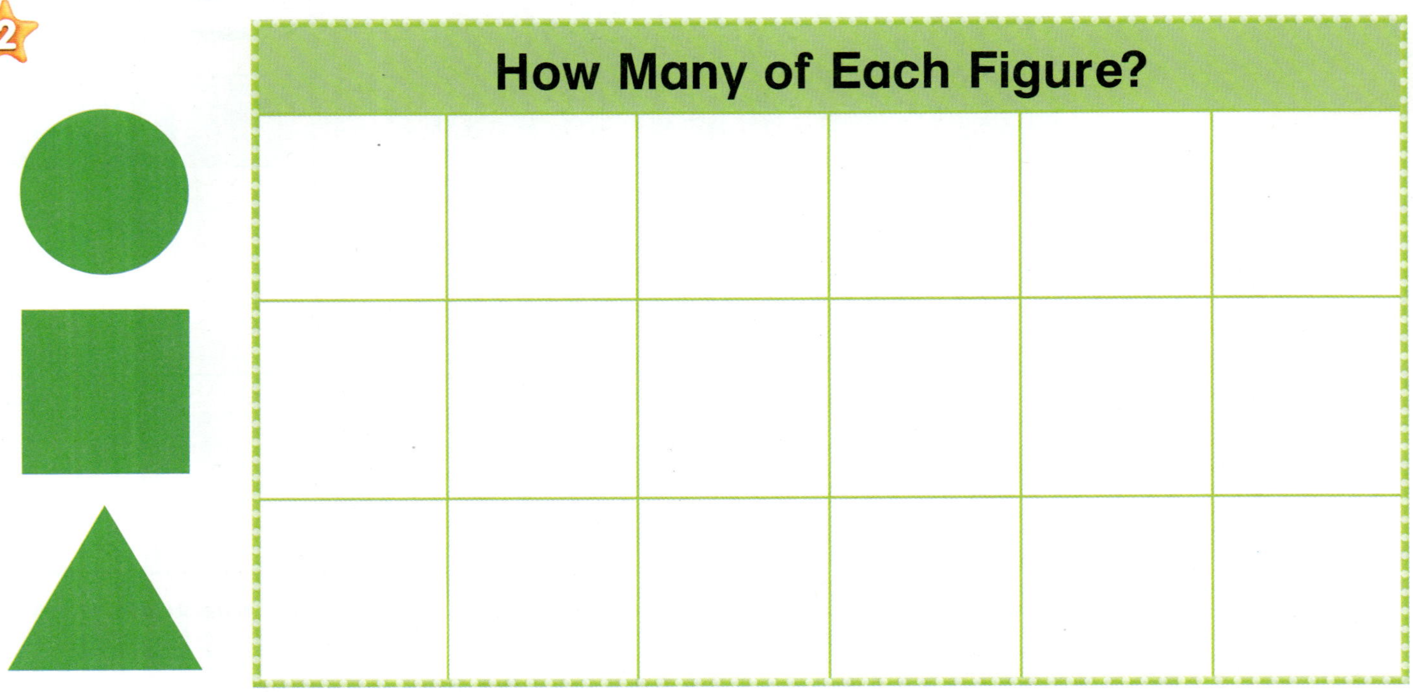

DIRECTIONS   **1.** Place 6 small green figures on the workspace. Sort them by shape.   **2.** Make a graph with your figures. Draw the figures in the graph.   **3.** Read the graph. Write how many there are of each figure.

HOME ACTIVITY · Draw a grid with two rows, and place objects of two kinds, such as pennies and dimes. Ask your child to explain which row has more objects.

Read Picture Graphs

DIRECTIONS   1. Read the graph. Write how many children like each kind of animal.
2. Circle the animal that more children like.

Chapter 5 • Lesson 3

Which Animal Do the Fewest Children Like?

1

 ______

 ______

 ______

2

DIRECTIONS 1. Read the graph. Write how many children like each kind of animal. 2. Circle the animal that the fewest children like.

 **HOME ACTIVITY** · Have your child explain how the graph on this page also shows which kind of animal the most children like.

Make Picture Graphs

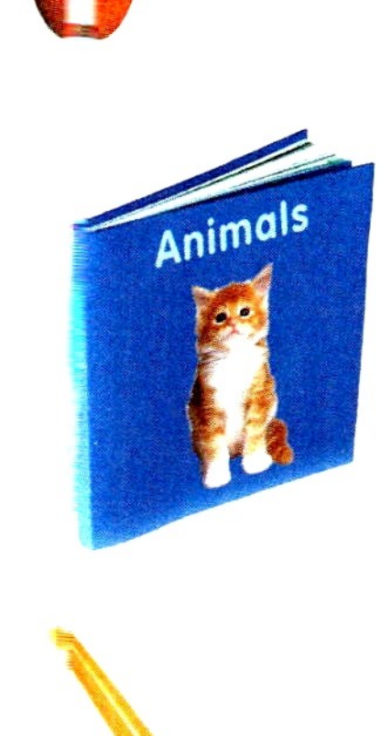

Are Fewer Children Reading or Painting?

2

____

____

____

____

DIRECTIONS **1.** Look at the centers. Make a picture graph about the children who are reading and painting. Circle the row with fewer children. **2.** Write how many. Circle the number that is less.

Which Kind of Animal Did the Most Children Paint?

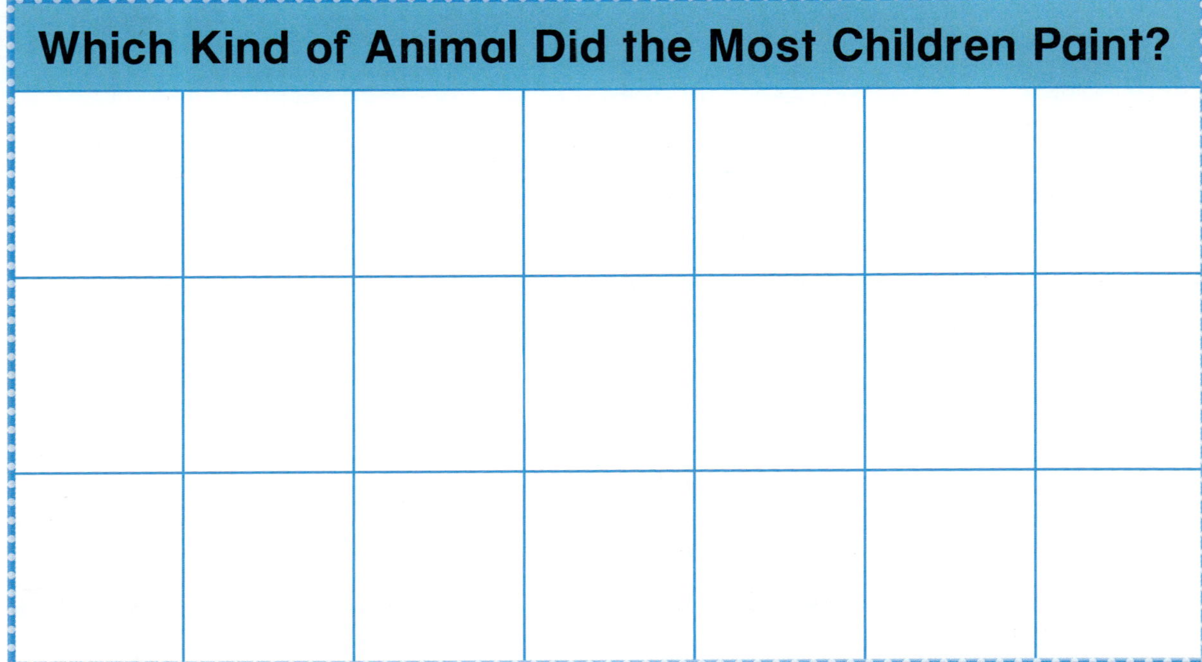

DIRECTIONS   1. Look at the paintings. Make a picture graph to show how many children painted each animal. Circle the row with the most children.   2. Write how many. Circle the greatest number.

130 one hundred thirty

Problem Solving Workshop
Strategy • Make a Graph

Which Kind of Shirt Are More Children Wearing?

1

2 

Which Kind of Shoe Are Fewer Children Wearing?

DIRECTIONS **1.** Ask five classmates whether their shoes have laces or no laces. Color a square on the graph for each response. **2.** Circle the kind of shoe that fewer children are wearing.

HOME ACTIVITY · Have your child ask five family members or friends whether they like summer or winter better and then make a graph to show this information.

✔ Mid Chapter 5 Review

Are There More Blue Bears or Green Bears?

Which Animal Do Fewer Children Like?

DIRECTIONS **1.** Count the bears. Write how many there are of each color. Circle the greater number. Circle the kind of bear that there are more of on the graph. **2.** Read the graph. Write how many children like each kind of animal. **3.** Circle the animal that fewer children like.

Chapter 5

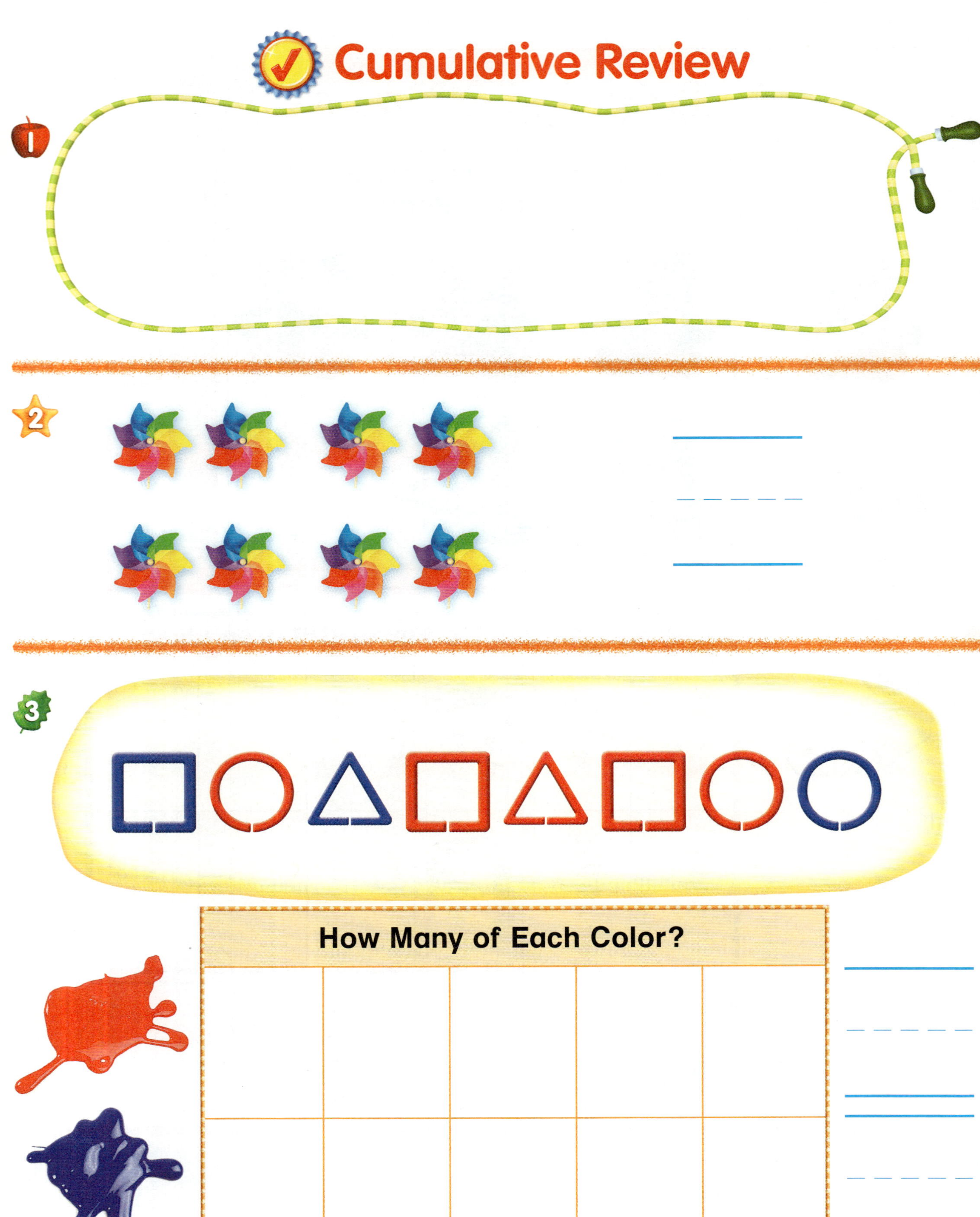

How Many of Each Color?

DIRECTIONS **1.** Use two colors of counters to make a pattern. Draw and color your pattern. Circle the part that repeats again and again. **2.** Write how many objects in the set. **3.** Draw and color the figures in the graph. Read the graph. Write how many figures there are of each color.

134 one hundred thirty-four

Deer With Antlers and Without Antlers
‖‖‖‖
‖‖‖‖

DIRECTIONS   **1.** Read the table. Write how many of each kind of deer.   **2.** Does this table show more deer with antlers or without antlers? Circle your answer.

OBJECTIVE • Read and interpret a tally table.

Chapter 5 • Lesson 6

one hundred thirty-five **| 35**

Wild Birds

	卌 III
	卌
	卌 II

 **2**

DIRECTIONS   1. Read the table. Write how many of each kind of bird.   **2.** Circle the kind of bird that there are the most of in this table. Mark an X on the kind of bird that there are the fewest of in this table.

HOME ACTIVITY • Draw a tally table for your child and have him or her read the tally table and explain the results.

136 one hundred thirty-six

Have You Fed Ducks?

Yes

No

Yes 

No 

DIRECTIONS   1. Ask five classmates if they have fed ducks. Record their answers in the tally table.   **2.** Write how many for each answer. Circle the greater number.

OBJECTIVE · Use a tally table to answer a simple two-choice question.

Have You Petted a Cat?

Yes

No

Yes   **No**

DIRECTIONS **1.** Ask five classmates if they have petted a cat. Record their answers in the tally table. **2.** Write how many for each answer. Circle the number that is less.

HOME ACTIVITY • Have your child ask family members or friends if they like frogs. Help your child make a tally table to show the results.

Name ___________________________

Purple and Green

DIRECTIONS 1. Make a spinner. Mark an X on the color on which you predict the clip is more likely to land. **2.** Spin ten times. Make a tally mark in the table after each spin. Circle the color on which the clip landed more often.

OBJECTIVE • Solve problems by using the skill *make a prediction*.

Purple and Green

DIRECTIONS **I.** Make a spinner. Mark an X on the color on which you predict the clip is less likely to land. **2.** Spin ten times. Make a tally mark in the table after each spin. Circle the color on which the clip landed less often.

HOME ACTIVITY · Have your child color a spinner red and blue so that it would be equally likely to land on either color.

140 one hundred forty

Spill the Counters

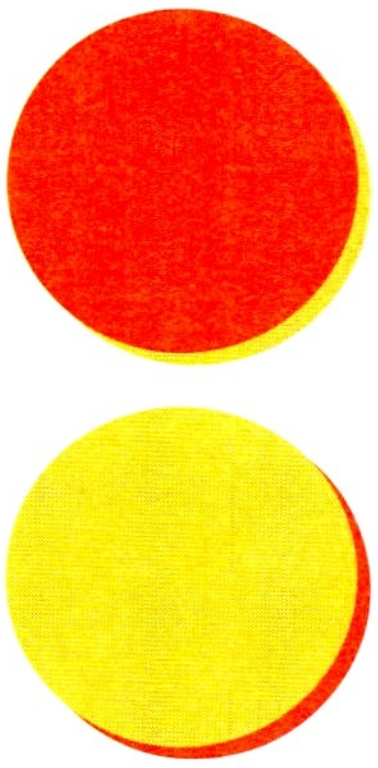

Player 1

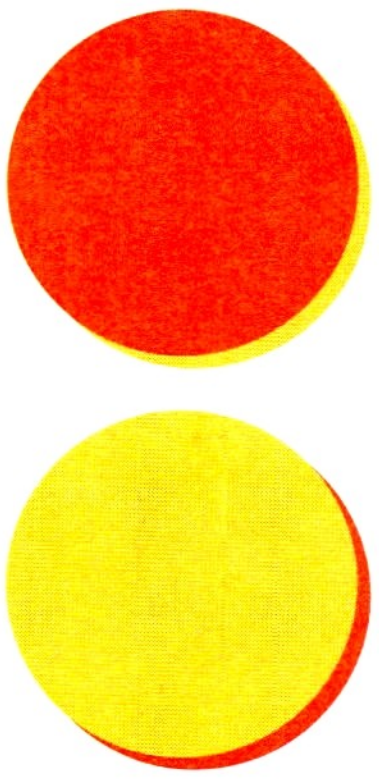

Player 2

DIRECTIONS   Play with a partner and decide who goes first. Spill the counters on the page. Sort the counters by color. Draw a counter on your chart for the color that has more. If there is an equal share of colors, draw a counter in the red row and the yellow row on your chart. The first player to fill a row on his or her chart wins.

MATERIALS 10 two-color counters

Math Power • Predict and Spin

Color	Predict	Tally
	_____	_____
	_____	_____
	_____	_____

DIRECTIONS Use a paperclip pnd a pencil to make a spinner. Look at the spinner. Predict how many times the spinner will land on each color if you spin ten times. Write your prediction. Make a tally mark in the table after each spin. Write how many tally marks. Compare your prediction with those numbers.

142 one hundred forty-two

Chapter 5 Review/Test

1.

Wild Birds	
I I I I	
I I I I I I	

____
- - - - - -
=======
- - - - - -

2.

Purple and Green

3.

DIRECTIONS 1. Read the table. Write how many of each kind of bird. Circle the kind of bird that there are more of in this table. **2.** Make a spinner. Spin ten times. Make a tally mark in the table after each spin. **3.** Circle the color with more tally marks.

Cumulative Review

Deer With Antlers And Without Antlers
llll
llll

DIRECTIONS **1.** Circle the child in front of the wheel. **2.** How many flowers in each set? Write the number. Circle the row that has more. Circle the number that is greater. **3.** Read the table. Write how many of each kind of deer. Circle the kind of deer that shows more on this table.

Geometry and Fractions

Theme: Marine Animals

Name ____

DIRECTIONS Look at the figures in the box. Find matching figures in the picture and color each figure the same color as the figure in the box.

FAMILY NOTE • This page checks your child's understanding of important concepts and skills needed for success in Chapter 6.

146 one hundred forty-six

Identify and Describe Solid Figures

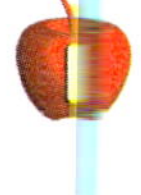 

sphere

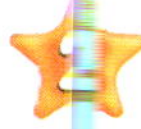 

cone

cube

cylinder

pyramid

  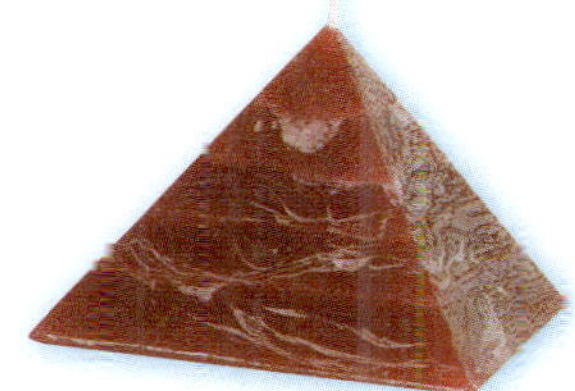

rectangular prism

DIRECTIONS 1–6. Name and describe the solid figure. Circle the object that is shaped like the solid figure.

OBJECTIVE • Identify and describe real-life objects or models of three-dimensional geometric figures.

Chapter 6 • Lesson 1

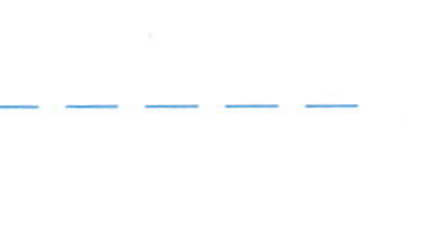

DIRECTIONS **1.** Find solid figures in the picture. Circle the objects shaped like cubes orange; spheres blue; cylinders green; cones red; rectangular prisms yellow; and pyramids purple. **2.** Write how many of each solid figure.

HOME ACTIVITY · Have your child find and name objects in your home that are shaped like a cube, a cone, a cylinder, a rectangular prism, a pyramid, and a sphere.

148 one hundred forty-eight

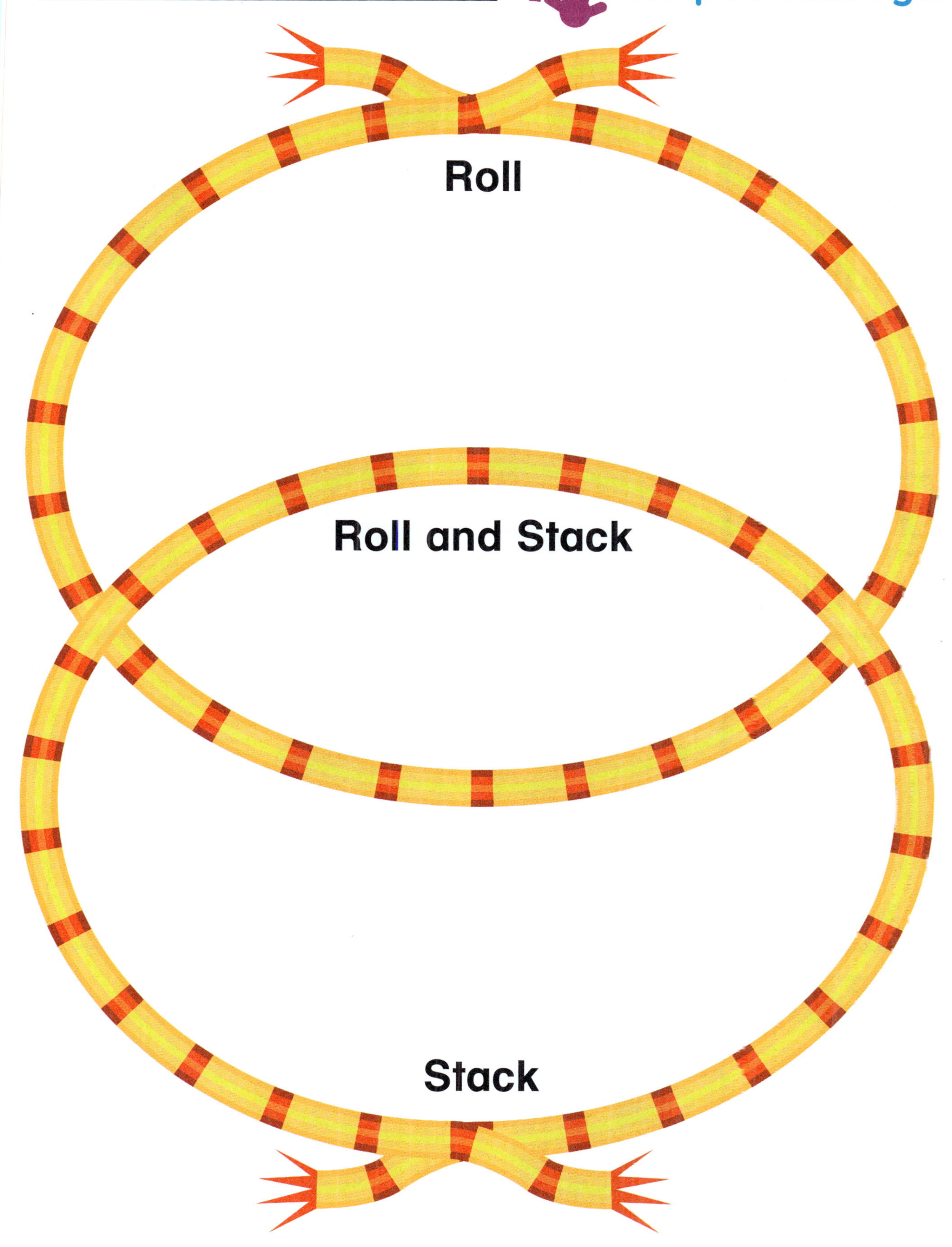

DIRECTIONS Sort solid figures or pictures of solid figures. Place the solid figures that roll in the top section. Place the solid figures that stack in the bottom section. Place the solid figures that roll and stack in the middle section. Draw the figures or glue the pictures.

1 roll

2 stack

3 slide

4 stack and slide

DIRECTIONS   1. Mark an X on the figure that does not roll.   2. Mark an X on the figures that do not stack.   3. Mark an X on the figure that does not slide.   4. Mark an X on the figure that does not stack and slide.

 **HOME ACTIVITY** · Have your child find and name objects in your home that roll, stack, or slide.

150   one hundred fifty

Plane Figures on Solids

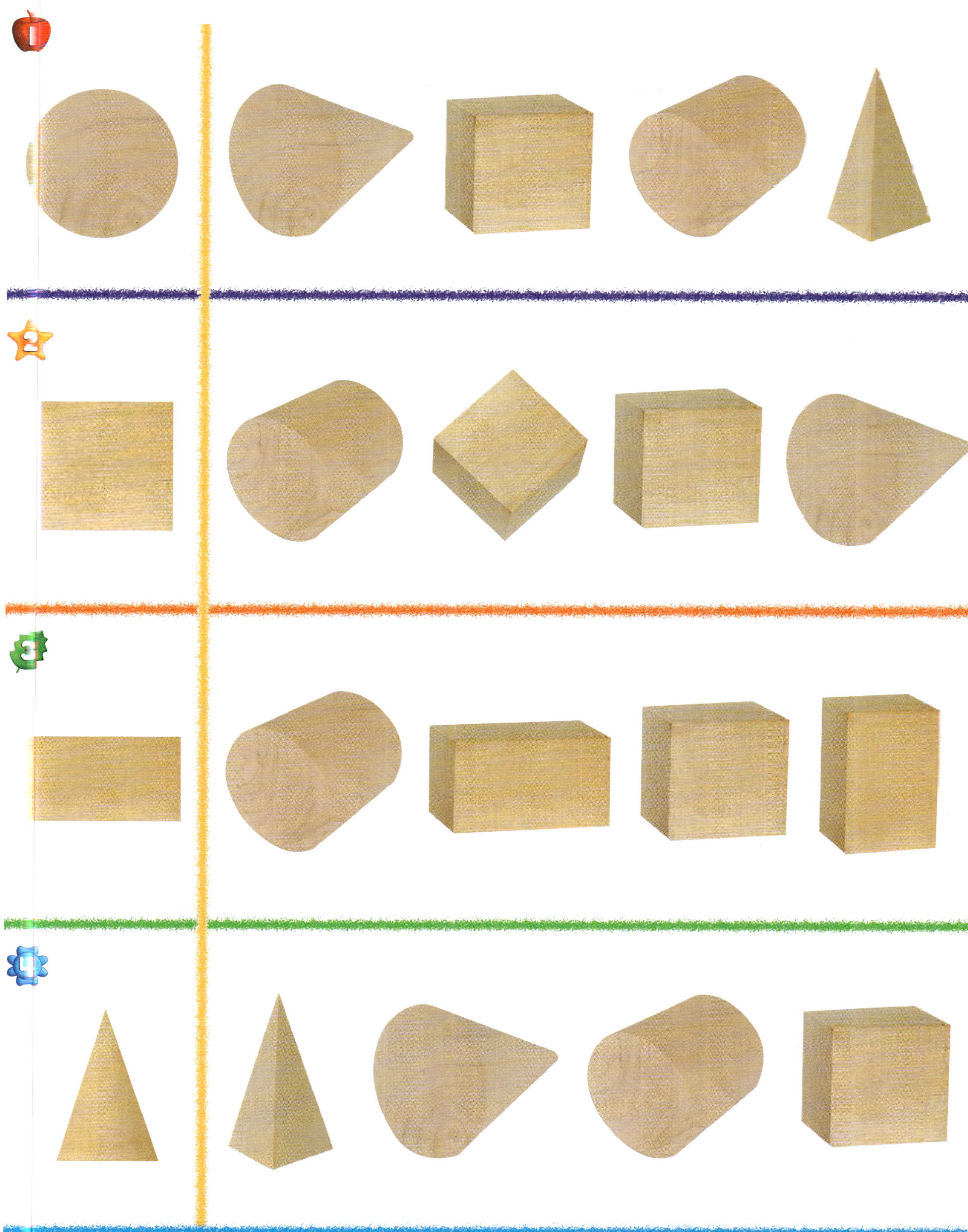

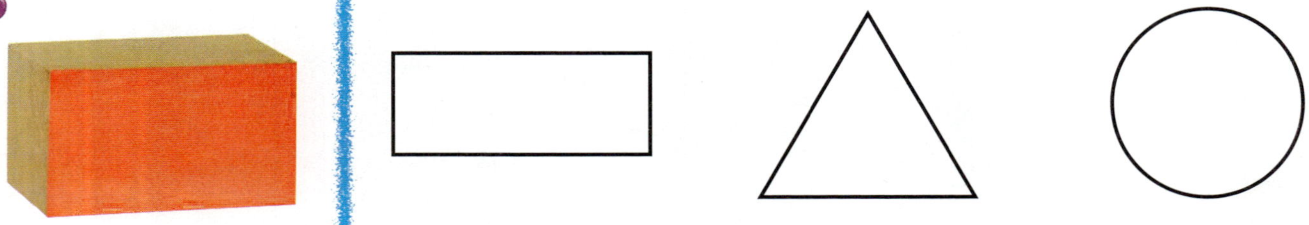

DIRECTIONS   **1–5. Find the plane figure that matches the shape of the surface of the solid figure. Color it to match.**

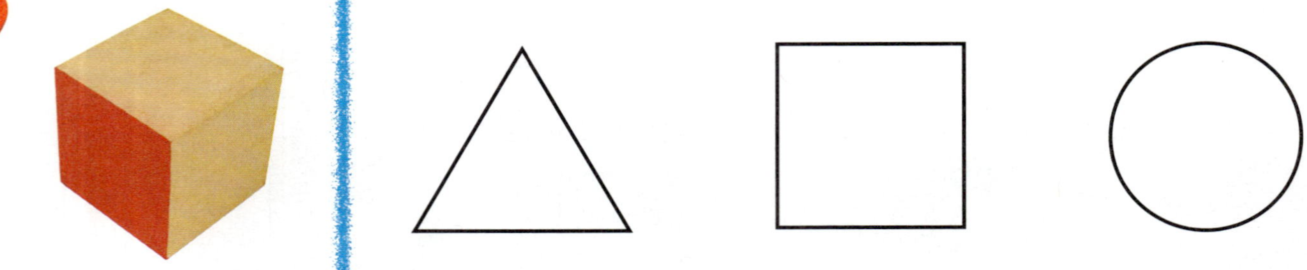

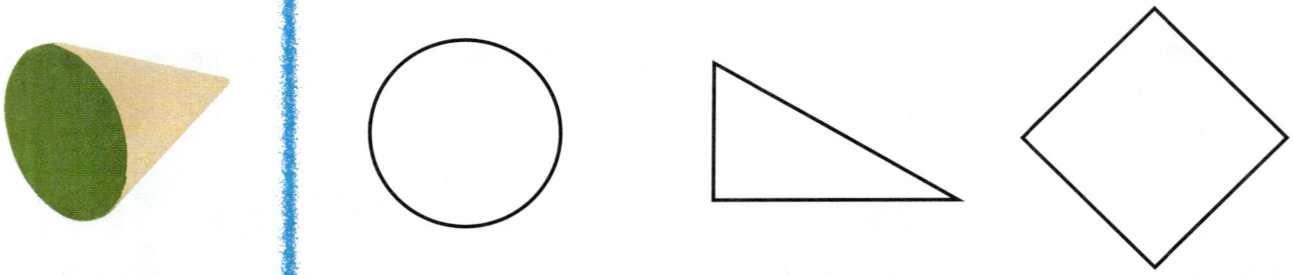

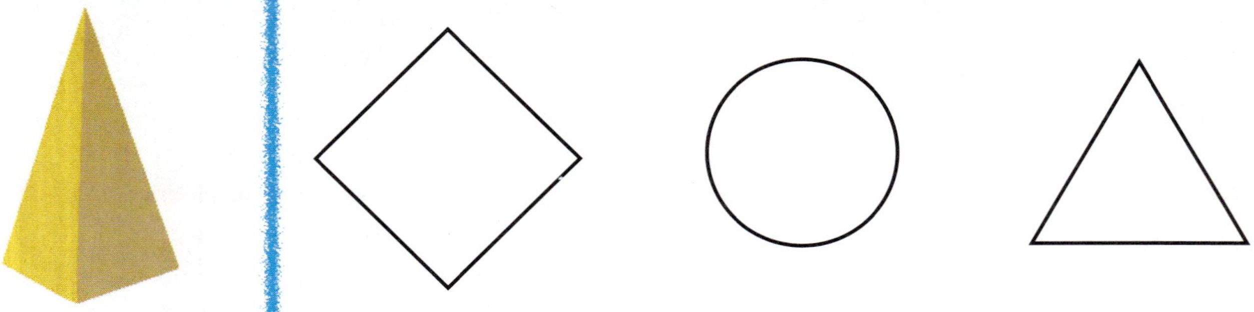

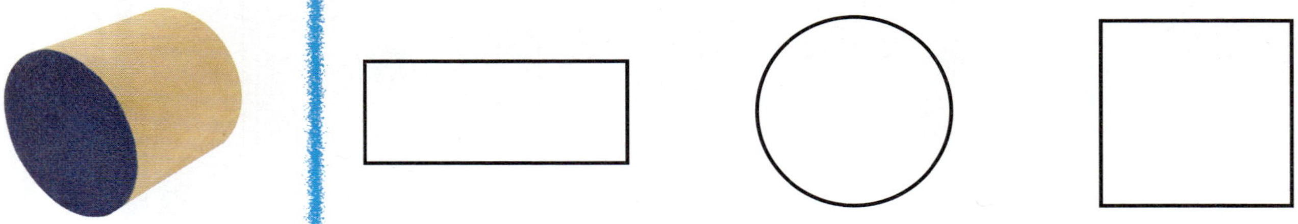

 **HOME ACTIVITY ·** Help your child trace around a surface of a solid object such as the bottom of a can or one side of a block to make a shape print. Have him or her name the shape.

152   one hundred fifty-two

Identify and Describe Plane Figures

1. circle

2. square

3. rectangle

4. triangle

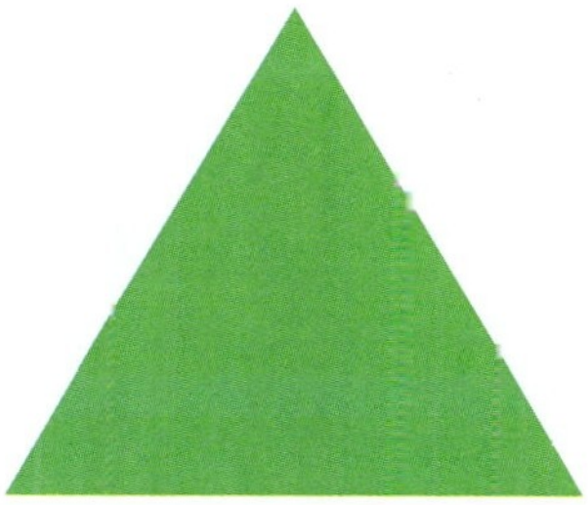

DIRECTIONS   1–4. Look at the figure at the beginning of the row. Circle the object that is the same shape.

HOME ACTIVITY • Have your child draw a picture using squares, circles, triangles, and rectangles. Have your child color each kind of figure a different color.

154 one hundred fifty-four

Compare Plane Figures

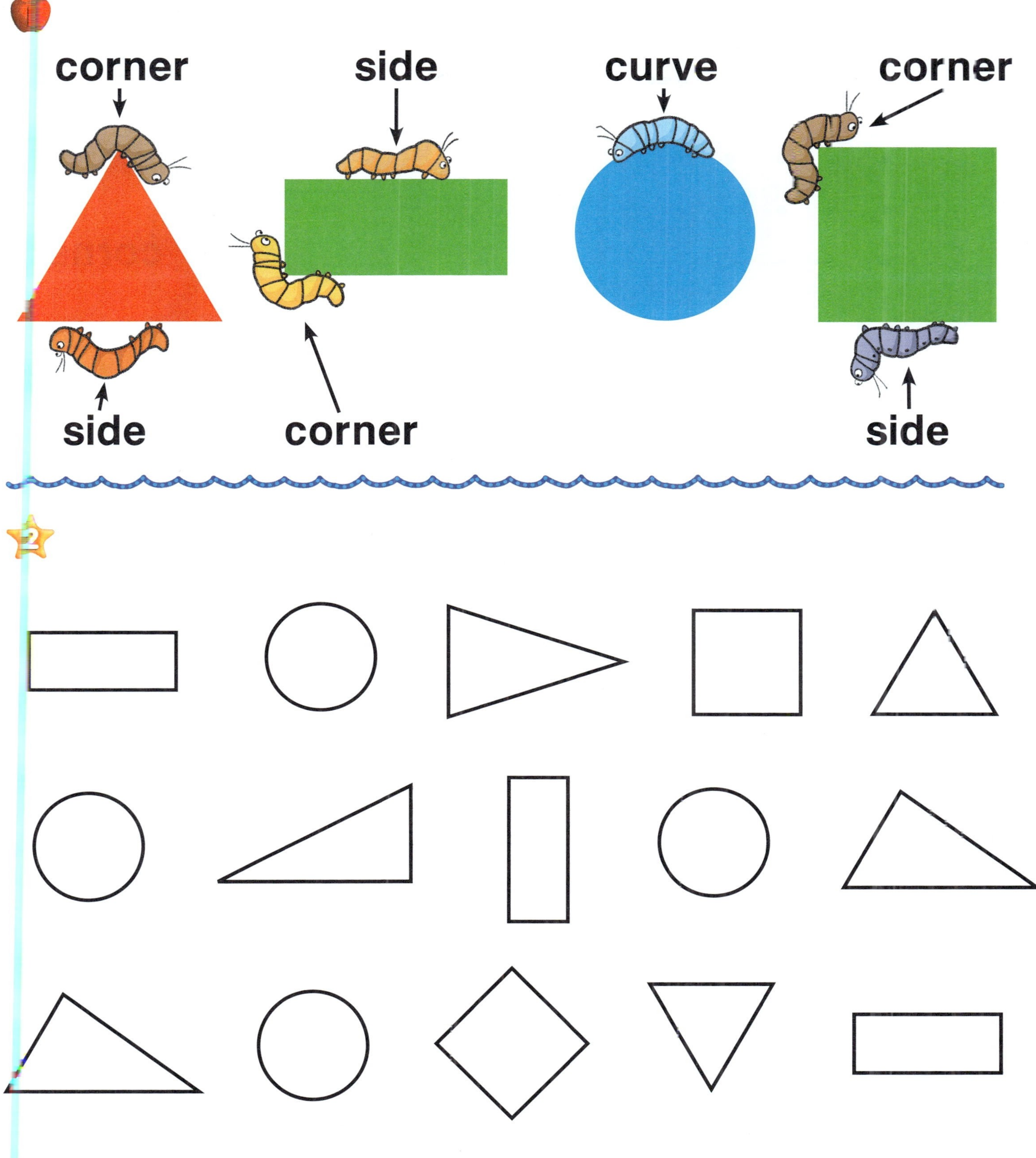

DIRECTIONS **1.** Look at the worms. Use the words **corner**, **curve**, and **side** to compare each figure. **2.** Use green to color the figures with four corners and four sides. Use blue to color the figures with curves. Use red to color the figures with three corners and three sides.

OBJECTIVE • Compare two-dimensional geometric figures by common attributes.

1

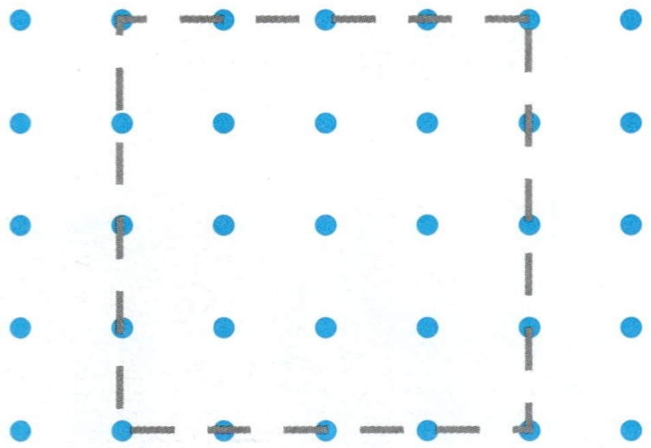

_______ sides

_______ corners

2

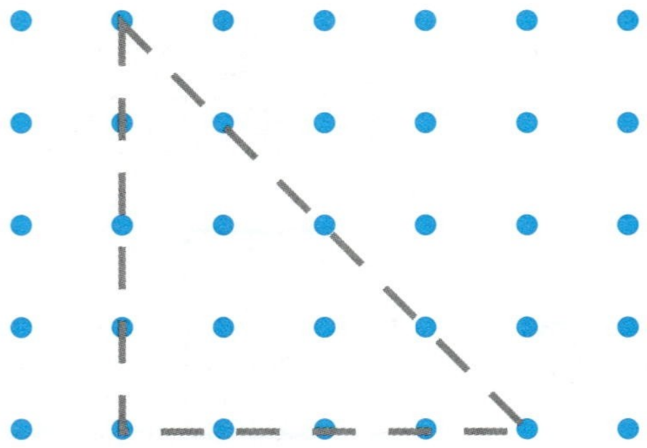

_______ sides

_______ corners

3

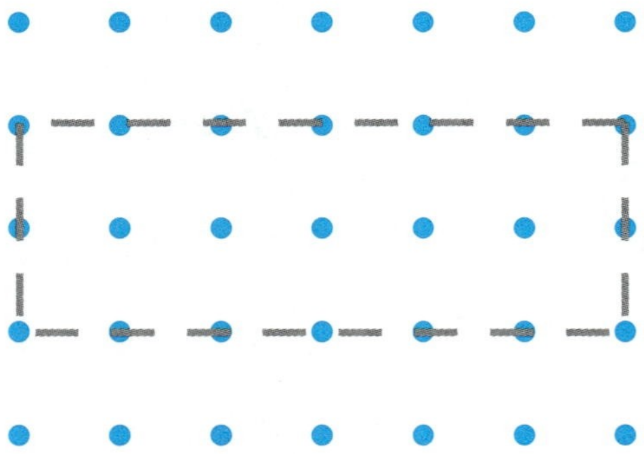

_______ sides

_______ corners

DIRECTIONS **1–3.** Trace the outline of the figure. Write how many sides. Write how many corners.

HOME ACTIVITY • Describe a figure for your child, such as a figure with 3 sides and 3 corners. Then ask your child to draw the figure.

Problem Solving Workshop
Strategy • Use Logical Reasoning

DIRECTIONS **1.** Use some or all of the figures to make a larger square. Trace around the figures to draw the square. **2.** Use some or all of the figures to make a rectangle. Trace around the figures to draw the rectangle.

OBJECTIVE · Solve problems by using the strategy *use logical reasoning*.

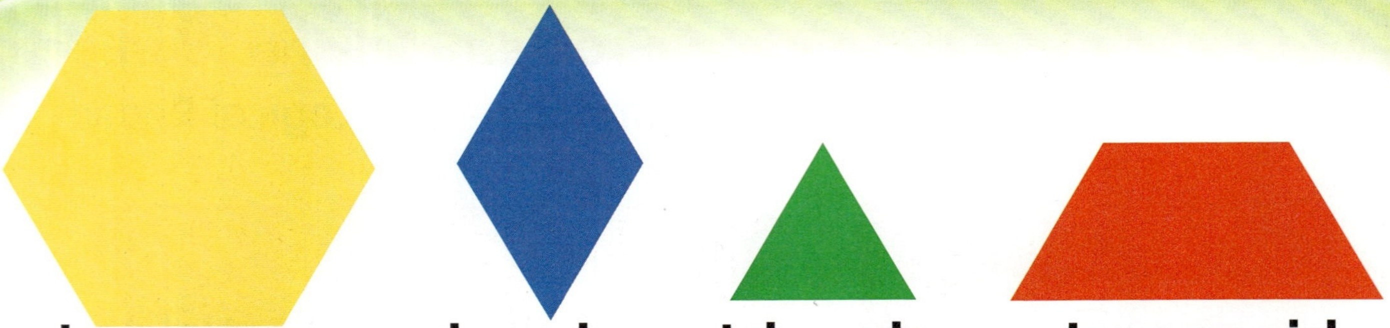

hexagon   **rhombus**   **triangle**   **trapezoid**

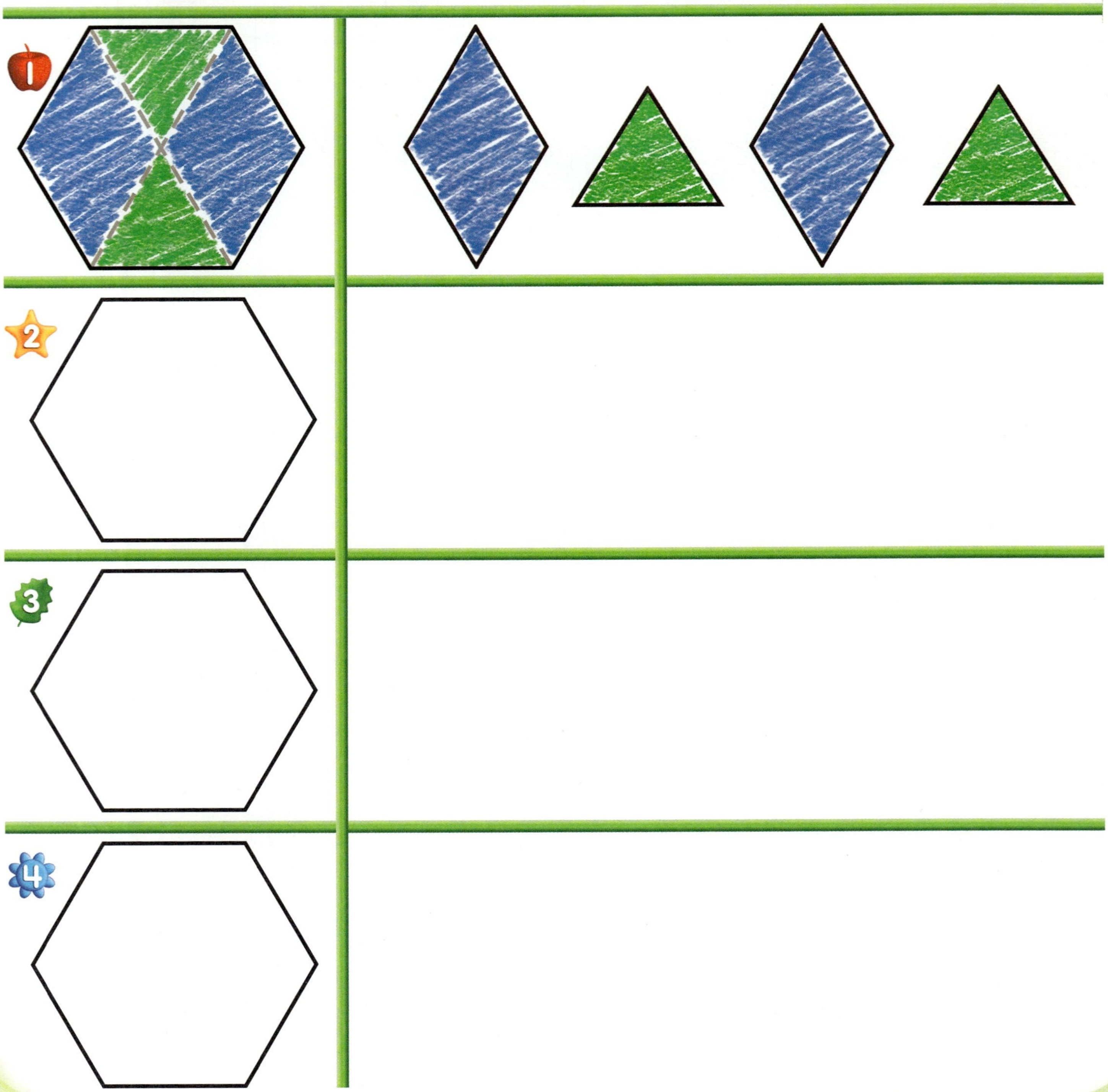

HOME ACTIVITY • Cut out a large rectangle.
Have your child draw lines on the rectangle to
make other figures, such as squares and
triangles. Help your child cut out and name the
new figures.

✓ Mid Chapter 6 Review

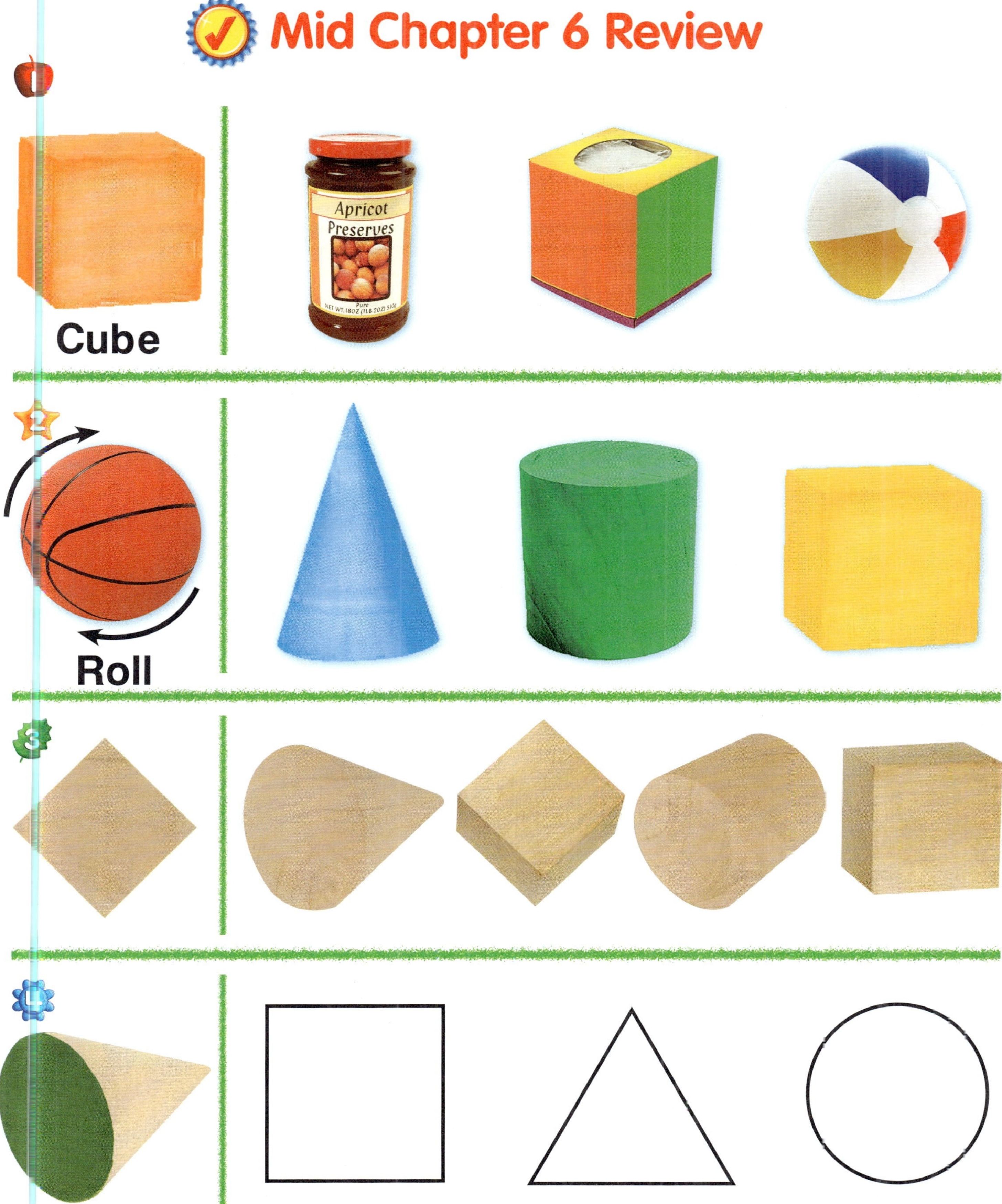

DIRECTIONS 1. Name and describe the solid figure. Circle the object that is shaped like the solid figure. 2. Mark an X on the figure that does not roll. 3. Circle the solid figures with a flat surface that could make the plane figure on the left. 4. Find the plane figure that matches the shape of the surface of the solid figure. Color it to match.

Cumulative Review

1

2

Which Color Has Fewer Cubes?

3

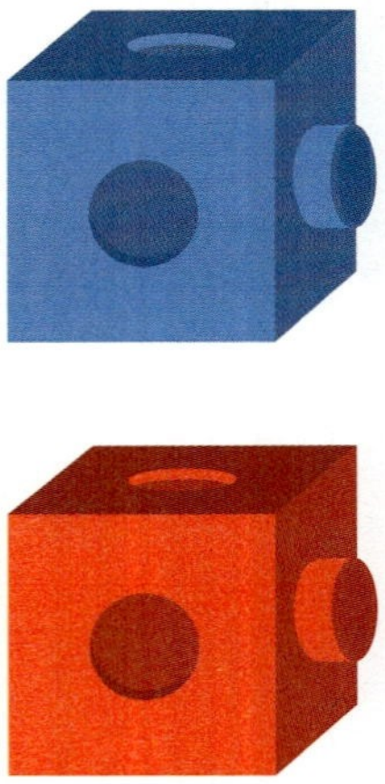

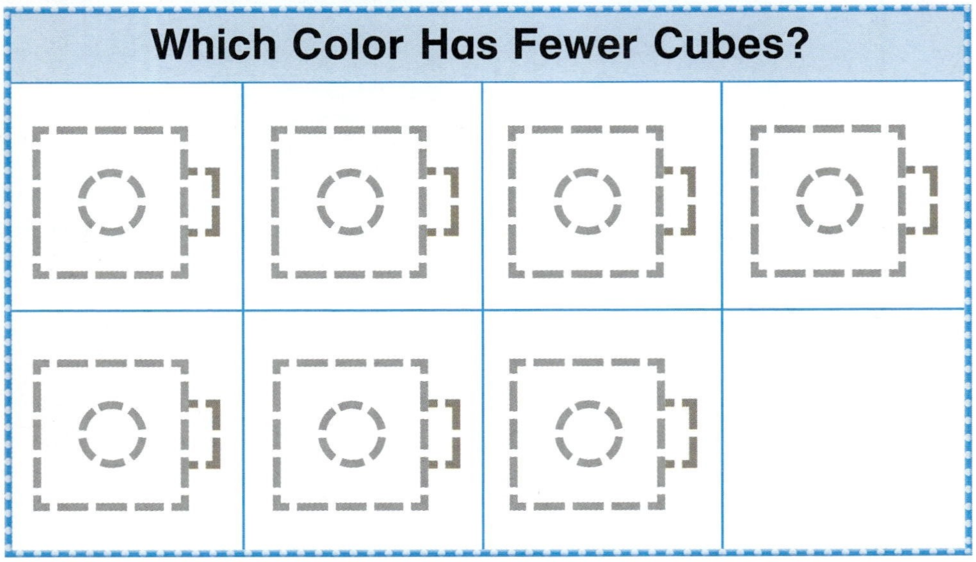

4

Stack and Slide

DIRECTIONS 1. Circle the bear that most likely comes next in the pattern. 2. How many dots? Draw cubes in the ten frame to show that number. Write the number. 3. Make a graph with blue and red cubes. Color the cubes. Count the cubes. Write how many of each color. Circle the number that is less. 4. Mark an X on the figure that does not stack and slide.

160 one hundred sixty

Symmetry

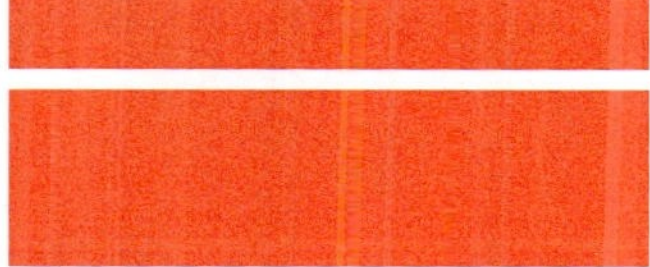

DIRECTIONS 1–4. Circle the figure with a line that makes two matching parts.

OBJECTIVE • Identify shapes that show a line of symmetry.

Chapter 6 · Lesson 7

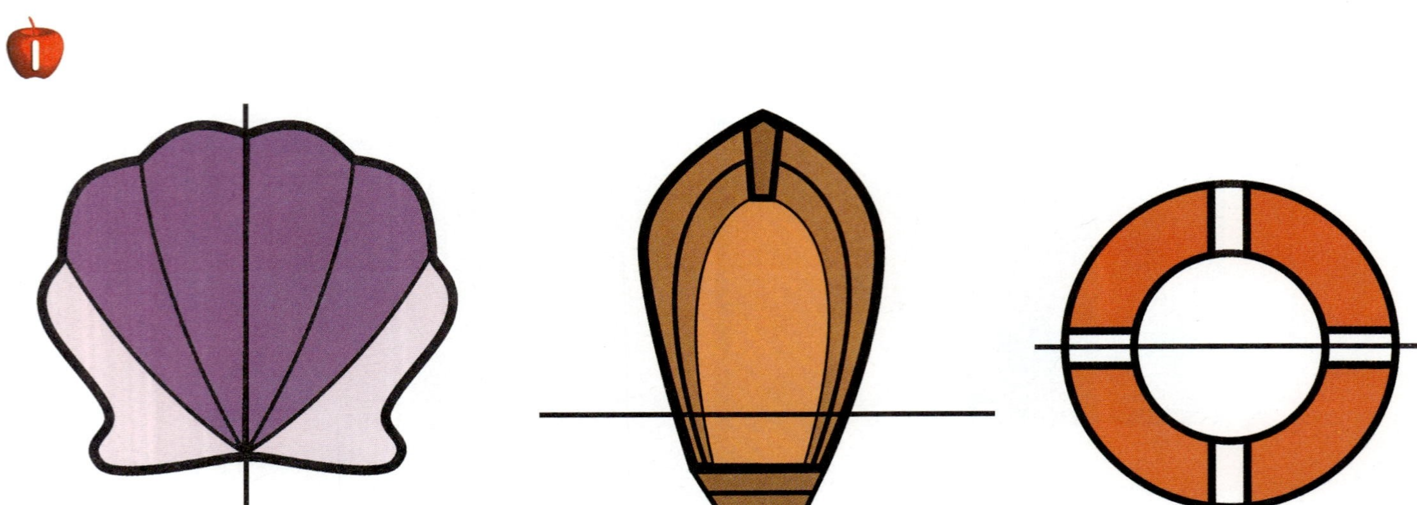

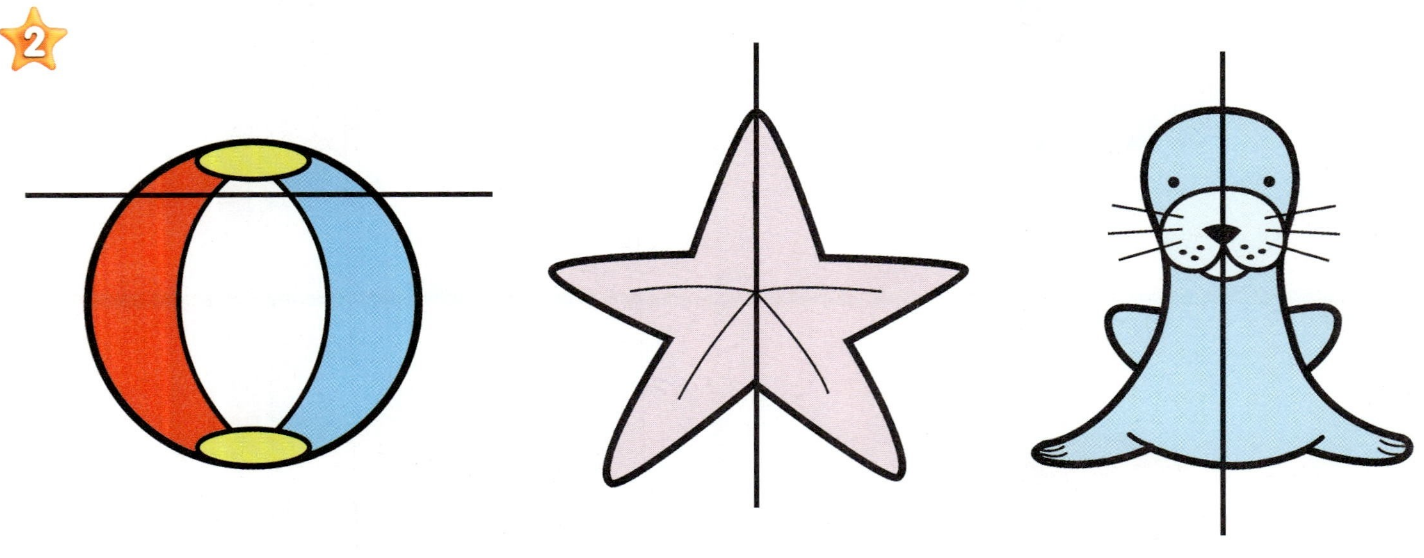

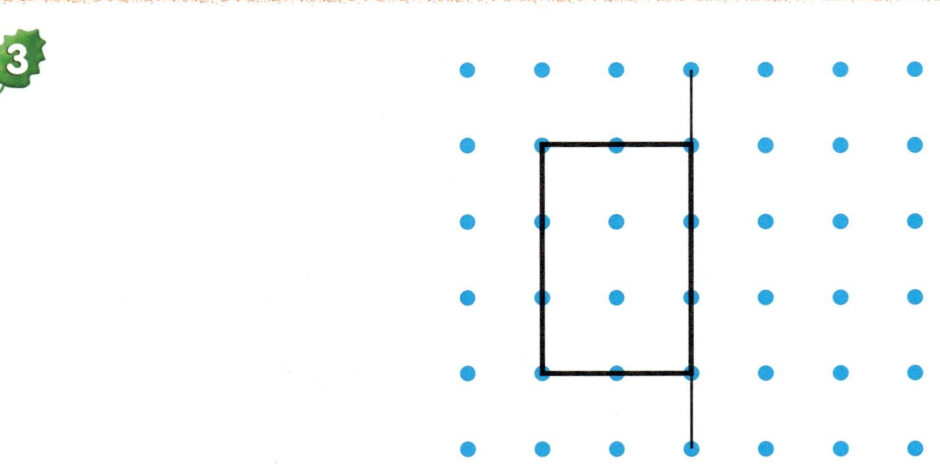

DIRECTIONS   **I–2.** Circle the objects with a line that makes two matching parts. **3.** Complete the rectangle that would show the line of symmetry.

HOME ACTIVITY • Cut out a paper square or circle. Ask your child to fold the figure to show two matching parts. Remind your child that the dividing line between these matching parts is called the line of symmetry.

162   one hundred sixty-two

equal parts   **unequal parts**

 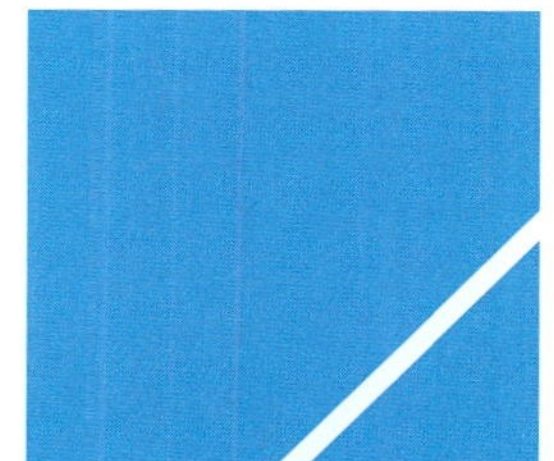 

DIRECTIONS   **1–3.** Circle the figures that have two equal parts.

OBJECTIVE • Recognize equal parts of a whole.

DIRECTIONS   **1–4.** Write the number that shows how many equal parts.

HOME ACTIVITY • Cut a piece of food into two or four equal parts. Ask your child to tell how many equal parts of the food there are.

HANDS ON

Whole and Half

whole

half

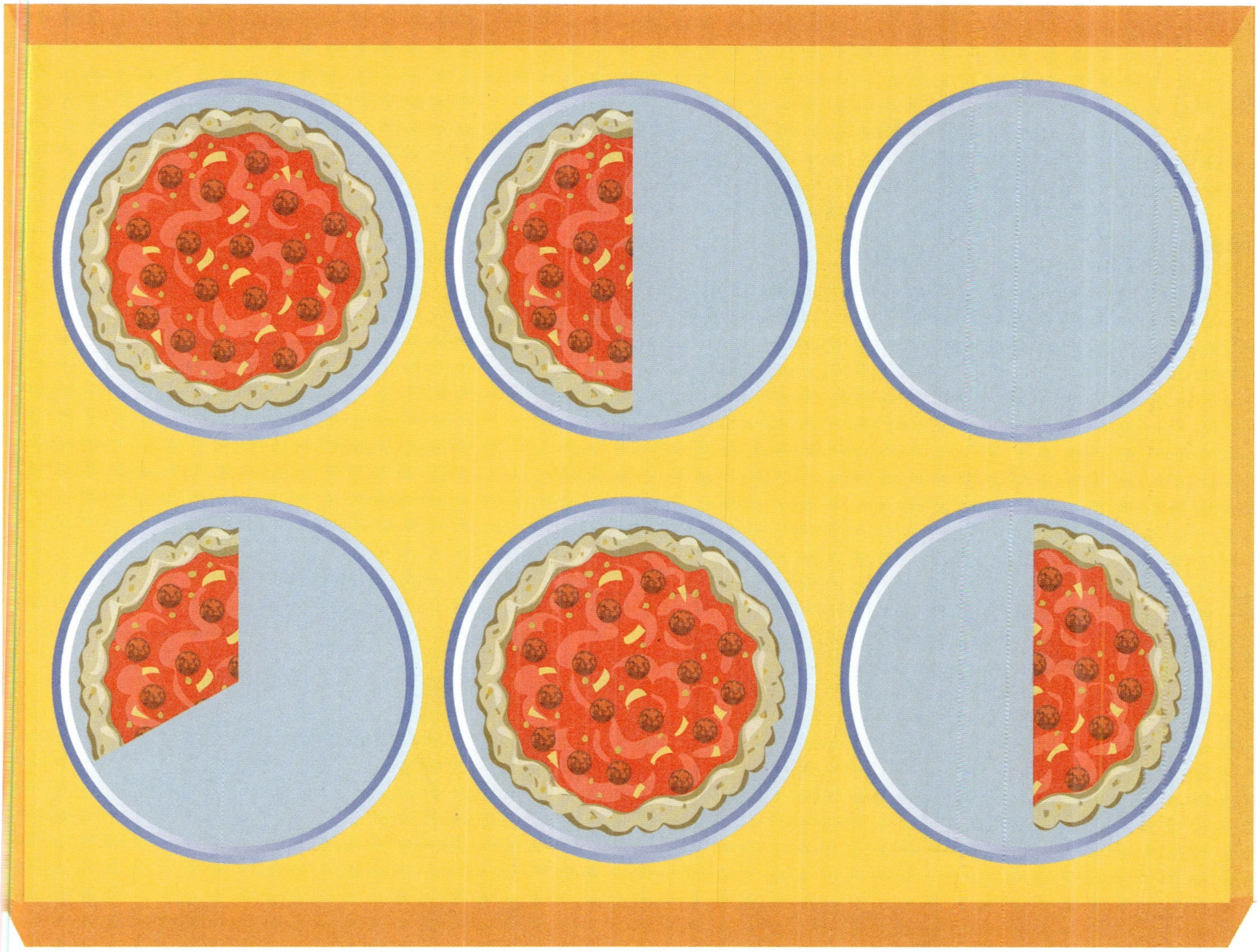

DIRECTIONS **I.** Use your pizza pieces to find the pizzas. Circle the whole pizzas. Mark an X on the half pizzas.

OBJECTIVE • Recognize a whole and one half.

Chapter 6 • Lesson 9

1

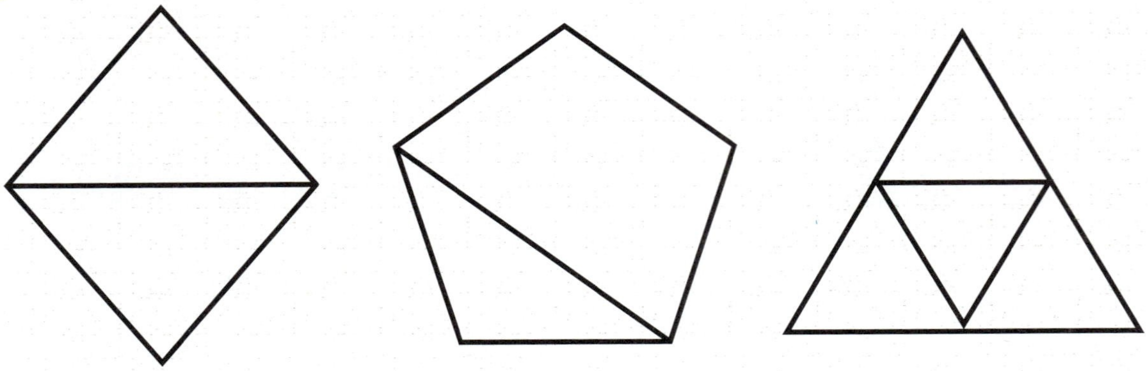

2

3

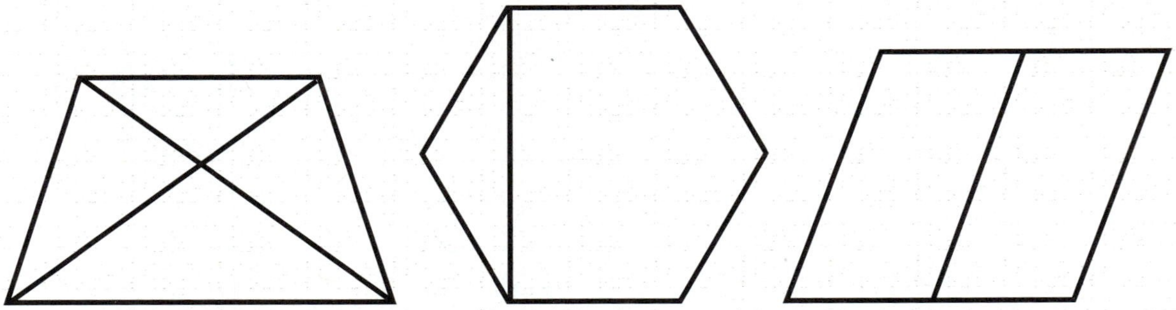

DIRECTIONS 1–3. Color one part of each figure. Circle the figures that have one half colored.

 **HOME ACTIVITY** · Ask your child to show you where to cut a whole food, such as a sandwich, to cut it into two halves.

Problem Solving Workshop
Skill • Use a Model

DIRECTIONS **1.** Place a counter on each fish. Write how many. **2.** Move the counters into the fish bowls. Place an equal share in each fish bowl. Draw the counters. Write how many are in each bowl.

OBJECTIVE • Solve problems by using the skill *use a model.*

Chapter 6 • Lesson 10

DIRECTIONS 1–3. Count the shells. How many shells would be in each pail for an equal share? Write the numbers.

HOME ACTIVITY • Give your child an even number of objects, such as paper clips or pencils. Ask your child to make two equal shares.

168 one hundred sixty-eight

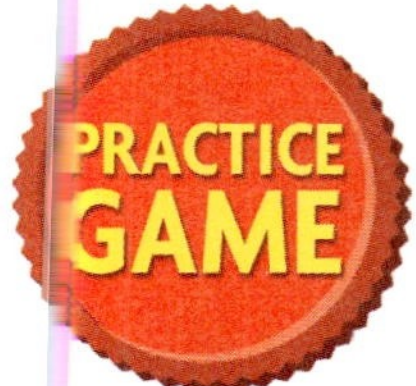

Number Picture

DIRECTIONS   Play with a partner. Decide who goes first. Toss the number cube. Color a figure in the picture that matches the number on the number cube. A player misses a turn if a number is rolled and all matching figures are colored. Continue until all figures in the picture are colored.

MATERIALS number cube 1-4, crayons

Chapter 6

one hundred sixty-nine **169**

Math Power • Seal Show Figures

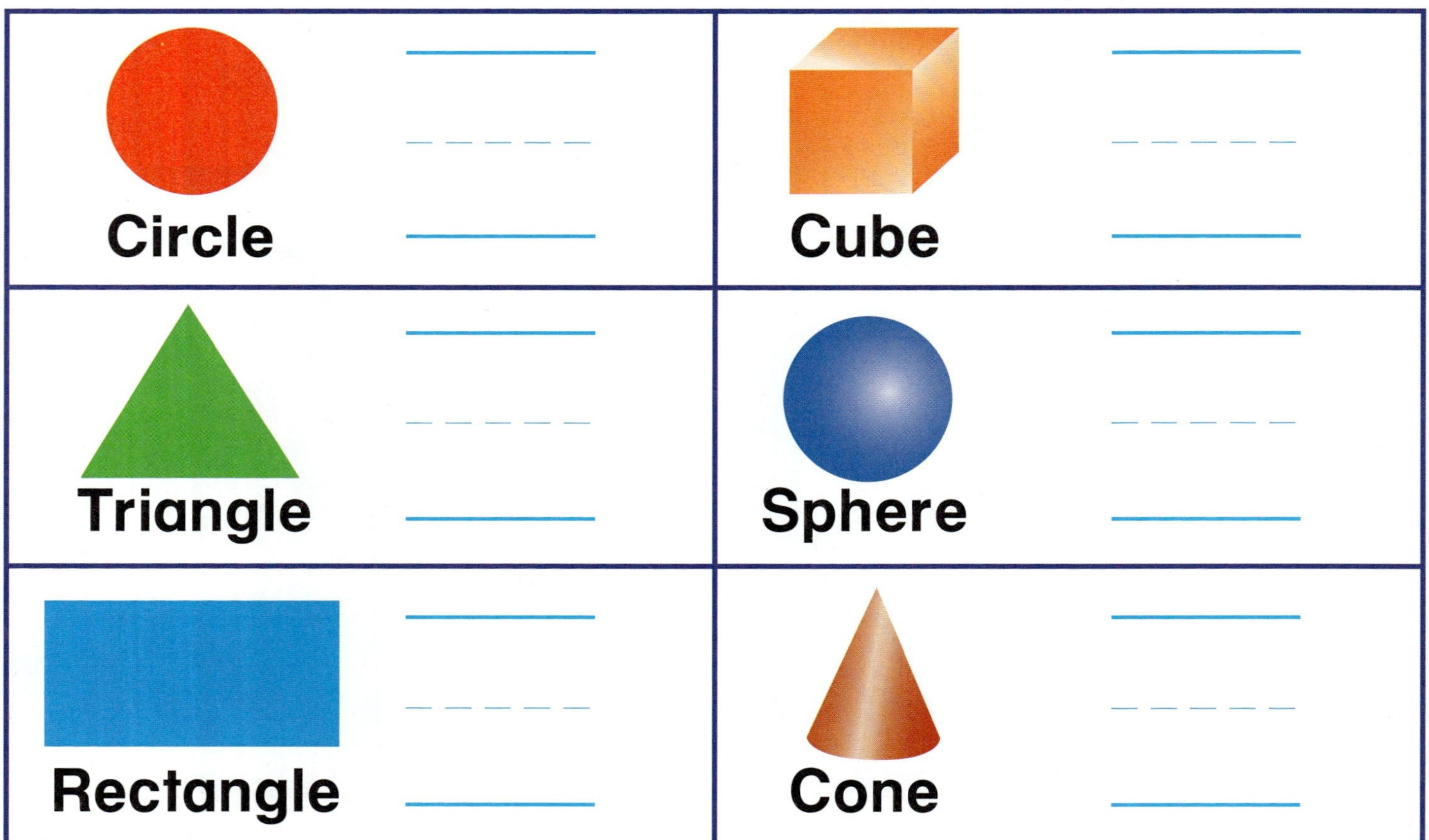

Circle		**Cube**	
Triangle		**Sphere**	
Rectangle		**Cone**	

DIRECTIONS **1.** Look at the picture. Use blue to circle the figures that are flat. Use red to circle the figures that are not flat. **2.** Write how many of each figure.

170 one hundred seventy

✓ Chapter 6 Review/Test

1 

2

3 

4 

DIRECTIONS 1–2. Circle the figure with a line that makes two matching parts. 3. Write the number that shows how many equal parts. 4. Count the shells. How many shells would be in each pail for an equal share? Write the numbers.

 Cumulative Review

1

2

Which Animal Do Most Children Like?							

3

DIRECTIONS   1. Circle the ninth car on the ride. Mark an X on the third car on the ride.   **2.** Read the graph. Write how many children like each kind of animal. Circle the animal that most children like.   **3.** Circle the whole pizza. Mark an X on the half pizza.

172   one hundred seventy-two

THE WORLD ALMANAC FOR KIDS

At the Pond

Some animals, such as frogs, have backbones. Some animals, such as snails, have no backbones.

Animals at the Pond

1

2

DIRECTIONS 1. Look at the picture. Make a graph about snails and frogs.
2. Write how many frogs and how many snails. Circle the number that shows more.

TALK Math Explain how a graph shows more and fewer.

Colorful Fish

Goldfish are animals with backbones. Goldfish may be many colors.

1

2

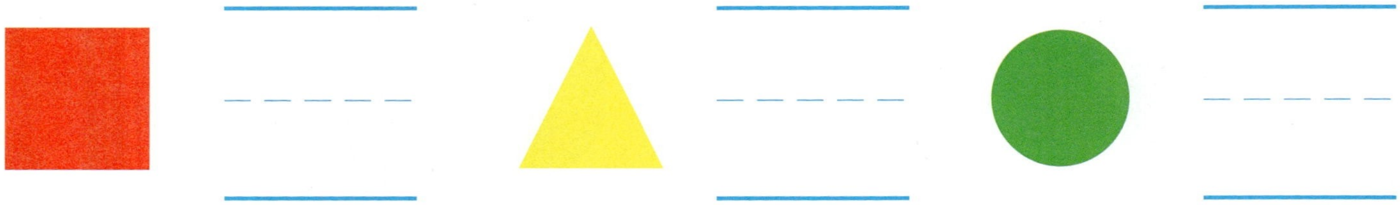

DIRECTIONS 1. You can use colorful figures to make fish. Use red to color the squares. Use yellow to color the triangles. Use green to color the circles. 2. Make a graph about the figures. How many of each figure do you see? Circle the greatest number.

TALK Math Graphs need a title. What could you name this graph?

174 one hundred seventy-four   **Unit 3 • The World Almanac For Kids**

Unit 4
READ Math Workshop
At The Market
written by Ann Dickson
In this story you will also TALK Math and WRITE Math.
Family Note: This story will help your child review numbers 6-10.
A
© Harcourt

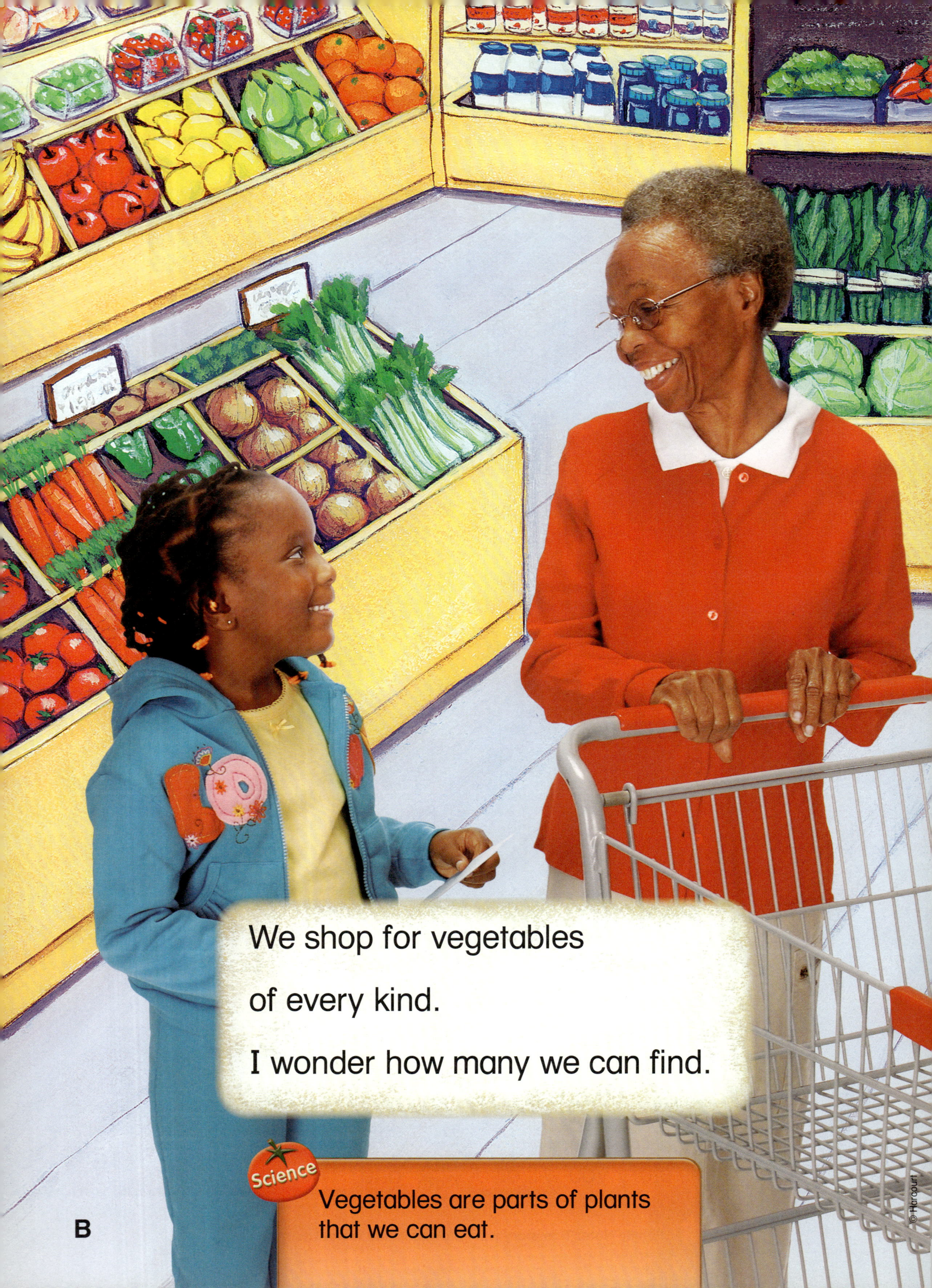

We shop for vegetables
of every kind.
I wonder how many we can find.
Science
Vegetables are parts of plants
that we can eat.
B

I count tomatoes into this sack.
How many peppers do you see on the rack?
Science
Which vegetables are fruits of plants?
C

Carrots have a crispy crunch!

How many carrots in the bunch?

Science

D

Which vegetables are roots of plants?

© Harcourt

I see the spinach by the wall.

How many round cabbages

do you see in all? _____

_____

_____

E

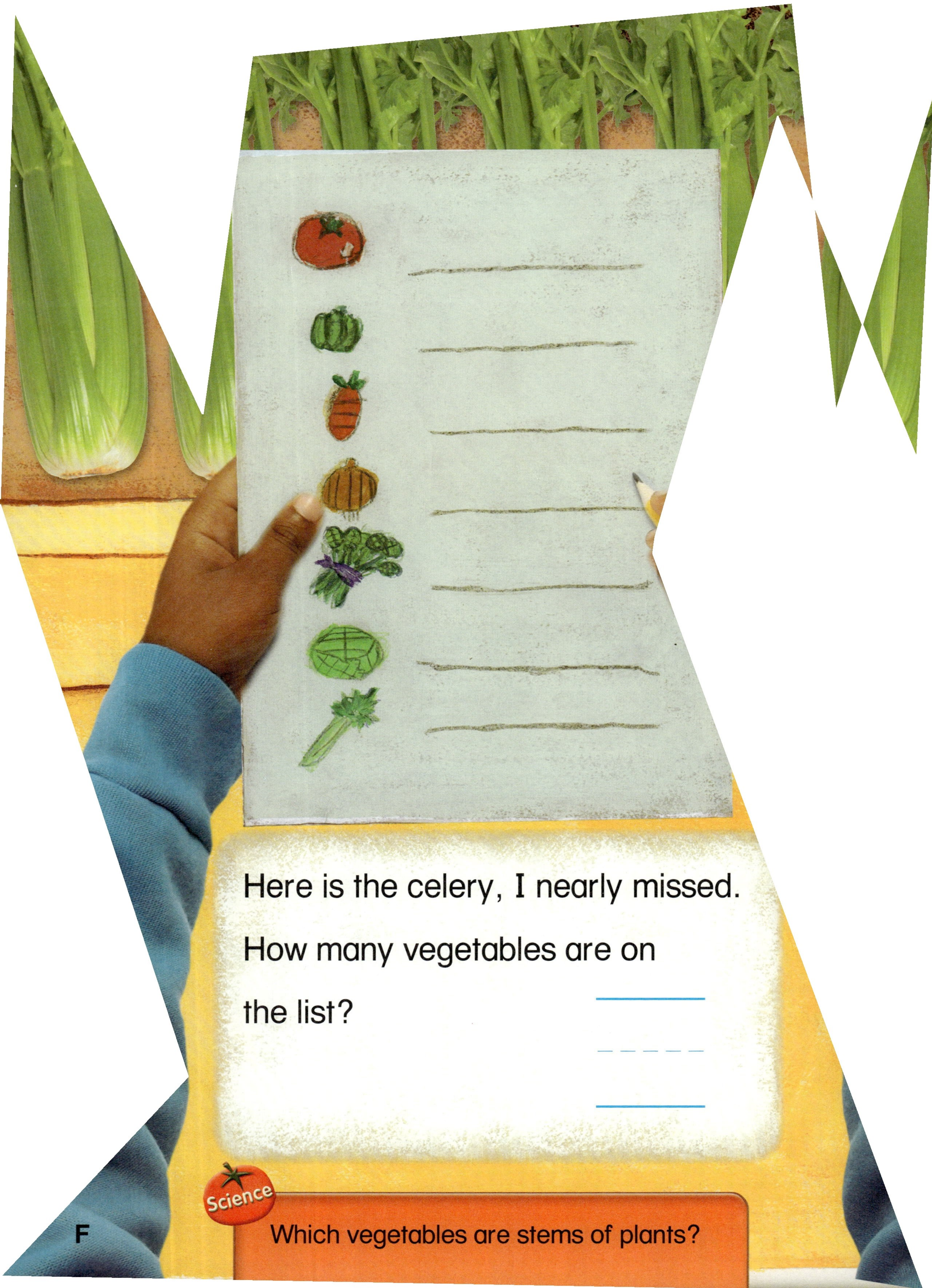
Here is the celery, I nearly missed.
How many vegetables are on
the list?

Science

Which vegetables are stems of plants?

F

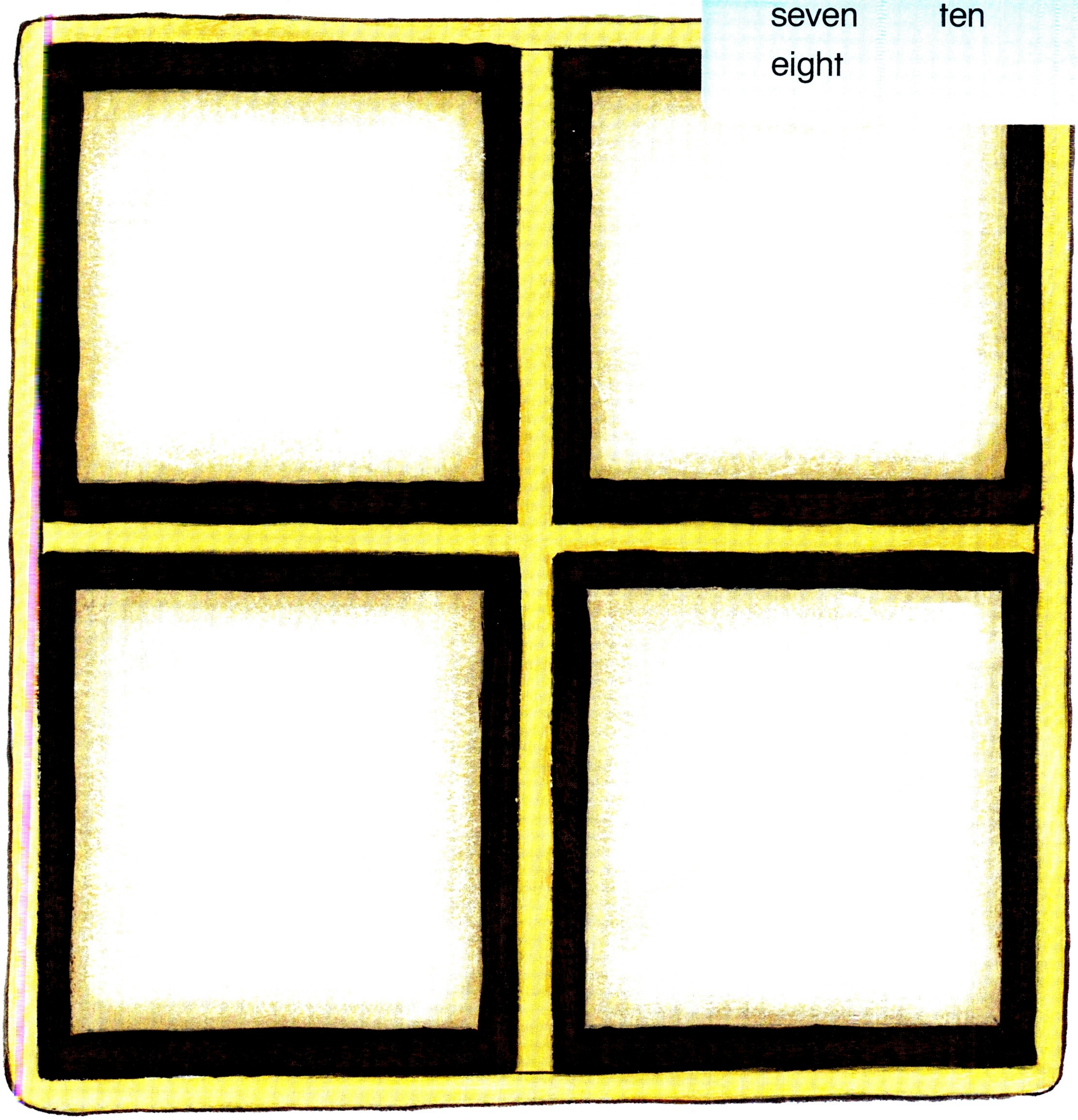

DIRECTIONS Make up a story about working in a market. Use the numbers 6 to 10. Draw the vegetables you want to sell.

G

Shopping List

vegetables	how many?
	_______
	_______
	_______
	_______
	_______

DIRECTIONS Fill in the shopping list to show how many you will buy.

H

Dear Family,

My class started Unit 4 today. I will learn how to count from 11 to 30 and identify coins. Here are some vocabulary words and activities for us to share.

Love, _______________________________

Vocabulary Power

Key Math Vocabulary

Eleven one more than 10

Vocabulary Activity

Math on the Move

Show your child a handful of pennies, nickels, dimes, and quarters and have him or her sort the coins and identify them.

Penny one cent

1 ¢

Technology
Multimedia Math Gloassary link ct
www.harcourtschool.com/hspmath

School Home CONNECTION

Remember This Your child may already know how to recognize numerals in the environment.

Calendar Activity

November						
Sunday	Monday	Tuesday	Wednesday	Thursday	Friday	Saturday
1	2	3	4	5	6	7
8	9	10	11	12	13	14
15	16	17	18	19	20	21
22	23	24	25	26	27	28
29	30					

Have your child place numeral cards to match the numerals on the calendar.

Practice (after pages 179 and 180)

Have your child point to the number that is directly after 12.

Practice (after pages 189 and 190)

Have your child point to the number that is directly before 30.

Literature

Look for these books in a library. Ask your child to point out math vocabulary words as you read each book together.

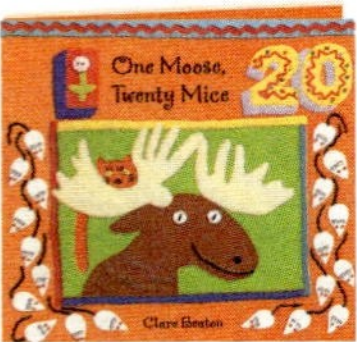

One Moose, Twenty Mice.
Beaton, Clare.
Barefoot Books, 2000.

Bunches of Buttons: Counting by Tens.
Dahl, Michael.
Picture Window, 2006.

The Coin Counting Book.
Williams, Rozanne Lanczak.
Charlesbridge, 2001.

CHAPTER
7
Numbers 11 to 30
Theme: Fruit and Vegetables

✓ Show What You Know

 _______________

 _______________

 _______________

 _______________

 _______________

DIRECTIONS How much fruit is in each crate? Write the number.

 **Family Note:** This page checks your child's understanding of important concepts and skills needed for success in Chapter 7.

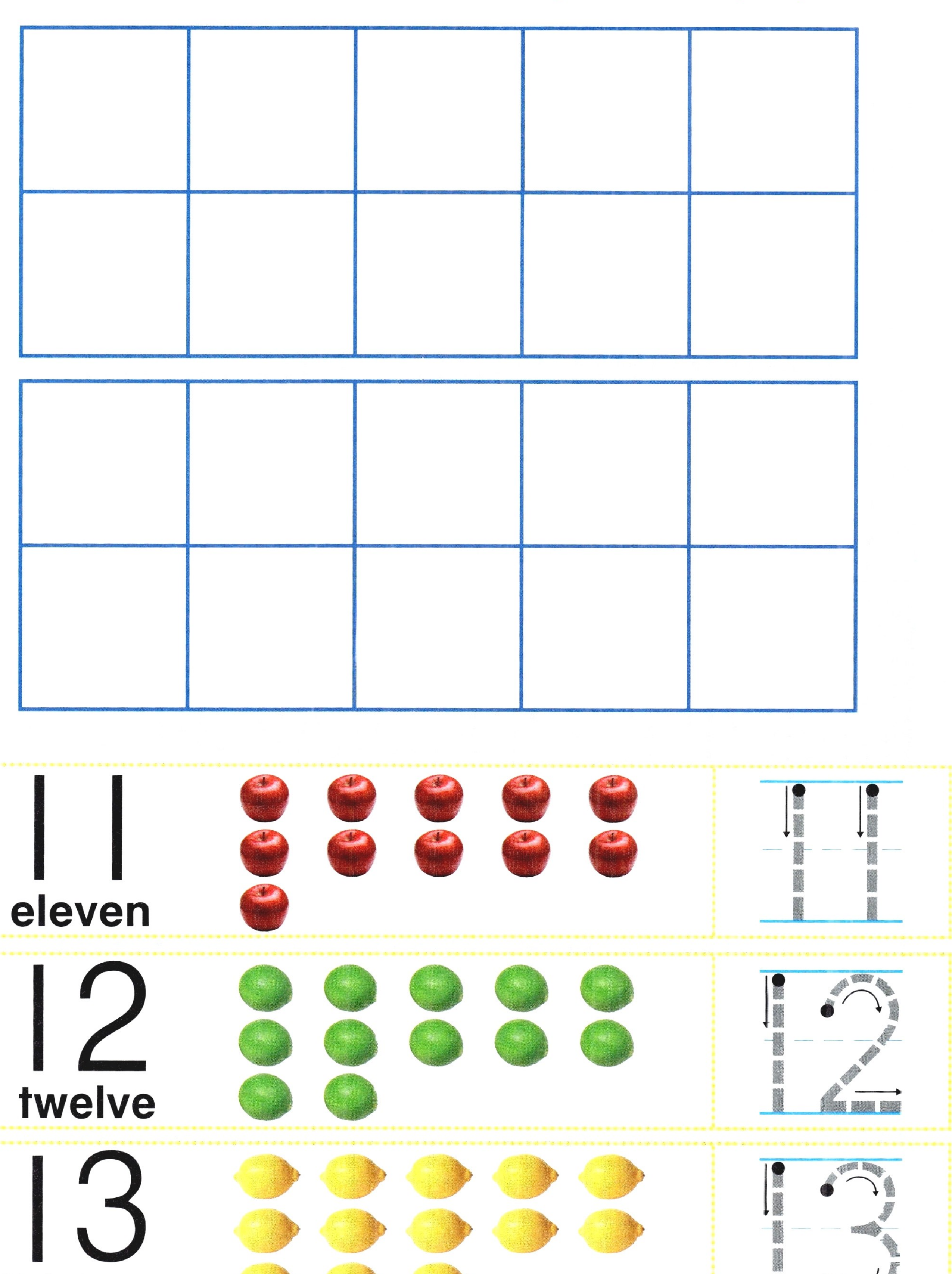

1 eleven 11

2 twelve 12

3 thirteen 13

DIRECTIONS   1–3. Use counters to model the number on the ten frames at the top of the page. Say the numbers as you count. Trace the number.

OBJECTIVE • Count, recognize, represent, and name objects for 11, 12, and 13.

Chapter 7 • Lesson 1

1

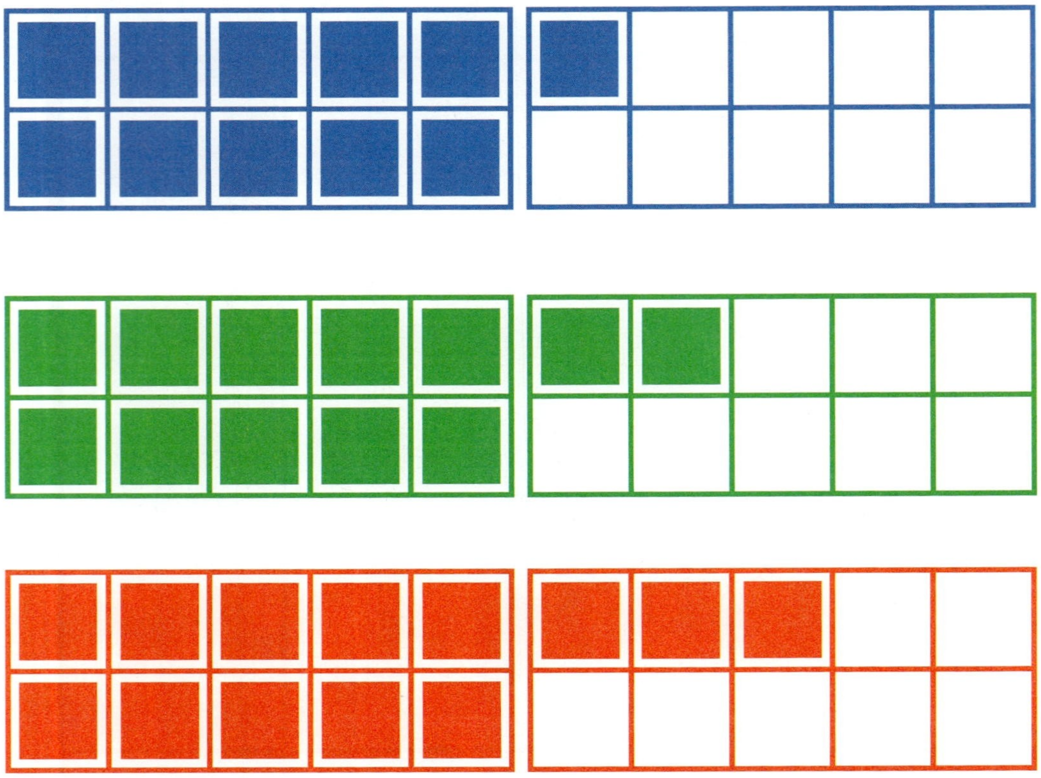

2

| 1 1

| 2

| 3

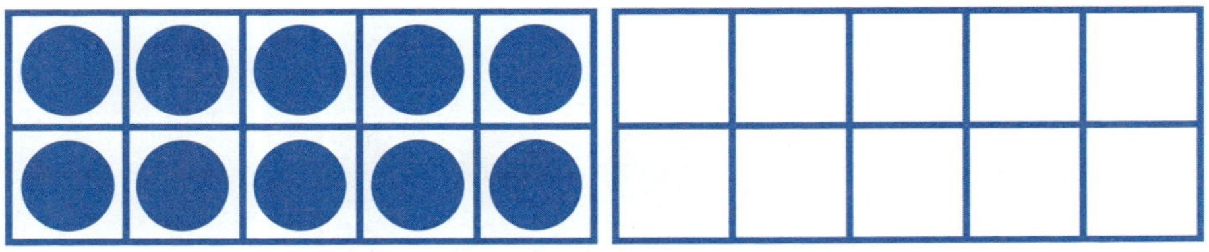

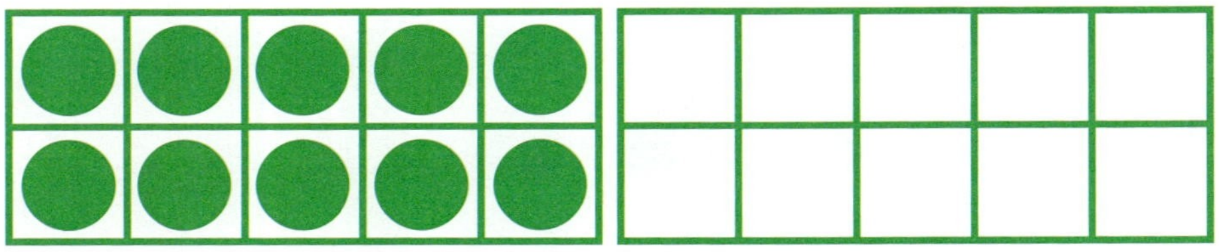

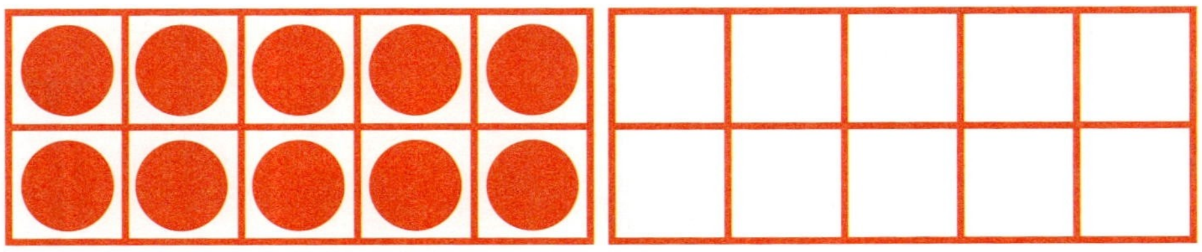

HOME ACTIVITY • Draw two ten frames side
by side on a sheet of paper. Have your child
model the numbers 11, 12, and 13, using
small objects such as buttons, pennies, or
dried beans.

180 one hundred eighty

© Harcourt

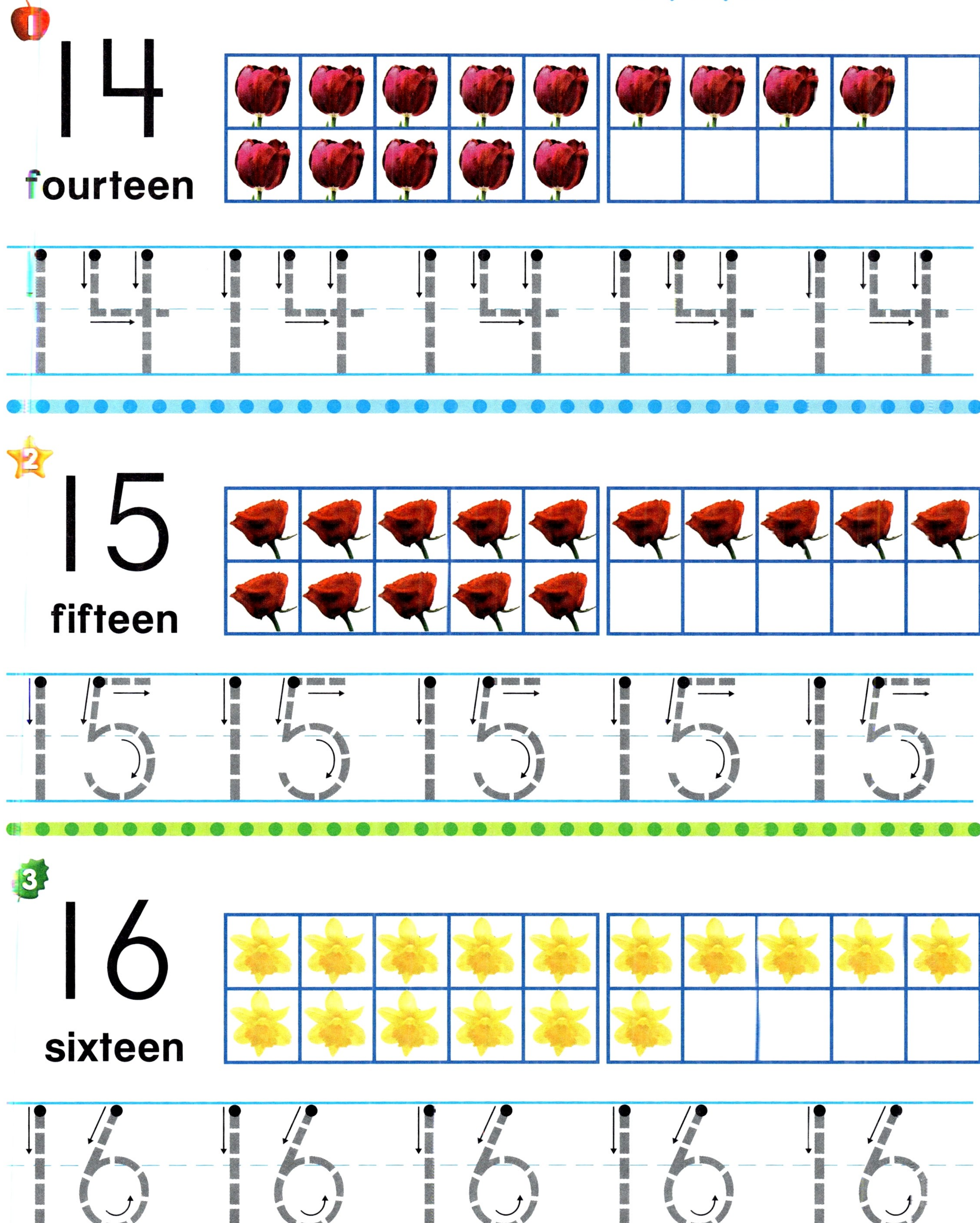

1 14
fourteen

2 15
fifteen

3 16
sixteen

DIRECTIONS 1–3. Count the flowers. Say the number as you trace it.

OBJECTIVE • Count, recognize, represent, and name objects for 14, 15, and 16.

Chapter 7 • Lesson 2

one hundred eighty-one **181**

1
2
14
15
16

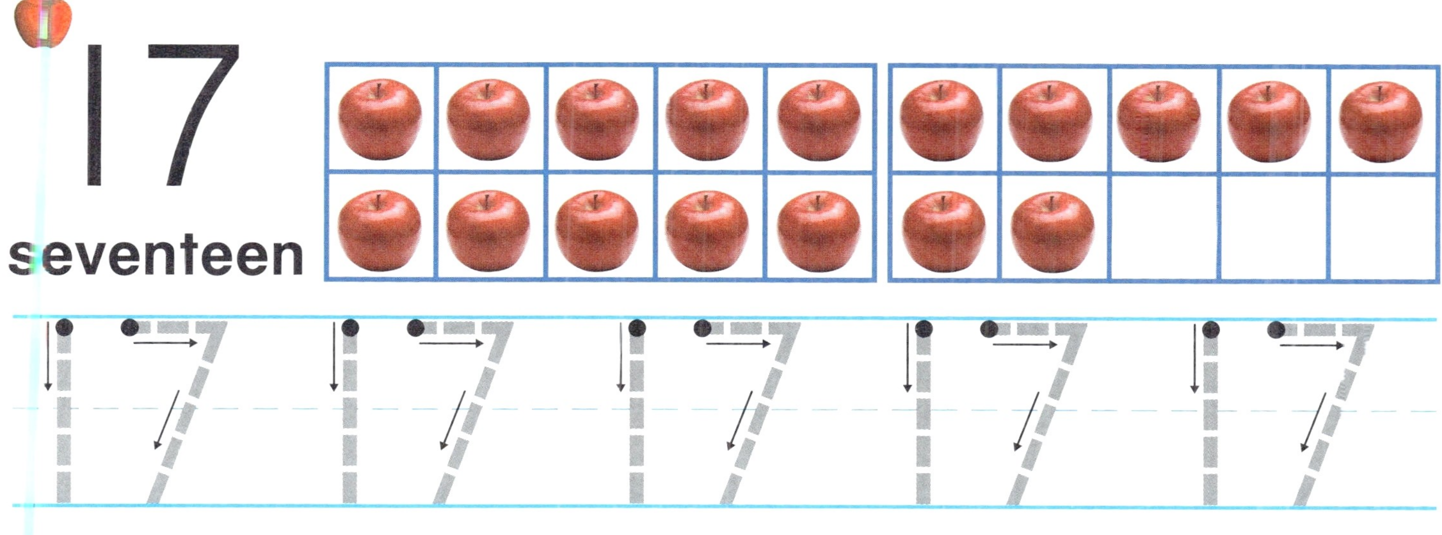

17
seventeen

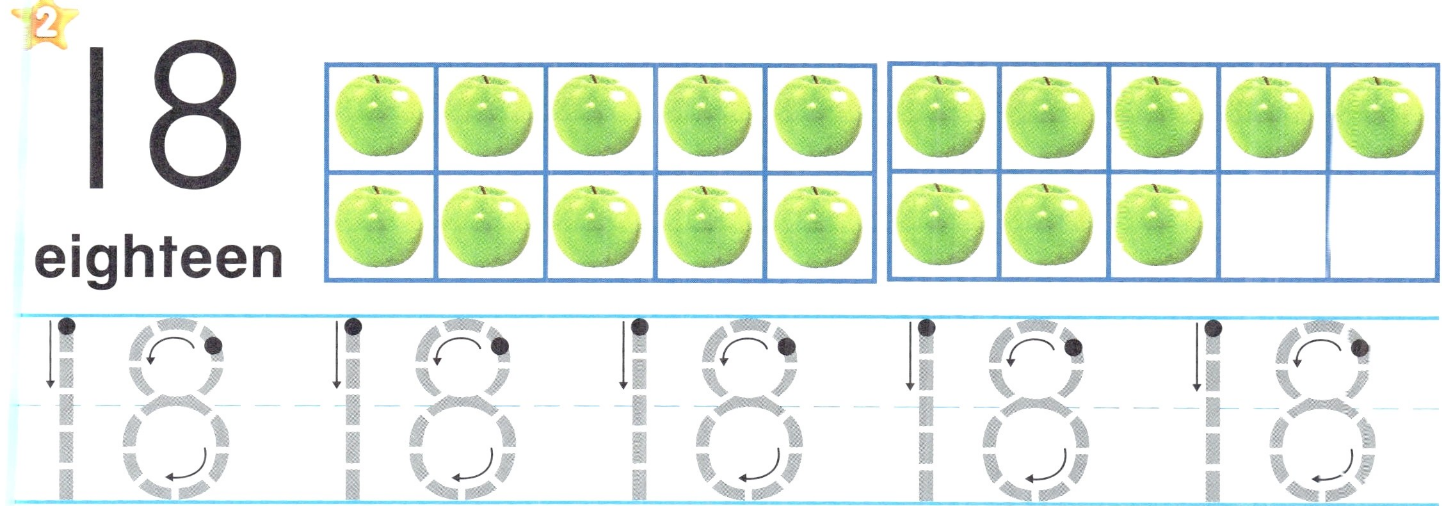

18
eighteen

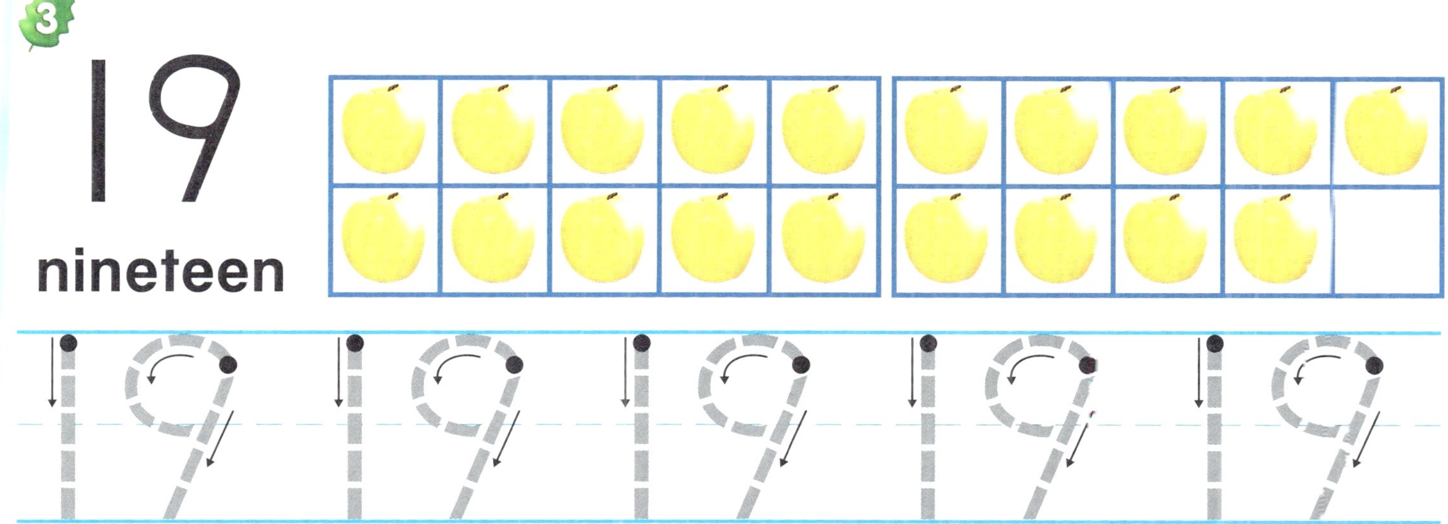

19
nineteen

DIRECTIONS 1–3. Count the apples. Say the number as you trace it.

OBJECTIVE • Count, recognize, represent and name objects for 17, 18, and 19.

1

2

17

18

19

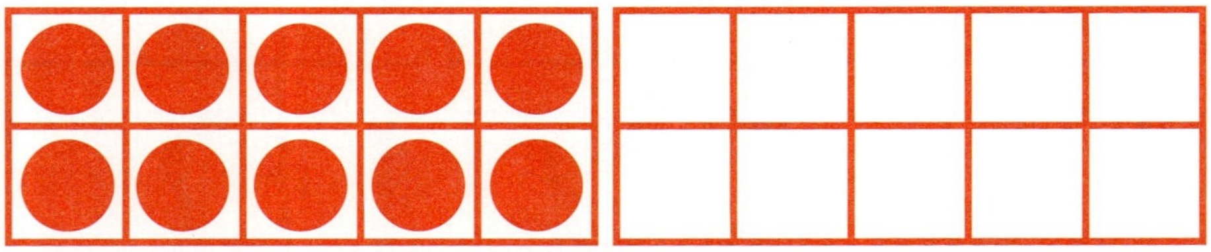

184 one hundred eighty-four

Problem Solving Workshop
Strategy • Use Logical Reasoning

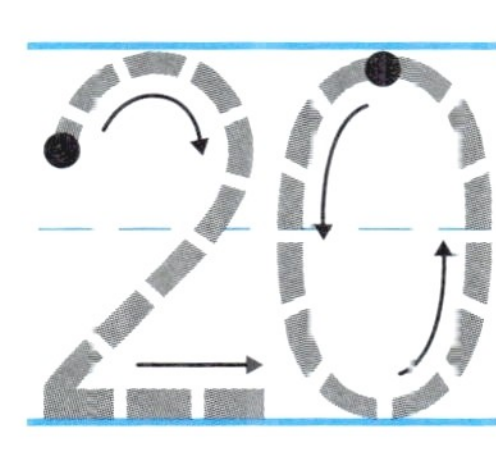

twenty

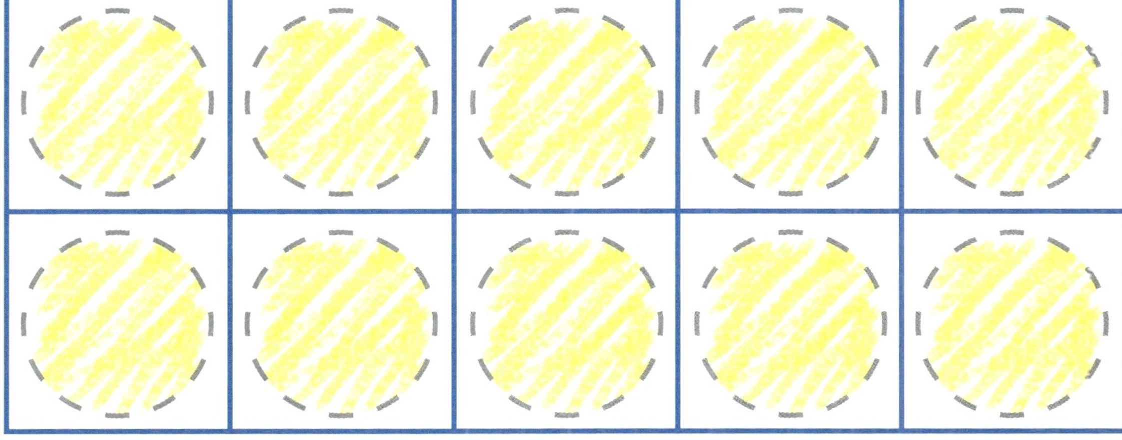

DIRECTIONS 1. Place more counters on the ten frame to model 20. Say the number. Trace the number. Trace the counters. **2.** Place more counters to model the number that is 2 less than 20. Write that number. Draw and color the counters.

OBJECTIVE • Solve problems by using the strategy *use logical reasoning.*

Chapter 7 • Lesson 4

1

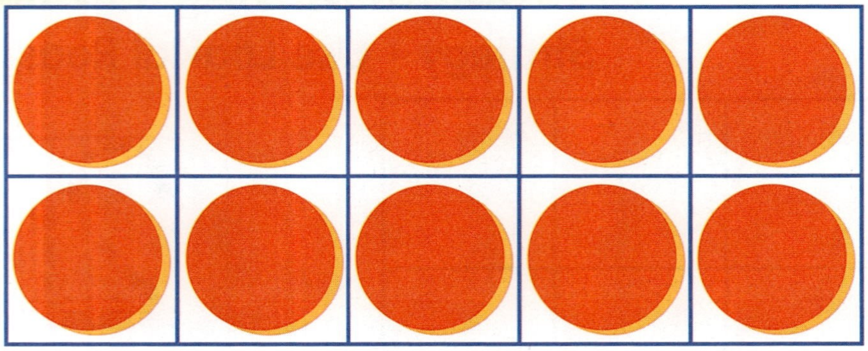

2

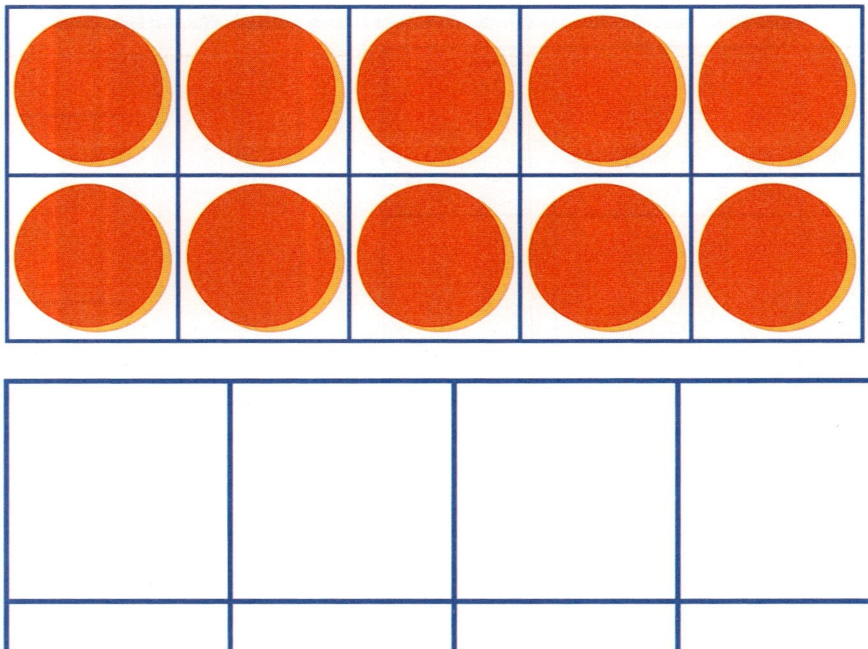

DIRECTIONS **1.** Draw and color more counters to model the number that is 2 more than 18. Write that number. **2.** Draw and color more counters to model the number that is 3 less than 20. Write that number.

HOME ACTIVITY • Ask your child to model 20 objects. Then have your child model 2 less than 20 objects. Ask your child to tell how many objects that will be.

186 one hundred eighty-six

Estimate Objects to 20

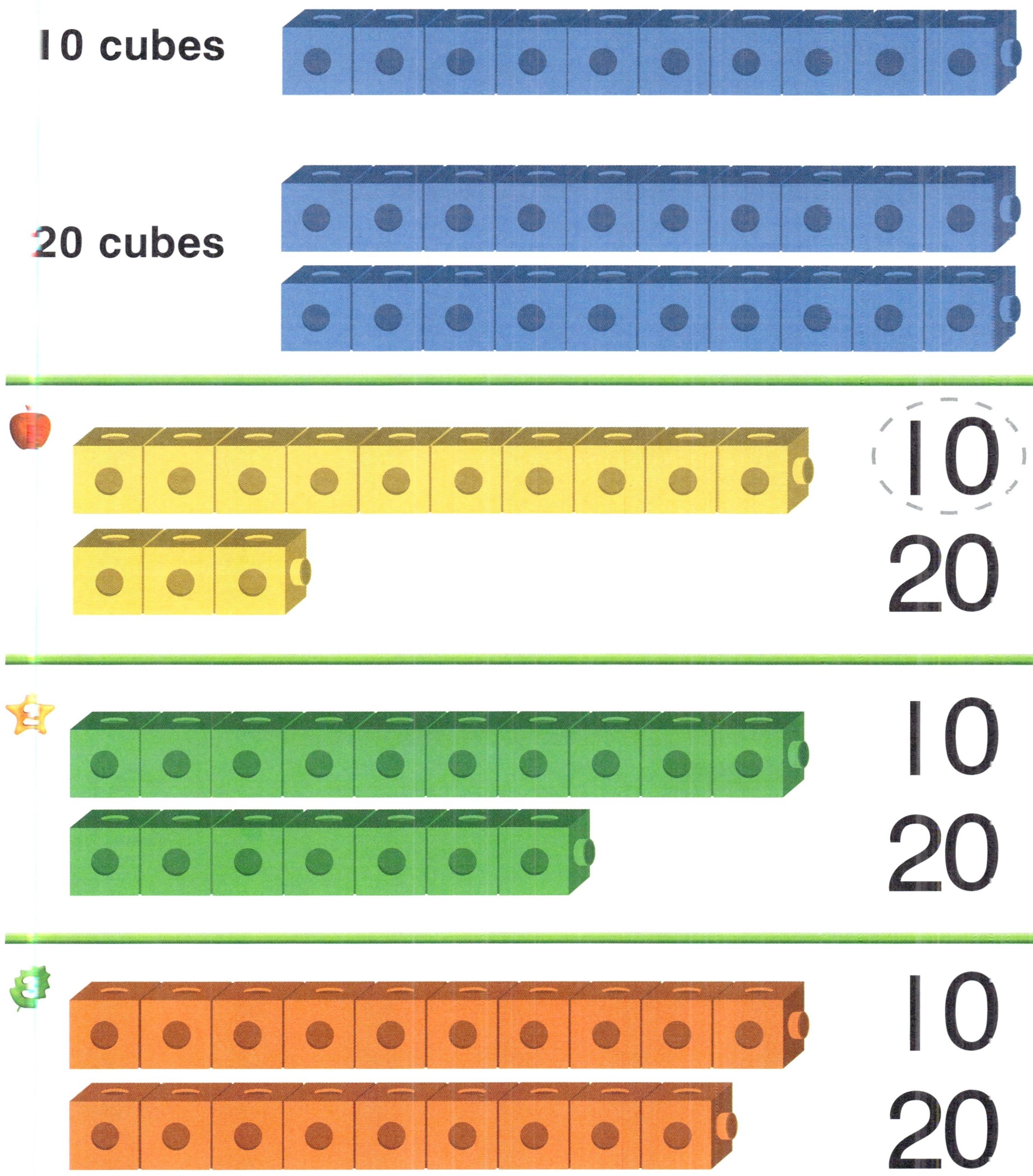

10 cubes

20 cubes

1. 10   20

2. 10   20

3. 10   20

DIRECTIONS   1–3. Look at the models at the top of the page. Without counting, circle to show whether each set is closer to 10 cubes or closer to 20 cubes.

OBJECTIVE • Use estimation for objects up to 20.

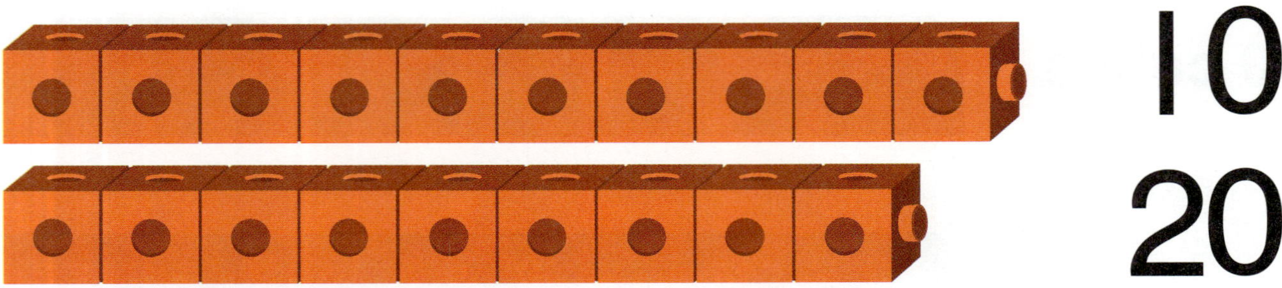

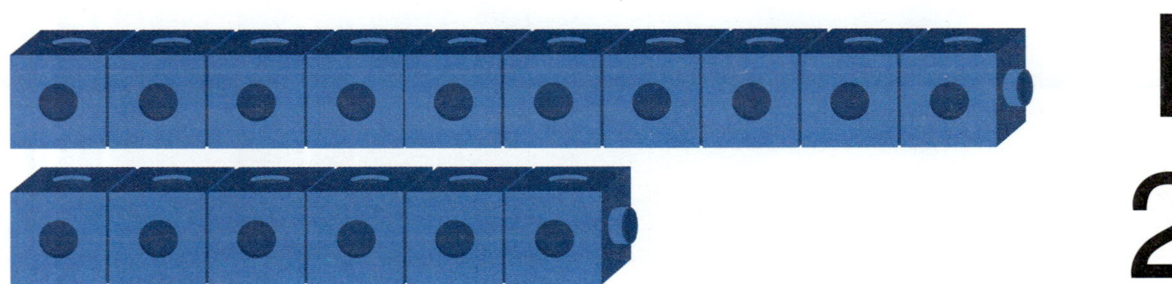

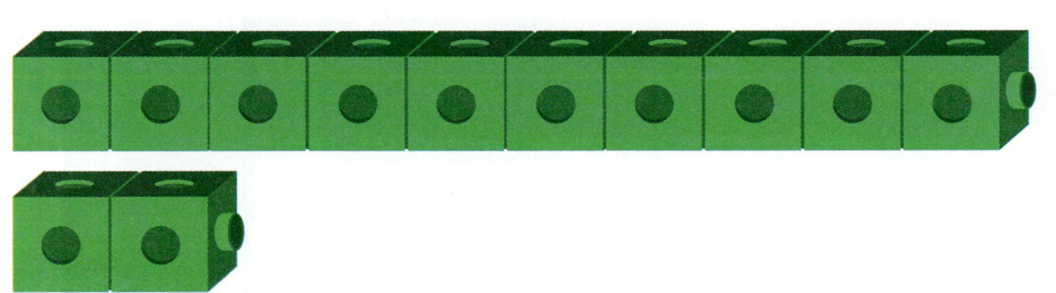

DIRECTIONS   1–4. Without counting, circle to show whether each set is closer to 10 cubes or closer to 20 cubes.

HOME ACTIVITY • Place 10 beans in one jar, 20 in another, and some in a third. Label the 10-bean and 20-bean jars. Have your child estimate whether the number of beans in the third jar is closer to 10 or to 20. Count to check.

188   one hundred eighty-eight

Name ______________________________

Mid Chapter 7 Review

1

2

14

fourteen

3

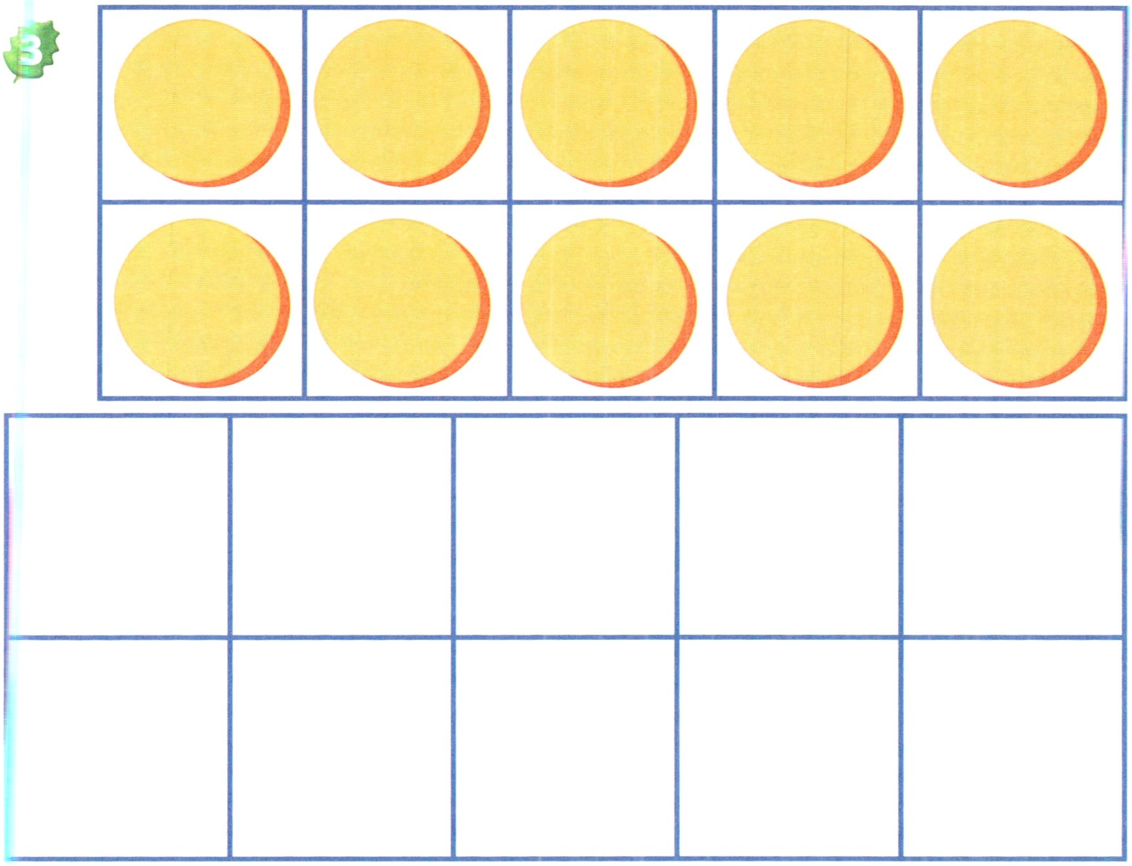

DIRECTIONS 1. How many color tiles? Write the number. 2. Count the flowers. Say the number as you trace it. 3. Place more counters to model the number that is 1 less than 20. Write that number. Draw and color the counters.

✓ Cumulative Review

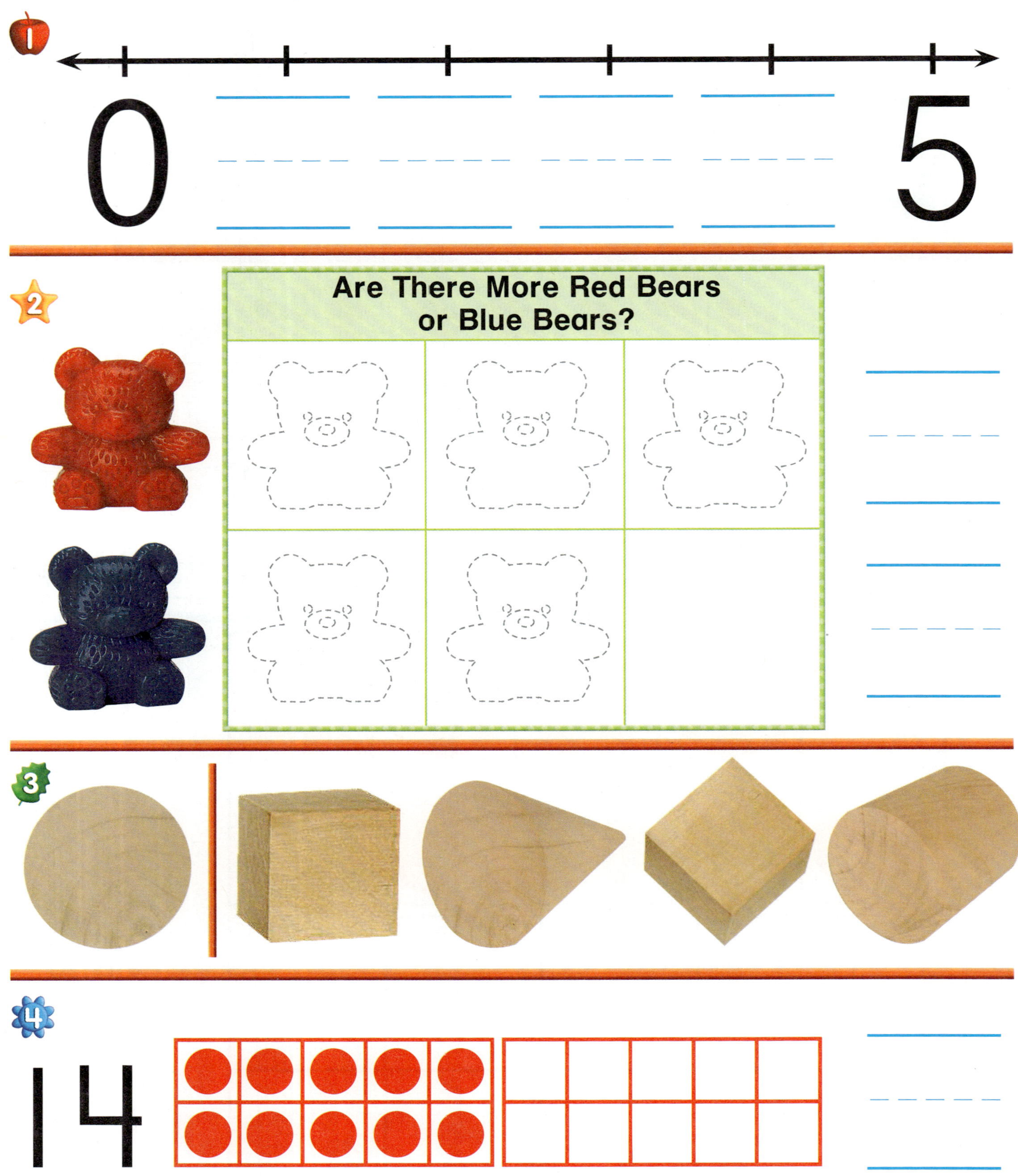

0   **5**

Are There More Red Bears or Blue Bears?

1 4

DIRECTIONS   **1.** Write the numbers in order on the number line.   **2.** Make a graph with red and blue bears. Color the bears. Count the bears. Write how many there are of each color. Circle the greater number.   **3.** Circle the solid figures with a flat surface that could make the figure on the left.   **4.** Draw more counters to show the number. Write the number.

190   one hundred ninety

Name ___________________________

1.

2.

3.

4.

5.

DIRECTIONS 1. How many counters? Trace the number. 2–5. How many counters? Write the number.

OBJECTIVE • Use ten frames to name the quantities 20 to 30.

DIRECTIONS 1–5. How many color tiles? Write the number.

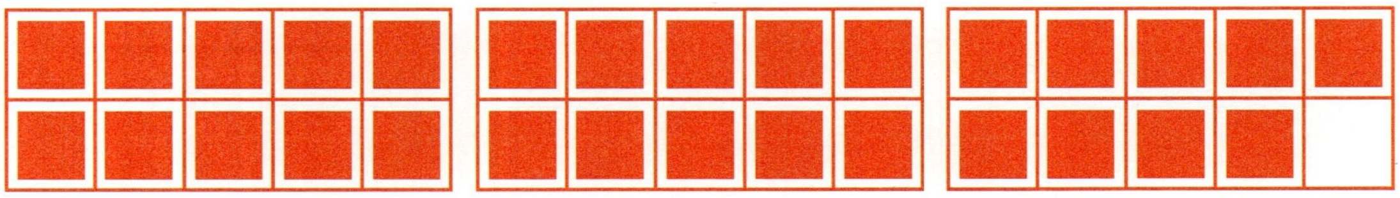

HOME ACTIVITY • Make a third ten frame from an egg carton. Place small objects such as dried pasta in the 3 ten frames to represent numbers between 20 and 30. Have your child count the objects and tell you the numbers.

192 one hundred ninety-two

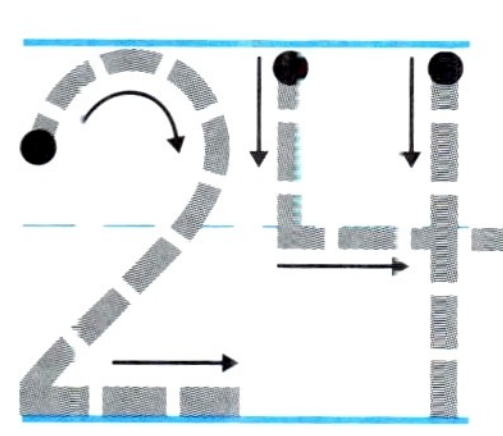

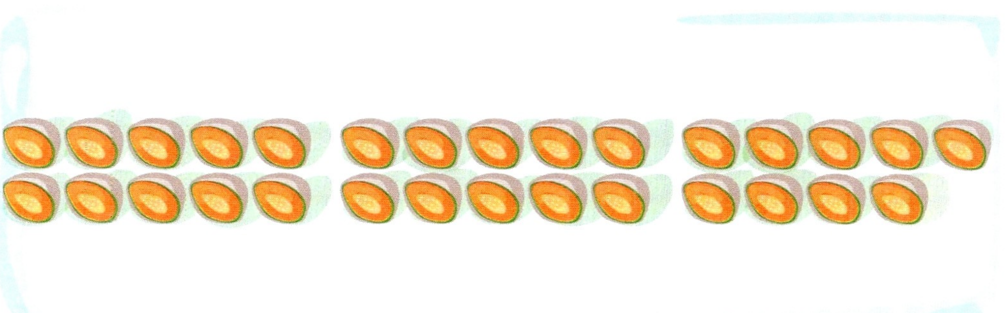

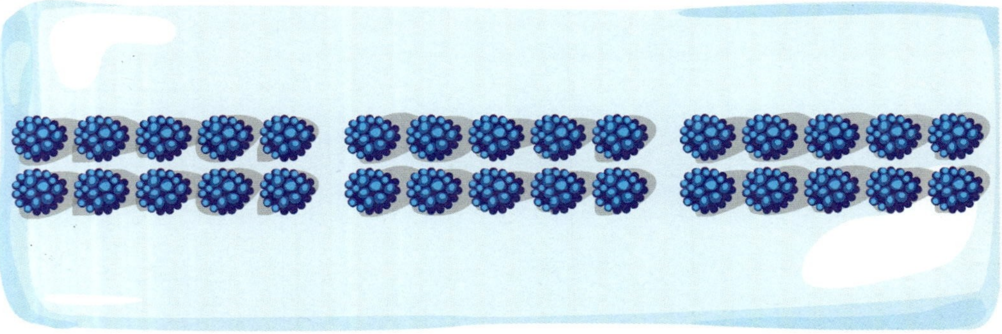

DIRECTIONS   1–4. How many berries? Write the number.

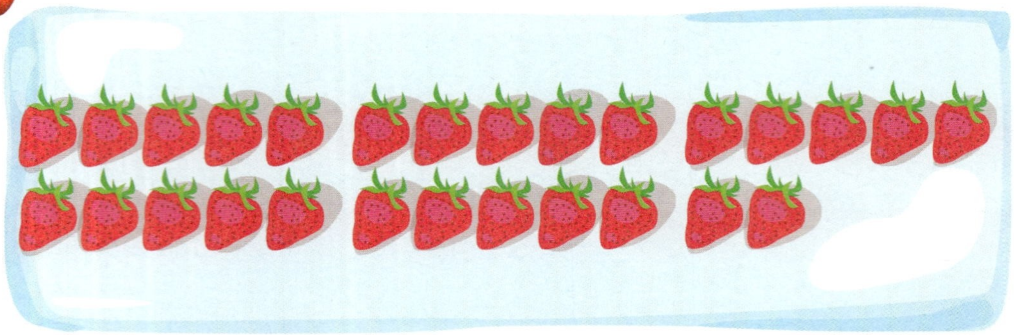

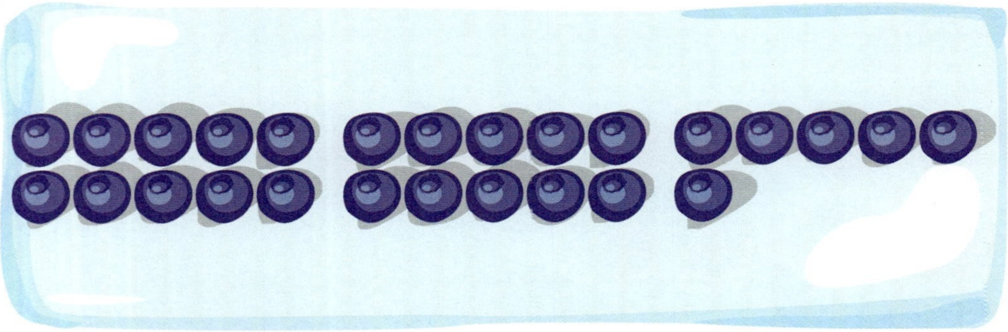

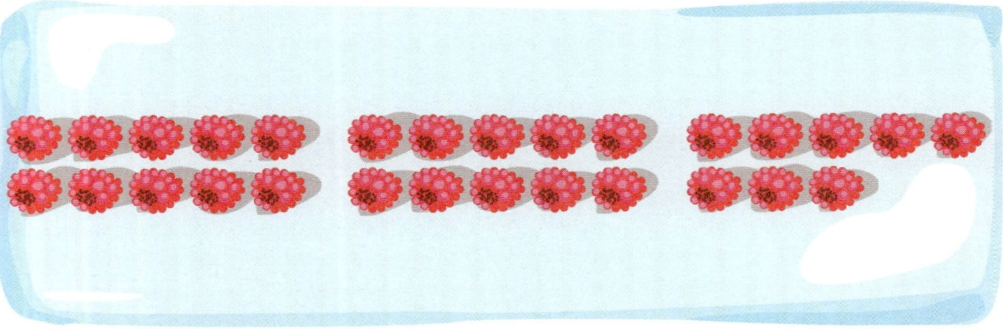

HOME ACTIVITY · Work with small objects such as dried beans or coins. Arrange them in sets similar to those in this lesson. Have children count the objects and say the number.

Problem Solving Workshop
Skill • Use Data from a Picture

Amy

John

DIRECTIONS Write how many apples are in each picture. Write how many bananas are in each picture. Circle the number that shows more bananas. Circle the fruit of which one picture shows 2 more than the other picture.

OBJECTIVE • Solve problems by using the skill *use data from a picture*.

Chapter 7 • Lesson 8

Chase

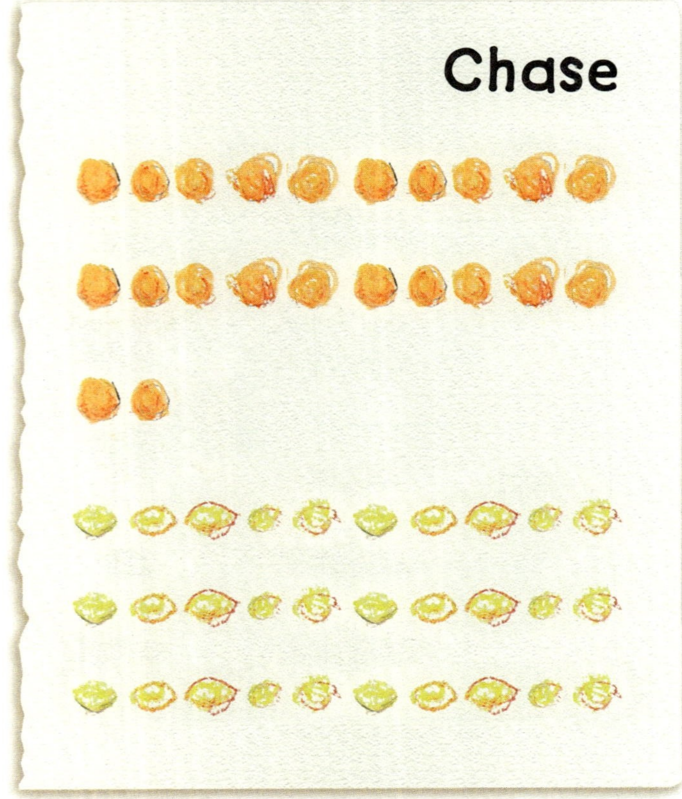

Mischa

DIRECTIONS Write how many oranges are in each picture. Write how many lemons are in each picture. Circle the number that shows fewer lemons. Circle the fruit of which one picture shows 2 fewer than the other picture.

HOME ACTIVITY · Have your child count objects in your home such as spoons and forks. Write how many in each group. Then have your child circle the greater number. Repeat with a different number of objects.

196 one hundred ninety-six

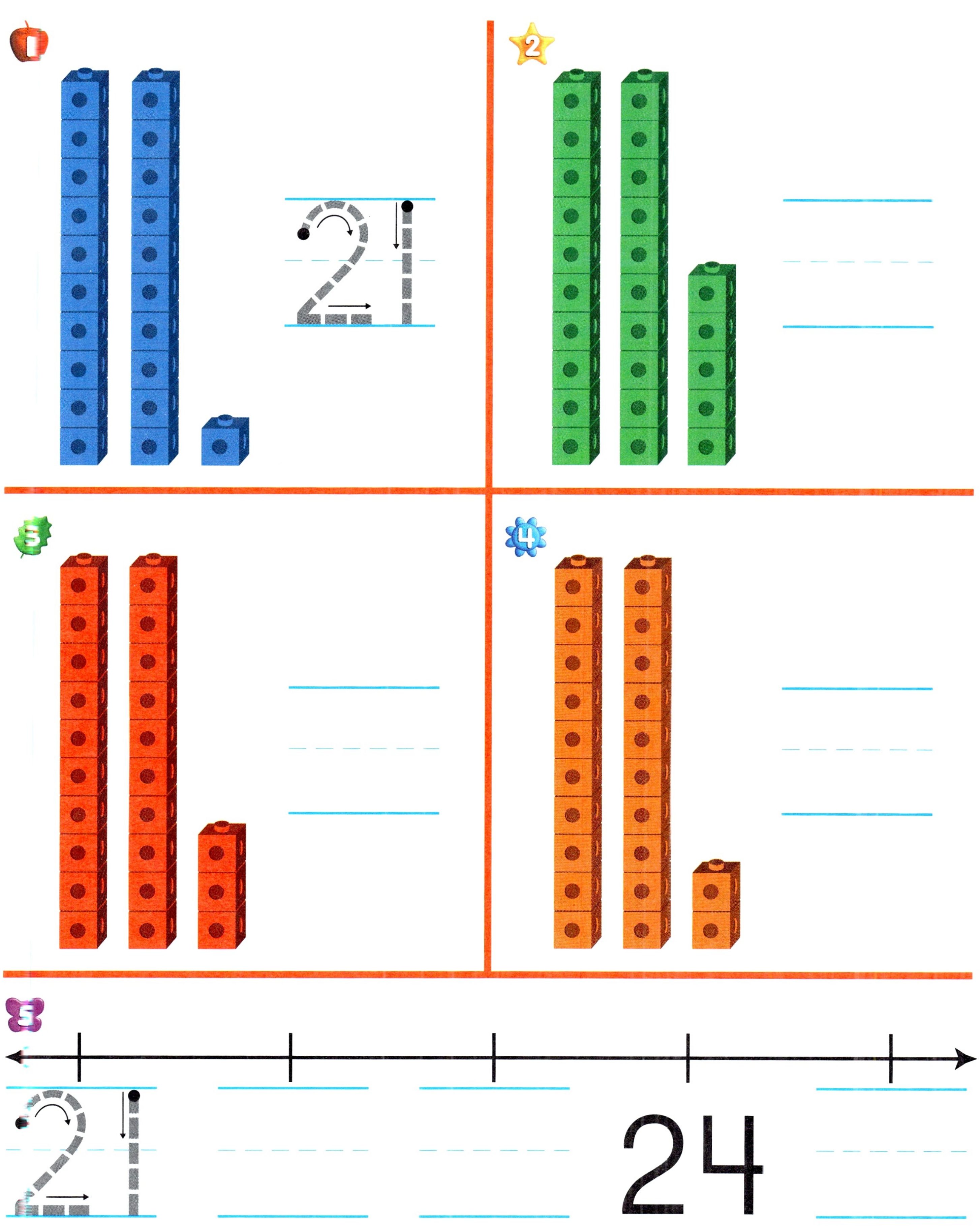

DIRECTIONS 1. How many cubes? Trace the number. 2–4. How many cubes? Write the number. 5. Write those numbers in order on the number line.

OBJECTIVE • Use a number line to order numbers to 30.

1

2

3

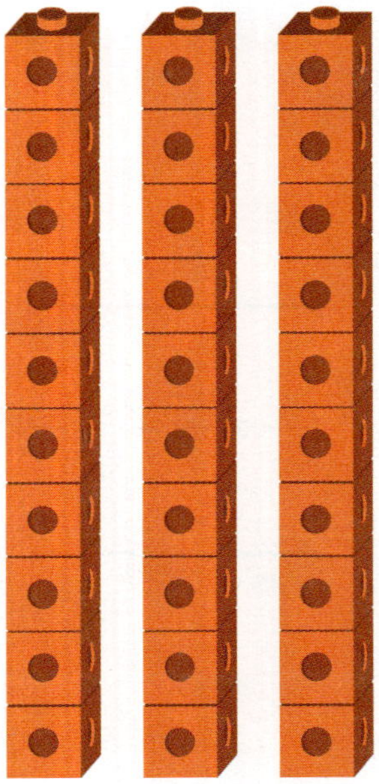

4

5

25

29

DIRECTIONS **1–4.** How many cubes? Write the number. **5.** Write those numbers in order on the number line.

 **HOME ACTIVITY** • Ask your child to count aloud from 1 to 30. Then say a number between 1 and 29, and ask your child to tell what numbers come before and after it.

198 one hundred ninety-eight

Sweet and Sour Path

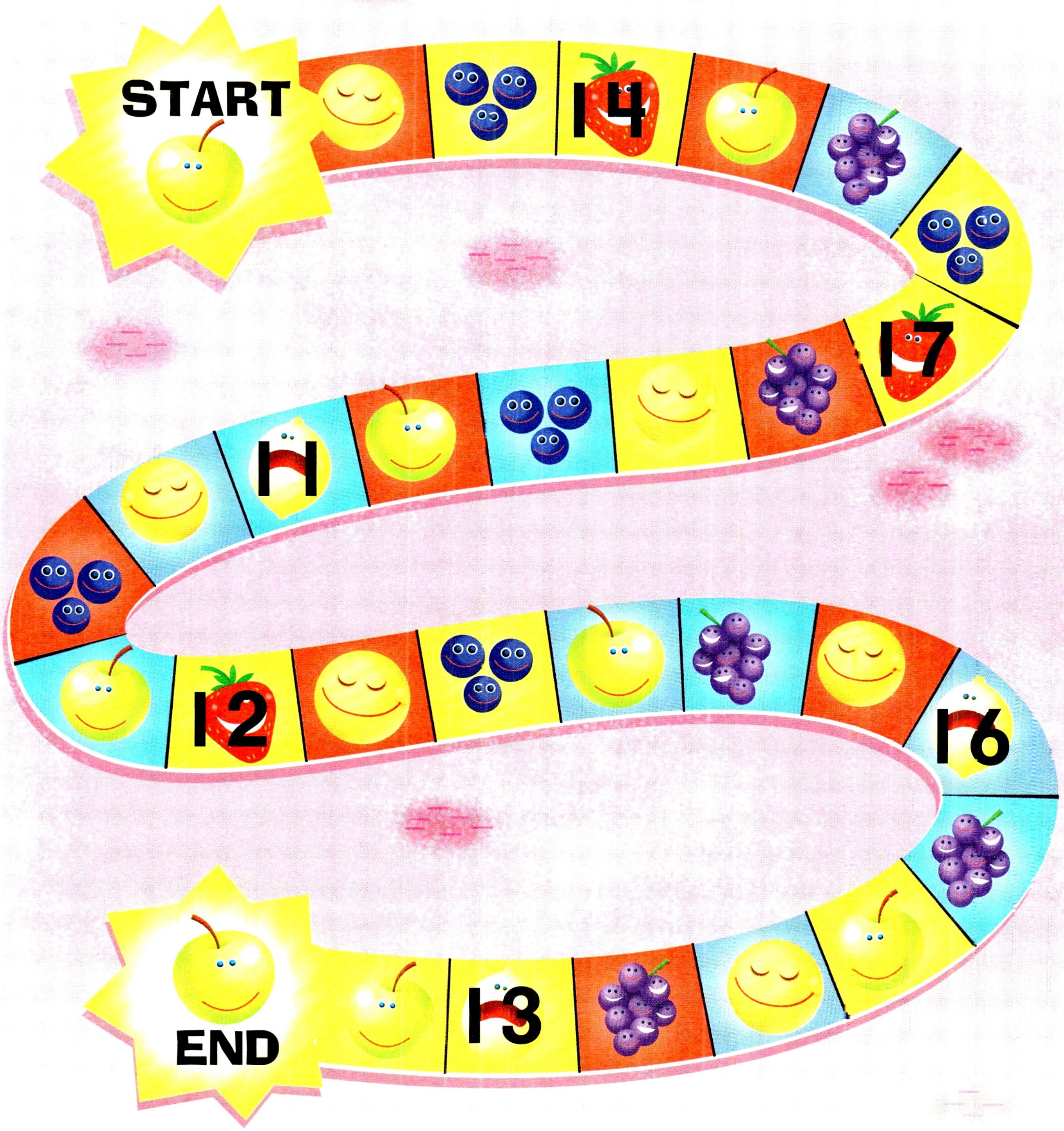

DIRECTIONS   Play with a partner and decide who goes first. Place game markers on START. Take turns. Toss the number cube. Move that number of spaces. If a player lands on a lemon, the player reads the number and moves back that many spaces. If a player lands on a strawberry, the player reads the number and moves forward that many spaces. The first player to reach END wins.

MATERIALS   two game markers, number cube (1-6)

Math Power • Order Numbers

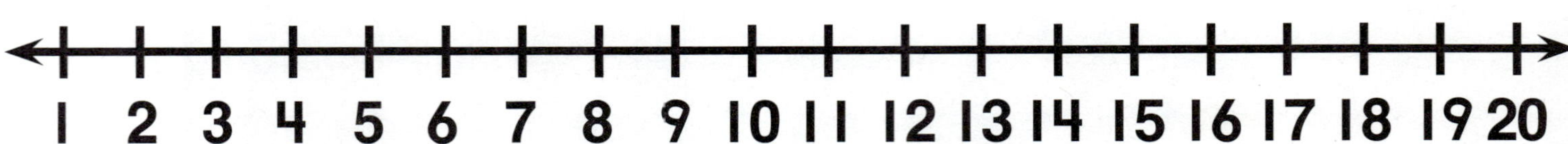

Before		After
	10	
	13	

	Between	
18		20
10		8

DIRECTIONS   **1.** Use the number line to count forward to 20, then backward from 10.   **2.** Write the number that comes directly before and after the numbers shown.   **3.** Write the number that comes between the numbers shown.

200 two hundred

Name ____________________

Chapter 7 Review/Test

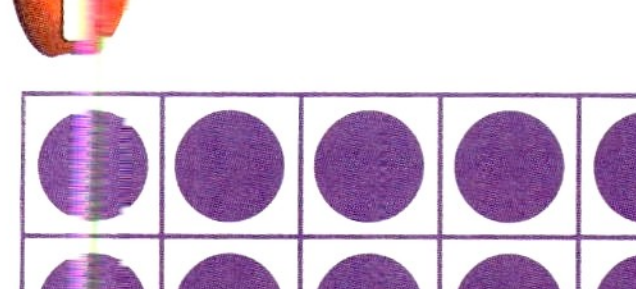

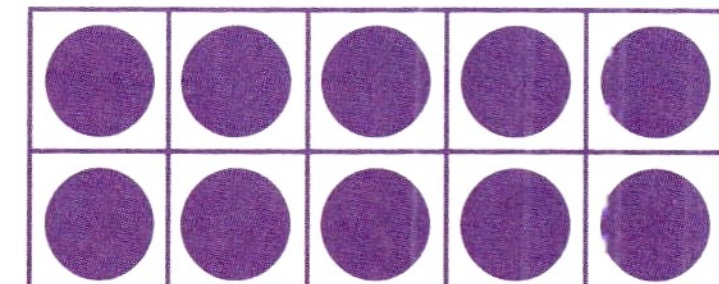

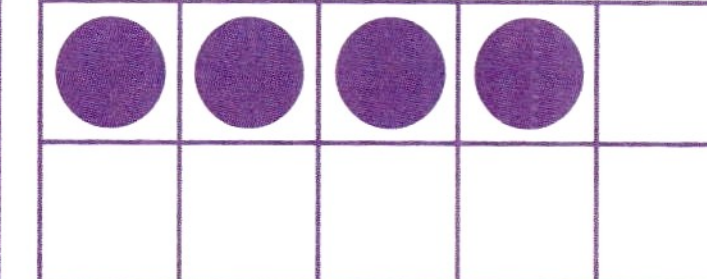

1

2

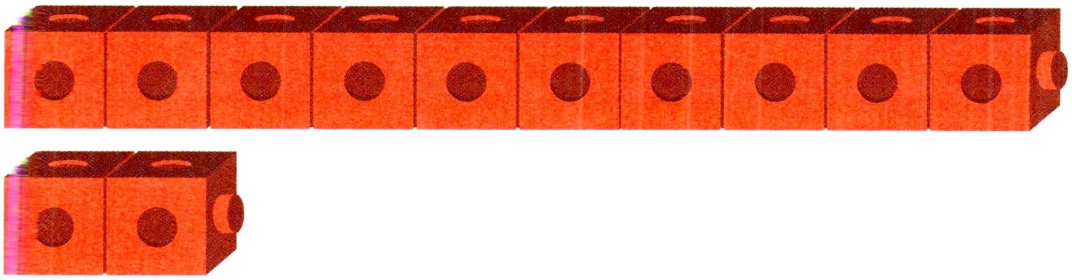

10

20

3

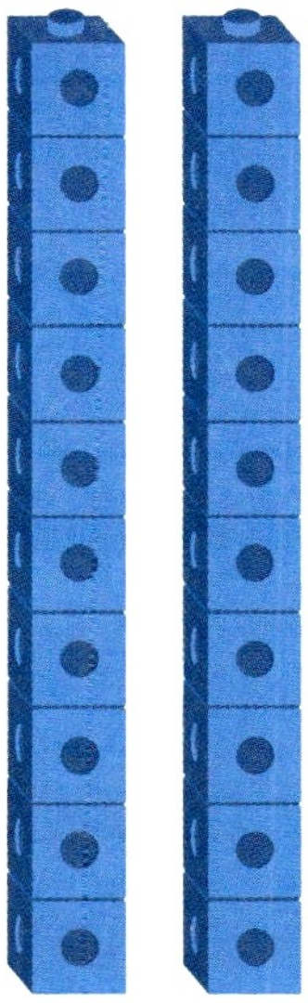

4

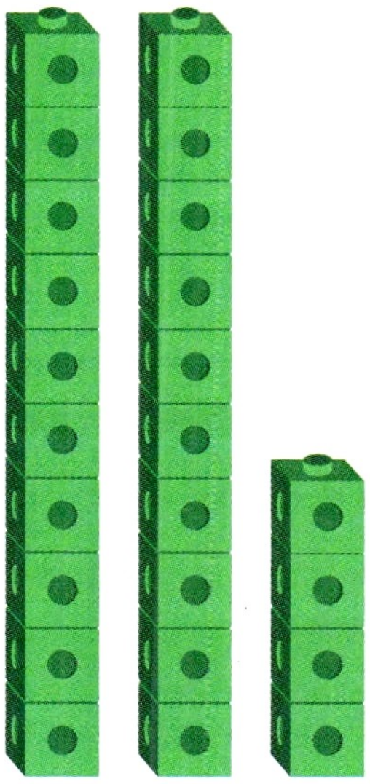

5

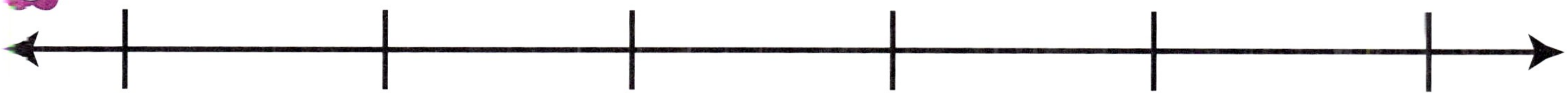

___ 21 22 23 ___ 25

DIRECTIONS 1. How many counters? Write the number. 2. Without counting, circle to show whether the set is closer to 10 cubes or closer to 20 cubes. 3–4. How many cubes? Write the number. 5. Write those numbers in order on the number line.

 Cumulative Review

first

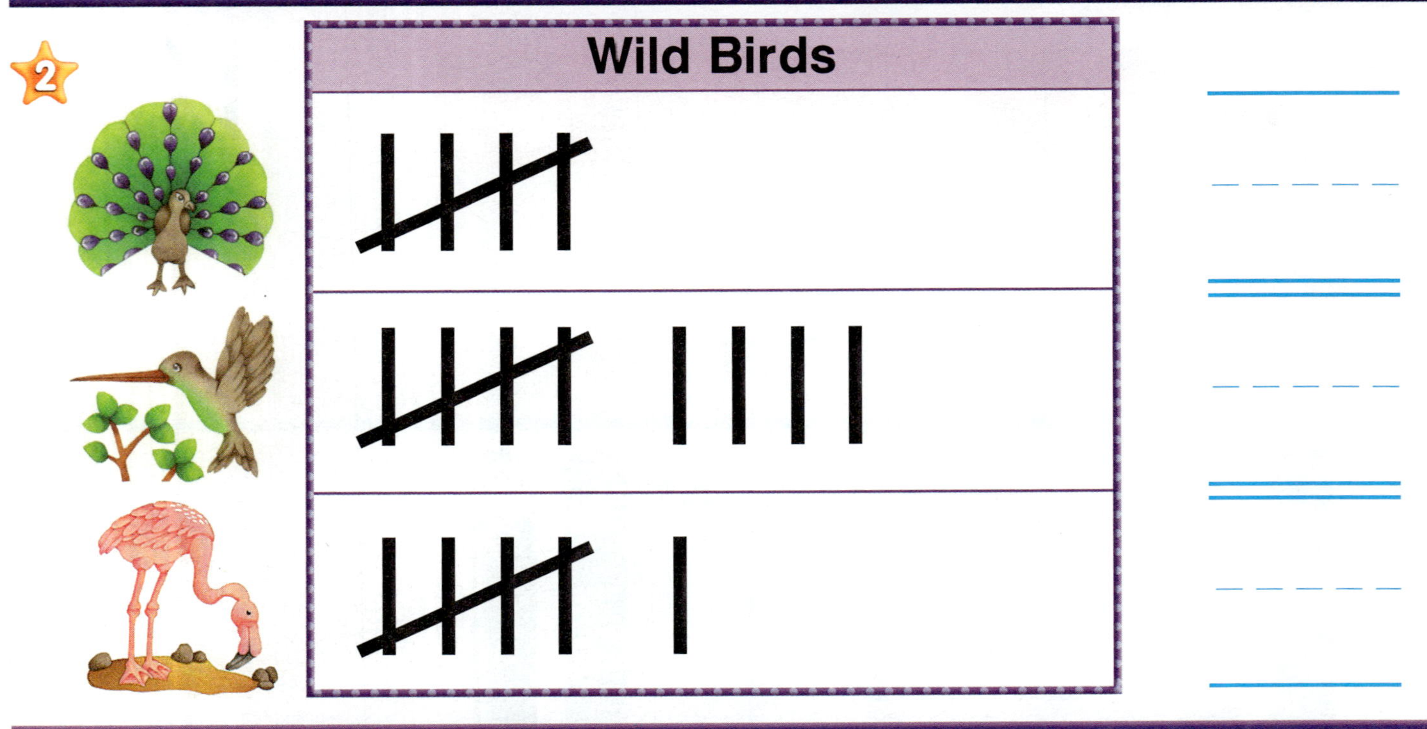

Wild Birds

DIRECTIONS **1.** Circle the seventh duck. Mark an X on the last duck. **2.** Read the table. Write how many of each kind of bird. Circle the kind of bird that there are the most of in this table. Mark an X on the kind of bird that there are the fewest of in this table. **3.** Complete the square that would show the line of symmetry. **4.** How many berries? Write the number.

202 two hundred two

CHAPTER
8
Money
Theme: Money
Giving

DIRECTIONS Place a coin on each coin in the workspace. Sort the coins by color. Move the coins to the sorting rings. Draw and color the coins.

Family Note: This page checks your child's understanding of important concepts and skills needed for success in Chapter 8.

204 two hundred four

Penny

  or 1¢  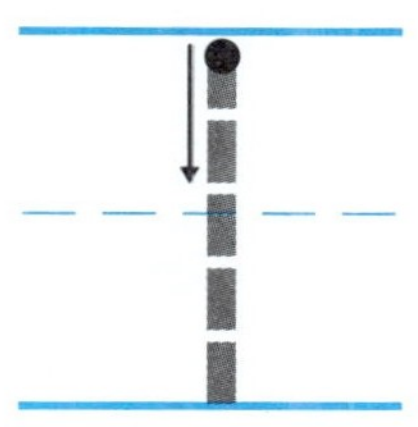 

---

1 

---

2 

---

3 

DIRECTIONS 1–3. Count the pennies. Write how many cents.

OBJECTIVE · Identify a penny and its value.

1 5¢

2  8¢

3  3¢

4 7¢

DIRECTIONS 1–4. Draw the pennies you need to buy the toy.

 **HOME ACTIVITY** · Show your child one to ten pennies. Have your child count the pennies and tell their value.

206 two hundred six

  **or**  **5¢** 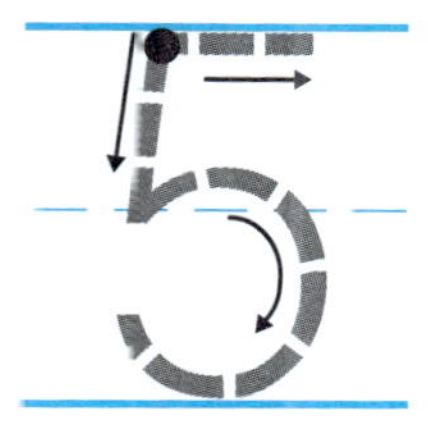  ¢

 **1**

  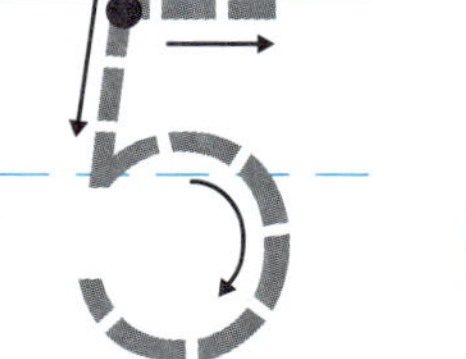 5 ¢

 **2**

 _______ ¢

 **3**

 _______ ¢

 **4**

   _______ ¢

 **5**

    _______ ¢

 **6**

  _______ ¢

DIRECTIONS   1–6. Write how many cents. Circle the coin or set of coins that shows 5¢.

OBJECTIVE • Identify a nickel and its value.

1

4¢

2

5¢

3

3¢

4

5¢

DIRECTIONS 1–4. Draw the coin or coins you need to buy the toy.

HOME ACTIVITY • Show your child a handful of coins. Have him or her identify each nickel. Now have your child use pennies to show the value of a nickel.

208 two hundred eight

 **or** 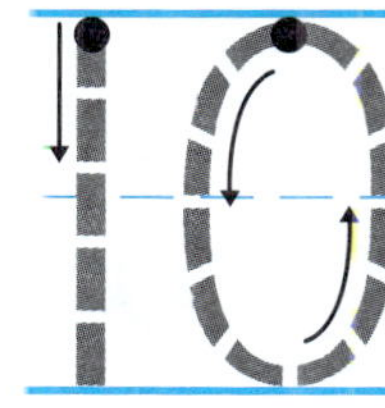

10¢

¢

 **1**

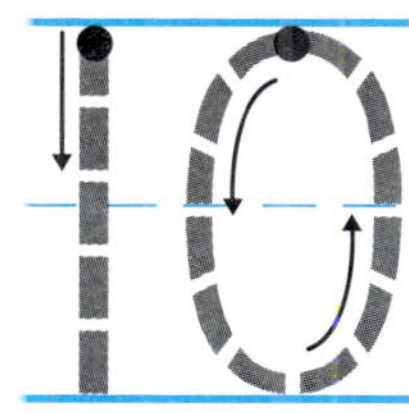¢

 **2**

_____ ¢

 **3**

_____ ¢

 **4**

_____ ¢

DIRECTIONS   1–4. Write how many cents. Draw a circle around the coin or set of coins that shows 10¢.

OBJECTIVE • Identify a dime and its value.

DIRECTIONS   1–3. Using dimes or pennies, draw the coin or coins you need to buy the toy.

 **HOME ACTIVITY** · Show your child a handful of coins. Have him or her identify each dime. Now have your child use pennies to show the value of a dime.

210   two hundred ten

✓ Mid Chapter 8 Review

$¢$

$¢$

DIRECTIONS **1.** Draw the pennies you need to buy the toy. **2–3.** Write how many cents. Circle the coin or set of coins that shows 5¢. **4.** Using dimes or pennies, draw the coin or coins you need to buy the toy.

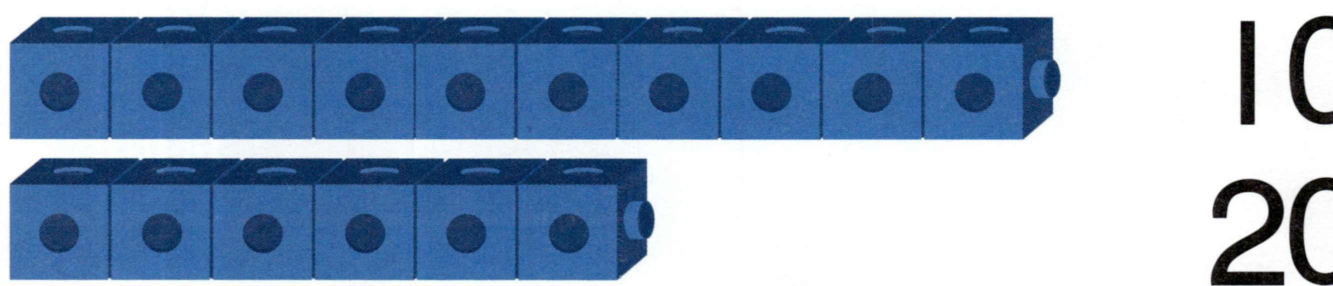

10
20

DIRECTIONS   **1.** Count the shells. How many shells would be in each pail for an equal share?   Write the numbers.   **2.** Without counting, circle to show whether the set is closer to 10 cubes or closer to 20 cubes.   **3.** Using dimes or pennies, draw the coin or coins you need to buy the toy.

212   two hundred twelve

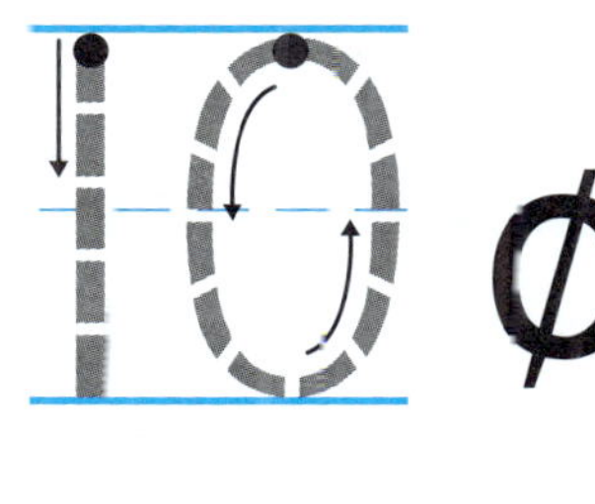

2

3

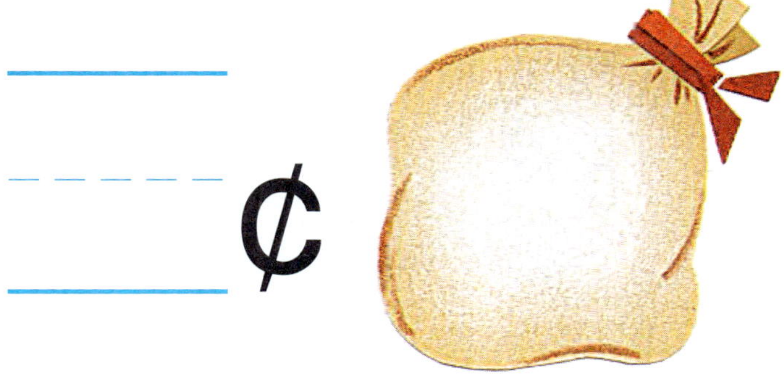

DIRECTIONS **1.** Trace the pennies to show the value of the coin. Trace how many cents. **2.** Sort those pennies into two equal shares. Draw the pennies. **3.** Write how many pennies in each share. Draw one coin that has the same value as the pennies.

OBJECTIVE • Trade pennies for equivalent coins.

Chapter 8 • Lesson 4

214 two hundred fourteen

Problem Solving Workshop
Strategy • Draw a Picture

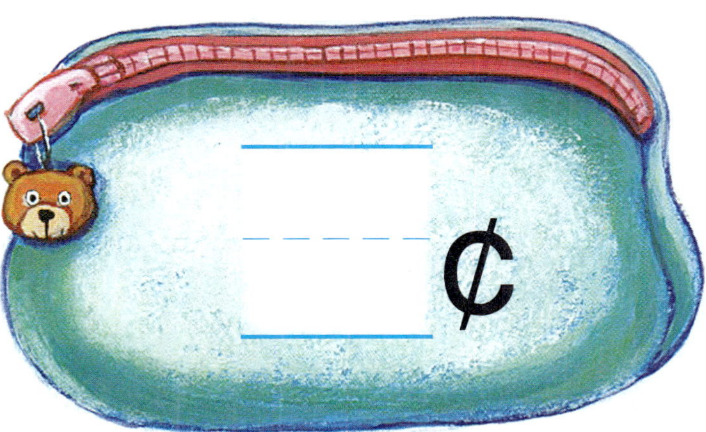

DIRECTIONS **I.** You need 4 pennies to buy an eraser. Draw the pennies and the eraser. A pencil is 2 more pennies than an eraser. Draw the coins you need and the pencil. **2.** Write how many cents you need to buy the pencil.

OBJECTIVE • Solve problems by using the strategy *draw a picture.*

Chapter 8 • Lesson 5

DIRECTIONS **1.** An apple is 5 cents. An orange is 2 more pennies than an apple. A banana is 3 pennies fewer than an orange. Draw the fruit and the coins you need to buy each one. **2.** Write how much for the banana.

HOME ACTIVITY · Give your child ten pennies. Then display several small items with self-stick note prices of 10¢ or less. Have your child select an item and show the coins needed to buy it.

216 two hundred sixteen

 or 

quarter
25¢

or

100¢   dollar

DIRECTIONS **1–2.** Name the coin or bill on the left. Circle the coin or bill with the same value on the right.

Chapter 8 • Lesson 6

two hundred seventeen **217**

1

10 cents

25 cents

100 cents

2

10 cents

25 cents

100 cents

3

10 cents

25 cents

100 cents

DIRECTIONS 1–3. Name the coin or bill on the left. Circle the value of the coin or bill on the right.

HOME ACTIVITY · Show your child a handful of pennies, nickels, dimes, and quarters. Have your child sort the coins into groups and then count the coins in each group.

218 two hundred eighteen

Problem Solving Workshop
Skill • Use a Pattern

1	2	3	4	5	6	7	8	9	10
11	12	13	14	15	16	17	18	19	20
21	22	23	24	25	26	27	28	29	30
31	32	33	34	35	36	37	38	39	40
41	42	43	44	45	46	47	48	49	50
51	52	53	54	55	56	57	58	59	60
61	62	63	64	65	66	67	68	69	70
71	72	73	74	75	76	77	78	79	80
81	82	83	84	85	86	87	88	89	90
91	92	93	94	95	96	97	98	99	100

DIRECTIONS Place a penny on each number as you count from 1 to 10. Trace around the 10th penny. Touch each number as you count from 11 to 100. Circle the last number in each row. What pattern do you see?

OBJECTIVE • Solve problems by using the skill *use a pattern.*

Chapter 8 • Lesson 7

1

10

20

30

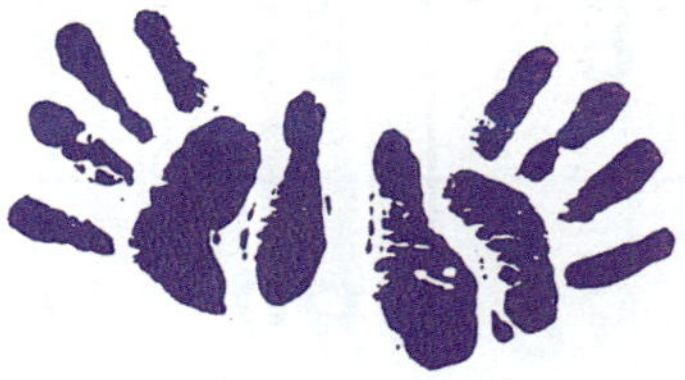

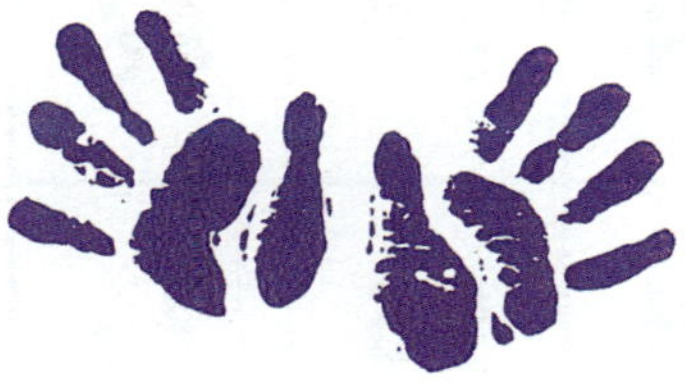

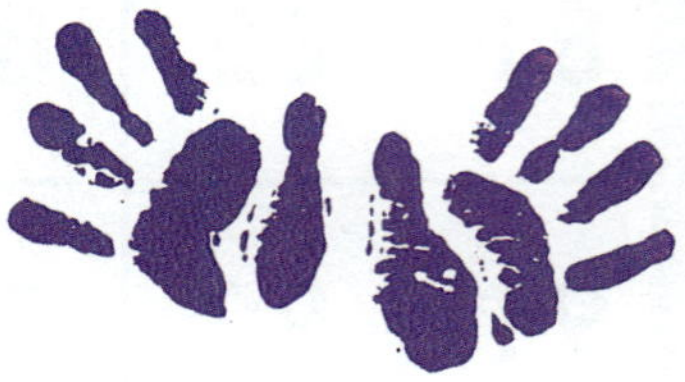

DIRECTIONS **1.** Count by tens. Trace each number. **2.** Count by tens. Write the number.

HOME ACTIVITY • Have your child count by tens as you hold up ten fingers repeatedly.

220 two hundred twenty

Count Groups of Coins

     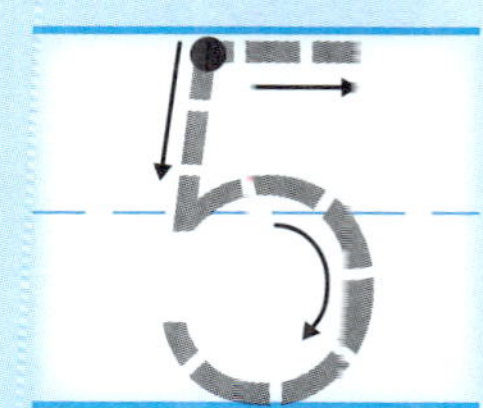

     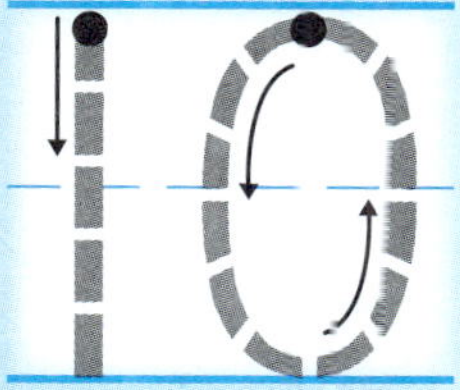

     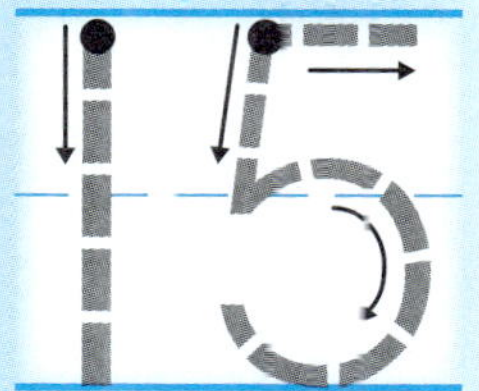

DIRECTIONS Count by fives.
Trace each number.

OBJECTIVE • Count groups of coins by twos and fives.

Chapter 8 • Lesson 8

two hundred twenty-one **221**

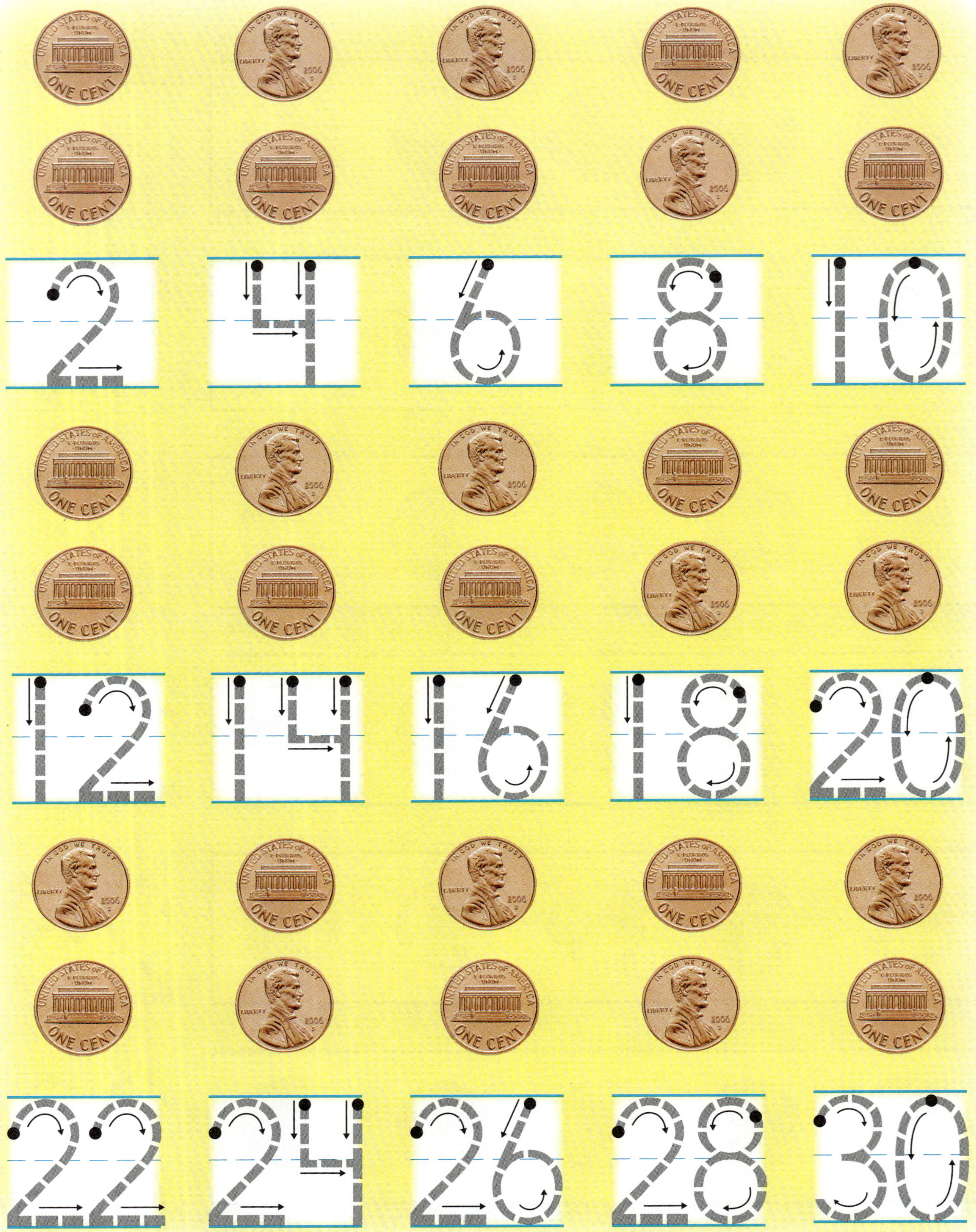

2 4 6 8 10

12 14 16 18 20

22 24 26 28 30

DIRECTIONS Count by twos.
Trace each number.

HOME ACTIVITY · Have your child line up pairs of socks and practice counting by twos.

222 two hundred twenty-two

First to the Market!

DIRECTIONS Play with a partner. Place the coin cards face down. Decide who goes first. The first player takes a card and identifies the value of the coin. Move your marker forward that many spaces. Continue taking turns. The first player to reach the market wins the game.

MATERIALS 10 penny, nickel, and dime coin cards, game markers

Math Power • Counting Money

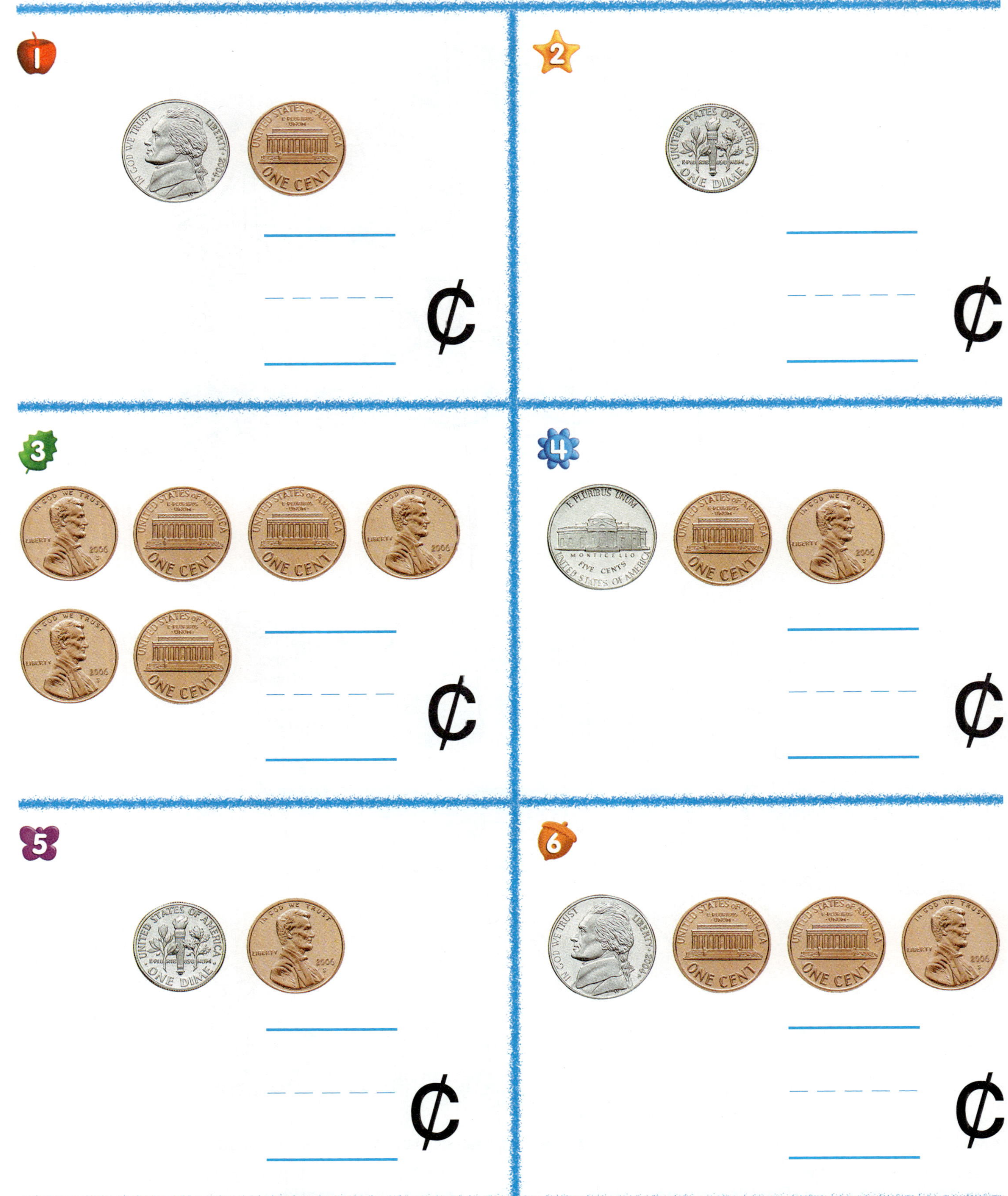

DIRECTIONS 1–6. Use count on to tell the value of the coins. Write how many cents.

 Chapter 8 Review/Test

10 cents

25 cents

100 cents

     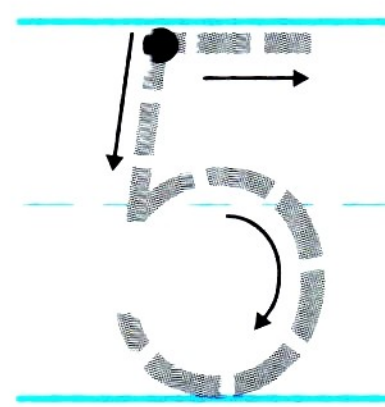

5

     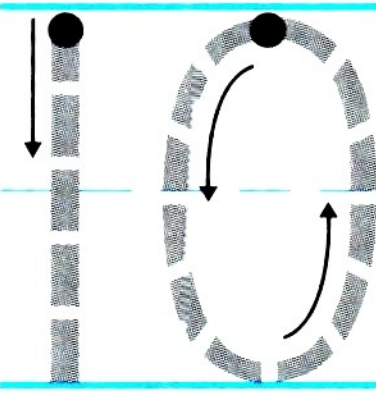

10

     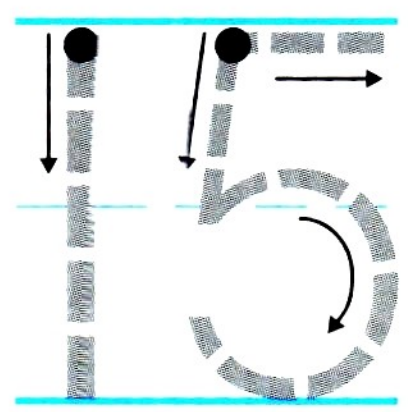

15

DIRECTIONS **1.** Use one nickel and some pennies to show the value of the coin. Draw the coins. **2.** Name the bill on the left. Circle the value of the bill on the right. **3.** Count by fives. Trace each number.

Chapter 8 two hundred twenty-five **225**

DIRECTIONS   1–2. Write the number that shows how many equal parts.   3. How many counters? Write the number.   4. Count by twos. Trace each number.

226   two hundred twenty-six

Apple Seeds

Worms that eat apples are really caterpillars that turn into moths.

DIRECTIONS Follow the trail to the caterpillar's home. Draw the number of seeds in each apple. Circle groups of 10 seeds.

TALK Math About how many seeds do you think there would be in one apple?

Grapes Galore

1

2

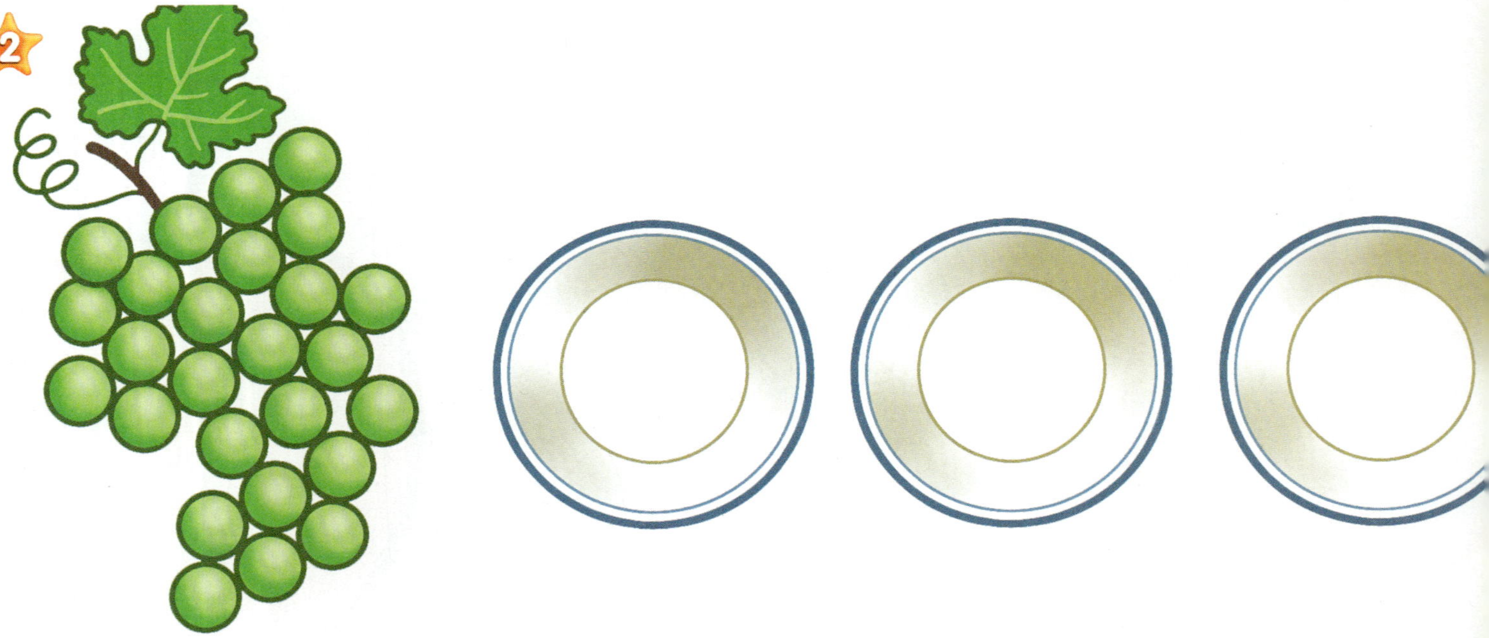

DIRECTIONS 1–2. Count the grapes. Draw the grapes on the plates in groups of ten.

TALK Math Explain how you would group 30 grapes in groups of ten.

228 two hundred twenty-eight

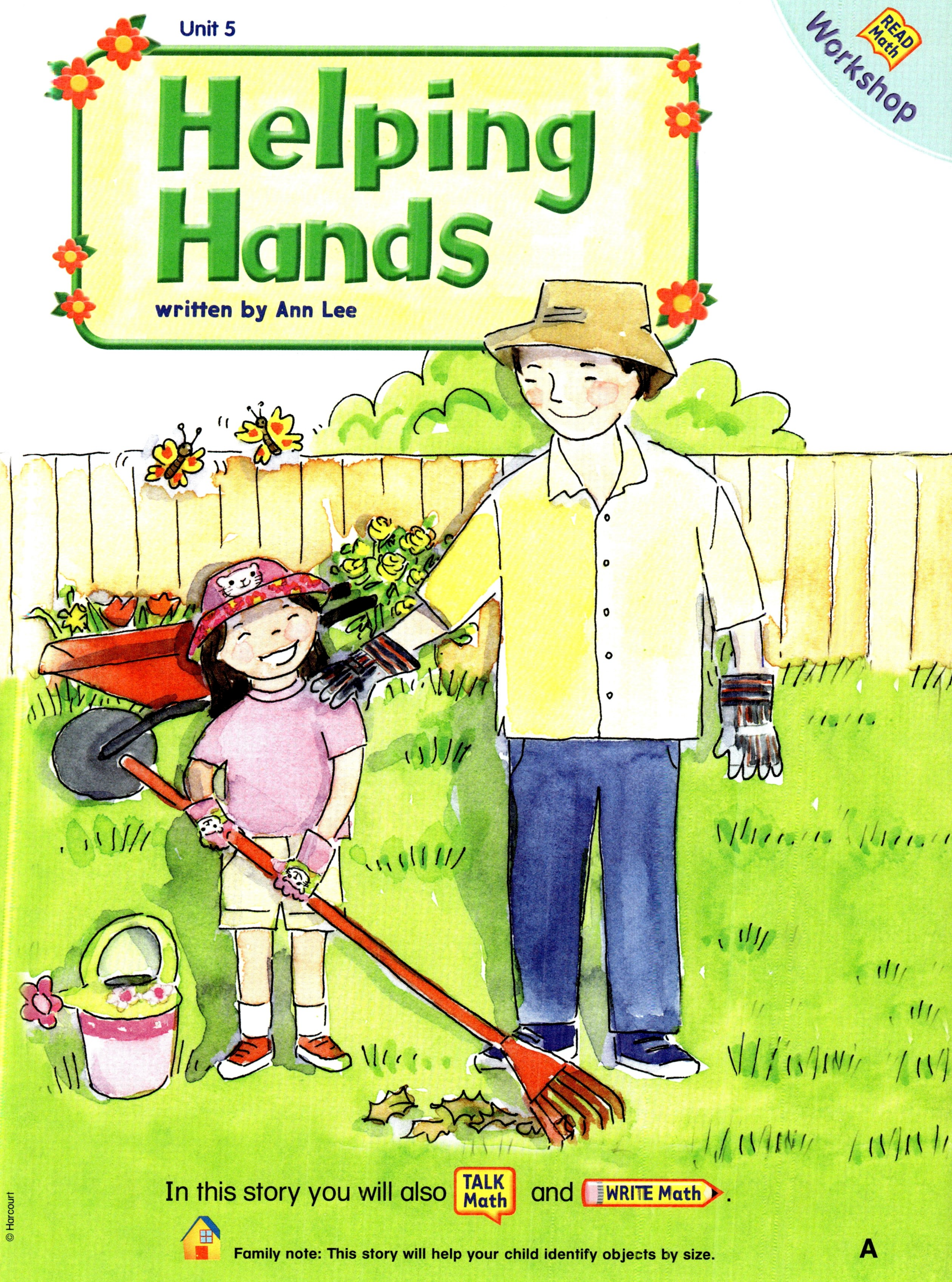

Unit 5
READ Math
Workshop
Helping Hands
written by Ann Lee
In this story you will also TALK Math and WRITE Math.
© Harcourt
Family note: This story will help your child identify objects by size.
A

Today I help Dad in the garden.

We wear our gloves.

Circle the bigger glove.

Science
What plants do you see?

B

Dad puts on his sun hat.

I put on mine.

Circle the smaller hat.

Science

How are most plants the same?

C

Dad fills his watering can.

I fill one, too.

Circle the watering can that holds more.

D

Dad picks some flowers.

I pick some, too.

Circle the smallest flower.

E

We surprised Mom!

Circle who has the biggest smile.

F

Name _______________________________

My Math Story
Literature Activity

DIRECTIONS Draw a story about plants.
Tell which plants are smaller and which plants are bigger.

G

How Big? How Small?

DIRECTIONS Look at the pictures. **1.** Draw a butterfly that is smaller. **2.** Draw a watering can that is bigger. **3.** Draw a flower that is the same size.

H

School Home CONNECTION

Dear Family,

My class started Unit 5 today. I will learn how to measure objects. I will also learn about calendar, time, and temperature. Here are some vocabulary words and activities for us to share.

Love, _______________________________

Vocabulary Power

Key Math Vocabulary

Measure to find size, weight, capacity, length, height, etc.

Clock an instrument that tells time

Vocabulary Activity

Math on the Move

Show your child 3 objects of different lengths and ask him or her to place them in order starting with the shortest.

Technology
Multimedia Math Glossary link at
www.harcourtschool.com/hspmath

School Home CONNECTION

Remember This Your child may already know how to compare the length of two objects by holding them together.

Calendar Activity

January

Sunday	Monday	Tuesday	Wednesday	Thursday	Friday	Saturday
				1	2	3
4	5	6	7	8	9	10
11	12	13	14	15	16	17
18	19	20	21	22	23	24
25	26	27	28	29	30	31

Ask your child if there are more Mondays or more Fridays in this month.

Practice (after pages 263 and 264)

Have your child circle a day on the calendar. Then have him or her tell you what day it will be tomorrow and what day it was yesterday.

Practice (after pages 267 and 268)

Have your child circle the first day of the month and then mark an x on the last day of the month.

Literature

Look for these books in a library. Ask your child to point out math vocabulary words as you read each book together.

The Best Bug Parade.
Murphy, Stuart J.
HarperCollins, 1996.

Mighty Maddie.
Murphy, Stuart J.
HarperCollins, 2004.

Daddy Goes to Work.
Asim, Jabari.
Little, Brown and Company, 2006.

CHAPTER
9
Measurement
Theme: How Does Your Garden Grow?
© Harcourt
two hundred thirty-one 231

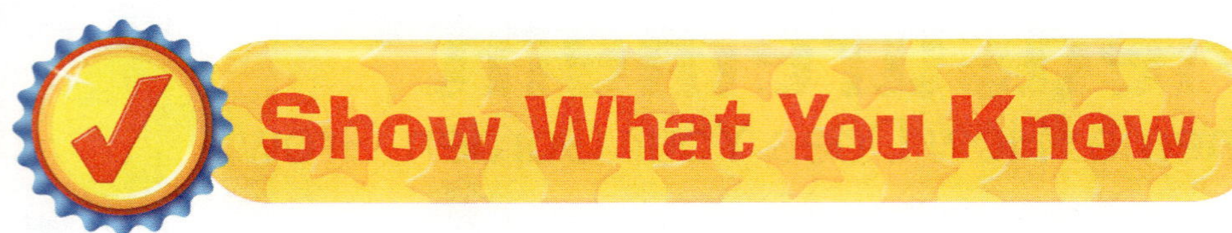

Show What You Know

1

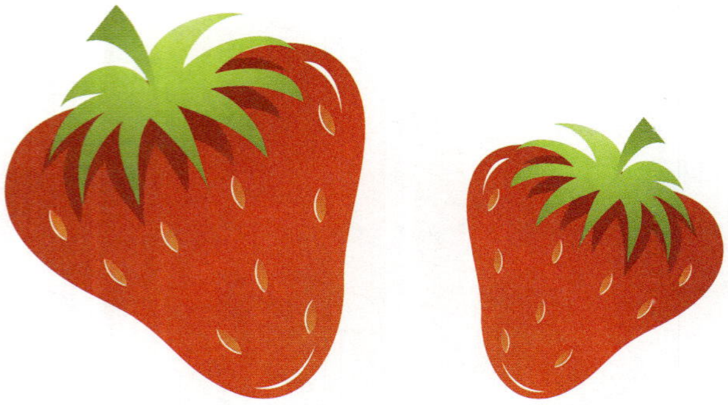

2

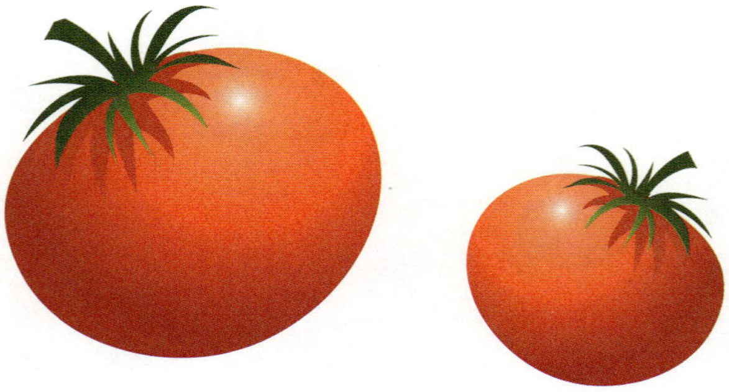

3

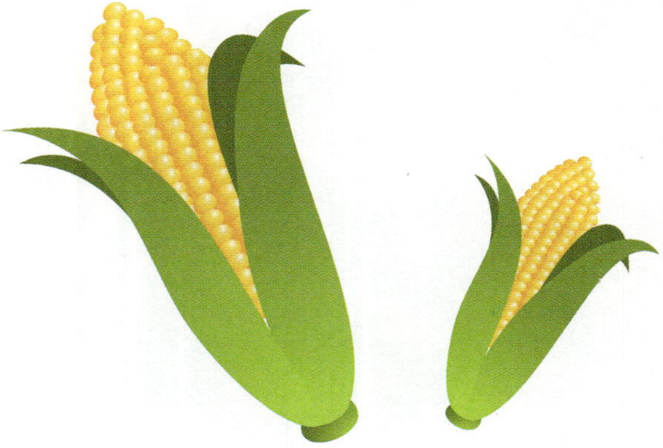

4

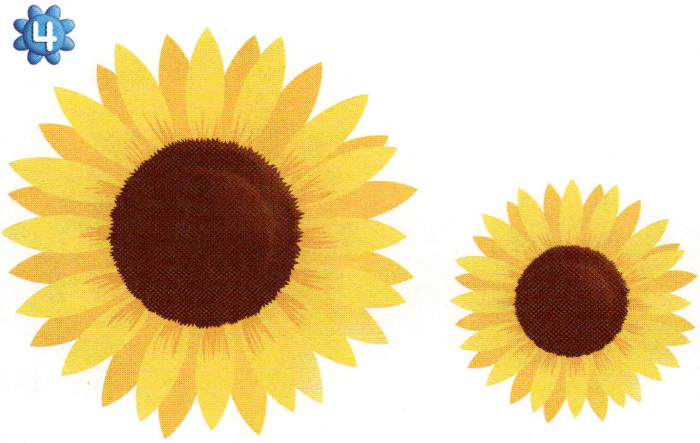

5

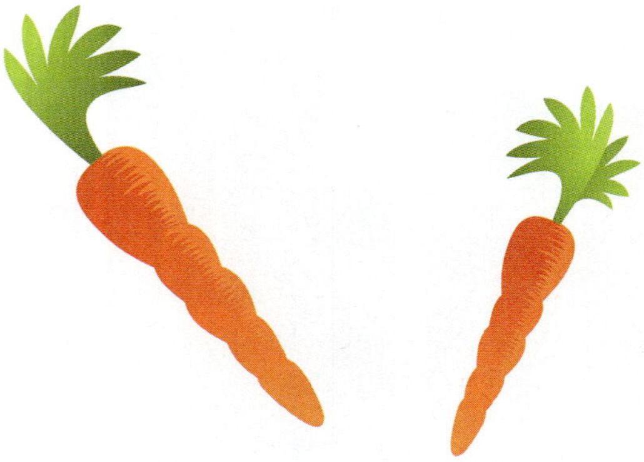

6

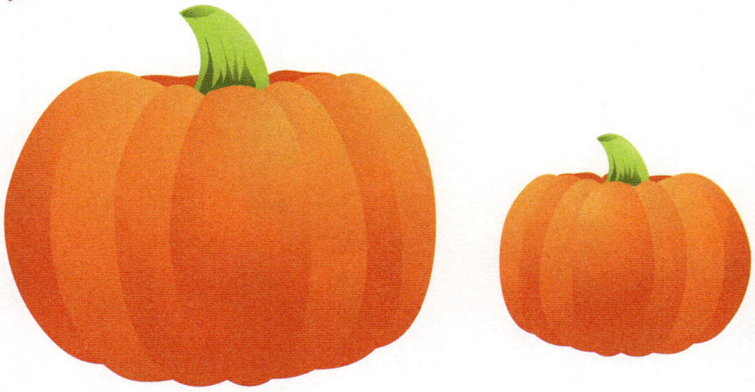

DIRECTIONS **1–3.** Circle the object that is bigger. **4–6.** Circle the object that is smaller.

 **Family Note:** This page checks your child's understanding of important concepts and skills needed for success in Chapter 9.

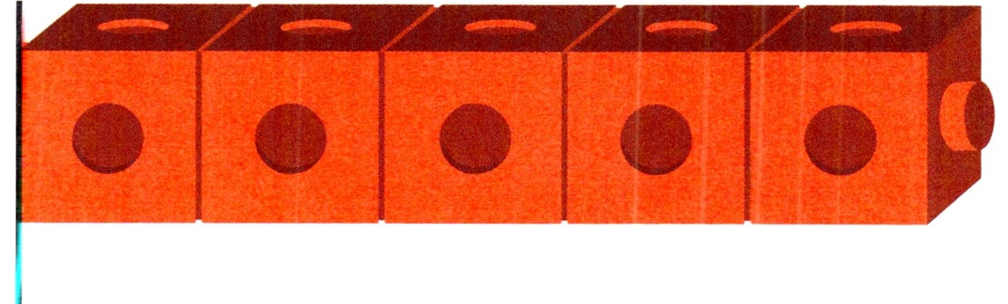

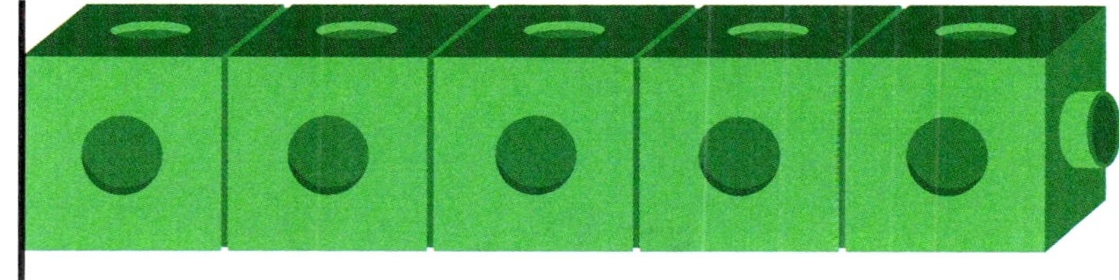

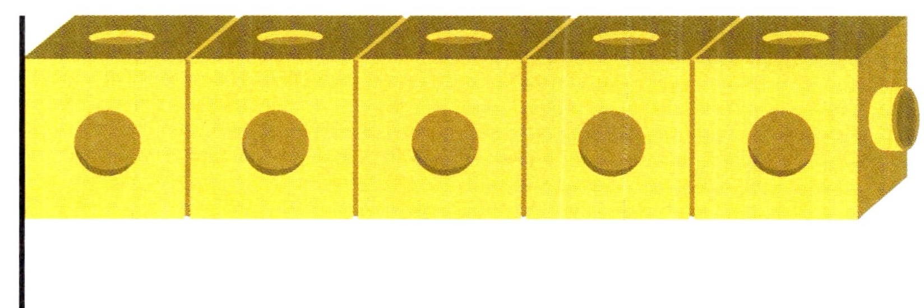

DIRECTIONS   1. Make a cube train that is the same length. Draw the cube train.
2. Make a cube train that is shorter. Draw the cube train.   **3.** Make a cube train that is longer. Draw the cube train.

OBJECTIVE • Compare objects by length.

DIRECTIONS   **1. Make a cube train that is shorter. Draw the cube train.   2. Make a cube train that is taller. Draw the cube train.
3. Make a cube train that is the same height. Draw the cube train.**

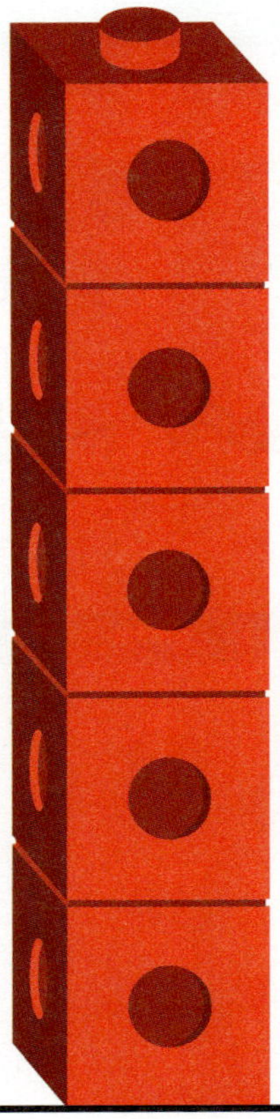

HOME ACTIVITY • Show your child a pencil, and ask him or her to find an object that is longer than the pencil. Repeat with an object that is shorter than the pencil.

234   two hundred thirty-four

Order Length

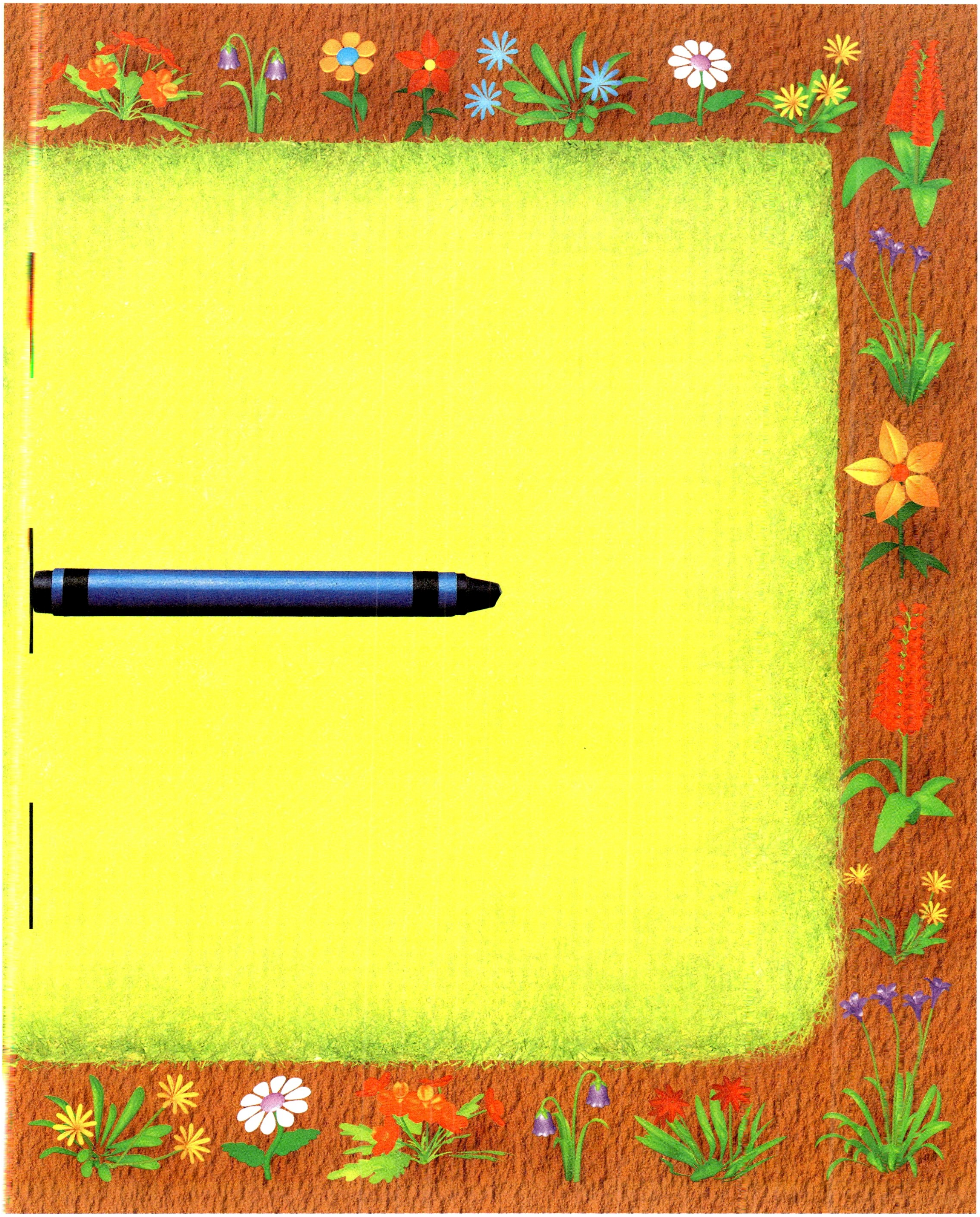

DIRECTIONS Find a classroom object that is shorter than the crayon and an object that is longer than the crayon. Draw the objects in order from shortest to longest.

OBJECTIVE • Order objects by length.

1

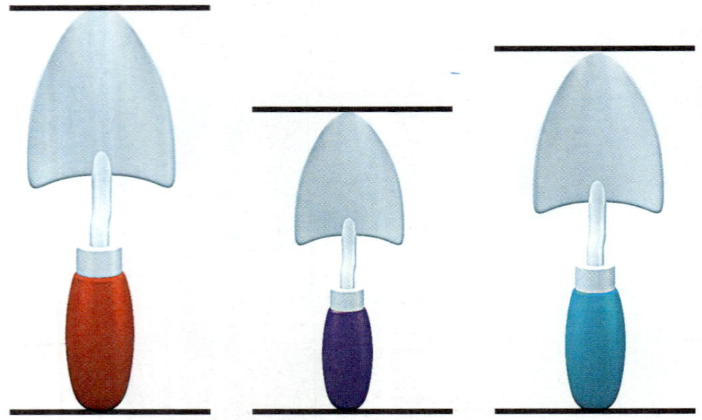

3 1 2

2

3

4

DIRECTIONS 1–4. Write the numbers *1, 2,* and *3* to order the objects from shortest to longest.

 **HOME ACTIVITY ·** Give your child three shoes of different lengths. Have him or her trace around each shoe on paper and write *1, 2,* and *3* in the shoe shapes to order them from shortest to longest.

236 two hundred thirty-six

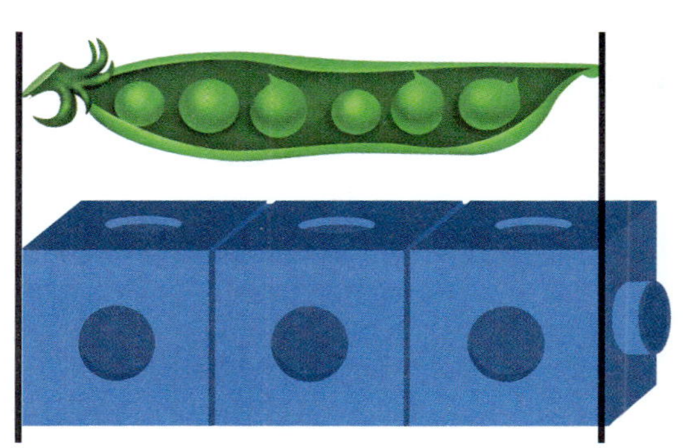

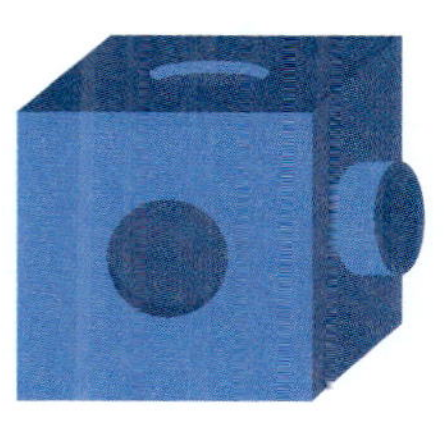

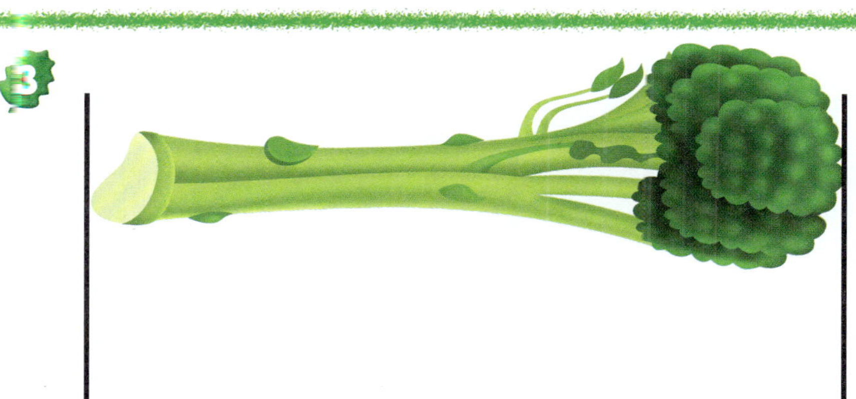

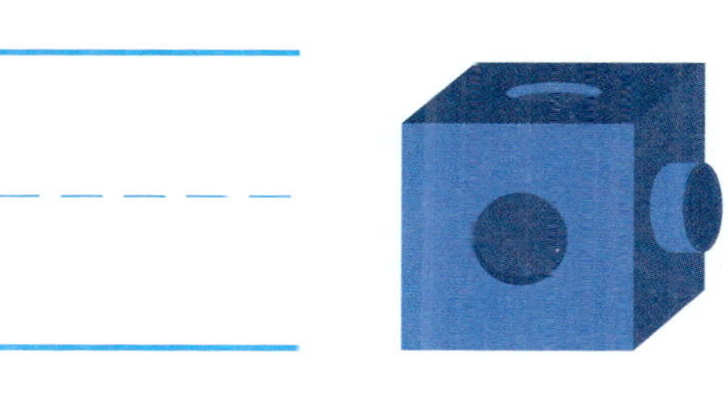

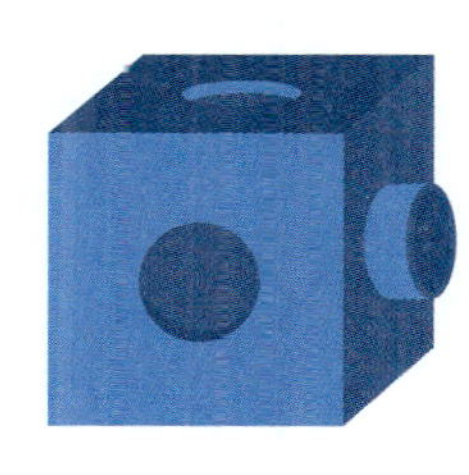

DIRECTIONS 1–4. Use cubes to measure the vegetable. Write about how many cubes long it is.

1.

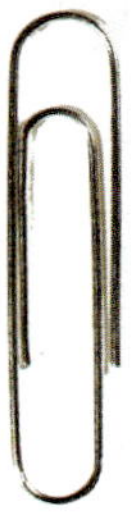

2.

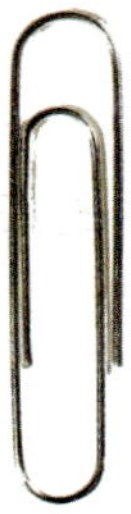

3.

4.

DIRECTIONS 1–4. Use paper clips to measure the vegetable. Write about how many paper clips long it is.

 **HOME ACTIVITY** · Give your child a raw vegetable like a stalk of celery or a carrot. Help him or her trace around the outline on paper and use paper clips to measure its length.

238 two hundred thirty-eight

Problem Solving Workshop
Strategy • Estimate and Measure

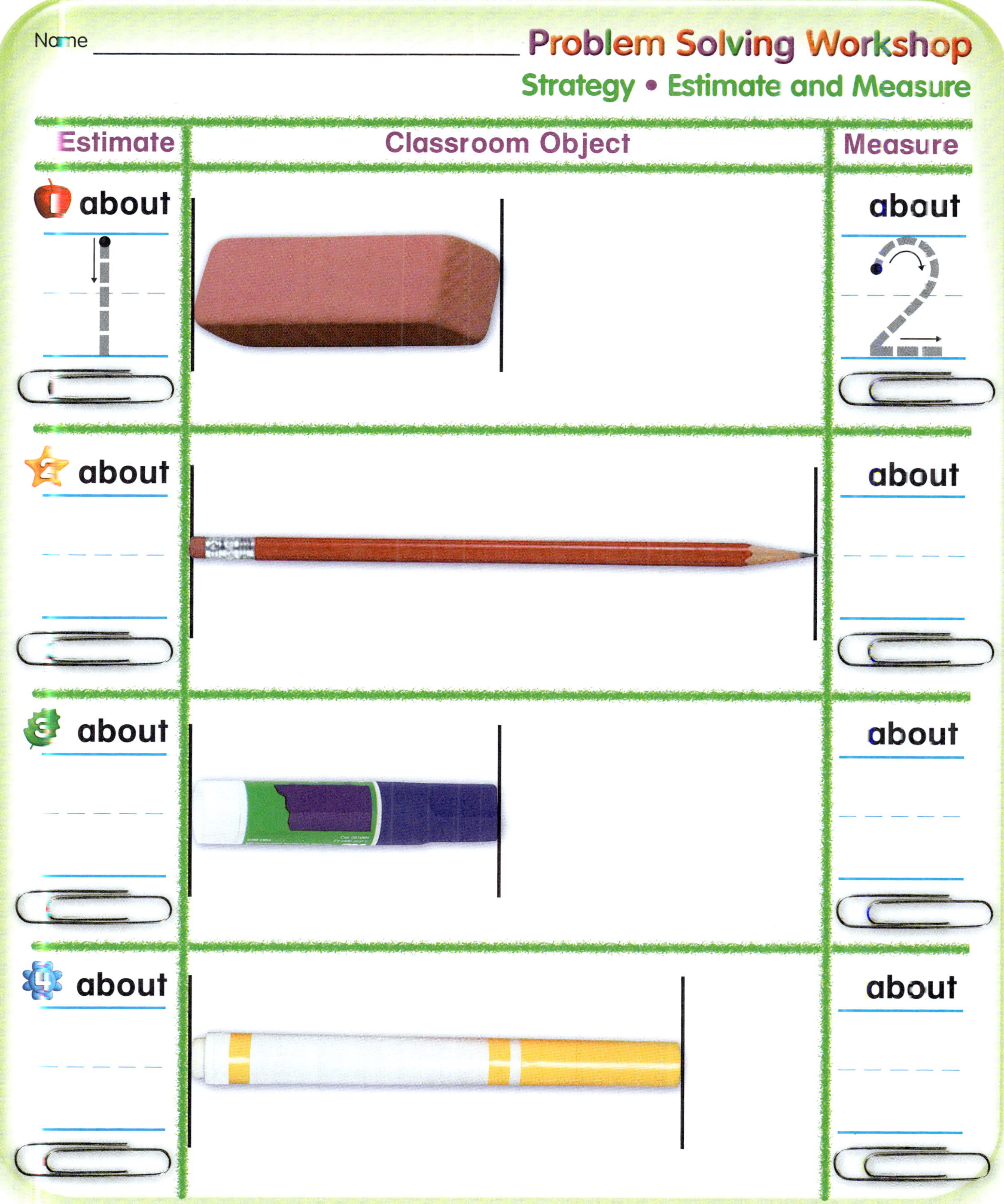

DIRECTIONS 1–4. Find the object in the classroom. Estimate about how many paper clips long it is. Write your estimate. Use paper clips to measure the object. Write about how many paper clips long it is.

OBJECTIVE • Solve problems by using the strategy *estimate and measure.*

Estimate	Classroom Object	Measure

1   about ___________ / about ___________

2   about ___________ / about ___________

3   about ___________ / about ___________

DIRECTIONS 1–3. Estimate about how many shoes long the object is, and write your estimate. Measure the object and write the measurement.

HOME ACTIVITY · Ask your child to estimate and then measure about how many hand lengths long the kitchen table is.

 # ✓ Mid Chapter 9 Review

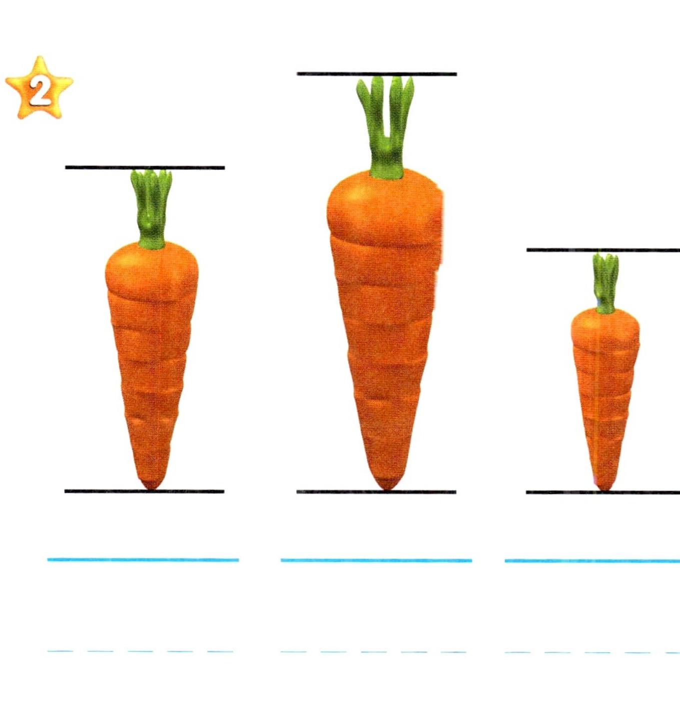

Estimate	Classroom Object	Measure
about	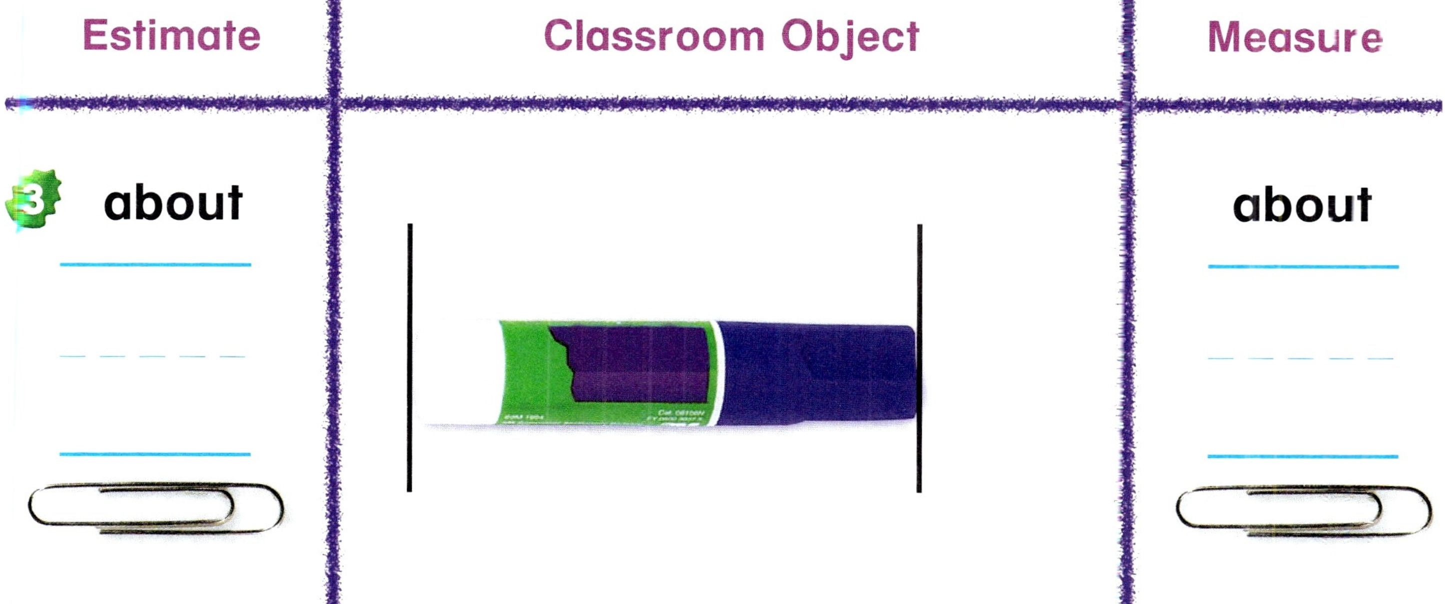	**about**

DIRECTIONS 1. Make a cube train that is shorter. Draw the cube train. 2. Write the numbers *1, 2,* and *3* to order the objects from shortest to longest. 3. Find the object in the classroom. Estimate about how many paper clips long it is. Write your estimate. Use paper clips to measure the object. Write about how many paper clips long it is.

Name _______________________

Cumulative Review

 **1**

 **2**

 **3**

  |   

 **4**

Estimate	**Classroom Object**	**Measure**
about		about

DIRECTIONS **1.** Circle the figure with a line that makes two matching parts. **2.** How many pieces of fruit? Write the number. **3.** Name the coin on the left. Circle the coin with the same value on the right. **4.** Estimate about how many shoes long the object is and write your estimate. Measure the object and write the measurement.

about

18

handfuls

about

____

handfuls

about

____

handfuls

about

____

handfuls

DIRECTIONS Use drinking cups like the cups pictured. Fill each cup with handfuls of rice. Write about how many handfuls each cup holds.

OBJECTIVE · Explore capacity.

Chapter 9 · Lesson 5

	about
	about
	about
	about

DIRECTIONS Use drinking cups like the cups pictured. Fill each cup with scoops of rice. Write about how many scoops each cup holds.

HOME ACTIVITY • Show your child two different-sized cups. Have your child use a small scoop to tell you how many scoops are in each cup.

244 two hundred forty-four

 **Compare Capacity**

holds more

holds the same

holds less

holds more

holds the same

holds less

holds more

holds the same

holds less

  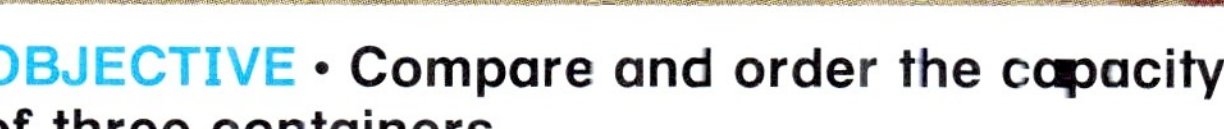

DIRECTIONS   I. Use sand to fill a drinking cup like the one pictured. **2–4.** Pour the sand from the cup you filled in the apple into a drinking cup like the one pictured. Does this cup hold more, less, or the same amount of sand as the first cup? Circle your answer.

OBJECTIVE • Compare and order the capacity of three containers.

Chapter 9 • Lesson 6

DIRECTIONS   Fill three different-sized drinking cups with sand. Use a different color to draw the cups in order, beginning with the cup that holds the least amount of sand.

 **HOME ACTIVITY** • Show your child a pan. Have him or her find a pan that holds less and a pan that holds more. Then ask your child to place the pans in order from the pan that holds the least to the pan that holds the most.

 **left**    **right**

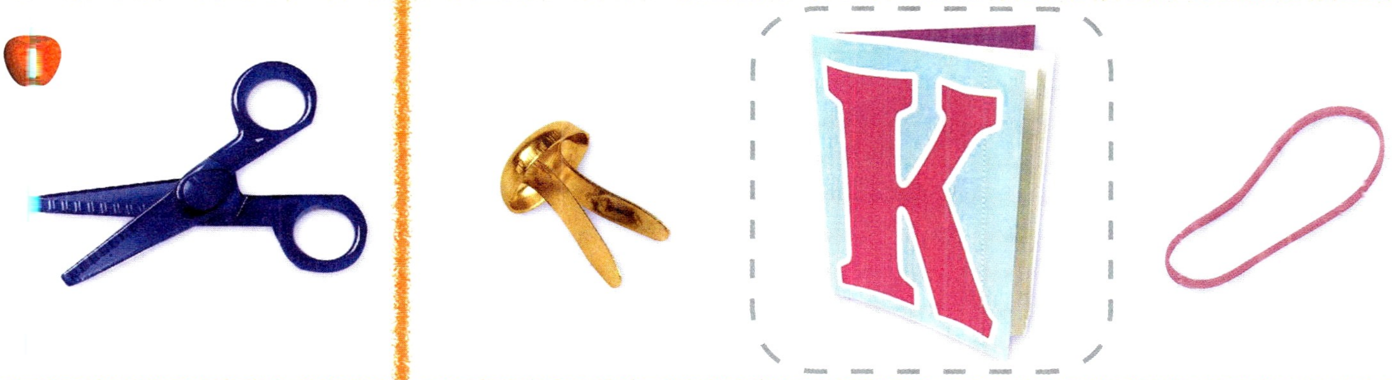

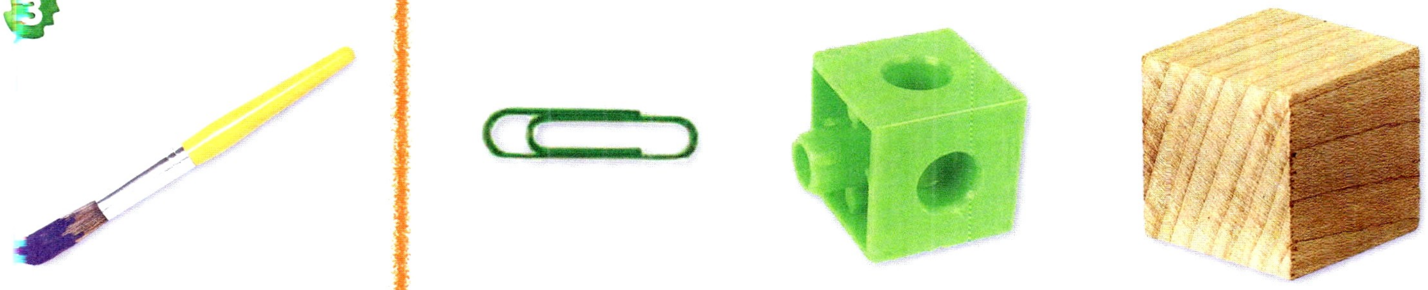

 **left**  **right**

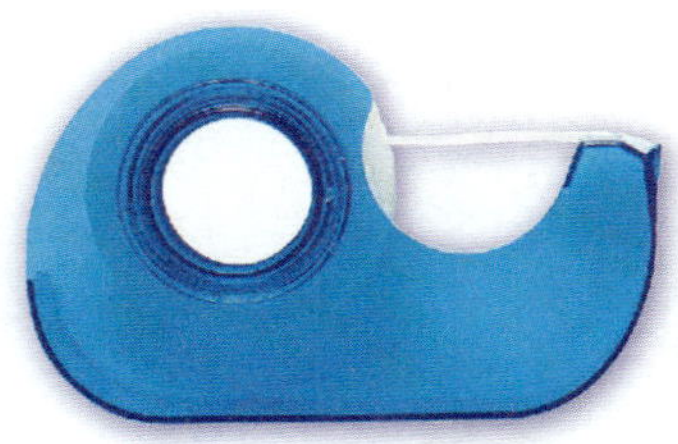

 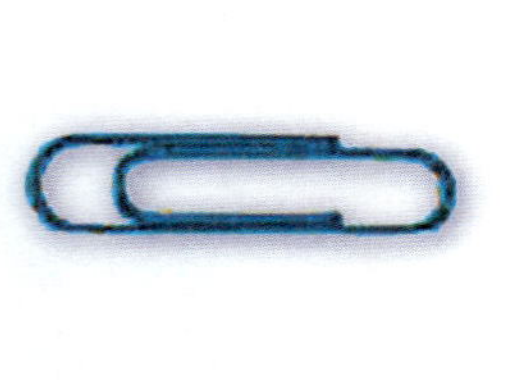 

DIRECTIONS   1–4. Find the first object in the row, and hold it in your left hand. Find the rest of the objects in the row, and take turns holding each object in your right hand. Circle the object that is lighter than the object in your left hand.

 **HOME ACTIVITY ·** Give your child a small household object. Have him or her find another household object that is lighter.

Compare Weight

1.

2.

DIRECTIONS Find a book in the classroom.
1. Find a classroom object that is lighter than the book and draw it in the work space.
2. Find a classroom object that is heavier than the book and draw it in the work space.

OBJECTIVE • Compare and order objects by weight.

Chapter 9 • Lesson 8

DIRECTIONS   Find three classroom objects that have different weights. Draw the objects in order from lightest to heaviest.

HOME ACTIVITY · Give your child three objects of clearly different weights. Have him or her place them in order from lightest to heaviest.

HANDS ON
Explore Area

DIRECTIONS   **1.** Use color tiles to find the garden that has the same area as the model garden at the top of the page. Circle the garden.

OBJECTIVE • Explore the area of a surface.

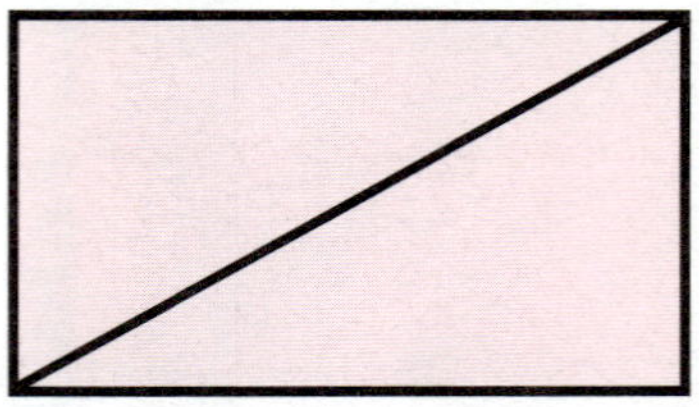

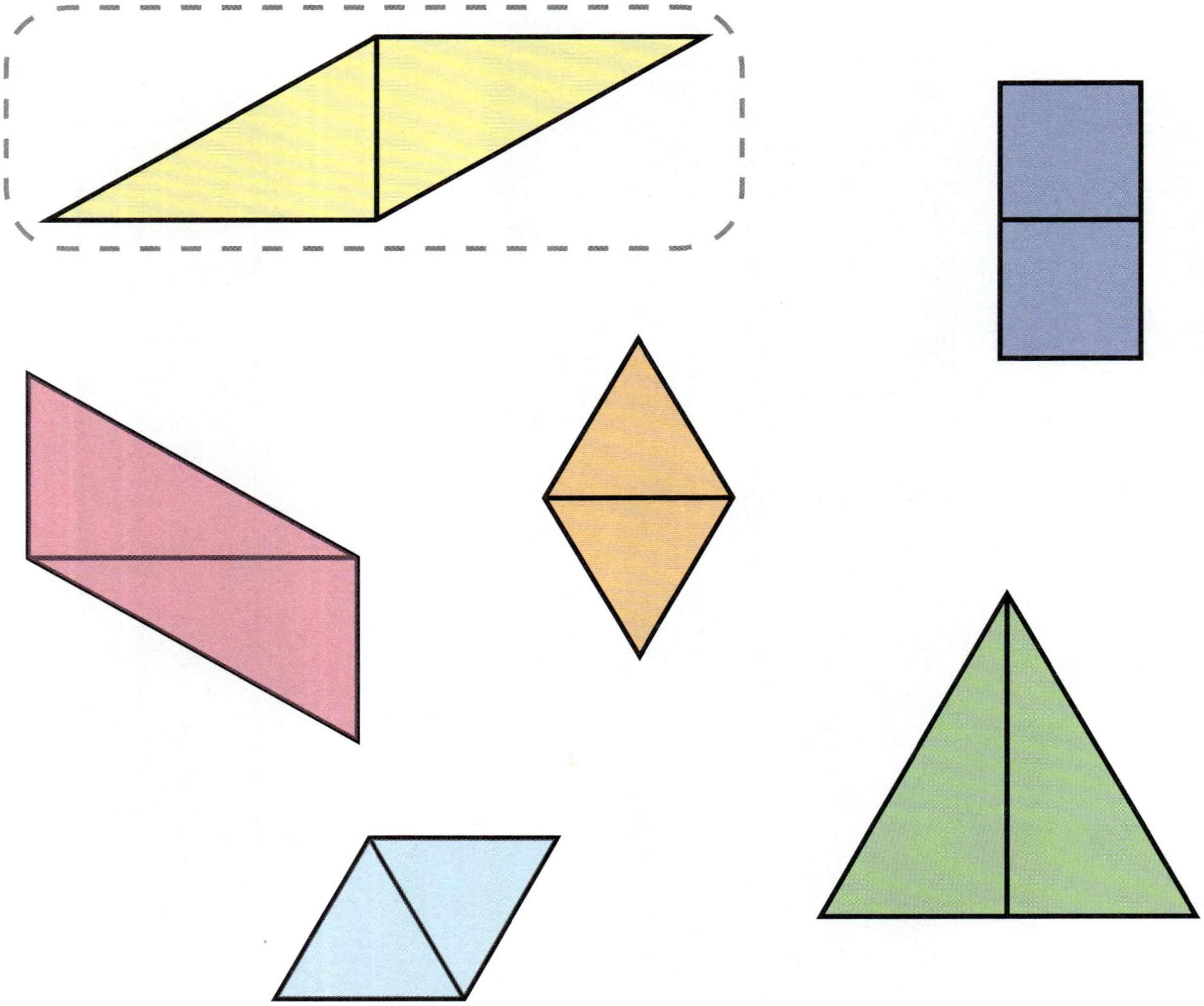

Problem Solving Workshop
Skill • Use Estimation

estimate

 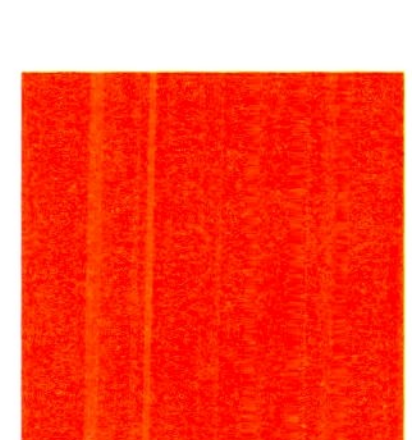

measure

 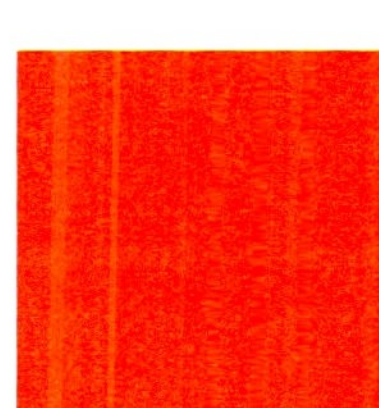

DIRECTIONS Estimate how many color tiles it will take to cover the area of the letter. Write your estimate. Use color tiles to measure the area. Write how many color tiles it takes. Trace and color the tiles.

OBJECTIVE • Solve problems by using the skill *use estimation.*

Chapter 9 • Lesson 10

estimate

____

measure

____

DIRECTIONS Estimate how many color tiles it will take to cover the area of the number. Write your estimate. Use color tiles to measure the area. Write how many color tiles it takes. Trace and color the tiles.

HOME ACTIVITY • Cut out 1-inch squares. Use these squares to draw a block numeral. Have your child estimate how many squares it will take to cover the area. Then have him or her use the squares to measure and check the estimate.

254 two hundred fifty-four

Connecting Cube Challenge

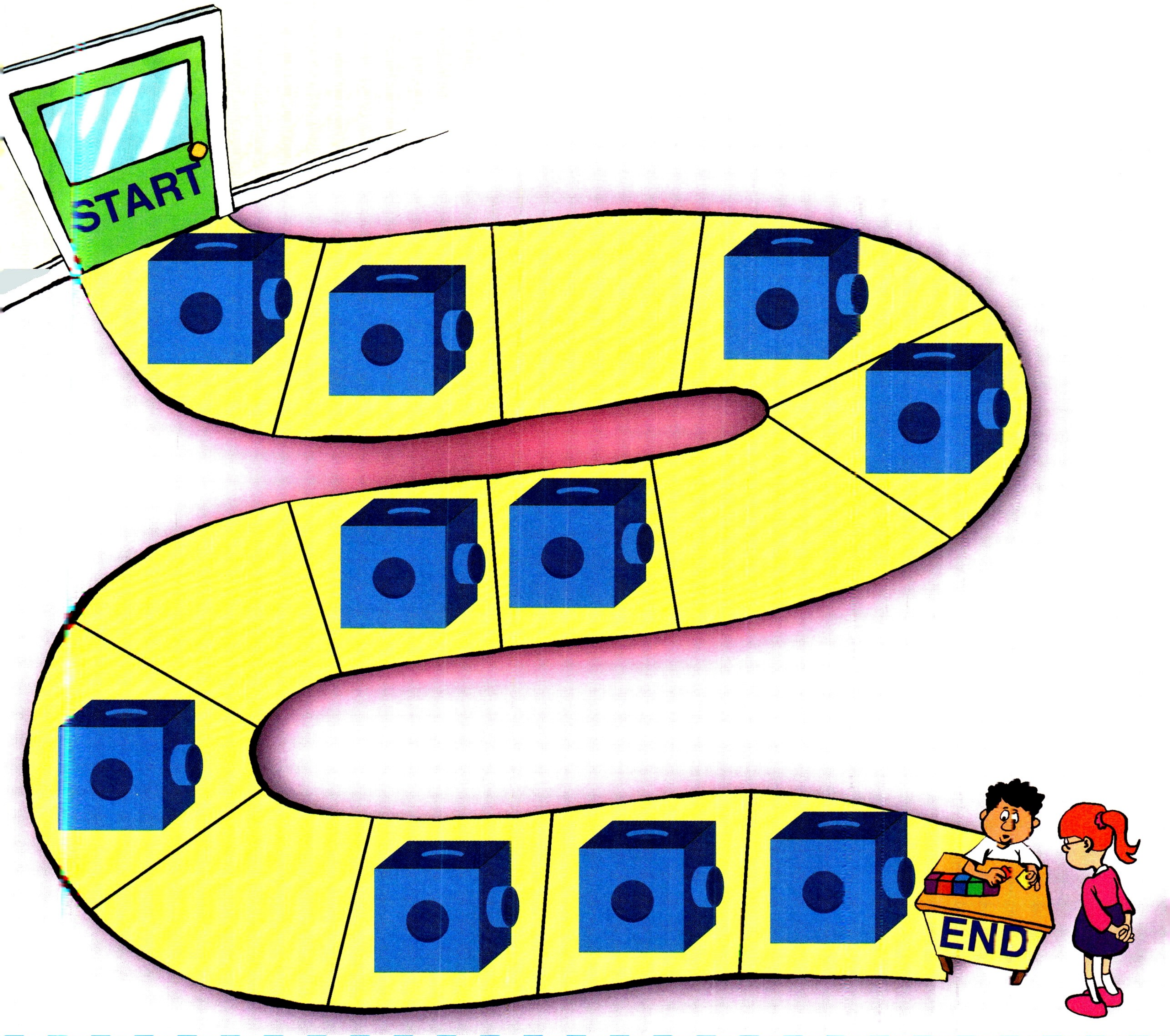

DIRECTIONS: Take turns with a partner tossing the number cube. Move your marker that number of spaces. If a player lands on a cube he or she takes a cube and makes a cube train. At the end of the game, players compare cube trains. The player with the longer cube train must find a classroom object longer than his or her cube train. The player with the shorter cube train must find a classroom object shorter than his or her cube train. If the cube trains are the same length, players must find a classroom object the same length as the cube trains.

MATERIALS: game markers, number cube (1-6), connecting cubes

Chapter 9

Math Power • Which Holds the Most?

Estimate	Container	Measure
about	COFFEE	about
about		about
about		about

DIRECTIONS Find containers like the ones pictured. Estimate about how many cups of rice will fill each container. Write your estimate. Use cups of rice to fill each container. Write about how many cups were used to fill each container. Circle the container that holds the most rice.

256 two hundred fifty-six

✓ Chapter 9 Review/Test

holds more

holds the same

holds less

DIRECTIONS   **1.** Use sand to fill the red drinking cup. Pour the sand from the red cup into the blue cup. Does the blue cup hold more, less, or the same amount of sand as the red cup? Circle your answer.   **2.** Find the first object in the row, and hold it in your left hand. Find the rest of the objects in the row, and take turns holding each object in your right hand. Circle the object that is heavier than the object in your left hand.   **3.** Find three classroom objects that have different weights. Draw the objects in order from lightest to heaviest.

Cumulative Review

1

2

3

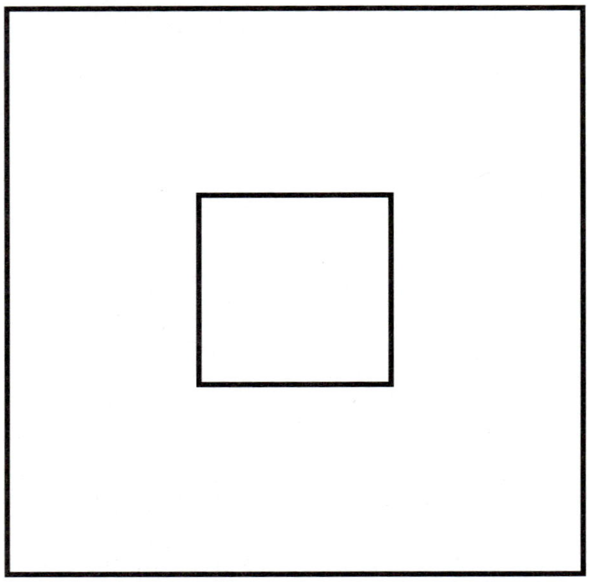

Estimate

Measure

DIRECTIONS 1. How many color tiles? Write the number. **2.** Use pennies to show the value of the coin. Draw the pennies. **3.** Estimate how many color tiles it will take to cover the area of the number. Write your estimate. Use color tiles to measure the area. Write how many color tiles it takes. Trace and color the tiles.

258 two hundred fifty-eight

Explore Calendar, Time, and Temperature

Theme: Day Planner

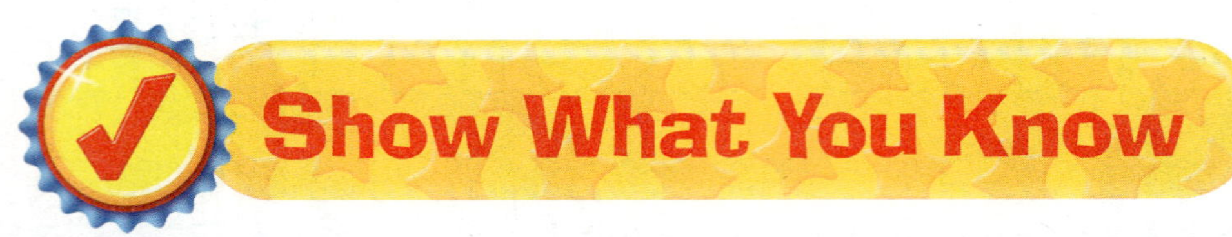

First	Next	Last

DIRECTIONS 1. Draw a picture to show what would come first. 2. Draw a picture to show what would come next. 3. Draw a picture to show what would come last.

FAMILY NOTE: This page checks your child's understanding of important concepts and skills needed for success in Chapter 10.

260 two hundred sixty

Days of the Week

Tuesday

Friday

Sunday

Wednesday

Saturday

Monday

Thursday

DIRECTIONS **1.** Point to and say each day of the week. **2.** Number the days in order, beginning with Sunday.

OBJECTIVE • Identify the days of the week.

Chapter 10 • Lesson 1

June

Sunday	Monday	Tuesday	Wednesday	Thursday	Friday	Saturday
	1	2	3	4	5	6
7	8	9	10	11	12	13
14	15	16	17	18	19	20
21	22	23	24	25	26	27
28	29	30				

2. Wednesdays 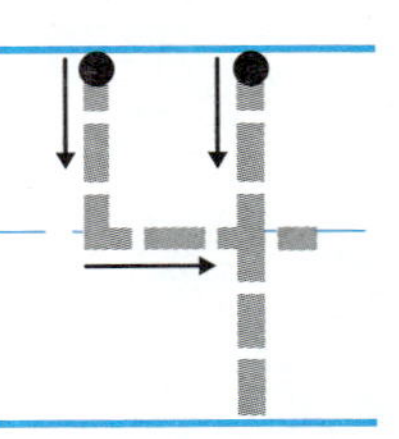

3. Mondays

4. Fridays

 **5.** Days in June

DIRECTIONS   I. Use red to color all the Sundays. Use blue to color all the Fridays.
2. Write how many Wednesdays are in this month.   **3.** Write how many Mondays are in this month.   **4.** Write how many Fridays are in this month.   **5.** Write how many days are in June.

HOME ACTIVITY • Show your child a calendar for the current month. Have him or her point to the days of the week as you both say them aloud. Have your child count the number of Wednesdays in the month.

Explore Sequence of Events

DIRECTIONS Draw a line from *today* to the name of the day. Trace the word. Trace the name of the day before today. Draw a line from that day to *yesterday*. Trace the name of the day after today, and draw a line to *tomorrow*.

OBJECTIVE • Use the days of the week to describe a sequence of events.

morning

afternoon

evening

---

morning

afternoon

evening

---

morning

afternoon

evening

DIRECTIONS   Look at each picture. Circle the time of day that this would probably happen. Use numbers to show the order.

HOME ACTIVITY · Have your child draw three pictures, showing what he or she does in the morning, in the afternoon, and in the evening. Have him or her number the pictures to show the order.

Name ______________________________

October

Sunday	Monday	Tuesday	Wednesday	Thursday	Fr day	Saturday
				1	2	
4	5	6		8		10
11	12	13			16	
18	19	20	21		23	
25	26			29	30	31

DIRECTIONS Use red to color the name of the month. Use yellow to color the names of the days of the week. Write the missing numbers. Use green to color the first day of the month. Use blue to color the last day of the month.

OBJECTIVE • Recognize parts of a calendar.

Chapter 10 • Lesson 3

December

Sunday	Monday	Tuesday	Wednesday	Thursday	Friday	Saturday
		1	2			5
6		8	10		12	
13	14	16		18	19	
20		22	24		26	
27		30	31			

DIRECTIONS Trace the name of the month at the top. Trace the numbers and write the missing numbers.

HOME ACTIVITY · Show your child the current month on a calendar. Have him or her point to and say the name of month and the names of the days of the week.

January

Sunday	Monday	Tuesday	Wednesday	Thursday	Friday	Saturday
				1	2	3
4	5	6	7	8	9	10
11	12	13	14	15	16	17
18	19	20	21	22	23	24
25	26	27	28	29	30	31

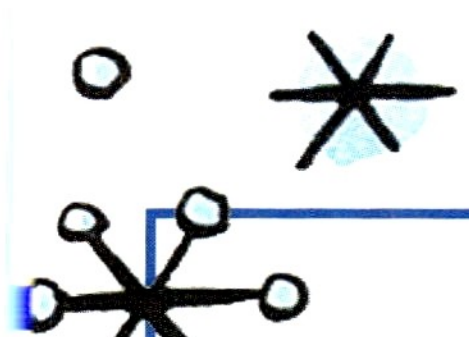

1.
Monday
(Tuesday)
Wednesday

2.
20
18
23

3.
Monday
Wednesday
Saturday

4.
3
4
5

DIRECTIONS **1.** Circle the day that comes right before Wednesday. **2.** Circle the number that is the third Tuesday of this month. **3.** Circle the day that is the tenth of this month. **4.** Circle the number of Wednesdays in this month.

OBJECTIVE • Solve problems by using the skill *use a calendar.*

January	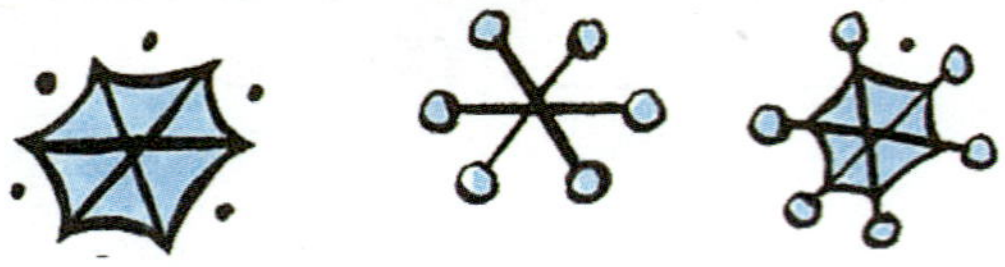
February	
March	
April	
May	
June	
July	
August	
September	
October	
November	
December	

1

February

March

May

2

July

November

January

3

12

10

14

4

April

June

July

DIRECTIONS 1. Circle the month that comes right before April. 2. Circle the first month of the year. 3. Circle the number of months in one year. 4. Circle the month that comes right after May.

HOME ACTIVITY • Show your child an annual calendar. Have your child name the months of the year as he or she points to them.

268 two hundred sixty-eight

Problem Solving Workshop
Strategy • Draw a Picture

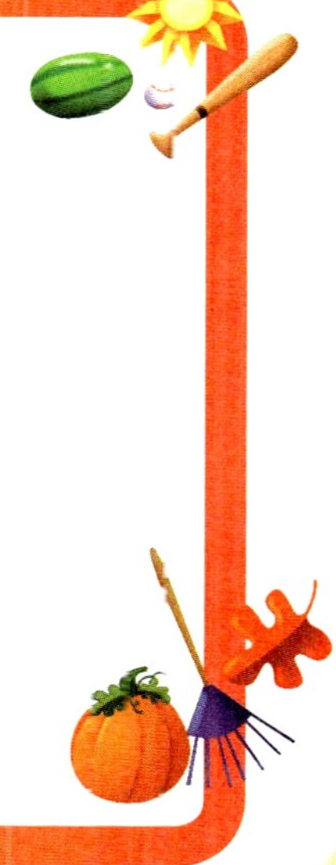

DIRECTIONS **1.** Talk about each picture. Circle your favorite season. **2.** Draw something that you like to do in your favorite season.

OBJECTIVE • Solve problems by using the strategy *draw a picture.*

Chapter 10 • Lesson 5

1. spring

2. summer

3. fall

4. winter

 **HOME ACTIVITY ·** Write the names of the seasons on separate sheets of paper. Have your child cut out and paste magazine pictures of things that relate to each season.

270 two hundred seventy

Explore Temperature

DIRECTIONS   1–6. Use red to circle the picture if it most likely shows hot weather. Use blue to circle the picture if it most likely shows cold weather.

OBJECTIVE • Explore temperature

Chapter 10 • Lesson 6

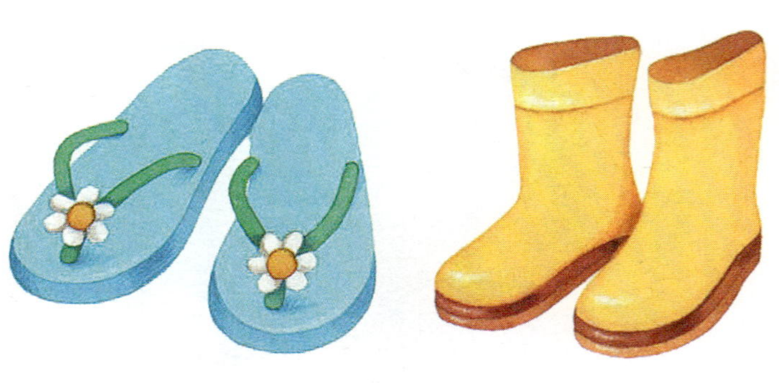

DIRECTIONS   1–4. Circle the clothing that you would most likely wear if you were in this picture.

HOME ACTIVITY · Listen to or watch a weather forecast with your child, and talk about the weather. Ask your child what clothing he or she will wear to dress for the weather.

272   two hundred seventy-two

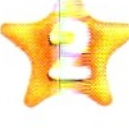 1 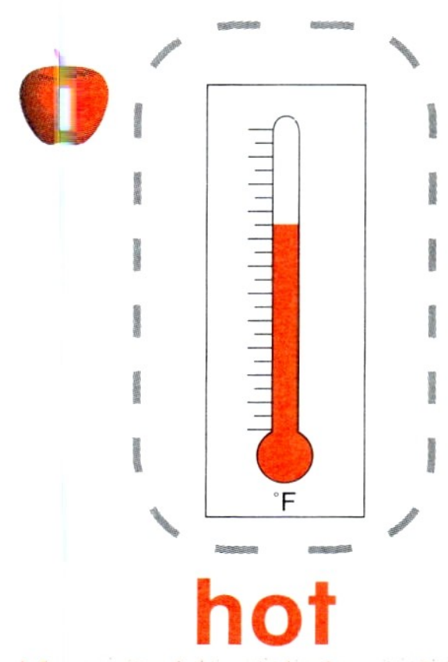  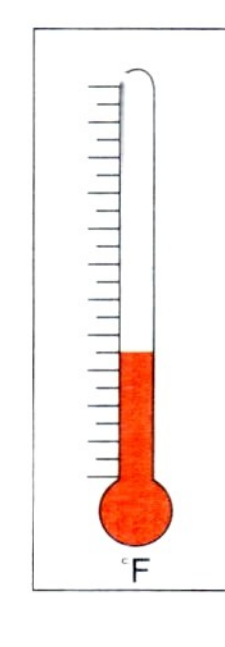

hot   cold

 2 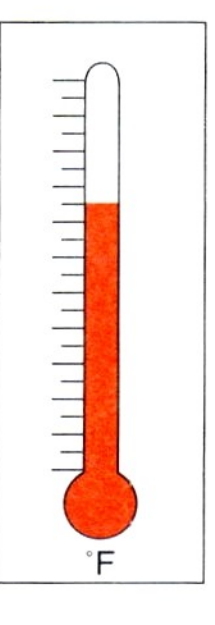  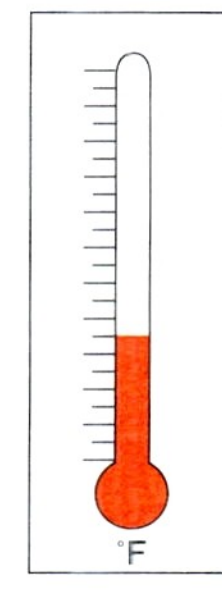

hot   cold

 3 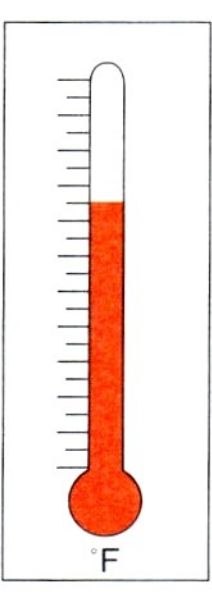  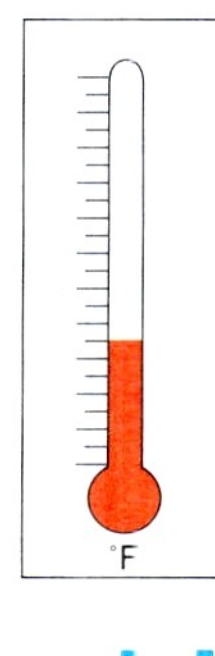

hot   cold

4 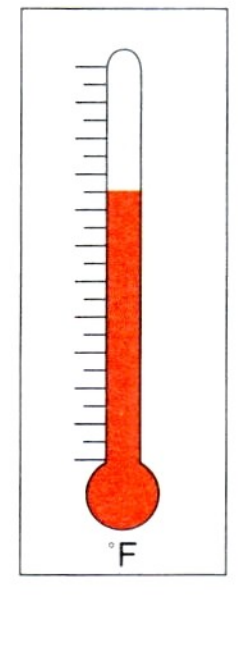 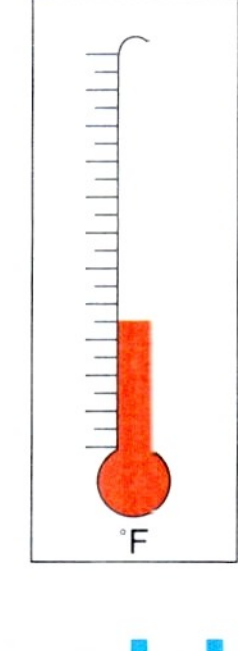

hot   cold

DIRECTIONS   1–4. Circle the thermometer that would most likely go with the picture.

OBJECTIVE • Use temperature to describe situations.

1

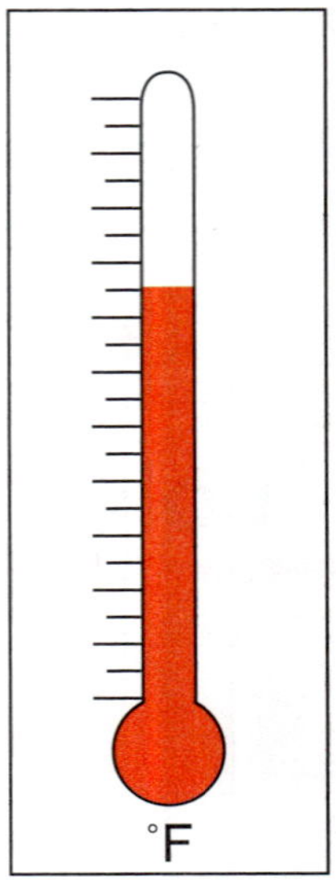

°F

hot

2

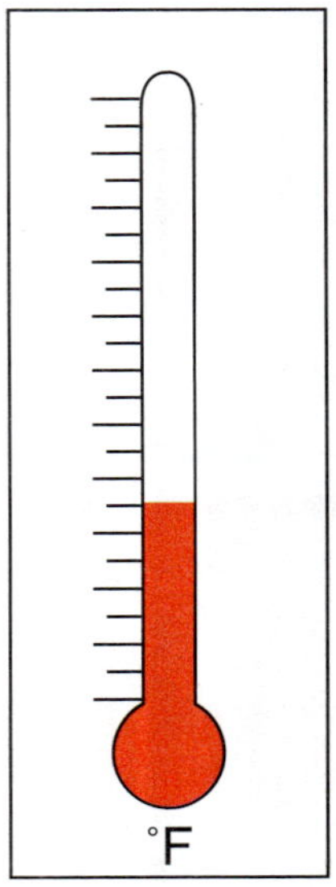

°F

cold

DIRECTIONS 1–2. Draw a picture to show what you would most likely do in this temperature.

HOME ACTIVITY · Ask your child to name an activity that he or she likes to do in cold weather. Then ask your child to name an activity that he or she likes to do in hot weather.

274 two hundred seventy-four

✓ Mid Chapter 10 Review

June

Sunday	Monday	Tuesday	Wednesday	Thursday	Friday	Saturday
	1	2	3	4	5	6
7	8	9	10	11	12	13
14	15	16	17	18	19	20
21	22	23	24	25	26	27
28	29	30				

2 **Tuesdays**

____

3 **Days in June**

____

4

hot   cold

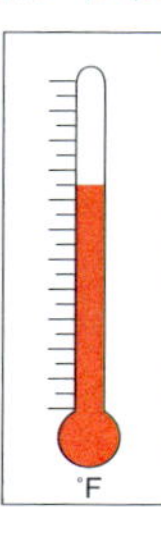

December

Sunday	Monday	Tuesday	Wednesday	Thursday	Friday	Saturday
		1	2	3	4	5
6	7	8	9	10	11	12
13	14	15	16	17	18	19
20	21	22	23	24	25	26
27	28	29	30	31		

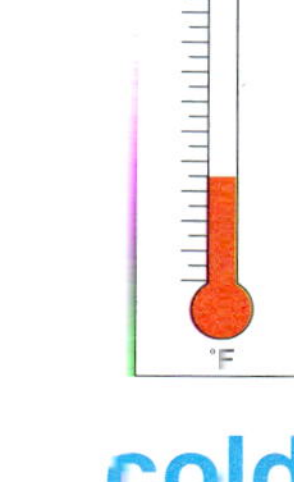

5 **Thursday**

Friday

Sunday

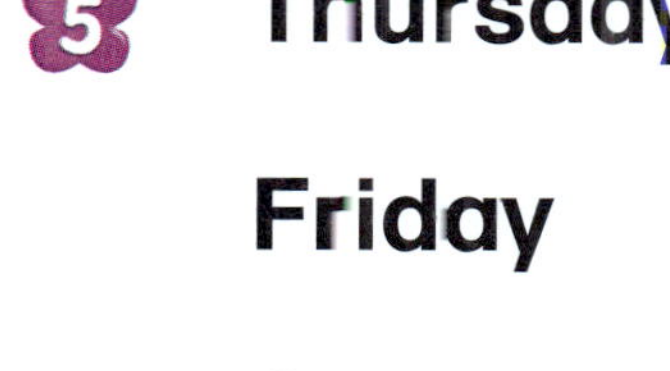

6 **8**

21

23

DIRECTIONS 1. Use blue to color all the Mondays. Use red to color all the Saturdays. **2.** Write how many Tuesdays are in June. **3.** Write how many days are in June. **4.** Circle the thermometer that would most likely go with the picture. **5.** Circle the day that comes right before Saturday. **6.** Circle the number that is the third Monday of this Month.

Name ______________________

✓ Cumulative Review

1 | |
eleven

2 ____¢

3 ____¢

Estimate	Classroom Object	Measure
4 about		about

5 Sunday · Wednesday · Monday · Thursday · Friday · Tuesday · Saturday

DIRECTIONS **1.** Say the number as you count. Write the number. **2–3.** Write how many cents. Circle the coin or set of coins that shows 5¢. **4.** Find the object in the classroom. Estimate about how many paper clips long it is. Write your estimate. Use paper clips to measure the object. Write about how many paper clips long it is. **5.** Point to and say each day of the week. Number the days in order, beginning with Sunday.

More Time, Less Time

1  

2  

3  

4  

DIRECTIONS 1–4. Circle the activity that usually takes more time.

OBJECTIVE • Use time to compare events according to duration.

Chapter 10 • Lesson 8

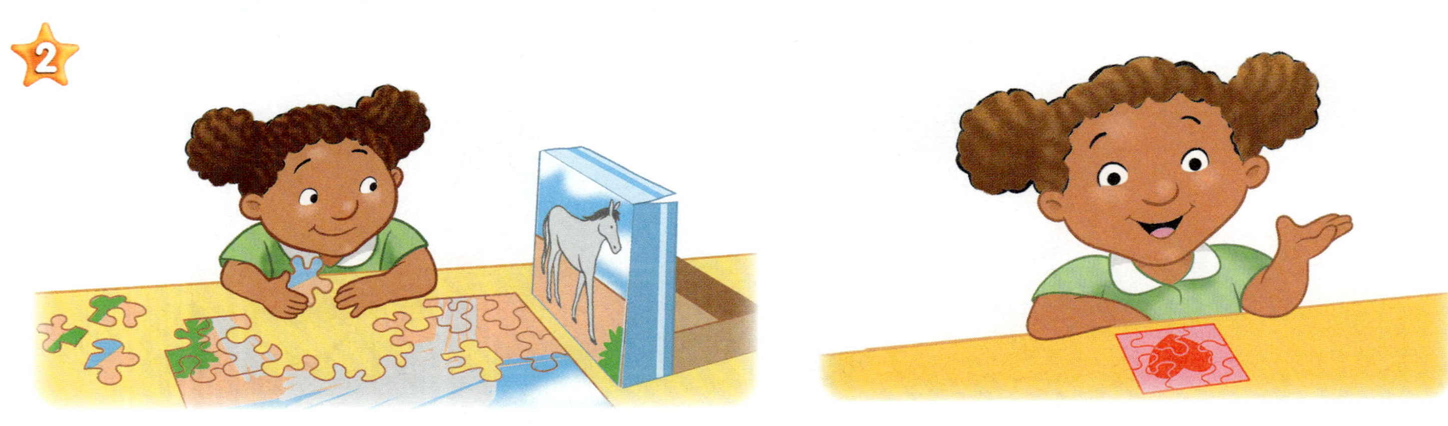

DIRECTIONS **1–4.** Circle the activity that usually takes less time.

HOME ACTIVITY • Ask your child which of two chores, such as making the bed or setting the table would take more time. Have your child do both chores whilst you time them, and then compare which chore actually took more time.

278 two hundred seventy-eight

Name ______________________________

Use a Clock

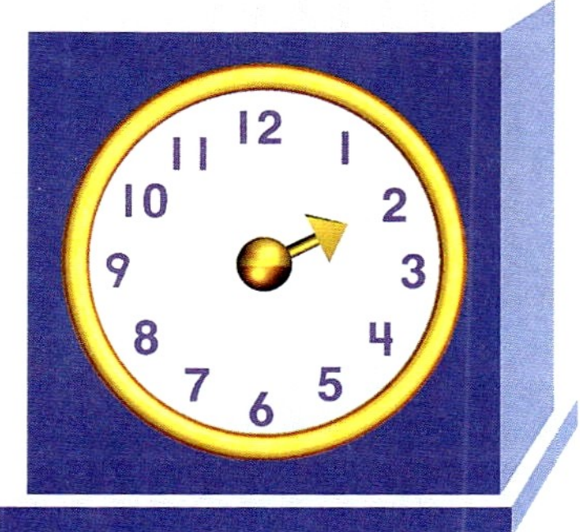

about **2** o'clock

1

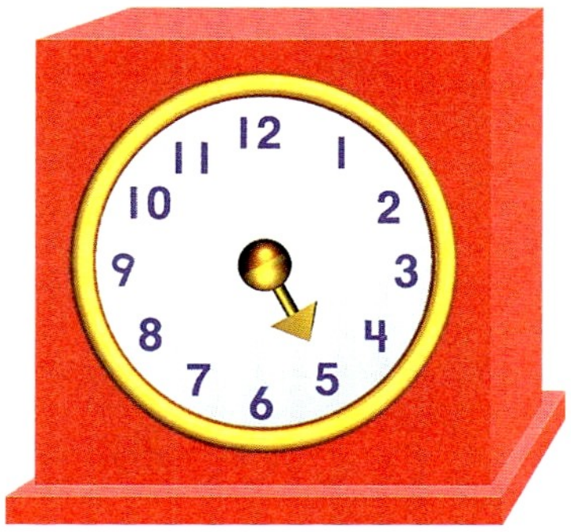

about ______ o'clock

2

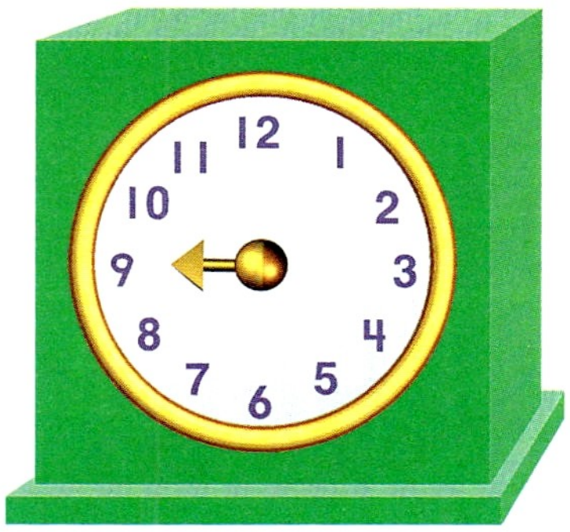

about ______ o'clock

3

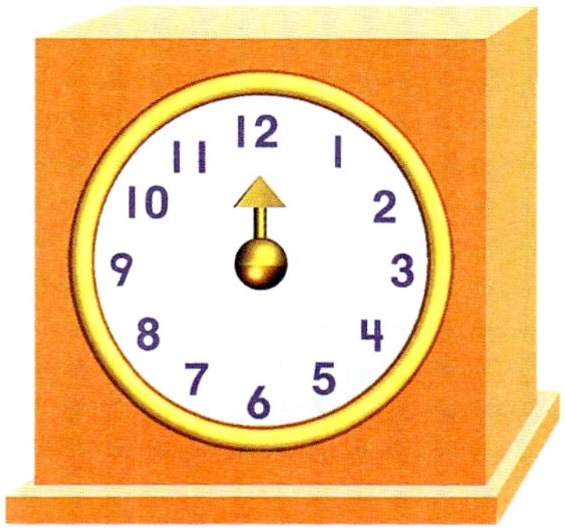

about ______ o'clock

DIRECTIONS **1–3.** About what time does the clock show? Write your answer.

OBJECTIVE • Recognize and explore the hour hand of a clock.

| before 6 o'clock | about 6 o'clock | after 6 o'clock |

1

before 2 o'clock

about 2 o'clock

after 2 o'clock

2

before 7 o'clock

about 7 o'clock

after 7 o'clock

3

before 11 o'clock

about 11 o'clock

after 11 o'clock

DIRECTIONS 1–3. Circle the time shown on the clock.

HOME ACTIVITY · Look at or draw a simple clock. Ask your child questions such as: *Where does the hour hand go to show about 8 o'clock? About 1 o'clock? About 4 o'clock?*

9 o'clock

1

3 o'clock

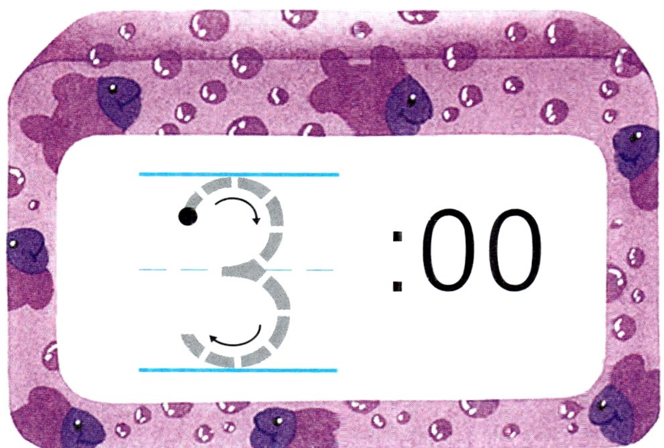

2

_______ o'clock

3

_______ o'clock

DIRECTIONS 1–3. Look at the clock. Write the time two ways.

OBJECTIVE • Identify time to the hour using an analog and digital clock.

Chapter 10 • Lesson 10

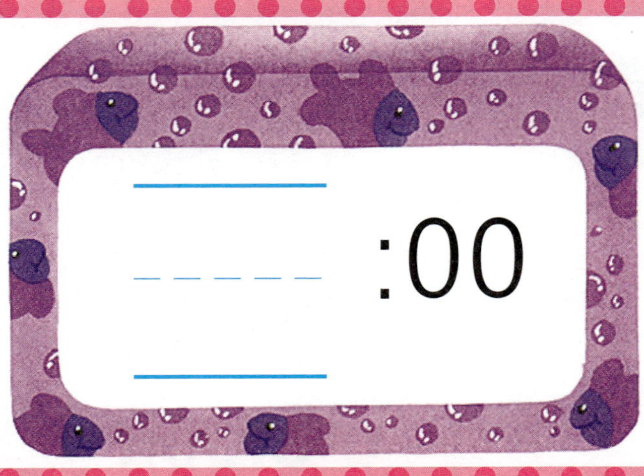

DIRECTIONS **1–2.** Look at the picture. Draw the hour hand to show about what time it might be. **3–4.** Look at the picture. Write a number to show about what time it might be.

HOME ACTIVITY · Help your child tell time to the hour on clocks at home and in the community.

282 two hundred eighty-two

Action Days

Sunday
Touch your toes.

Monday
Touch your head.

Saturday
Stand on one foot.

Friday
Touch your nose.

Tuesday
Touch your shoulders.

Thursday
Clap your hands.

Wednesday
Touch your knees.

	Sunday	Monday	Tuesday	Wednesday	Thursday	Friday	Saturday
Player 1							
Player 2							

DIRECTIONS Play with a partner. Decide who goes first. Take turns spinning the spinner. Say the name of the day you land on. Act it out. Put a check mark (✓) on the chart. The first player to check off all seven days of the week wins the game.

MATERIALS paper clip, pencil

Math Power • This Month

Sunday	Monday	Tuesday	Wednesday	Thursday	Friday	Saturday

DIRECTIONS Make a calendar for this month. Write the name of the month at the top. Write the numbers on the calendar beginning on the first day of the month.

284 two hundred eighty-four

✓ Chapter 10 Review/Test

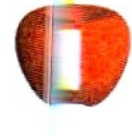

**before
3 o'clock**   **about
3 o'clock**   **after
3 o'clock**

_____
_____ **o'clock**

:00

DIRECTIONS   **1.** Circle the activity that usually takes more time.
2. Circle the time shown on the clock.   **3.** Look at the
clock. Write the time two ways.

✓ Cumulative Review

1

1	2	3	4	5	6	7	8	9	10
11	12	13	14	15	16	17	18	19	20
21	22	23	24	25	26	27	28	29	30
31	32	33	34	35	36	37	38	39	40
41	42	43	44	45	46	47	48	49	50

2 left   right

DIRECTIONS   **1.** Place a penny on each number as you count from 1 to 10. Trace around the 10th penny. Touch each number as you count from 11 to 50. Circle the last number in each row. What pattern do you see?   **2.** Find the first object in the row, and hold it in your left hand. Find the rest of the objects in the row, and take turns holding each object in your right hand. Circle the object that is lighter than the object in your left hand.   **3.** Circle the activity that usually takes less time.

THE WORLD ALMANAC FOR KIDS

Rainy Days

ALMANAC Fact

Problem Solving

Clouds form when many small water droplets join to make large drops. The large drops fall as rain or snow.

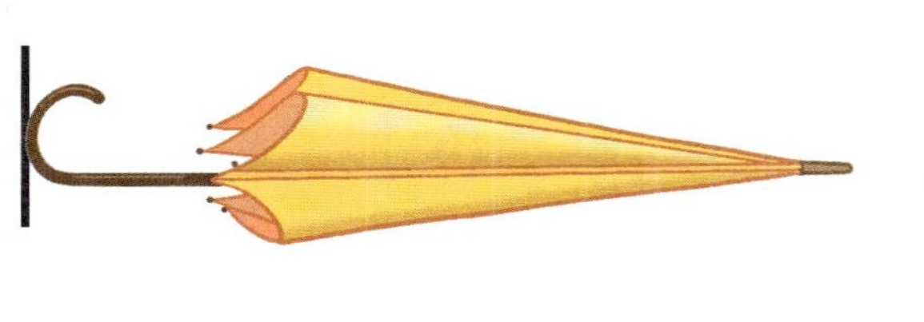

DIRECTIONS 1. Circle the longest umbrella. Mark an X on the shortest umbrella. 2. Draw a picture of a longer umbrella.

TALK Math Tell how you would put the umbrellas in order from shortest to longest.

April Showers

In some places, April is the rainiest month!

April

Sunday	Monday	Tuesday	Wednesday	Thursday	Friday	Saturday
			1 ☀	2 ☀	3 ☀	4 ☀
5 ☀	6 ☀	7 🌧	8 🌧	9 ☀	10 ☀	11 ☀
12 ☀	13 🌧	14 🌧	15 ☀	16 🌧	17 ☀	18 ☀
19 ☀	20 ☀	21 🌧	22 🌧	23 🌧	24 ☀	25 🌧
26 🌧	27 ☀	28 🌧	29 ☀	30 🌧		

DIRECTIONS **1.** On what day of the week did it always rain? Use red to circle the name of the day. On what day of the week was it always sunny? Use yellow to circle the name of the day.
2. Circle the picture that shows what the weather was like on April 18.

 **What is the weather like today?**

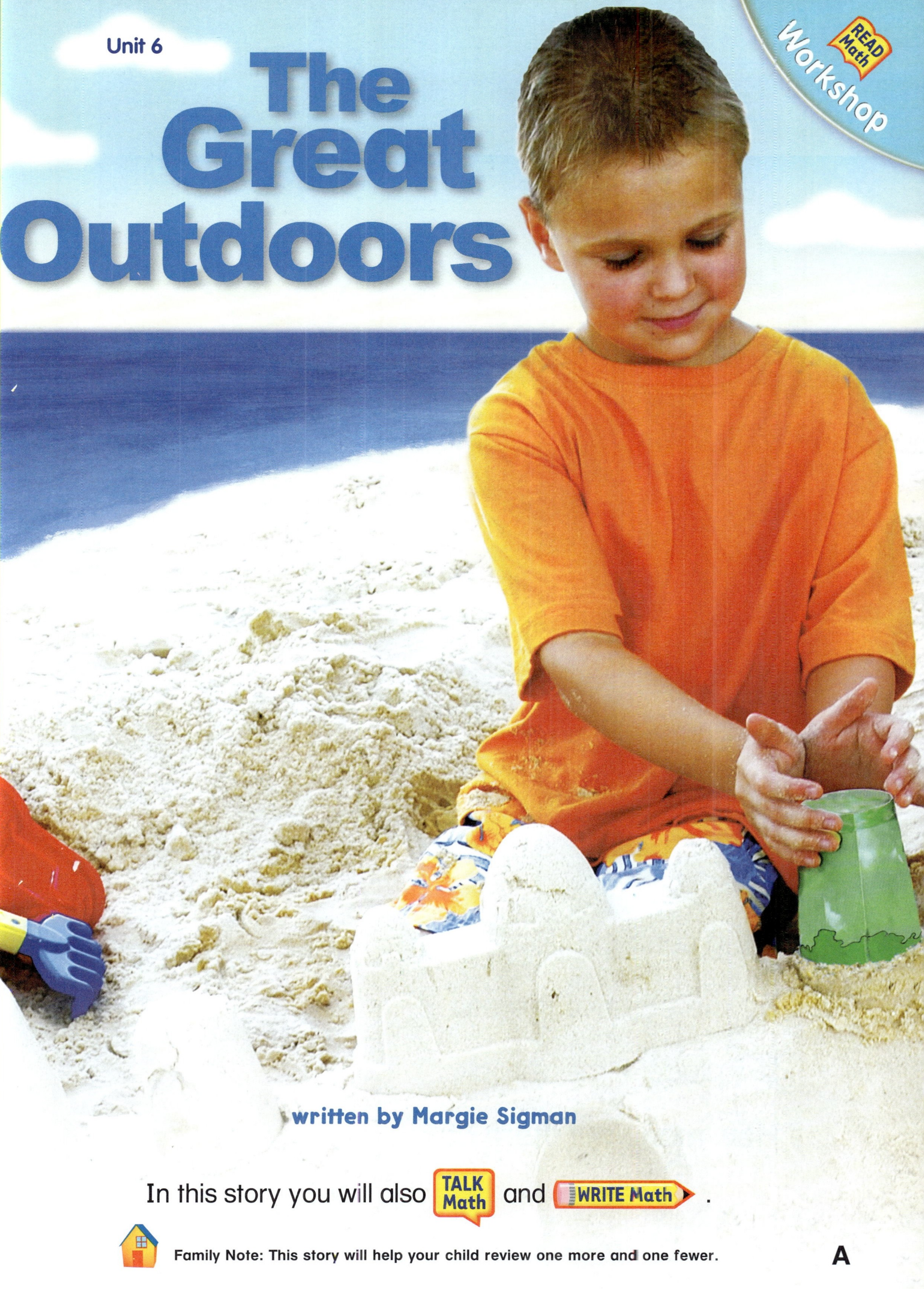

Unit 6
READ Math
Workshop
The Great Outdoors
written by Margie Sigman
In this story you will also TALK Math and WRITE Math .
Family Note: This story will help your child review one more and one fewer.
A

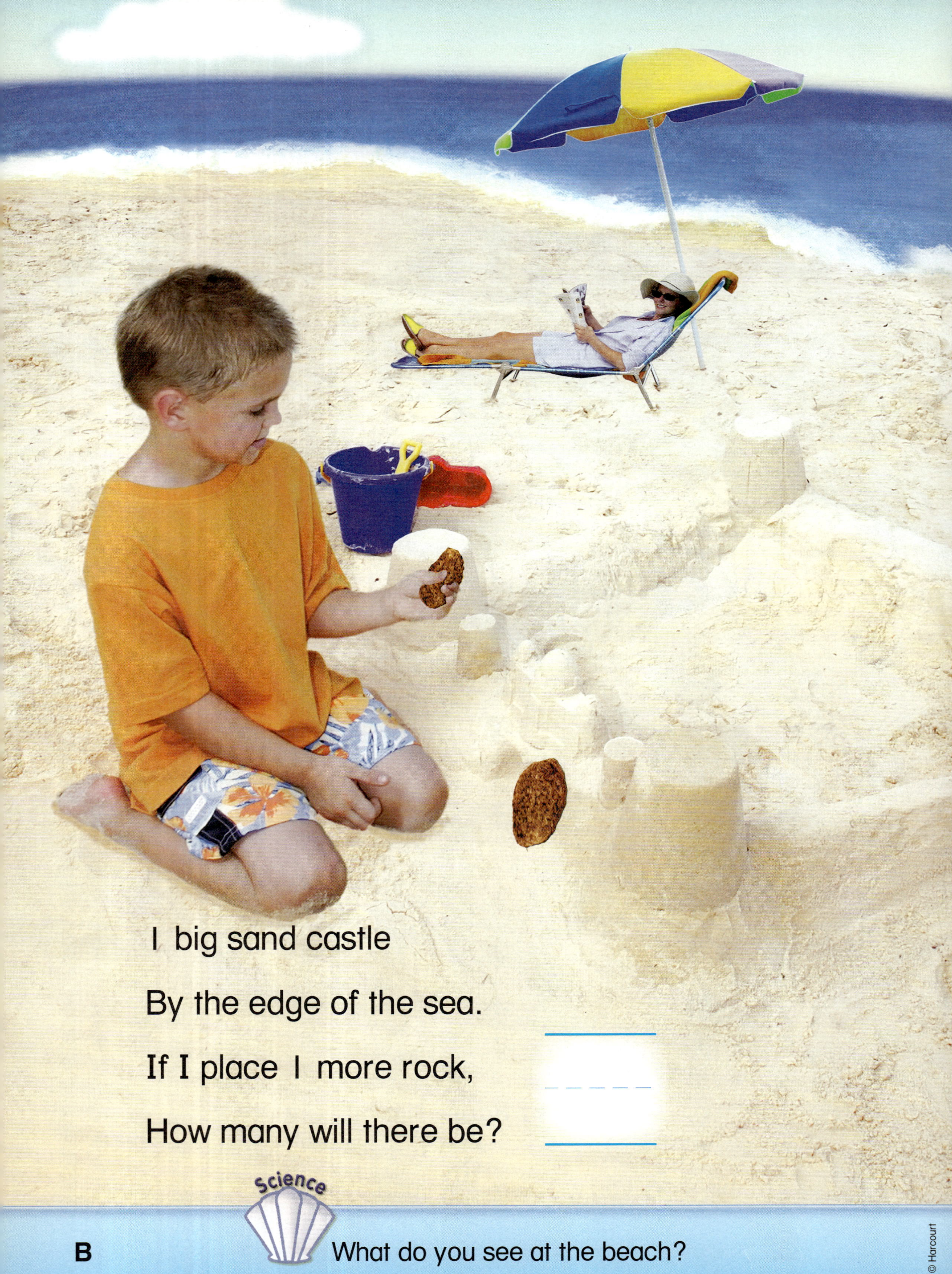

1 big sand castle

By the edge of the sea.

If I place 1 more rock,

How many will there be?

Science

What do you see at the beach?

2 shells on my castle

By the edge of the sea.

If I place 1 more shell,

How many will there be?

Science

What floats on the ocean?

C

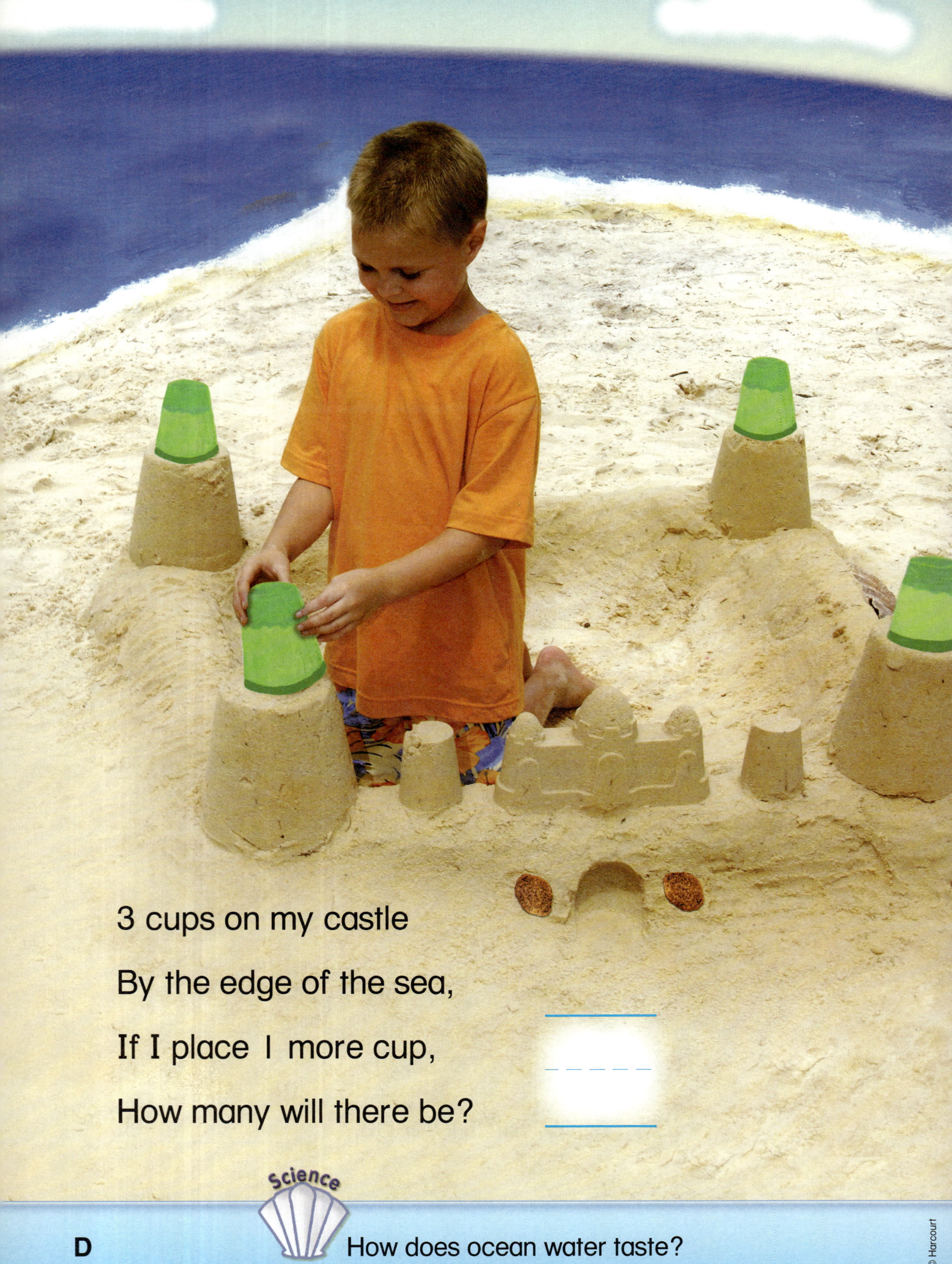

How does ocean water taste?

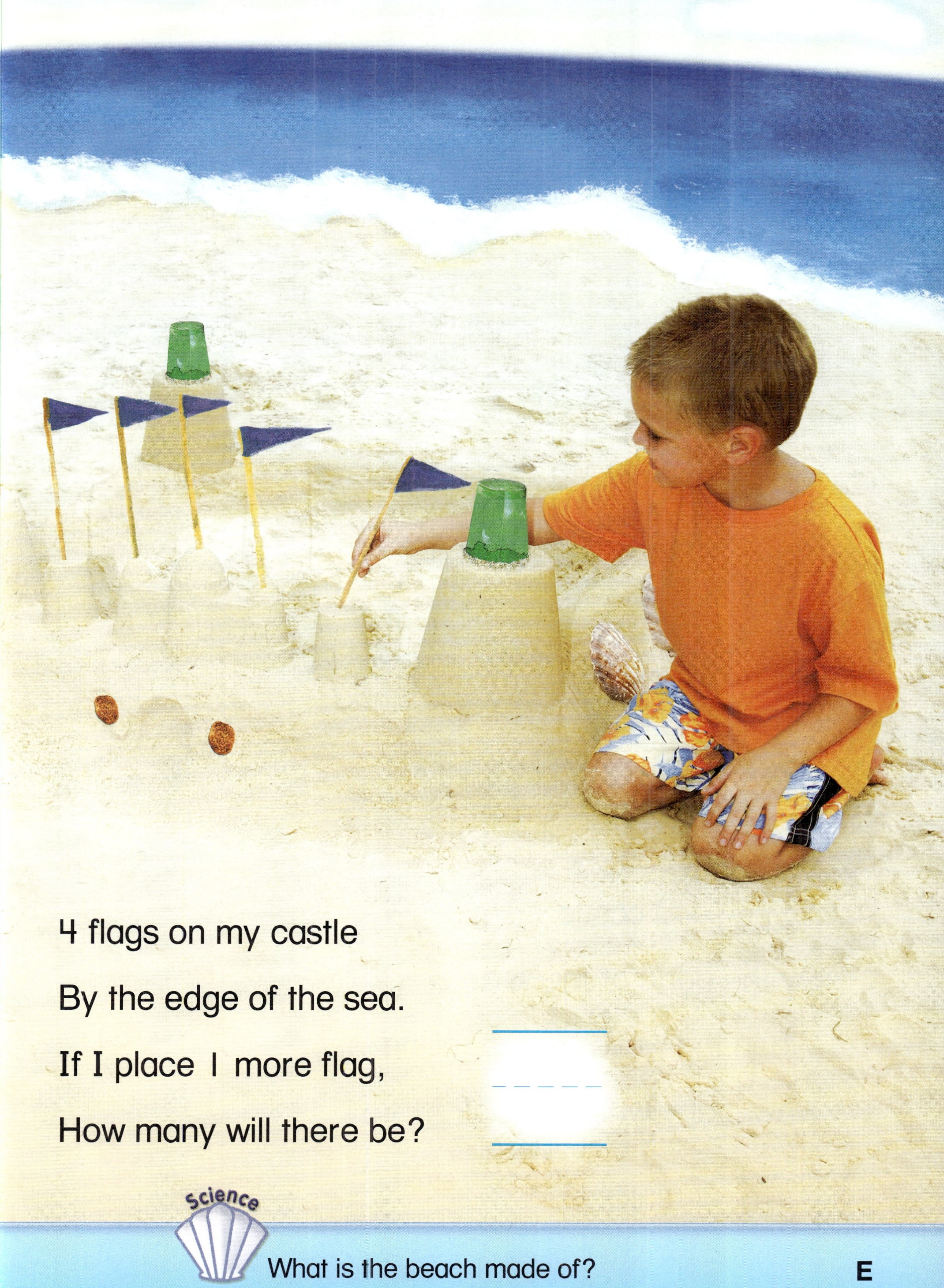

4 flags on my castle

By the edge of the sea.

If I place 1 more flag,

How many will there be?

What do waves do?

Name ____

© Harcourt

DIRECTIONS Draw a sand castle. Draw 8 objects on the sand castle. Share a story about your sandcastle with a classmate.

G

One More and One Fewer

1

2

DIRECTIONS **1.** Draw a set with one more shell.
2. Draw a set with one fewer shell.

H

Dear Family,

My class started Unit 6 today. I will learn about addition and subtraction. Here are some vocabulary words and activities for us to share.

Love, ____

Vocabulary Power

Key Math Vocabulary

Add to combine; to join two separate sets and find the total quantity

Subtract the process of finding out how many are left when a number of items are taken away from a set

Vocabulary Activity

Math on the Move

Show your child a set of 5 objects and a set of 2 objects. Ask him or her how many objects in all.

GO ONLINE

Technology
Multimedia Math Gloassary link at
www.harcourtschool.com/hspmath

School Home CONNECTION

Remember This Your child may already know how to tell you how many objects there will be if you add one more to a set.

Calendar Activity

March						
Sunday	Monday	Tuesday	Wednesday	Thursday	Friday	Saturday
1	2	3	4	5	6	7
8	9	10	11	12	13	14
15	16	17	18	19	20	21
22	23	24	25	26	27	28
29	30	31				

Ask your child to add all the Wednesdays and all the Saturdays in this month.

Practice (after pages 301 and 302)

Have your child use red to circle the days in one week he or she goes to school. Now have him or her use blue to circle the days in one week he or she does not go to school. Write an addition sentence to show this.

Practice (after pages 327 and 328)

Have your child color all the days in one week. Now have your child mark an x on the days in one week that he or she does not go to school. Write a subtraction sentence to show this.

Literature

Look for these books in a library. Ask your child to point out math vocabulary words as you read each book together.

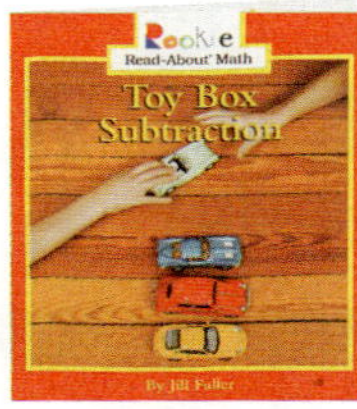

Toy Box Subtraction.
Fuller, Jill.
Children's Press, 2005.

Addition Annie.
Gisler, David.
Children's Press, 2002.

Construction Countdown.
Olson, K. C.
Henry Holt, 2004.

Addition
Theme: Summer Fun

1

2

DIRECTIONS 1-2. Circle the set that has more.

Family Note: This page checks your child's understanding of important concepts and skills needed for success in Chapter 11.

Problem Solving Workshop
Strategy • Act It Out

DIRECTIONS 1-2. Listen to and act out the story. Write the number that shows how many children in all.

OBJECTIVE • Solve problems by using the strategy *act it out.*

DIRECTIONS **1.** Listen to and act out the story. Write the number that shows how many books in all. **2.** Listen to and act out the story. Write the number that shows how many blocks in all.

HOME ACTIVITY • Tell your child a short story about adding 2 objects to a group of 5. Have your child use toys to act out the story and then write the number that shows how many objects in all.

294 two hundred ninety-four

3

1

4

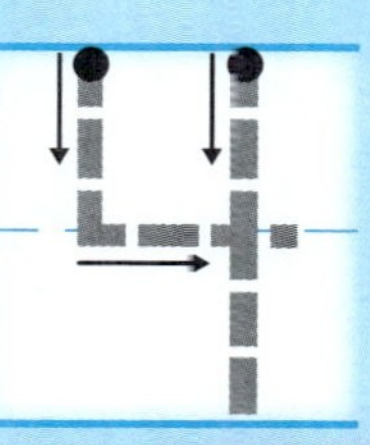

2

4

8

2

DIRECTIONS **1–3.** Listen to the story. Model the story with cubes. Draw the cubes. Write the number that shows how many in all.

OBJECTIVE • Use concrete objects to model addition.

3

3

2

6

4

5

HOME ACTIVITY · Tell your child a short
vacation story about adding 3 objects to a
group of 4. Have your child use small objects
such as beans to make each group in the story
and then write the number that shows how
many objects in all.

296 two hundred ninety-six

Joining Groups

1

$$2 \quad \text{and} \quad 2 \quad \text{is} \quad 4$$

2

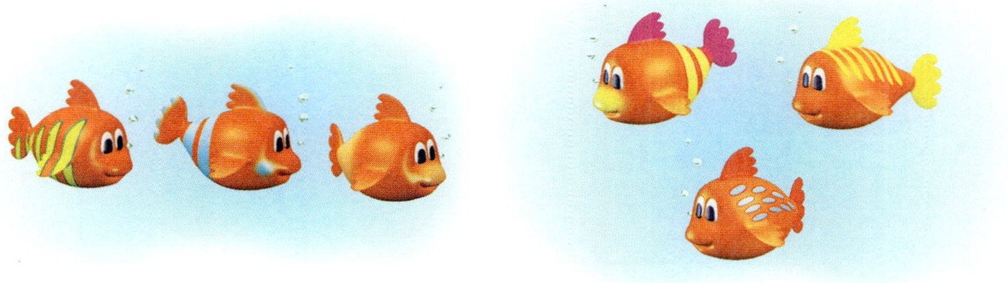

____ and ____ is ____

3

____ and ____ is ____

DIRECTIONS   **1–3.** Place cubes on the objects in each group. Write how many in each group. Circle the two groups. Write how many in all.

OBJECTIVE • Use objects and pictures to understand joining groups.

1

_____ and _____ is _____

2

_____ and _____ is _____

3

_____ and _____ is _____

DIRECTIONS 1–3. **Write how many in each group. Circle the two groups. Write how many in all.**

 **HOME ACTIVITY** · Have your child draw a group of 2 beach balls and a group of 7 beach balls. Have your child write how many beach balls are in each group. Then have him or her write how many beach balls in all.

298 two hundred ninety-eight

Name ___________________________________

1

4   and   3   is   7

2

6   and   2   is   8

3

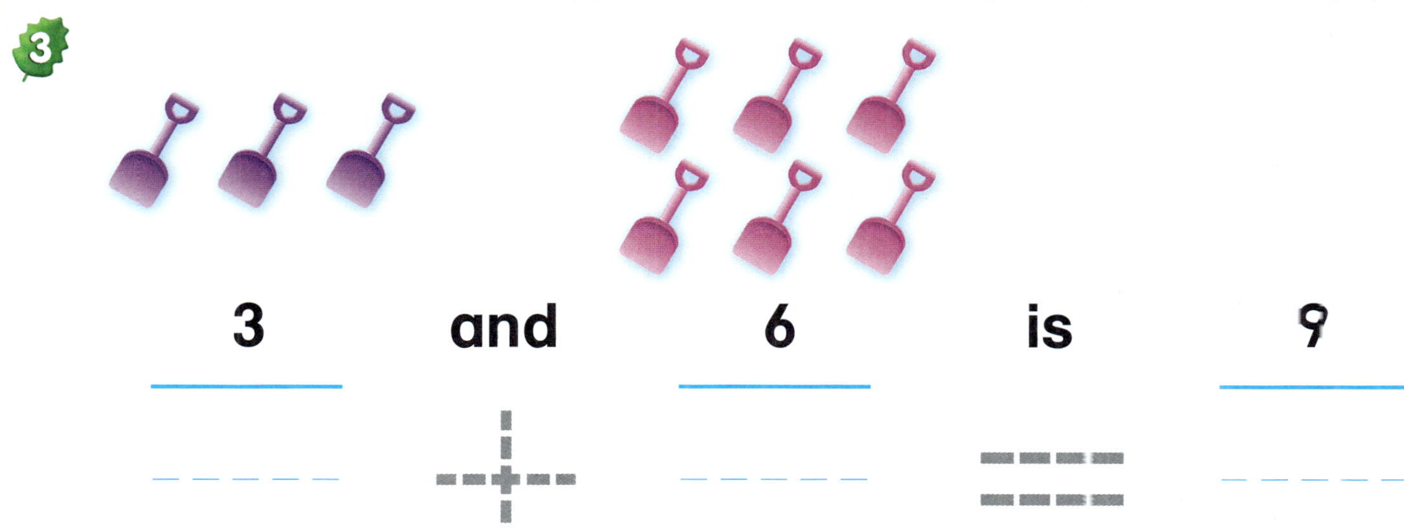

3   and   6   is   9

DIRECTIONS   **1–3.** Write how many in each group. Circle the two groups. Trace the symbols. Write how many in all.

OBJECTIVE • Use symbols to represent addition sentences.

Chapter 11 • Lesson 4

1

2   and   5   is   7

2 + 5 = 7

2

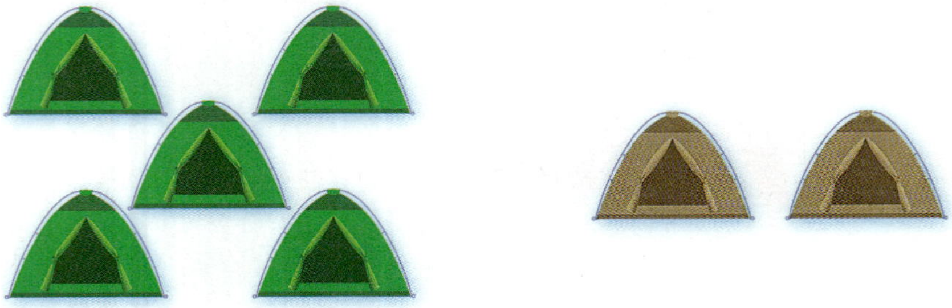

5   and   2   is   7

___ + ___ = ___

3

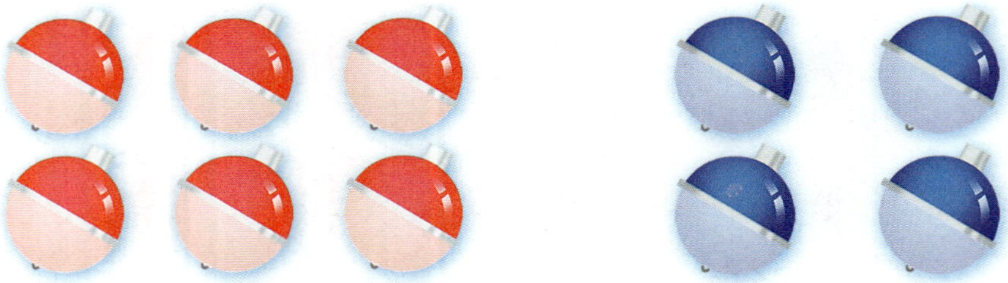

6   and   4   is   10

___ + ___ = ___

DIRECTIONS 1–3. Write how many in each group. Circle the two groups. Trace the symbols. Write how many in all.

HOME ACTIVITY • Have your child use small objects to model one of the addition sentences on this page. Then have him or her combine the groups before the = to show the same amount as the number after the =.

 Mid Chapter 11 Review

1

3   4   _______

2

_______   _______   _______

_____ **and** _____ **is** _____

_______   _______   _______

3

2   **and**   **6**   **is**   **8**

_______   ┼   _______   ═   _______

_______   _______

DIRECTIONS **1.** Model the numbers with cubes. Draw the cubes. Write the number that shows how many in all. **2.** Write how many in each group. Circle the two groups. Write how many in all. **3.** Write how many in each group. Circle the two groups. Trace the symbols. Write how many in all.

Cumulative Review

1

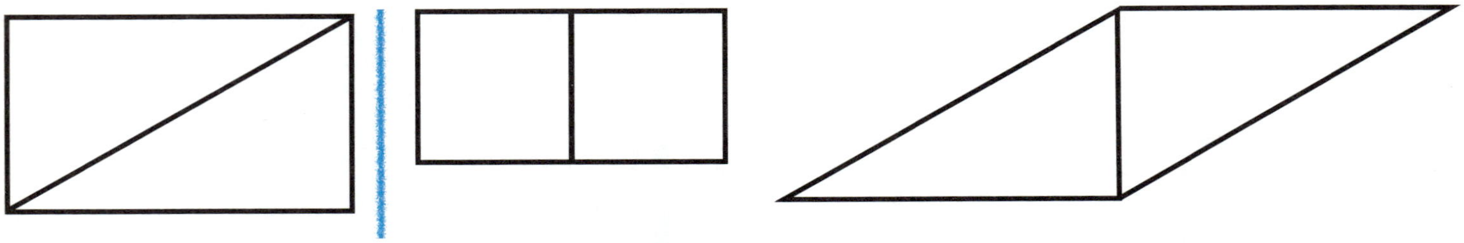

2 spring

3

4   2   _____

DIRECTIONS **1.** Find two plane figures that make the figure at the beginning of the row. Use these two figures to find the figure that has the same area as the figure at the beginning of the row. Circle the figure. **2.** Look at the name of the season. Draw something that happens in that season. **3.** Model the numbers with cubes. Draw the cubes. Write the number that tells how many in all.

302 three hundred two

Addition Patterns

1
$$1 + 1 = \underline{}$$

2
$$2 + 1 = \underline{}$$

3
$$3 + 1 = \underline{}$$

4
$$4 + 1 = \underline{}$$

DIRECTIONS 1–4. How many shells? Draw one more shell. Write the number of shells in all to complete the addition sentence.

OBJECTIVE • Represent an addition pattern of one more in addition sentences.

1 5 + 1 = ___

2 6 + 1 = ___

3 7 + 1 = ___

4 8 + 1 = ___

5 9 + 1 = ___

DIRECTIONS 1–5. How many shells? Draw one more shell. Write the number of shells in all to complete the addition sentence.

HOME ACTIVITY · Draw objects in a column beginning with a set of 1 to a set of 9. Have your child draw one more object beside each set, and write how many in all.

Addition Sentences 

1.

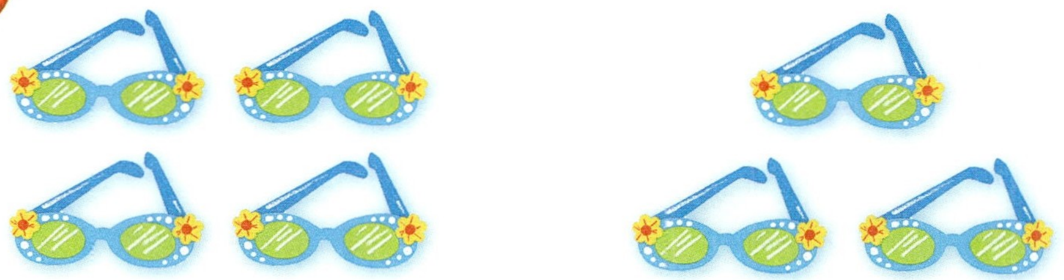

$$4 + 3 = 7$$

2.

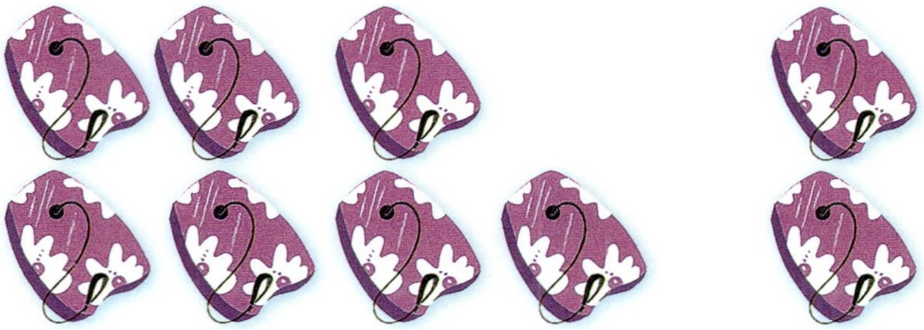

$$\_\_\_ + \_\_\_ = \_\_\_$$

3.

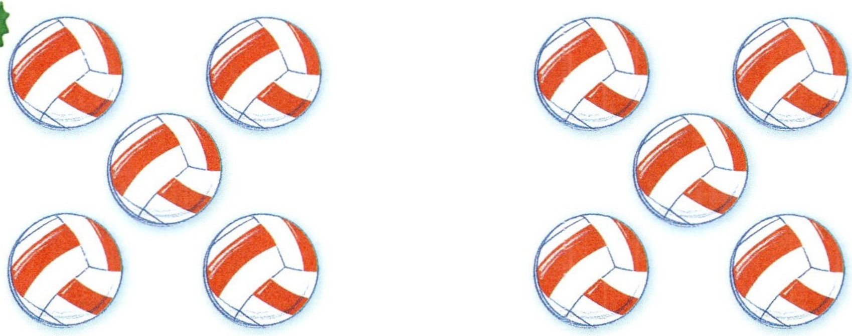

$$\_\_\_ + \_\_\_ = \_\_\_$$

DIRECTIONS Tell a story about the objects. Complete the addition sentence.

1

_____ + _____ = _____

2

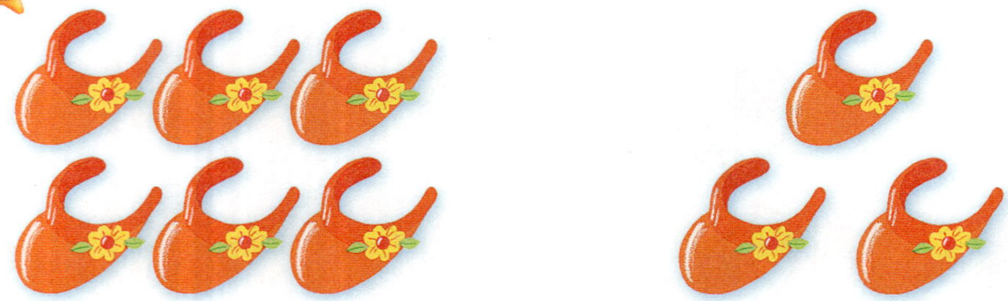

_____ + _____ = _____

3

_____ + _____ = _____

DIRECTIONS 1–3. Tell a story about the objects. Complete the addition sentence.

 **HOME ACTIVITY** • Give your child 6 socks of one color and 4 socks of another color. Ask your child to tell a story about the socks. Then write this addition sentence, and have your child complete it: _ + _ = _.

306 three hundred six

Name ______________________________

Create and Model Addition Problems

1

2

DIRECTIONS I–2. Tell an addition story. Model your story with counters. Color the counters. Use count on to find the sum. Complete the addition sentence.

OBJECTIVE • Use concrete objects to create and model an addition problem.

Chapter I I • Lesson 7

three hundred seven **307**

308 three hundred eight

$$4¢ \ + \ \underline{}¢ \ = \ 6¢$$

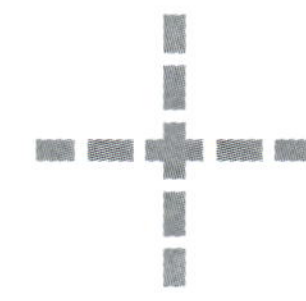

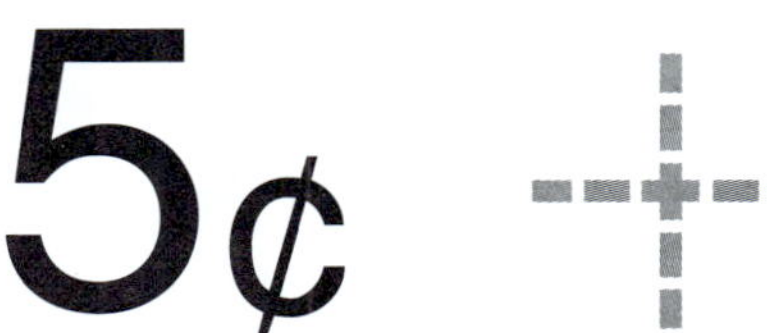

$$5¢ \ + \ \underline{}¢ \ = \ 8¢$$

DIRECTIONS 1–2. Use pennies to find the missing number. Draw the pennies. Write the missing number.

Chapter 11 · Lesson 8

$$4¢ \; + \; \underline{}¢ \; = \; 7¢$$

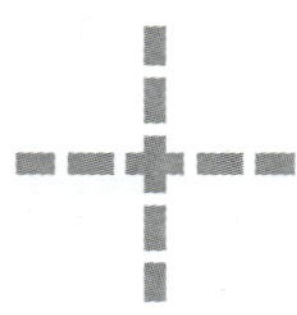

$$6¢ \; + \; \underline{}¢ \; = \; 10¢$$

DIRECTIONS **1–2.** Use pennies to find the missing number. Draw the pennies. Write the missing number.

HOME ACTIVITY • Show your child an object with a price tag of up to 10 cents. Show your child a group of pennies less than the amount of the object. Ask your child to tell you how many more pennies they need to buy the object.

310 three hundred ten

Problem Solving Workshop
Skill • Use a Model

1

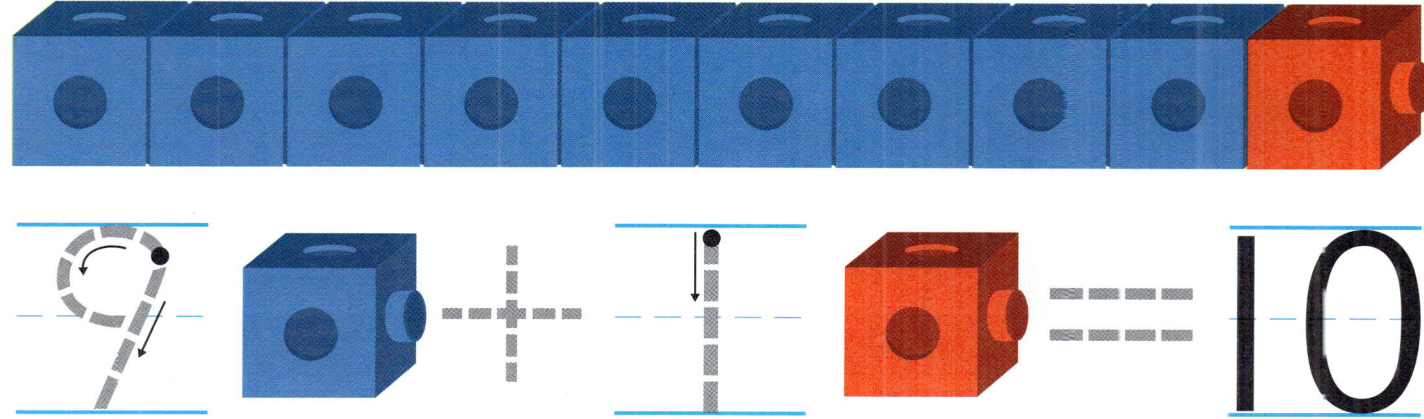

9 + 1 = 10

2

___ + ___ = 10

3

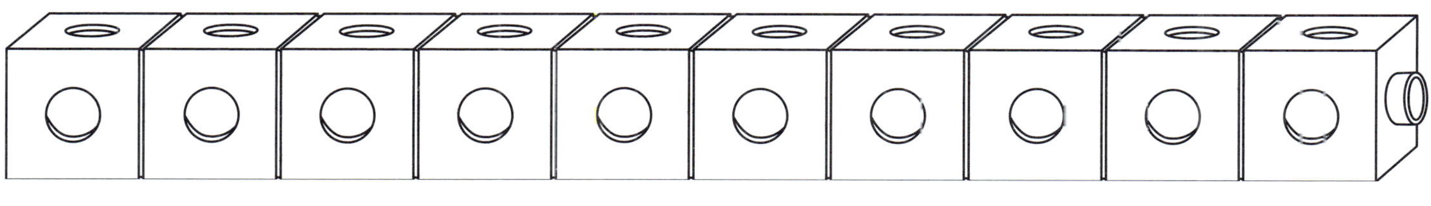

___ + ___ = 10

DIRECTIONS 1–3. Use two colors of cubes to show different ways to make 10. Color the cubes. Complete the addition sentence for each model.

OBJECTIVE • Solve problems by using the skill *use a model*.

1

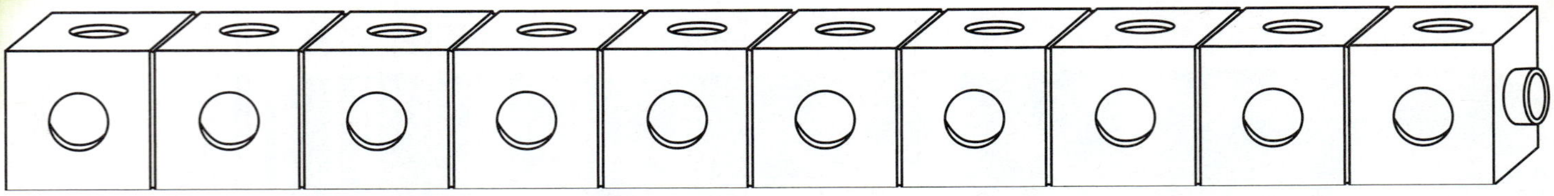

2

3

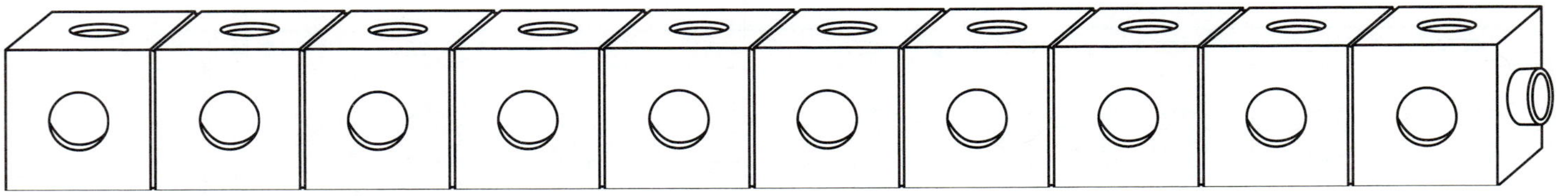

 **HOME ACTIVITY** • Give your child ten pennies. Have your child arrange the coins to show different combinations of heads and tails. Write the addition sentences.

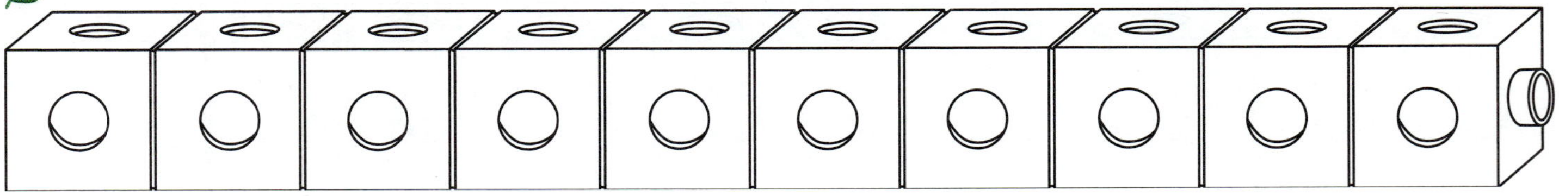

312 three hundred twelve

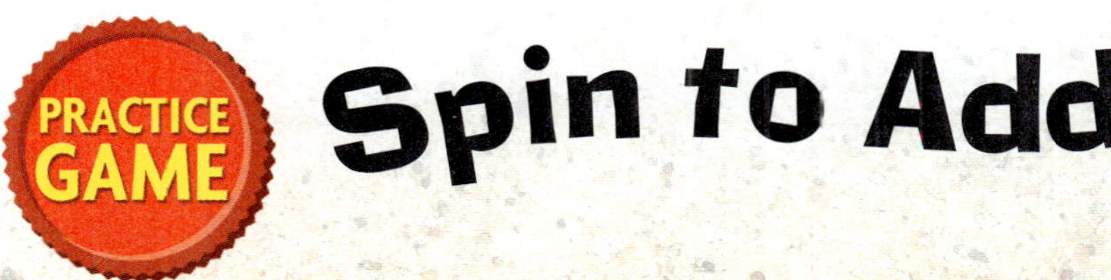

Spin to Add

0 1 2 3 + 4 5 6 7

Spin to Add	
Player 1	
Player 2	

DIRECTIONS Play with a partner. Decide who goes first. Take turns spinning to get a number from each spinner. Use cubes to model your numbers and make a cube train to show how many in all. Compare your cube train with your partner's. Make a tally mark on the table for the player who has more cubes. The player who has the most tally marks after five spins wins the game.

MATERIALS Two paper clips, pencils, connecting cubes

Math Power • Doubles and Near Doubles

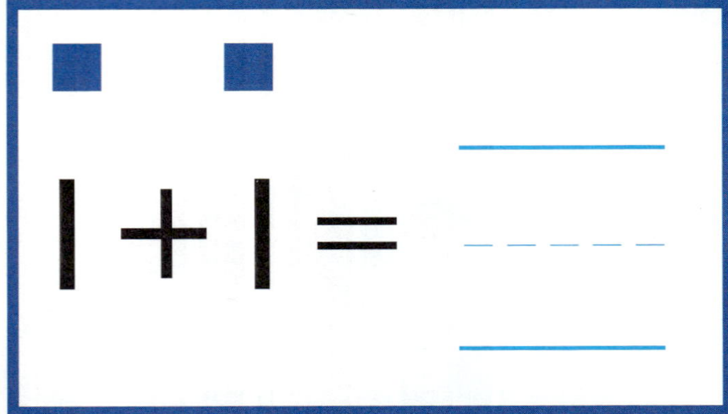

$1 + 1 =$ _____

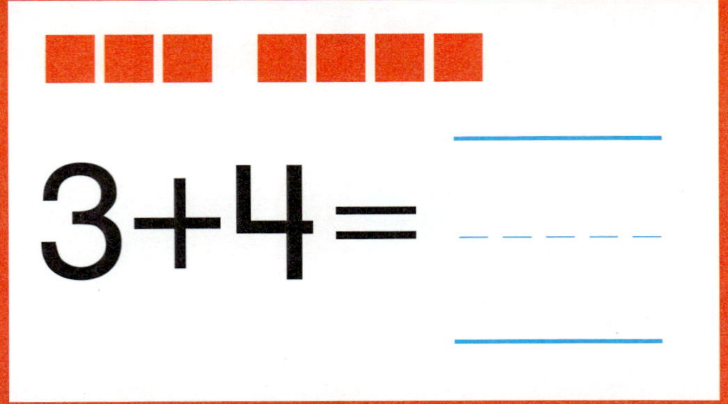

$3 + 4 =$ _____

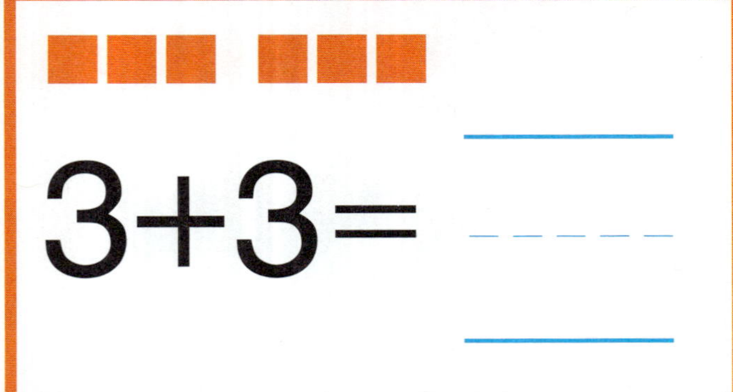

$3 + 3 =$ _____

$2 + 3 =$ _____

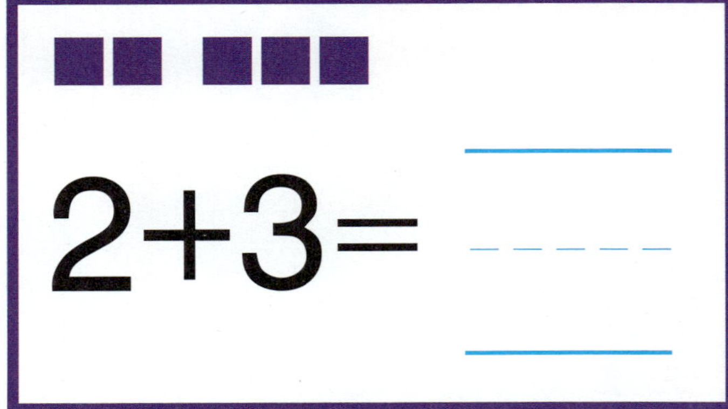

$4 + 4 =$ _____

$1 + 2 =$ _____

$2 + 2 =$ _____

$4 + 5 =$ _____

DIRECTIONS Complete the addition sentences for each model. Draw a line to the addition sentence that shows one more.

314 three hundred fourteen

Chapter 11 Review/Test

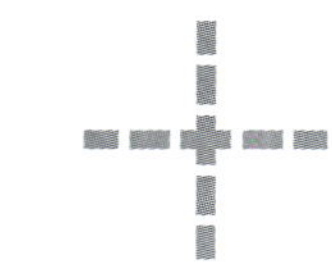

$$7 \quad + \quad 1 \quad = \quad \underline{}$$

 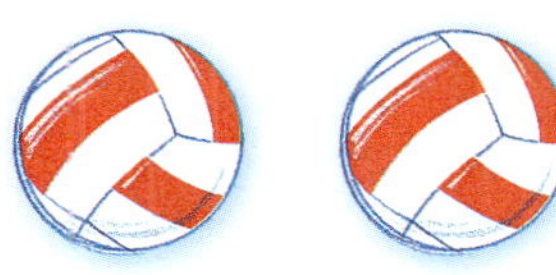

$$\underline{} \quad + \quad \underline{} \quad = \quad \underline{}$$

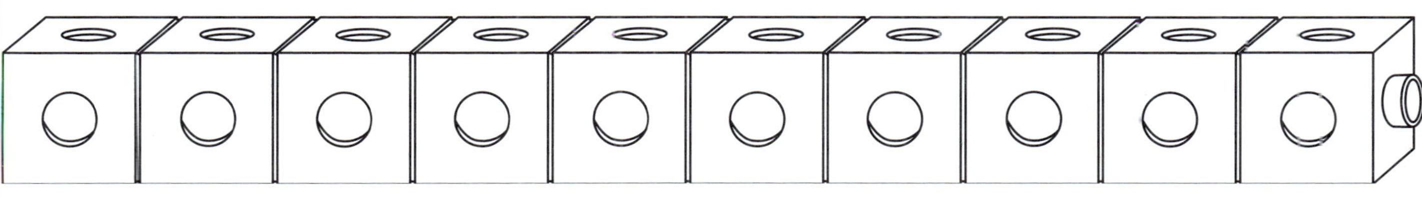

  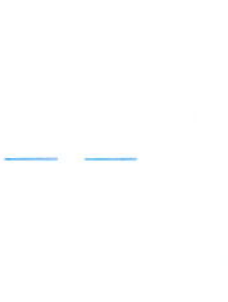 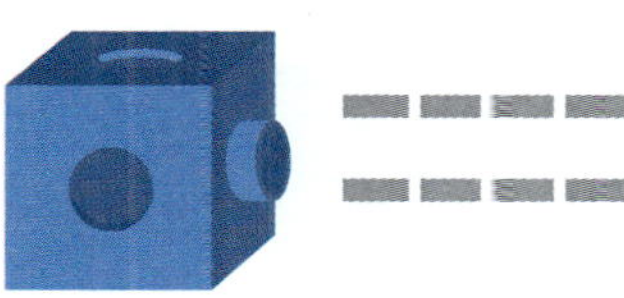 

$$\underline{} \quad + \quad \underline{} \quad = \quad 10$$

DIRECTIONS **1.** How many shells? Draw one more shell. Write the number of shells in all to complete the addition sentence. **2.** Tell a story about the objects. Complete the addition sentence. **3.** Use two colors of cubes to show a way to make 10. Color the cubes. Complete the addition sentence.

1. 

3. 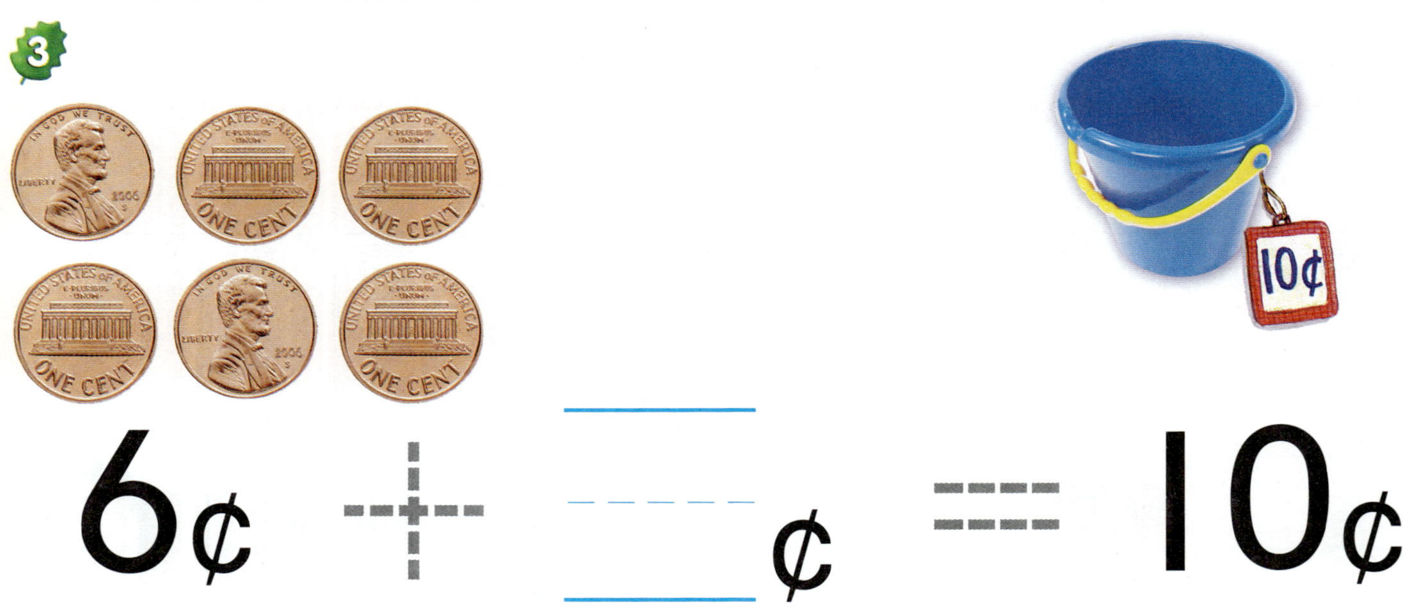

DIRECTIONS **1.** Find the first object in the row, and hold it in your left hand. Find the rest of the objects in the row, and take turns holding each object in your right hand. Circle the object that is heavier than the object in your left hand. **2.** Circle the time shown on the clock. **3.** Use pennies to find the missing number. Draw the pennies. Write the missing number.

Subtraction
Theme: Ocean Life

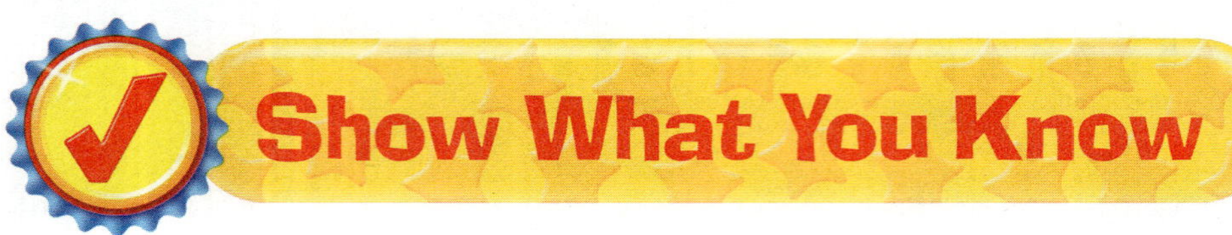

Show What You Know

1

2

3

Family Note: This page checks your child's understanding of important concepts and skills needed for success in Chapter 12.

318 three hundred eighteen

Problem Solving Workshop
Strategy • Act It Out

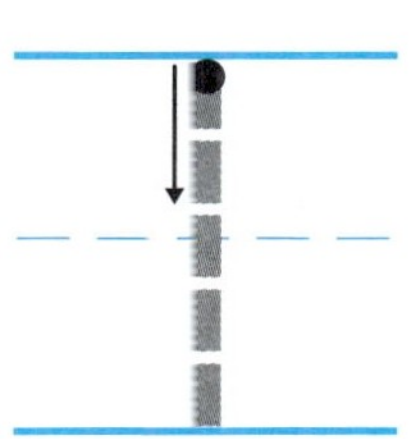

DIRECTIONS 1–2. Listen to and act out the story. Write the number that shows how many children are left.

OBJECTIVE • Solve problems by using the strategy *act it out*.

DIRECTIONS   **1.** Listen to and act out the story. Write the number that shows how many books are left.   **2.** Listen to and act out the story. Write the number that shows how many cups are left.

HOME ACTIVITY · Tell your child a short subtraction story. Have your child use toys to act out the story and then write the number that shows how many toys are left.

320   three hundred twenty

Model Subtraction

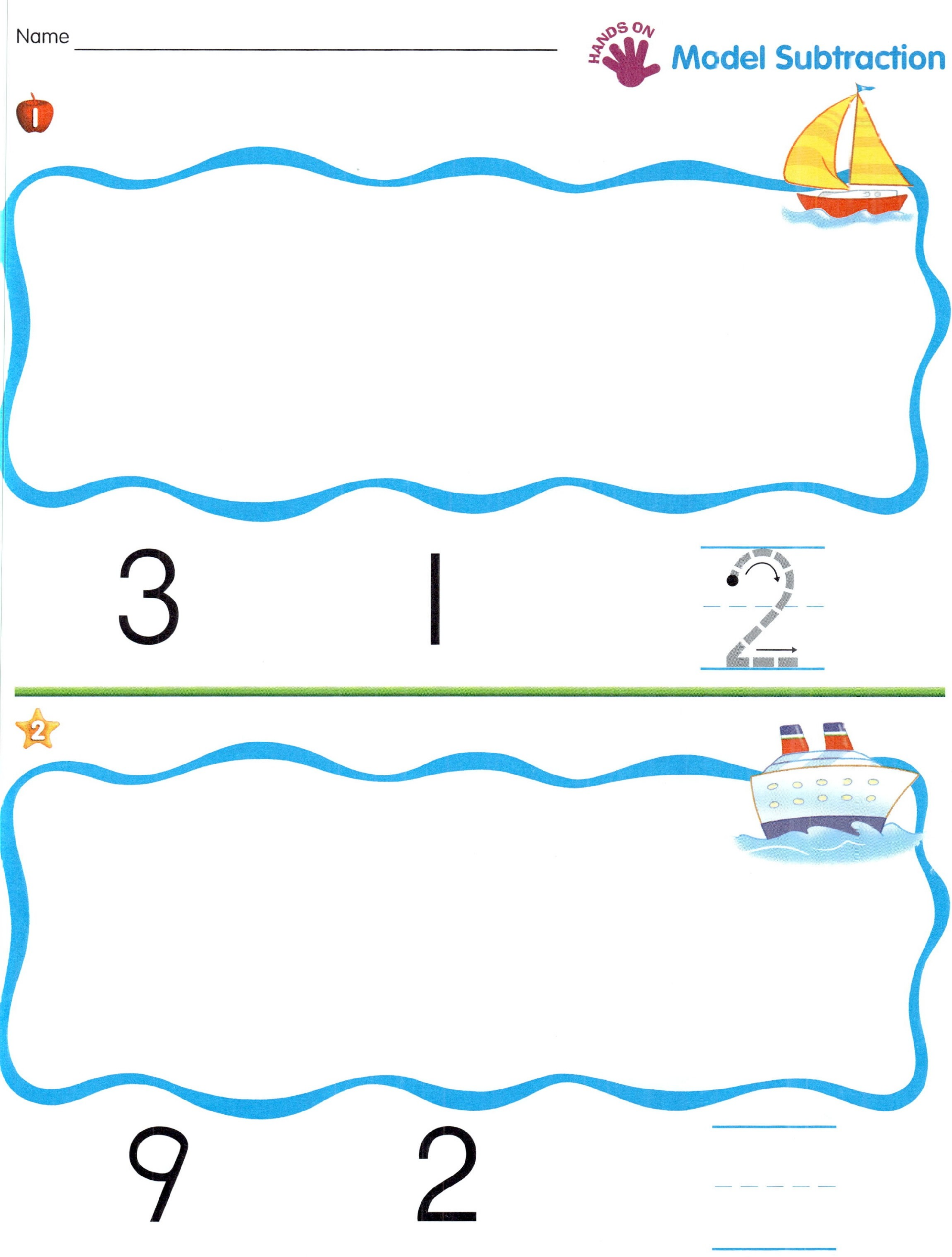

1

3   1   2

2

9   2

4   3

7   5

DIRECTIONS **1–2.** Listen to the story. Model the story with cubes. Write the number that shows how many are left.

HOME ACTIVITY • Tell your child a short subtraction story. Have your child act out the story using objects and tell how many objects are left.

1

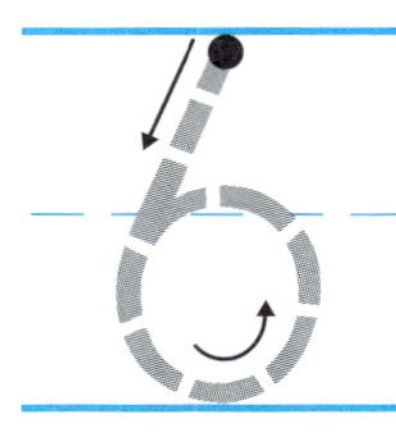 take away  **4** is 

2

take away **7** is

3

take away **5** is

DIRECTIONS 1–3. Write how many there are in all. Mark an X on the animals that are taken away. Write how many are left.

OBJECTIVE • Use pictures to understand separating groups.

DIRECTIONS 1–3. Write how many there are in all. Mark an X on the animals that are taken away. Write how many are left.

HOME ACTIVITY • Have your child draw a group of ten or fewer balloons and then mark an X on some balloons to show that they have popped. Have your child write the number that tells how many balloons are left.

324 three hundred twenty-four

Introduce Symbols to Subtract

1

7   take away   4   is   3

2

10   take away   6   is   4

3

8   take away   2   is   6

DIRECTIONS 1–3. Write how many fish there are in all. Mark an X on the fish that are taken away. Complete the subtraction sentence to show how many are left.

OBJECTIVE • Use symbols to represent subtraction sentences.

1.

8   take away   5   is   3

2.

9   take away   3   is   6

3.

10   take away   5   is   5

DIRECTIONS   **1–3.** Write how many fish there are in all. Mark an X on the fish that are taken away. Complete the subtraction sentence to show how many are left.

HOME ACTIVITY · Ask your child to choose one subtraction sentence on the page. Have your child point to the sign used to represent *take away* and the sign that shows *is equal to*. Ask your child to tell you which number shows how many in all, which shows how many are being taken away, and which shows how many are left.

326   three hundred twenty-six

✓ Mid Chapter 12 Review

1

8   1   _____

2

_____ take away **6** is _____

3

8   take away   5   is   3

DIRECTIONS   **1.** Listen to the story. Model the story with cubes. Write the number that shows how many are left.   **2.** Write how many there are in all. Mark an X on the animals that are taken away. Write how many are left.   **3.** Write how many fish there are in all. Mark an X on the fish that are taken away. Complete the subtraction sentence to show how many are left.

✓ Cumulative Review

1

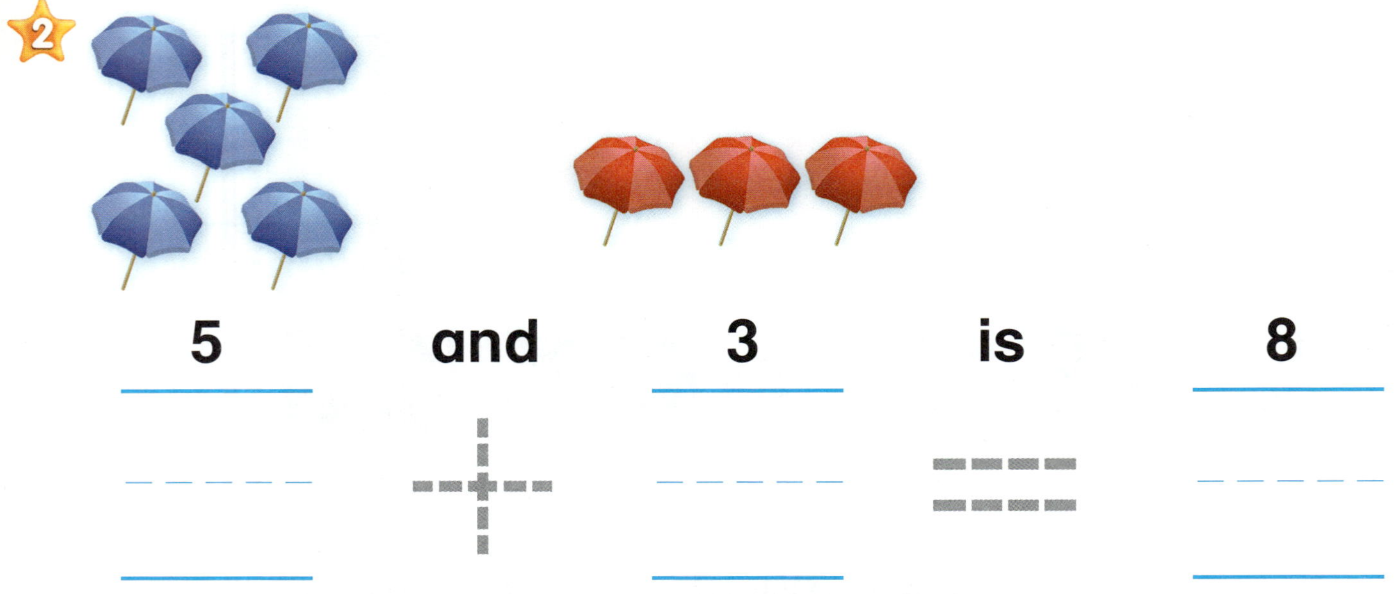

2

5	and	3	is	8

$+$

10	take away	5	is	5

3

DIRECTIONS   **1.** Make a cube train that is the same length. Draw the cube train.   **2.** Write how many in each group. Circle the two groups. Trace the symbols. Write how many in all.   **3.** Write how many fish there are in all. Mark an X on the fish that are taken away. Complete the subtraction sentence to show how many are left.

328   three hundred twenty-eight

Subtraction Patterns

1

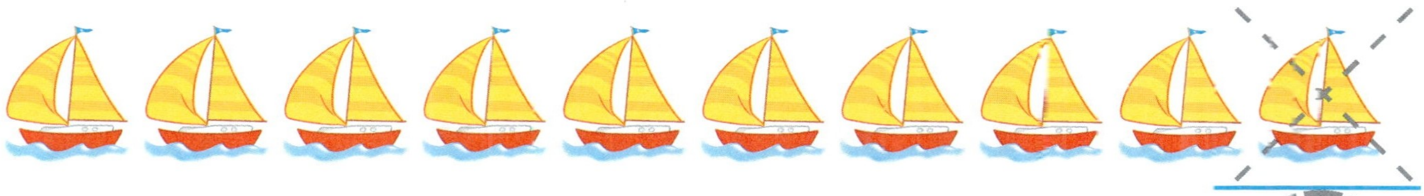

10 − 1 = 9

2

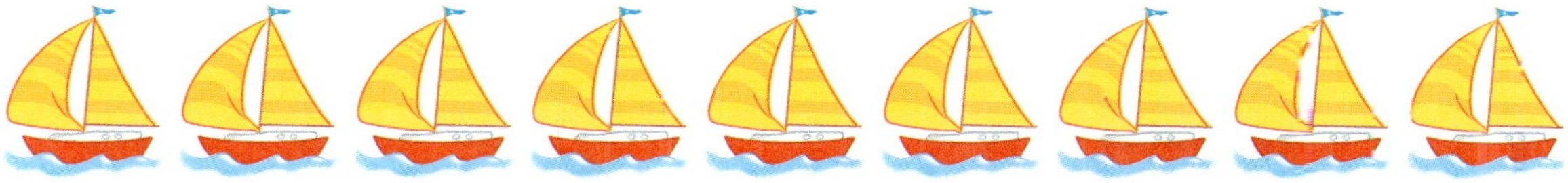

9 − 1 =

3

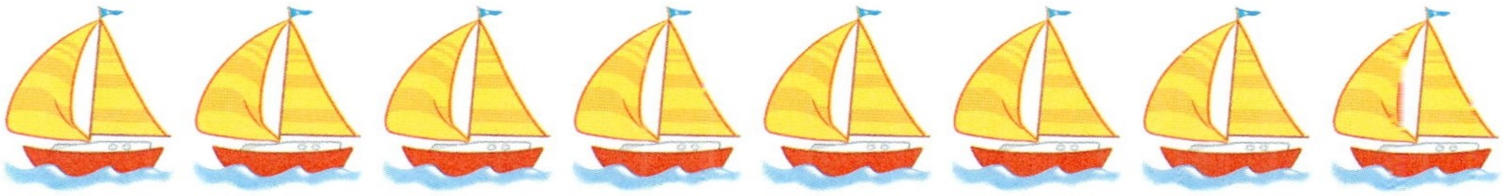

8 − 1 =

4

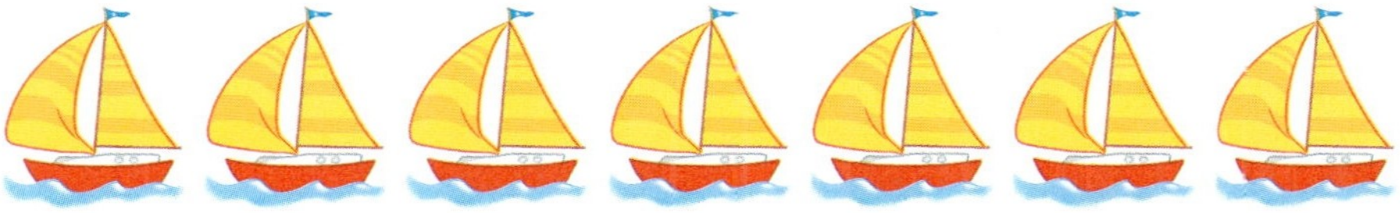

7 − 1 =

DIRECTIONS 1–4. How many boats are there in all? Mark an X on the boat that is taken away. Complete the subtraction sentence to show how many boats are left.

1.

6 --- | === _______

2.

5 --- | == _______

3.

4 --- | == _______

4.

3 --- | === _______

5.

2 --- | == _______

HOME ACTIVITY · Ask your child to use toys to demonstrate and describe the number pattern shown on this page.

330 three hundred thirty

Subtraction Sentences

1

4 − 3 = 1

2

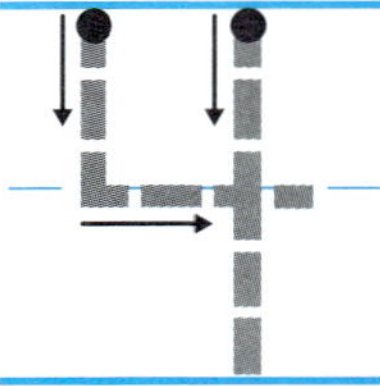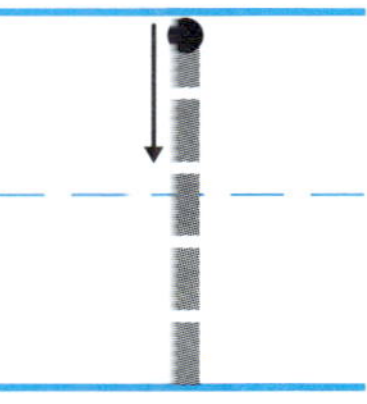

___ − ___ = ___

3

___ − ___ = ___

DIRECTIONS 1–3. Tell a story about the birds. Complete the subtraction sentence.

OBJECTIVE • Complete simple subtraction sentences.

Chapter 12 • Lesson 6

332 three hundred thirty-two

Name _______________________________

Create and Model Subtraction Problems

DIRECTIONS **I–2.** Tell a subtraction story. Model your story with counters. Draw the counters. Mark an X on the counters that are taken away. Complete the subtraction sentence.

OBJECTIVE • Use concrete objects to create and model a subtraction problem.

Chapter I2 • Lesson 7

three hundred thirty-three **333**

334 three hundred thirty-four

Use Pennies to Subtract

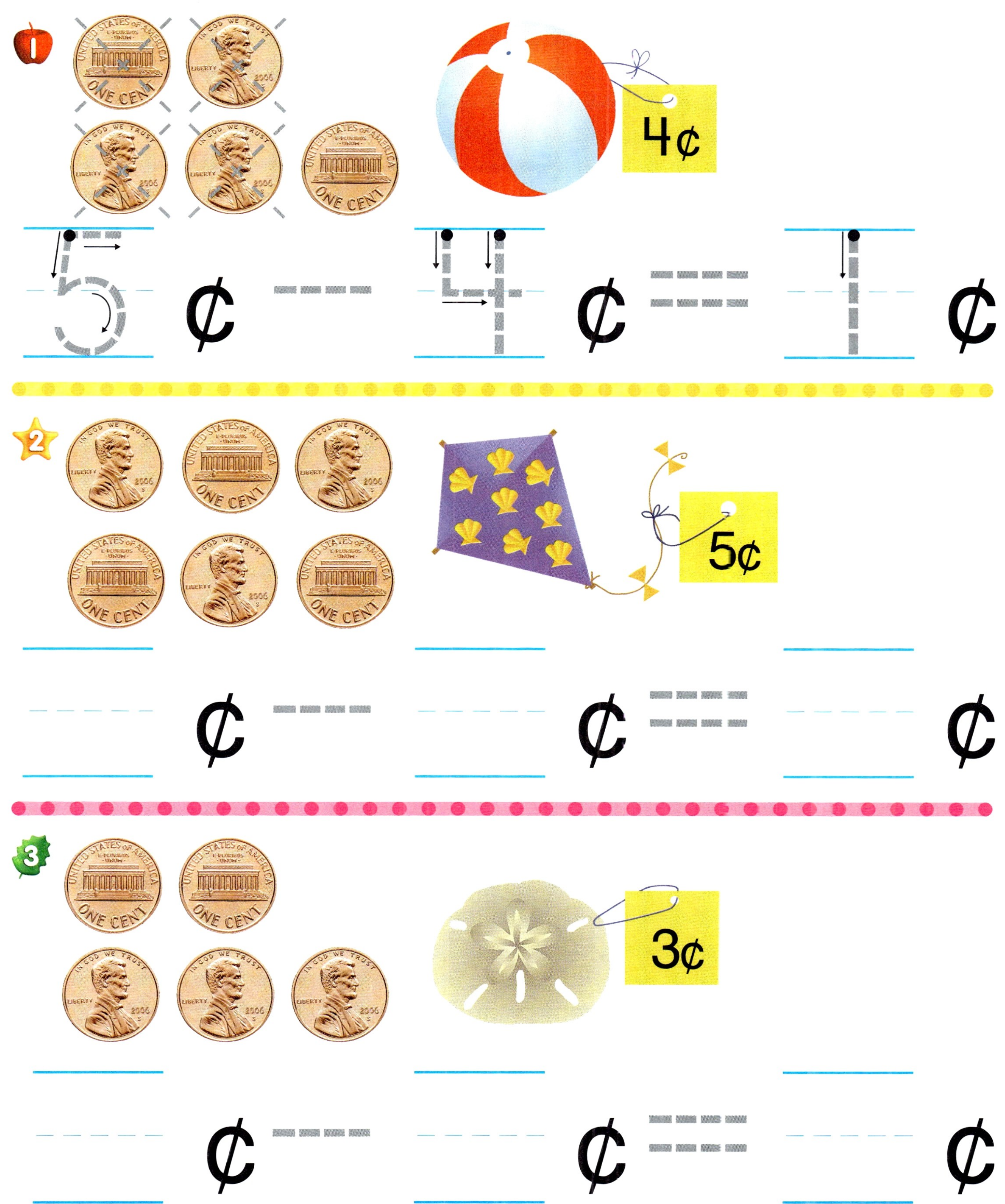

1

5 ¢ − 4 ¢ = 1 ¢

2

___ ¢ − ___ ¢ = ___ ¢

3

___ ¢ − ___ ¢ = ___ ¢

DIRECTIONS 1–3. Write how many pennies there are in all. Mark an X on the number of pennies it would take to buy the toy. Write that number. Then complete the subtraction sentence.

Chapter 12 • Lesson 8   three hundred thirty-five   **335**

1.

___ ¢ − ___ ¢ = ___ ¢

2.

___ ¢ − ___ ¢ = ___ ¢

3.

___ ¢ − ___ ¢ = ___ ¢

DIRECTIONS 1–3. Write how many pennies there are in all. Mark an X on the number of pennies it would take to buy the toy. Write that number. Then complete the subtraction sentence.

HOME ACTIVITY • Show your child a set of 8 pennies and a toy with a sticky-note price tag of 5¢. Write the following symbols: ___¢ − ___¢ = ___¢. Have your child complete the subtractioin sentence to show what would happen if he or she bought the toy with the money. Repeat with other groups of up to 10 pennies and with toys priced from 1¢ to 9¢.

Problem Solving Workshop
Skill • Use a Picture

1 2 more ⚓

2 _____ more 🥽

3 _____ more 🏐

DIRECTIONS 1–3. Draw lines to match the objects in the top row to the objects in the bottom row. Compare the groups. Circle the group that has more objects, and write how many more.

OBJECTIVE • Solve problems by using the skill *use a picture*.

1

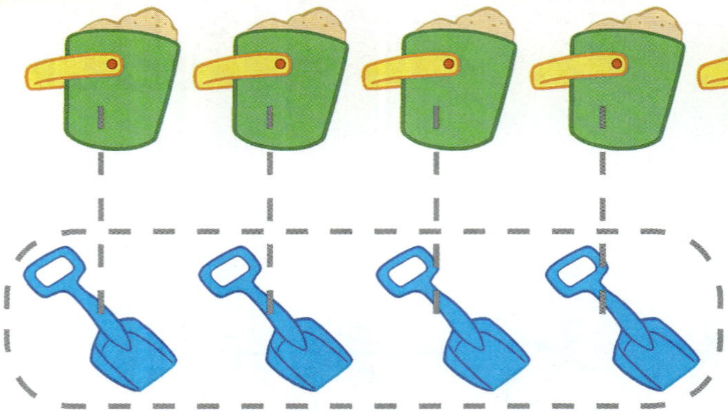

fewer

2

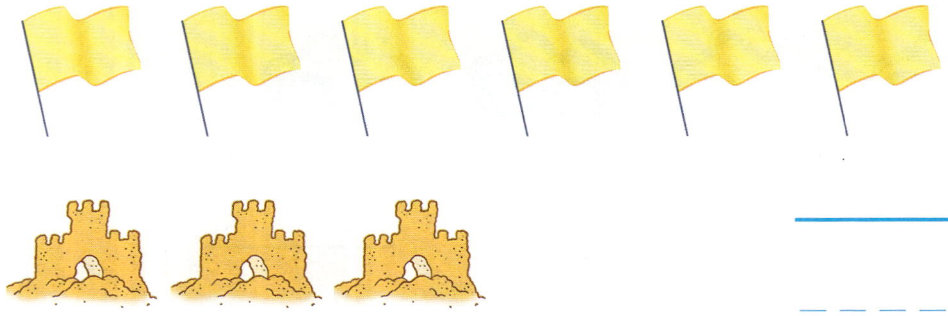

fewer

3

fewer 

DIRECTIONS **1–3.** Draw lines to match the objects in the top row to the objects in the bottom row. Compare the groups. Circle the group that has fewer objects, and write how many fewer.

HOME ACTIVITY • Show your child a row of 7 pennies and a row of 3 nickels. Have your child compare the groups, identify which has fewer coins, and tell how many fewer. Repeat with other groups of coins up to ten.

338 three hundred thirty-eight

Sailboat Subtraction

PRACTICE GAME

DIRECTIONS Play with a partner. Each player starts with an 8-cube train on the workspace. Decide who goes first. Take turns rolling the number cube. Subtract the number of cubes shown on the number cube. After each roll, tell your number sentence. If the number rolled is more than the cubes you have left, you must add that many cubes. The player who subtracts all their cubes wins the game.

MATERIALS number cube (1-3); 8 connecting cubes for each player

Math Power • Add and Subtract

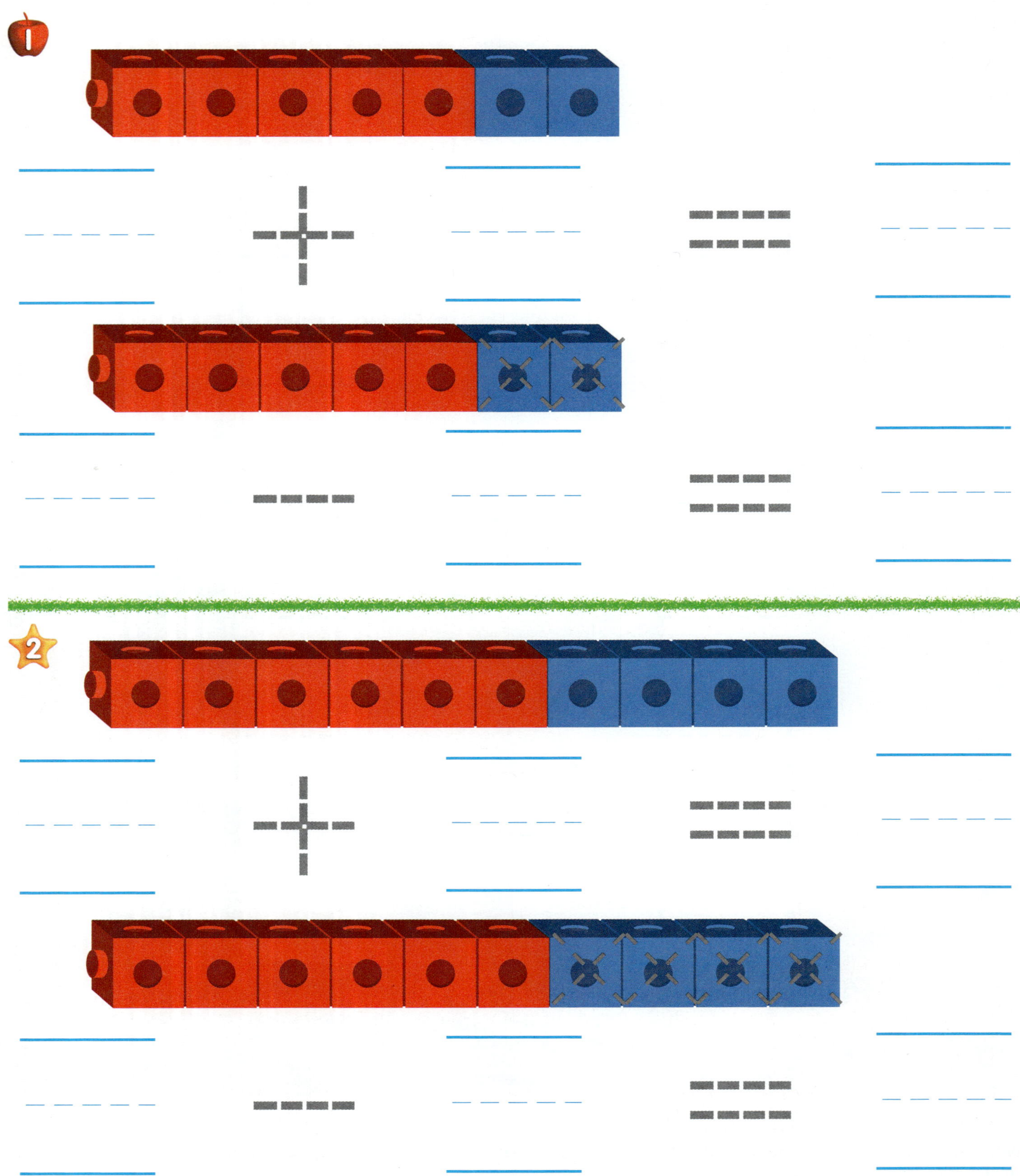

DIRECTIONS 1–2. Use cubes to add and to subtract. Complete the sentences.

✔ Chapter 12 Review/Test

1.

$$5 - 1 = \underline{\qquad}$$

2.

$$\underline{\qquad} - \underline{\qquad} = \underline{\qquad}$$

3.

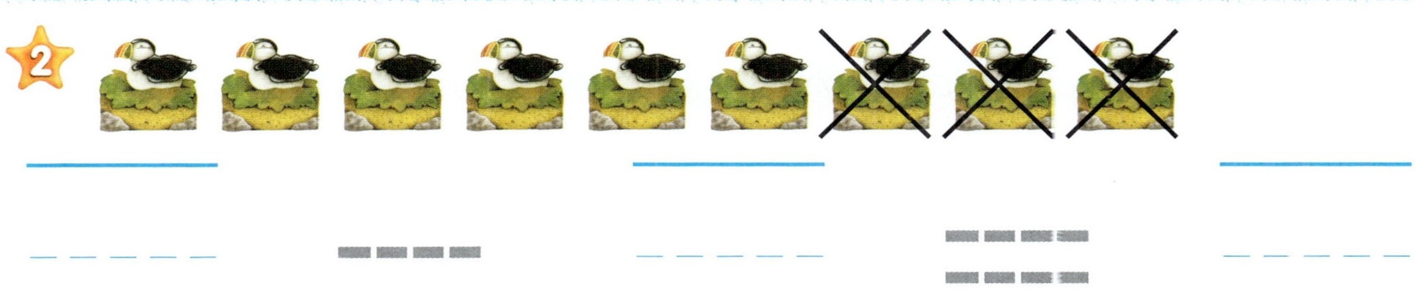

$$\underline{\qquad} - \underline{\qquad} = \underline{\qquad}$$

DIRECTIONS **1.** How many boats are there in all? Mark an X on the boat that is taken away. Complete the subtraction sentence to show how many boats are left. **2.** Tell a story about the birds. Complete the subtraction sentence. **3.** Tell a subtraction story. Model your story with counters. Draw the counters. Mark an X on the counters that are taken away. Complete the subtraction sentence.

DIRECTIONS **1.** Circle the activity that usually takes more time. **2.** Tell an addition story. Model your story with counters. Draw the counters. Use count on to find the sum. Complete the addition sentence. **3.** Tell a subtraction story. Model your story with counters. Draw the counters. Mark an X on the counters that are taken away. Complete the subtraction sentence.

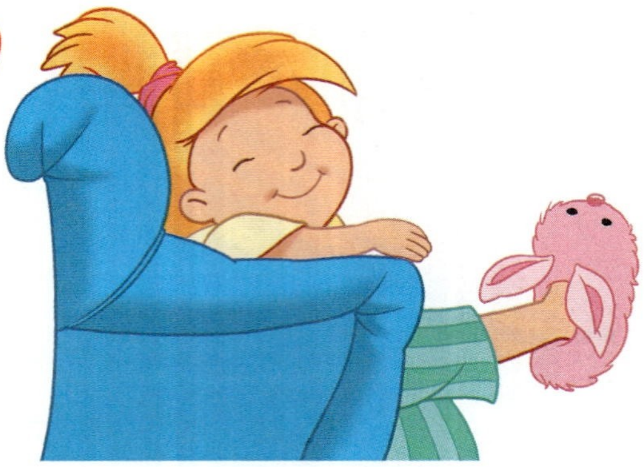

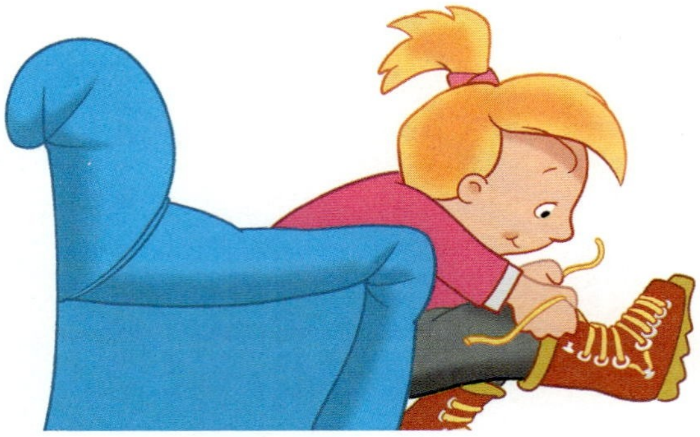

THE WORLD ALMANAC FOR KIDS

Colorful Coral

ALMANAC Fact

Coral is not a plant or a rock. It is a tiny animal called a coral polyp.

1. ___ + ___ = ___

2. ___ + ___ = ___

DIRECTIONS 1. Tell an addition story about the red corals in the picture. Complete the addition sentence. 2. Tell an addition story about the purple corals in the picture. Complete the addition sentence.

TALK Math Tell other addition stories about the corals you see on the page.

Fishy Subtraction

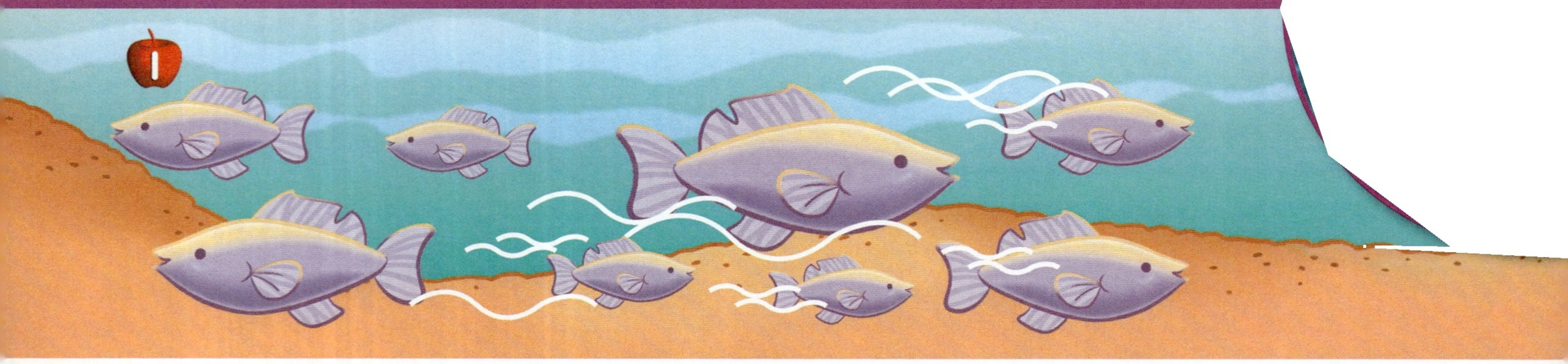

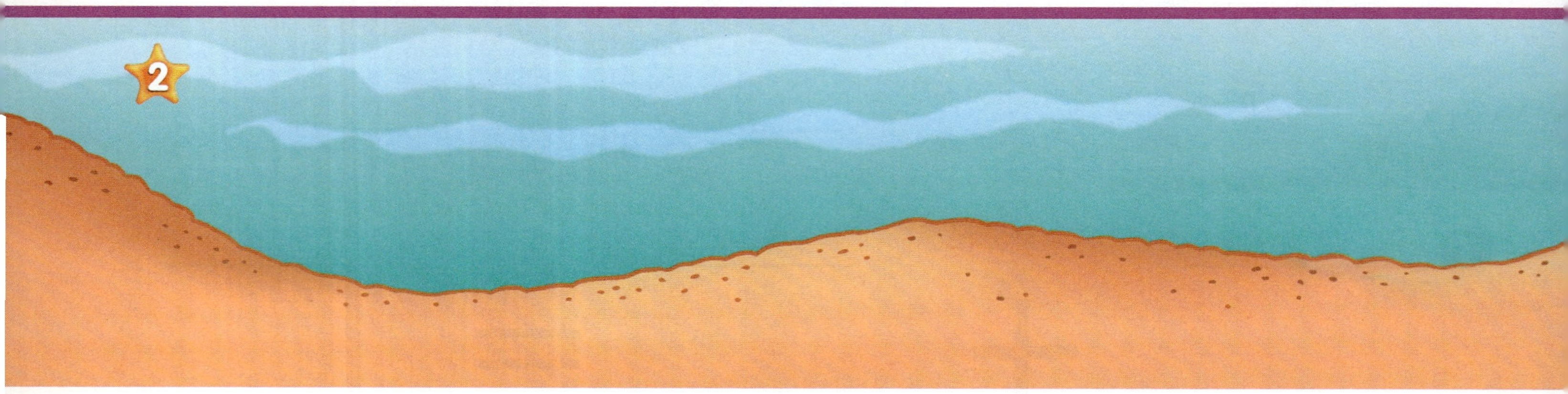

1.

___ − ___ = ___

2.

___ − ___ = ___

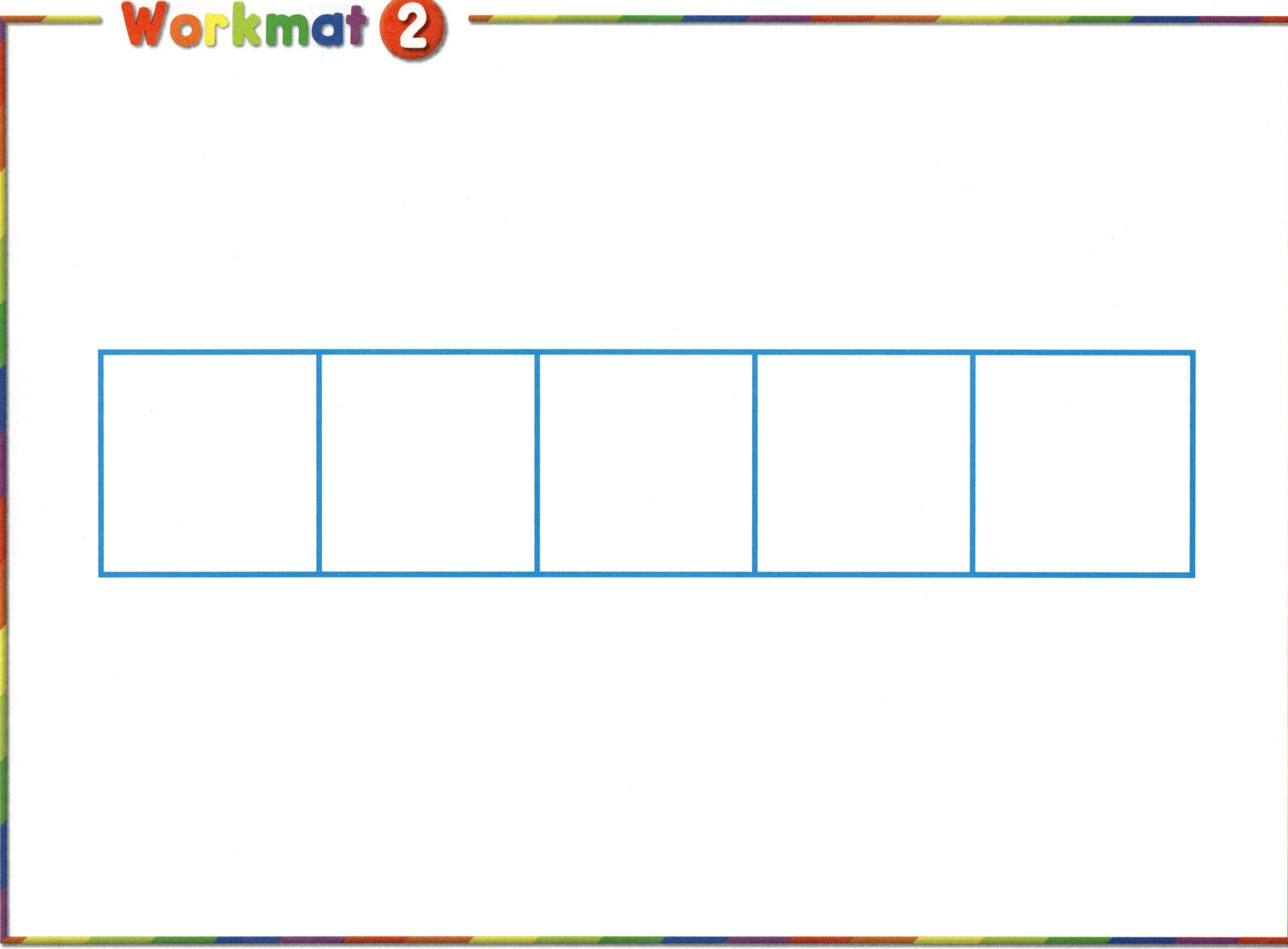

workmat 2 (five frame)

Workmat **3**

workmat 3 (ten frame)

Workmat 4

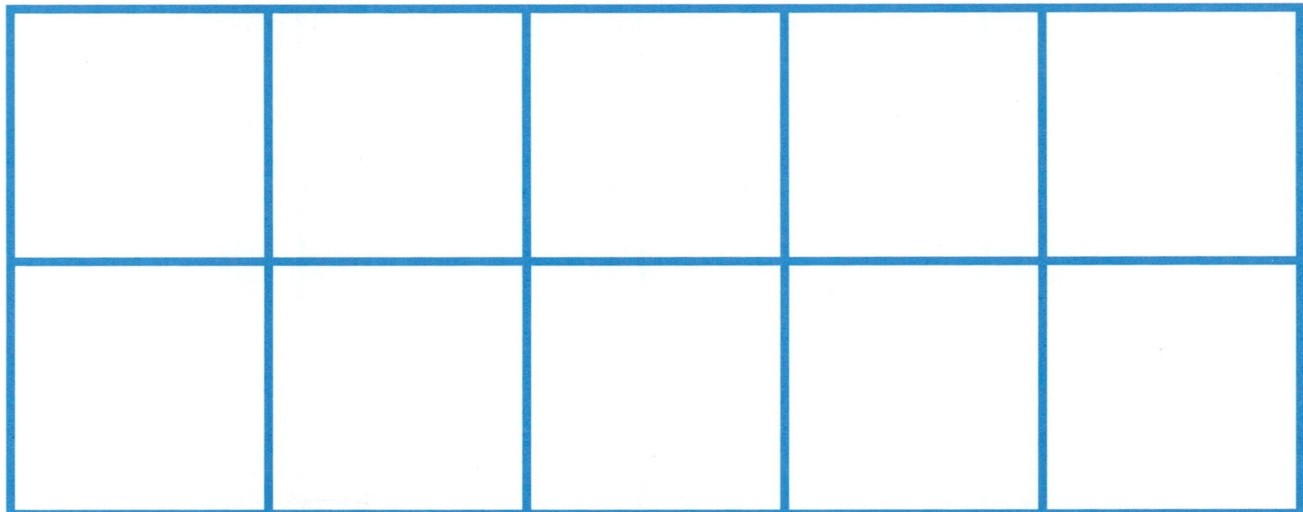

workmat 4 (ten frames)

Photo Credits

Page Placement Key: (t) top, (b) bottom, (c) center, (l) left, (r) right, (bg) background, (i) insert.

Front Cover: (l) ImageState/Alamy; (r) Philip Lee Harvey/Getty Images.

Back Cover: (l) Philip Lee Harvey/Getty Images; (r) Juniors Bildarchiv/Alamy.

Table of Contents
iv-xii Jeff Rotman/Getty Images.

UNIT 1
Chapter 1
3 Laurence Mouton/PhotoAlto/Jupiterimages; 20 (bl) Mihaela Ninic/Alamy; 21 (b) Losevsky Pavel/Shutterstock RF;
28 (br) Scott Rothstein/Shutterstock.

Chapter 2
56 (tc) C Squared Studios/Getty Images; (tr) Grant Heilman/Grant Heilman Photography.

UNIT 2
Storybook
F (t) blickwinkel / Alamy; (t) Digital Archive Japan/Alamy; (t) Eureka/Alamy; (t) Poprugin Aleksey/Shutterstock;
H (tl) Chris Turner/Shutterstock; (tr) Jan Kopec/Getty; (bl) Terrance Klassen/Alamy; (br) Darrell Gulin/CORBIS.

Chapter 3
59 Photodisc Royalty Free/Fotosearch.

Chapter 4
89 Johnathan Smith; Cordaiy Photo Library Ltd./CORBIS; 101 (tl) Dirk Anschutz/ Getty Images; (cl) Getty Images RF;
(bl) Juniors Bildarchiv/Alamy; 102 (bl) D. Hurst/Alamy; 114 (t) Shutterstock; (b) Shutterstock;
117 (tr) Inga Spence/Visuals Unlimited; 118 (bg) Paul Taylor/Getty Images; B (cr) Federico Gambarini/dpa/Corbis;
C (tl) Jan Kopec/Getty; (c) Chris Turner/Shutterstock; D (t) Darrell Gulin/CORBIS; (cr & b) Terrance Klassen/Alamy;
E (tl) Randall Ingalls/Alamy; (tc) Peter Arnold, Inc./Alamy; (cr) Mira.

UNIT 3
Storybook
E (c) Olga Lyubkina/Shutterstock; G (tl) Shutterstock; H (t) Olga Lyubkina/Shutterstock.

Chapter 5
121 Johnny Johnson/Getty Images

Chapter 6
145 Jeff Rotman/Getty Images; 147 (tr) D. Hurst/Alamy; (bc) D. Hurst / Alamy; (c) PhotoDisc, Inc / Harcourt;
(b) ShutterStock RF; (cr) Stephen Coburn/Shutterstock; 150 (tl) Ingvald Kaldhussater/Shutterstock;
152 (bl) Harcourt Telescope; 154 (cl) Mehmet Alci/Shutterstock RF; (c) Patsy A. Jacks/Shutterstock RF;
159 (tr) Stephen Coburn/Shutterstock; 164 (tr) Foodfolio/Alamy Images; 171 (cl) Foodfolio/Alamy Images;
173 (tc) GK Hart/Vikki Hart/Getty Images; (tr) Steven Burr Williams/Getty Images.

UNIT 4
Chapter 7
177 Ariel Skelley/CORBIS; 180 (bg) Rosemary Calvert/Gettyimages; 182 (inset) Martin Ruegner/Gettyimages;
183 (c) Elena Elisseeva/Shutterstock RF; (b) Elena Elisseeva/Shutterstock RF; 184 (bg) Schnare & Stief/gettyimages.

Chapter 8
228 (r) Bill Smith Studio

UNIT 5
Chapter 9
231 Dorit Lombroso Photography; 240 Borut Gorenjak/Shutterstock; 242 (b) Borut Gorenjak/Shutterstock;
248 (c) Michael Thompson/Shutterstock RF.

Chapter 10
259 Royalty-Free/Corbis; 286 (cr) Michael Thompson/Shutterstock RF; 288 (r) Getty Images.

UNIT 6
Chapter 11
291 Getty Images RF.

Chapter 12
317 Randy Wells/Corbis; 343 (t) Jupiterimages; 344 (r) Getty/Harcourt.

All other photos © Harcourt School Publishers. Harcourt Photos provided by the Harcourt Index, Harcourt IPR, and Harcourt photographers; Weronica Ankarorn, Eric Camden, Don, Couch, Doug Dukane, Ken Kinzie, April Riehm, and Steve Williams.

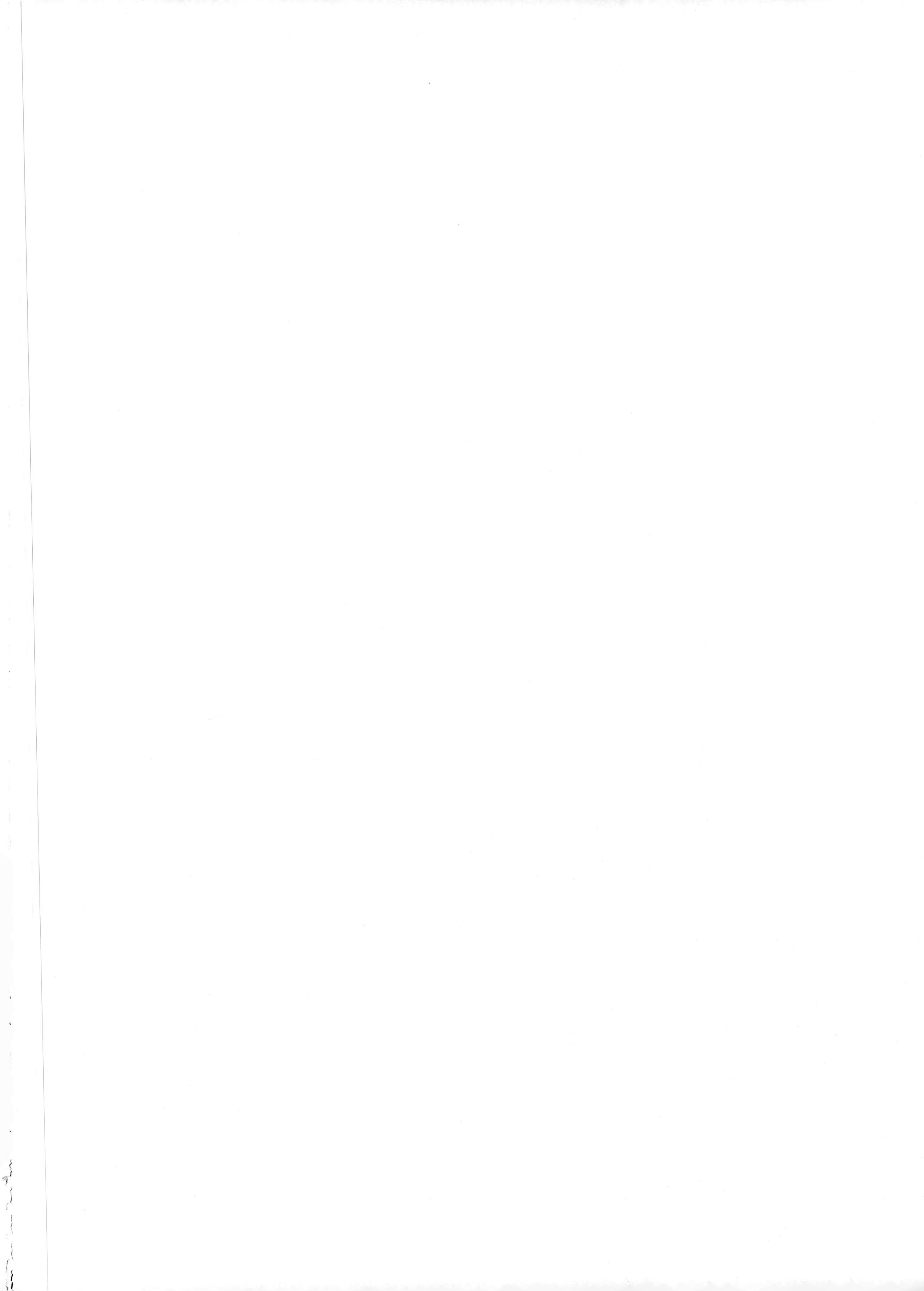